Novgorod the Great
Lake Ilmen

Uglich

Tver

VOLGA

Nizhny
Novgorod

VOLGA

Moscow

Mozhaysk

Vyazma

OKA

Vitebsk

Orsha
Smolensk

Kaluga

Serpukhov

Boundary of
Muscovy

OKA

Tula

M U S C O V Y

OKA

52°

Bryansk

Starodub

Oryol
Kromy

Yelets

Novgorod

Sevsk

Kursk

Voronezh

Brahin
Chernigov

Rylsk

Putivl

S T E P P E

D I K O Y E

P O L E

Moravsk

Ostyor

Kiev

Priluki

Valuyki

DON

silov
stov

VISHNEVETSKY
ESTATES

DONETS

DNYEPER

C O S S A C K S

DON

"W I L D E R N E S S"

Azov

40°

SEA
OF AZOV

40°

DIMITRY

Dimitry, from an anonymous watercolor preserved in the Hessische Landes- und Hochschulbibliothek, Darmstadt, Germany. Undoubtedly painted from life, this portrait was brought to Darmstadt in October, 1605, almost certainly by Sigismund Myszkowski, Great Marshal of Poland and a staunch supporter of Dimitry's cause.
Courtesy of the Hessische Landes- und Hochschulbibliothek, Darmstadt.

Dimitry

Called the Pretender

Tsar and Great Prince of All Russia, 1605-1606

PHILIP L. BARBOUR

Illustrated with PHOTOGRAPHS
and with MAPS *and* TABLES
by Samuel H. Bryant

HOUGHTON MIFFLIN COMPANY · BOSTON
THE RIVERSIDE PRESS · CAMBRIDGE
1966

FOR
RUTH AND SKEE

Read and like, for much is in it worthy of observation.

Foreword to *Sir Thomas Smithes Voyage and Entertainment in Rushia.* London, 1605.

PREFACE

THIS IS THE STORY of a young man who appeared out of nowhere, claimed to be the Tsarevich Dimitry, son of Ivan the Dread, collected a band of followers, marched on Moscow, fought two battles, was crowned Tsar and murdered — all in the space of three years. So remarkable in the annals of history was this young man who called himself Dimitry that the German critic and author Rudolf von Gottschall wrote of him that "to present his genesis and rise [*Werden und Wachsen*] would have been a task for the genius of a Shakespeare."

Dimitry, whom others called "the Pretender," existed dramatically in fact, although his career reads like fiction. Yet there has been, to the best of my knowledge, no original history of his life in English, and for more than a century not even a translation of a history. In his own day, several short works were published in English about him, and these, along with some relatively recent excerpts from ancient documents, are all that is available. Indeed, even in English fiction there is virtually nothing about him, with the exception of a single drama.

Yet on the continent of Europe several dramatic works have dealt with Dimitry, either as the main character, or as an adjunct to the Tsars Boris Fyodorovich Godunov and Fyodor Ivanovich, his brother-in-law. One of the earliest of these, and certainly the most famous, is Aleksandr Sergeyevich Pushkin's *Boris Godunov*, universally known through the opera of the same name which Modest Petrovich Musorgsky based on it. In both the play and the opera, Dimitry and his Polish love, Marina Mniszech, have pregnant parts. That the plot of Pushkin's work is based on mistaken historical assumptions does not detract from its dramatic interest — on the contrary, historically the death of Boris was much more prosaic. Nevertheless, it was the opera (and particularly Chaliapin in the title rôle) which led me to read the play, to translate it, and finally to undertake the present work.

But Pushkin and Musorgsky are by no means the only dramatist and composer to be attracted by the subject. Antonín Dvořák wrote a four-act opera called *Dimitrij,* which was first performed in 1882 but is not known either in the United States or, I believe, in the United Kingdom. Far more important, however, are the numerous plays which have been written about Dimitry. To mention but a few (see the Bibliography for others), there is Friedrich von Schiller's unfinished drama *Demetrius* beside Friedrich Hebbel's *Demetrius,* heading a long list of German works. In Russian, in addition to Pushkin's *Boris Godunov,* there is a quaint old play by Aleksandr Petrovich Sumarokov, *Dimitry Samozvanets* (Dimitry the Pretender), and a much finer work by Aleksey Stepanovich Khomyakov, with the same title. Elsewhere, there is Lope de Vega's *El Gran Duque de Moscovia y Emperador Perseguido,* written before news of Dimitry's death reached Spain and far from a "great work." Prosper Mérimée tried his hand at the subject in the dramatic sketch *Les Débuts d'un Aventurier,* which followed close on the heels of his serious historical study, *Épisode de l'histoire de Russie — Les faux Démétrius.* And finally, mention must be made of the "intolerable tragedy" by Mary Pix, *The Czar of Muscovy,* comparable with Lope de Vega's work for its vast exercise of imagination. As I have mentioned, these are only a few of the dramatic works devoted to Dimitry's career.

On this basis alone, it is obvious that many have considered Dimitry a subject of great dramatic interest. Whether the true story of his life is equally interesting is for the reader to judge. But it may not be beside the point to suggest that, beyond the sheer drama of his unique life, there is a historical interest in it which is pertinent to the happenings of today.

It could well be claimed that the "medieval" period of Russia closed with the death of Ivan the Dread in 1584. A century and four years of freedom from Tatar hegemony, symbolized by the cessation of tribute paid to the Khan, should by all standards have sufficed to bring Moscow, so to speak, back into the European picture. In the case of Spain, which had been under more direct "Oriental" rule for even more centuries than Russia, freedom from Moors and Islam preceded by only a matter of months the voyage of Columbus which opened a New World to the Old. But by contrast, in Russia the end of tribute payments was virtually contemporary with the introduction of the rigid, hieratic court-procedure of the Eastern Empire, wiped from the political map by the Ottoman Turks a generation before. Where a certain amount of Slavic anarchy* mixed with Scandinavian Viking-marauder freedom had persisted until Ivan III (grandfather of the Dread) married the Byzantine Princess Sophia, after that marriage and the establishment of a strong Muscovite state the Tsar was converted into a despot who was called "Oriental" in the courts of western Europe, but who in actuality was reigning according to the immutable customs of the Court of Constantinople (before 1453).

Two fundamental questions arise in presenting the history of Dimitry. The first is, was the Tsarevich Dimitry really dead, and if so was he murdered or did he kill himself accidentally? My conclusions are that he was probably dead, and most likely killed himself.

The second question, which arises out of the first, is, If the Tsarevich Dimitry was dead, who was the Dimitry who was crowned Tsar in 1605? The answer to that, despite the reactionary article in the communist Great Soviet Encyclopedia (second edition), seems clearly to be that no-one knows. The man who was crowned Tsar by all accounts and signs firmly believed that he was heir to the throne. Therefore, if he was not the Tsarevich, he can also hardly have been a deliberate impostor. For that reason, the

---

* Nicolas Berdyaev (*The Russian Idea*) refers to the Russian people as "anarchist in their fundamental bent."

descriptive adjective often applied to him in Russian, *Samozvanets,* "self-styled," is not just. The matter is more fully discussed in Appendix E, *Who Was Dimitry?* (pp. 321–27).

To conclude, it is fortunate for the biographer of the 1960's that practically every known document pertinent to Dimitry's career has appeared in print, in full, or in extensive extracts. The publications of various Russian governmental agencies and individual scholars, not to mention the vast amount of research published by "outsiders," from the days of Karamzin to the Bolshevik Revolution, contain hundreds of pages of transcripts of manuscript documents, for the greater part painstakingly reproduced. These are referred to in the Notes and Comments.

The all but exhaustive documentary sources being thus at hand, the problem of Dimitry's biographer remains that of making his way through often conflicting contemporary accounts, and to the best of his ability and insight choosing the story which for the most reasons seems soundest. If I have followed the wrong path on occasion, which I trust has not been the case, it has not been to cover up Dimitry's shortcomings. My aim has been to present the facts so far as they are determinable, and to interpret them in the light of what appear to be the most conscientious contemporary chronicles and the most rational modern studies. Whatever my success in this, Dimitry himself must remain one of history's truly extraordinary figures.

Lastly, a brief personal note seems necessary. I would have liked to retrace Dimitry's route from Kraków to Moscow, but since that proved unfeasible (within the time at my disposal) I contented myself with following the greater part of Marina's, farther to the north. Descriptions of Moscow and the countryside as far as Warsaw are therefore based on personal impressions, converted, if I may so put it, into the currency of 1605. Nevertheless, what I have to say about the Russians (or Muscovites) and the Poles of Dimitry's era need not reflect my experiences with the people of today. If, then, this book at times reads like an eye-witness account of the much more recent French Revolution, with its mob-rule, deceit and bloodshed, it is only because it is not the historian's task to bowdlerize either the French Revolution or the first great popular revolt in Russia.

I am deeply indebted to many individuals and institutions for courteous help. Among these, Mme. E. Kirillova, of London, unquestionably deserves first mention, as my mentor when I was preparing my translation of Pushkin's *Boris Godunov* many years ago, who has again come to my aid, in connection with the accentuation of Russian names. Professor Morton Benson of the University of Pennsylvania has also given me the benefit of his vast experience in that same field.

Then, as on previous occasions, I am indebted for help to the New York Public Library and its staff, particularly in this instance to Dr. John L. Mish and his assistants in the Slavonic Room; and to the British Museum and the Public Record Office, London, and their staffs. In addition, I want to acknowledge invaluable aid from the Prints Division, and personally from Mrs. Maud Cole of the Rare Books Division, of the New York Public Library, and from the Polish Library, London, and Dr. J. Jasnowski, of the Polish Research Centre there. I am also grateful to the staff of the State Historical Museum, Moscow, and particularly to Mme. E. S. Ovchinnikova, Kandidat Nauk, for information, for producing items not immediately at hand, and for securing photographs of exhibits. Similarly, I am indebted to the Bibliothèque Slave, Paris, and its Director, Father M.-J. Rouët de Journel, S.J., for giving me access to the library and permission to photograph and reproduce a unique historical painting of the death of the Tsarevich Dimitry.

Special mention must be added of the efforts of Dr. Gisela Bergsträsser and Dr. G. Bott, of the Hessisches Landesmuseum, and Oberbibliotheksrat Dr. Knaus, of the Hessische Landes- und Hochschulbibliothek, Darmstadt, which resulted in locating an almost forgotten portrait of Dimitry, done by an unknown artist in 1604. This portrait probably comes closer to showing Dimitry's features than the contemporary woodcuts and engravings, and there can be no question of its genuineness.

Harvard University Library, Cambridge, and the Library of Congress, Washington, have courteously supplied me with information and photographic reproductions of one sort or another, as have also the Bibliothèque Nationale, Paris, and the Polish Library there, as well as the Vatican Library and Archives, Rome. To Columbia University Press I am indebted for a number of quotations from my translation of Pushkin's *Boris Godunov*. All these too have my thanks.

And to conclude, a number of personal friends and acquaintances have also given me much of their time, for which I should like to express my gratitude. Professor the Hon. Richard Hare, University of London, was most helpful to me on several occasions. M. Constantin de Grunwald, of Paris, spent an afternoon discussing the issues with me, and offered valuable suggestions. Dr. A. L. Jordan, of New York City, helped me with one of the Polish sources. And Dr. George Vernadsky, Emeritus Professor at Yale University, and Professor James H. Billington, of Princeton University, have not only read part or all of this book in manuscript, but kindly offered counsel and suggestions. Needless to say, any historical misconceptions that may be found are entirely my own.

PHILIP L. BARBOUR

Newtown, Connecticut
7 August 1965

CONTENTS

ILLUSTRATIONS

Russian armor in the 1500's. It had not changed greatly by 1605.

Silk kaftan of the time of Ivan Vasilyevich, the Dread.

Redrawing, after Olearius, of boyars' costumes, about 1650. They had not changed since Dimitry's day.

One of the streltsy, as drawn by Olearius. The costume had changed little since 1605.

Anonymous woodcut of Dimitry, "Great Tsar of Muscovy," published in a brochure by Grochowski in honor of Marina's marriage-by-proxy in Kraków, November 22, 1605.

Marina Mniszchówna, of Velké Končice, Great Tsaritsa of Muscovy. From Grochowski's Wedding Brochure, 1605.

FOLLOWING PAGE 228

Afanasy [Vlasyev], Ambassador of the same Tsar of Muscovy. From Grochowski's Wedding Brochure, 1605.

Dimitry receiving the Polish ambassadors. Contemporary oil painting.

The Coronation of Marina. A painting by an anonymous (Polish?) artist, of great historical importance.

The Wawel, Kraków, as drawn about 1576 by Georg Braun.

Smolensk under Polish attack in 1609–1611, by Franz Hogenberg.

A procession of the time of Tsar Mikhail Romanov, showing the Golden Palace in the center, with the Red Staircase before it.

A modern view of the three Kremlin cathedrals as seen from the Moskva River.

A photograph of Red Square today, as seen from near the Cathedral of the Blessed Idiot Basil.

MAPS

PRINCIPAL HISTORICAL FIGURES

OTHERS

Basmánov, Pyotr Fyódorovich, Boyar and favorite of Dimitry. Murdered in 1606 in his late thirties.

Buczyński, John and Stanislas [boo-CHEEN-ski], Dimitry's most trusted secretaries.

Gosiewski, Alexander Korwin [go-SYEV-ski], Starosta of Velizh, Sigismund's first ambassador to Dimitry.

Ignáty, Patriarch of Moscow under Dimitry.

Iov [Job], Patriarch of Moscow (the first) under Borís Godunóv.

Margaret, Captain Jacques, French mercenary soldier under Borís and Dimitry, writer.

Massa, Isaac Abrahamszoon, young Dutch merchant-apprentice resident in Moscow.

Merrick, Sir John, English merchant in Moscow.

Mniszech, Pan George, Palatine of Sandomierz, Polish Senator.

Mniszech, Stanislas, Starosta of Sanok, Pan George's eldest surviving son.

Mstislávsky, Fyódor Ivánovich, Prince, First Boyar.

Nagóy, Mikhaíl and Grigóry Fyódorovich, brothers of the Tsarítsa María.

Ostrogski, Constantine, Prince, Palatine of Kiev.

Ostrogski, Janusz, Prince, his son, Castellan of Kraków.

Otrépyev, Smirnóy, Dyak. Uncle of the monk Grigóry (Gríshka) with whom Borís Godunóv attempted to identify Dimítry.

Rangoni, Claudio, Prince-Bishop of Reggio (Emilia), Papal Nuncio in Kraków.

Románov, Fyódor Nikítich, nephew of Anastásia, Ivan the Dread's first wife; compelled to become a monk by Borís Godunóv, under the name of Filarét, restored to honors by Dimítry. Father of Tsar Mikhaíl, founder of the Románov dynasty.

Sapieha, Leo, Great Chancellor of Lithuania, and second political power in the Polish "Republic."

Smythe, Sir Thomas, Ambassador of King James I to Borís Godunóv.

Vishnevétsky [Wiśniowiecki], Adam, Prince, Polish magnate.

Vishnevétsky [Wiśniowiecki], Konstantín, Prince, his second cousin.

Vlásyev, Afanásy Ivánovich, Secretary of Council rank, occasional Ambassador and imperial Treasurer.

Zamoyski, John, Great Chancellor of Poland ("Prime Minister") and Commander-in-Chief of the Army. 1541–1605

Zebrzydowski [zeb-zhi-DUV-ski], Nicholas, Palatine of Kiev, a persistent trouble-maker.

NOTE: The Great Princes of Moscow up to the death of Tsar Fyódor Ivánovich were known only by their baptismal name, their patronymic and, on occasion, their sobriquet. All other Russians had surnames, with the exception of the common people.

Since Russian (and Polish) surnames are generally adjectival, they are usually declined. For this reason, a feminine suffix is added to most women's names: -a or -aya. By the same token, the feminine patronymic suffix is -evna or -ovna (Polish -w-) in place of the familiar masculine suffix -evich, -ovich or simply -ich.

For notes on the pronunciation of Russian and Polish, and for the system of transliteration used for the former, see Appendix A, (p. 301).

CHRONOLOGY

1530 August 25. Birth of Ivan IV "the Dread."

1533 September 7. Birth of Elizabeth I of England.
      December 3. Death of Vasily III. Ivan IV succeeds.

1547 January 16. Coronation of Ivan IV as Tsar, followed
      by marriage.
      January 28. Death of Henry VIII of England.

ca. 1551 Birth of Boris Godunov.

1553–54 First English merchants reach Russia via the White Sea.

1558 November 17. Elizabeth succeeds to the throne.

1560 Ivan IV's first wife dies. Beginning of "the terror."

1566 June 19. Birth of James VI of Scotland (James I of
      England).
      June 20. Birth of Sigismund III of Poland.

1582 Calendar revised by Pope Gregory XIII. Thursday,
      October 4, was followed by Friday, October 15. Prot-
      estant Europe and Orthodox Russia refused to accept
      the "new style" (n.s.).
      October 19/29. Birth of Tsarevich Dimitry, son of Ivan
      IV's seventh wife.
      November 19/29. Ivan IV kills his son Ivan.

1584 March 18/28. Ivan IV dies; Fyodor Ivanovich, aged 26,
      succeeds.

1591 May 15/25. Death of Tsarevich Dimitry in Uglich.

1598   January 7/17. Tsar Fyodor dies. Boris Godunov asked
        to become Tsar, but he hesitates.

        September 1/11. Boris crowned. (It was the first day
        of the year 7107 according to the Russian calendar.)
        Rumors arise that Tsarevich Dimitry is still alive.

1600   October 16/26. Lithuanian Chancellor Leo Sapieha
        arrives in Moscow to discuss peace treaty between
        Poland-Lithuania and Russia. Poland refuses to call
        Boris "Tsar," and Boris has his son Fyodor, aged 11,
        preside over first meeting. Further rumors about
        Tsarevich Dimitry.

1601   August. Sapieha signs peace treaty. Bad crops.

1602   Treaty ratified in Poland. Bad crops, famine.

1603   Summer. A young man in the service of Prince Adam
        Vishnevetsky, in Brahin (Byelorussia), "reveals" him-
        self as Dimitry, son of Ivan IV.

        September 27/October 7. Prince Adam informs the
        Polish Great Chancellor of Dimitry's appearance.
        Soon thereafter, he takes Dimitry to the estate of his
        cousin, Prince Konstantin Vishnevetsky.

1604   February. Dimitry arrives in Sambor and meets Marina,
        daughter of Pan George Mniszech.

        March 5/15. Dimitry received by the King.

        August 15/25. Dimitry leaves Sambor and assembles
        his army near Lvov.

        October 21/31. Dimitry enters Muscovy with his army.

        December 21/31. Dimitry's victory at Novgorod Sever-
        sky.

1605   January 21/31. Dimitry defeated at Dobrynichi; flees
        south to Putivl.

        April 13/23. Boris Godunov dies; his son Fyodor suc-

ceeds. Shortly thereafter, Basmanov appointed commander of Fyodor's army.

May 6/16. Camillo Borghese elected Pope (Paul V).

May 7/17. Basmanov deserts Fyodor for Dimitry.

ca. May 16/26. Dimitry leaves Putivl.

June 10/20. Young Tsar Fyodor murdered.

June 20/30. Dimitry enters Moscow.

July 18/28. Tsaritsa-nun Marfa, mother of Tsarevich
Dimitry, reaches Moscow. Dimitry crowned three
days later.

November 1/11. Dimitry's Ambassador Vlasyev arrives
in Kraków. Eleven days later, marriage by proxy
celebrated with Marina.

1606   February 20/March 2. Marina sets out for Moscow.

May 2/12. Marina enters Moscow.

May 8/18. Marina crowned and married to Dimitry.

May 17/27. Dimitry murdered.

May 19/29. Prince Vasily Shuysky "elected" Tsar.

June 1/11. Shuysky crowned.

May 29/June 8. Dimitry's body burned and ashes fired
from a cannon.

PROLOGUE

F OR SEVEN CENTURIES the descendants of Rurik the Viking had reigned over Russia. Twenty generations of them, father and son, brother and cousin, had succeeded to the heritage when Ivan IV assumed the title of Tsar and Great Prince of All Russia in 1547.

Tsar Ivan was madman mixed with genius. In a fit of rage he killed his only able son, and when Ivan died his ivory throne became the birthright of Fyodor, a childless weakling of twenty-six years, and Dimitry, one day short of seventeen months old.

Ivan, already called "the Dread" in his own lifetime, had set up a council of state to govern for Fyodor, but it soon fell apart due to the illness of Fyodor's uncle, Nikita Romanovich Zakharyin-Yuryev, and palace intrigue. Boris Godunov, the new Tsar's brother-in-law, became sole regent. Meanwhile, friends and relatives of Ivan's widow, Maria Nagaya, started a move to place her son, the infant Dimitry, on the throne. Godunov, to preserve order, had to dislodge this faction from the capital. Dimitry and his mother, along with other members of the Nagoy family, were sent north to Uglich, on the upper reaches of the Volga, to hold independent but somewhat beggarly court.

Dimitry's mother's family was old and respectable, but not conspicuous. No Nagoy had been noted for political influence, and only one or two achieved some sort of civic prominence. Yet the Tsaritsa's brothers and cousins took umbrage at their removal from Moscow. Exile in Uglich, they hinted, was not only a punishment. It was even dangerous. They outspokenly feared for the life of Dimitry because he was next in line of succession to the throne, after Fyodor. More pertinently, Dimitry was for the Nagoys both a reminder of an ephemeral family glory and a hope of a return to an importance in reality never theirs.

As the years passed, Fyodor and his wife, Irina Godunova, continued to have no heir, and the Tsaritsa's miscarriages hinted that no heir would ever come. Furthermore, Fyodor, whose sobriquet was "the Angelic Tsar," was obviously not long for this world, and while he lived he was completely in the hands of his wife and his baleful brother-in-law Boris, by then the Prince Regent. Under such circumstances, Dimitry's relatives could foresee that Boris would exert every effort to make himself Fyodor's heir and successor. He was not likely to fail.

The only living thing between Boris and eventually the throne was Dimitry. Even Giles Fletcher, Queen Elizabeth's ambassador to Moscow in 1588–1589, reported that Dimitry was "not safe (as I have heard) from attempts of making away by practice of some that aspire to the succession, if this emperour die without any issue."

It has been assumed that Fletcher got his information from Jerome Horsey (later knighted), who had been in Russia since 1573, spoke Russian fluently, and was a friend of Tsaritsa Maria's first cousin, Afanasy Nagoy. Whether he did or not, the appearance of this statement in a book published in London in 1591 shows that the Nagoys' fears were not kept dark.

In 1590 the government in Moscow appointed *Dyak* (Secretary) Mikhail Bityagovsky comptroller-auditor for Uglich, including the royal estate there. This apparently honest and loyal servant of the crown stirred up the bitterest hostility among the Nagoys. The Tsaritsa's brother, Mikhail, quarreled with him over the amounts of money which should be paid him, Mikhail, while the other Nagoys did little to conceal their suspicion that the new comptroller was a mere political agent whose real task was to do away with Dimitry. On the other side, Bityagovsky had protested to Mikhail about his and his brother's employment of conjurors to predict, and thereby speed, the appointed hour for the death of Fyodor.

But it was Dimitry whom the Rider of the Pale Horse sought — the Nagoys should have consulted other soothsayers. Although he had only turned six on October 19, 1588, he had already been noted to possess

> the father's quality that beginneth to appear. . . He is delighted (they say) to see sheep and other cattle killed, and to look on their throats while they are bleeding (which commonly children are afraid to behold), and to beat geese and hens with a staff till he see them lie dead.

The extent of credence to be given this statement should be influenced by the parenthetical "they say."

In addition, although this may have developed later, Dimitry suffered from violent epileptic fits, according to the sworn statement of his mother's cousin, Andrey Nagoy, and the testimony of his governess and his nurse. In 1591, he suffered just such a fit during Lent, which began on February 17 that year in Russia, another just before Easter (April 4), and a third on May 12, a Wednesday.

Dimitry's recovery from this third fit was rapid, and on Friday the Tsaritsa took him to church services. The next day, May 15, she again took him to church, and afterwards let him go play with four boys in the palace courtyard. His nurse and chambermaid were with him, and the governess was in the yard, not far away. What happened was described by the nurse in these words:

> On Saturday Dimitry played with a knife with the boys, and she had not been careful enough to notice when the black sickness [epileptic fit] seized him; and he had a knife in his hands, and he cut himself with that knife, and she took him in her arms, and he passed away in her arms.

The governess ran up, but it was too late.

Screams from the courtyard brought the Tsaritsa and Mikhail Nagoy at once. In her frantic fear for the Tsarevich's life, already tragically ended, Maria Nagaya caught up a stick of firewood and started beating the governess. The tocsin sounded from the Church of the Savior, echoed by a mad peal of bells from all over

the town, as the news spread like a brush-fire in a gale. Mikhail
Bityagovsky, who was dining with Grigory Nagoy's father-confes-
sor, sent a servant to learn what had happened, and was soon on the
scene himself. Mikhail Nagoy then began to roar that Dimitry had
been murdered by the man who had only just arrived, Bityagovsky.
And the Tsaritsa, crazed with despair, wildly importuned the governess to say that Bityagovsky's son (who had been with his father
all along) and two other delinquent children were the Tsarevich's
assassins.

By that time crowds of hysterical people had pushed into the
courtyard. Incited by the Tsaritsa and her brother, they hurled
imprecations at Bityagovsky, yelling that his son had murdered
Dimitry. Bityagovsky, whose crime was that he was the Tsar's
financial agent, attempted to calm them and possibly to explain
that his boy had not even been there at the time. The ringleaders
of the mob only turned on him, in answer. Bityagovsky fled, but
was cut down in a nearby building. The rabble swarmed out into
the streets, swords, clubs, and firebrands in hand. The town chief,
helpless to control the riot, dispatched messengers post haste to
Moscow.

Four days later a commission arrived, possibly with an armed
detachment, since the riots suddenly ceased. Promptly, and with
impartiality and an interest in getting at the truth which would
have been remarkable anywhere in that age, the depositions of
everyone who knew anything whatsoever about the events were
taken and duly recorded, with the notable exception of the Tsaritsa herself. No judgment was passed, no accusation made. A document called the *Slédstvennoye Délo,* or report of investigation,
was compiled containing all the details. Nothing more.

This report, which survives in mutilated or perhaps "edited"
form, established that the Tsarevich killed himself with a knife
during an epileptic fit. (It also cast light on the venom that poi-
soned Mikhail Nagoy even before the tragedy, and on the readiness
of the mob to take vengeance on an agent of Boris Godunov even
before he became Tsar.) But for one reason or another the results
of the inquiry were not fully and clearly circulated, and as a result

the Russian people drew their own conclusions. These were that Boris Godunov was the murderer of Dimitry Ivanovich, in intent and wish if not in actual execution. To this day he generally stands thus falsely accused.

Less than seven years after the death of Dimitry, Fyodor was carried away by the angels with whom his soul had always lived. His widow shortly thereafter entered a nunnery. The dynasty of Rurik the Viking in the line of Great Prince Ivan I "Kalitá" ("Money-bags") was extinguished.

Popular acclaim, which never knows what tergiversation is, did not tarry long in calling for the election of Boris Godunov, a Tatar by descent, as Tsar and Great Prince of Holy Russia. Dimitry's "murder" was apparently forgotten.

It may of course be held that this acclaim was in no small measure prompted by Boris's loyal supporters, if not by the man himself. Nevertheless, there can be little doubt that Boris was better fitted to rule the country than any other man then living and available. Regrettably, there can be no doubt at all that Boris's ability was less important in Muscovy than his greatest shortcoming. He was not of the Blood of Rurik. He had not even married one of that Blood.

Those distant cousins of Ivan the Dread who were of that Blood, therefore, abetted by the disgruntled noblemen of Boris's own rank before his elevation to the throne, lost little time in plotting his overthrow. All the gifts with which nature and experience had endowed Boris were ignored, as were the best interests of the state. Great princes and lesser nobles put their petty selves before all else, and deceit, lying, conspiracy and sedition gnawed at law and order, and progress.

The death of the Tsarevich Dimitry was then resurrected to be placed on the whispered list of Boris's offenses. Since direct accusation was too dangerous even to be whispered, other means were found to profit by his now universally suspected complicity. And subtle dialectics were invented to start a controversy and a rumor that the Tsar's command to remove Dimitry from his path to power had been foiled.

The Tsarevich had not been murdered, soft voices purred. He had been whisked away in the night, in time. A playmate had been stabbed in his stead. Dimitry himself lived. Well hidden from the Tsar's henchmen, he was waxing strong in mind and body, under loving care. Soon he would return.

CHAPTER 1

THE MAN WHO
CALLED HIMSELF DIMITRY

Not long before the end of the sixteenth century, Prince Adam Vishnevetsky (or Wiśniowiecki) acquired a place called Brahin. Prince Adam was a scion of the royal house of Gedimin, virtual father of modern Lithuania, and had a strain of the Blood of Rurik.* Brahin was, and is, a great oasis in reverse — a relatively arid molehill in a vast swamp — in the southeastern sector of the Pripet Marshes, where Central Europe merges into Eastern Europe.

The acquisition of this bit of solid ground was only one of several annexations to the vast estates Prince Adam and his sister Eve inherited from their forefathers during the 1500's, after the family seat of Vishnevets became conspicuously inadequate for so important a clan. Indeed, by 1600 the Vishnevetskys had spread from the small valley where the Horyn River is born, in Volhynia, down to the Dnyeper and across. There, on the far side just south of the Muscovite border, they owned sparsely inhabited expanses of steppe and forest, sprinkled with towns and villages, as large as today's state of Maryland or the kingdom of Belgium. It was Brahin, however, which Prince Adam preferred. The Vishnevetskys were Polish magnates. Brahin was only two hundred and sixty or so miles from the center of the estates, yet was on the Polish side of the Dnyeper. That facilitated getting to Kraków and the Court.

Early in 1603 a rabble of Muscovites swarmed out of the old Russian principality of Chernigov to harass the Vishnevetsky do-

* See Appendix B, Table VI, (p. 312).

main. With neither excuse nor explanation, they seized two fortified towns, Priluki and Świecino Horodiszcze, and held them despite protests, with considerable loss of blood on both sides. Prince
Adam, unequipped for major warfare, appealed to the Palatine (or
Voyvode) of Kiev, then chief city of southeastern Poland. The
Palatine, Prince Constantine Ostrogski, formulated a legal complaint and sent it to the King, Sigismund III Vasa. Sigismund, as
royal head of the Polish Republic,* as it was called, then initiated
the long process of diplomatic representation in Moscow. Meanwhile, Prince Adam fumed.

About the same time, Prince Adam had employed a new youth
as a personal attendant, or *valet-de-chambre,* at Brahin — in itself
nothing remarkable, for his staff was very large. The young man
had come from Hoshcha, a small town nearly two hundred and
fifty miles to the west, possibly, though no-one knows, with some
sort of introduction from there. However it was, one day during
the summer of 1603 Prince Adam called for a bath. The new valet,
assigned to the chore for the first time, was inordinately slow, and
His Highness was either in a hurry or by nature impatient. He got
very much exercised over the delay. Then, as a contemporary
chronicler put it,

> the Prince asked him to bring something to the bathroom, and he
> did not bring what he was supposed to bring. Then the Prince got
> very angry and fetched him a slap on the face, and called him a
> whoreson; at which the valet carried on as if he took such actions
> keenly to heart. He began to weep bitterly, and said to the Prince:
>
> If you, Prince Adam, knew who I am, you would not rail at me
> for a whoreson, much less box my ears over such a trifle. But since
> I professed to be a servant, I must bear it with patience.
>
> The Prince then asked: Well, who are you? What is your name?

To this the valet answered that he was in reality the youngest
son of Tsar Ivan the Dread. His life had been threatened by Boris
Godunov, he said, but he had escaped, and people had helped him
get to Brahin.

At that he showed the Prince a gold cross set with diamonds,

* See Notes and Comments, Chapter 1, 1, p. 332.

which his god-father had given him when he was christened, and, as the chronicler continues,

> prostrated himself at the Prince's feet after the Muscovite manner, and said: Prince Adam of Vishnevets! Now that it has come about that you know who I am, I throw myself at your mercy. Do with me what you will. I no longer want to live in such misery. But if you want to help me, you shall be richly requited, when God comes to my aid.

Thus the writer, Konrad Bussow, explained how the valet revealed himself to Prince Adam Vishnevetsky as Dimitry, the son of Ivan the Dread. For lack of any other known name for him, he must be called Dimitry.

There is no report of how much more of his story Dimitry told at that time, but it is obvious that what he did tell fell on avid ears. Rancor fattened upon Prince Adam's liver over the loss of his two towns to the Muscovites. If indeed the young man before him was Ivan's son, then Tsar Boris Godunov was an impostor, as well as a would-be assassin. Somehow, revenge on the Muscovite marauders might be his if this Dimitry was the Dimitry supposed to have been killed in Uglich. If he only were!

By the time the valet had finished declaring who he was and had thrown himself at his feet, Prince Adam's mind was made up. The sobbing figure in a lackey's trappings had opened dazzling prospects to him, and with inspired impetuosity he helped Dimitry rise. He excused himself volubly for his unpardonable language and more unpardonable slap. Then he motioned to Dimitry to stay where he was and strode down the hall to his private apartments.

There he loftily commanded his startled spouse to order a state dinner for that very evening, to entertain the Tsar and Great Prince of all Russia. That done, and leaving the Princess Aleksandra in an easily imaginable state of confusion as to how or when her imperial guest had arrived, Prince Adam hurried off to collect a dozen liveried attendants to bring brocaded kaftans and robes bordered with sables to the bathroom.

An astoundingly self-possessed youth stood waiting. With friendly dignity, the ex-valet allowed himself to be washed and clothed in the handsomest raiment the opulent family had at its disposal. That accomplished, he was conducted by Prince Adam to the courtyard, where six of the finest riding-horses in the Vishnevetsky stables were presented to him, along with a showy *araba,* a carriage after the Turkish style. Prince Adam then handed him a gold-chased sword, a gem-studded dagger and other jeweled arms, while intoning what he obviously considered a proper presentation speech: "Would Your Majesty rest content for the moment with a gift of so little value, as from a Prince of like little value. In whatever way I can serve you further, I will spare neither effort nor fortune, and I will provide you also with all good things."

Then, by way of confirmation of this promise, he added a coachman and grooms, and personal attendants for Dimitry's exclusive service. For all this, the recipient of so much largesse expressed his gratitude in no less reverential language, promising with God's aid to repay Prince Adam.

History provides no details of the happenings of the next few days. Nevertheless, it can be assumed that Prince Adam and Dimitry had further conversations during which the former became more and more convinced of Dimitry's authenticity. Although the diamond cross was not mentioned again, other supporting evidence appeared in the persons of "many important Muscovites" who recognized him as being who he said he was, and of an Orthodox monk or two who also brought corroboration.

Word soon reached Moscow of Dimitry's appearance in Poland. Tsar Boris, "not a little frightened by this news," as Bussow put it, quickly and secretly sent a trusted messenger to Prince Adam, with a promise to give over to him several Muscovite forts and towns along the border, together with a sizable sum in money, if he would "surrender the rogue [*vor,* in Russian]" to him.

The effect of this move was quite the opposite of what had been expected. Prince Adam, who shortly before would have given a good deal to get back the two towns in dispute, now had prospects of much more to be collected from Moscow through the agency of the young man named Dimitry. The messenger was sent home, not empty-handed, but with words designed to throw the Tsar off the trail. Prince Adam had no intention of revealing his plans to Boris.

Dimitry the while brought great joy to the Prince by quickly setting to work to regain his throne. With the Prince's fullest aid, messengers were dispatched down the valley of the Dnyeper and across the steppe to the peaceful Don and the turbulent Cossacks who roamed its banks. The galloping envoys from Brahin were to enlist volunteers along the Dnyeper and Don alike. Yet what specifically took place in that black-earth land, now called the Ukraine, cannot be known. The Cossacks wrote their annals with the sabre, not the pen. Recruitment as carried out *viva voce* in the open air. Scribes who might have written down their warlike boasts instead gladly took up the sword.

The enthronement of a recognized son of dread Ivan was a fitting appendage to their métier of warring for almost any cause, especially a just one. Had they not flocked to the call of the ill-starred champion of freedom, Nalivayko, only a handful of years before? And here was another champion of freedom.

Legend has it that Dimitry himself had once ridden with the Cossacks, and well he might have. His superb horsemanship was soon to win acclaim in knightly Poland. But that detail did not matter. It did not matter if any horseman of the steppe had even heard of him. The prospect of setting him on the throne of the Tsars was a beautiful thing to the Cossacks, who had no cause to love the reigning autocrat, Boris Godunov. Besides, the boundless cultivated plains and the well-stocked coffers of Muscovy were more appetizing than any raids on petty principalities such as they carried out from time to time. Accordingly one ataman after another swore to call up a *druzhina*, a band (literally, of friends), and build an army for Dimitry. On rode the messengers, east and south.

By this time, Prince Adam had come to the conclusion that Brahin was not an entirely safe place for so valuable a guest. It was a scant twenty miles from the Muscovite town of Lyubech, which had been guarding the Russian border for eight centuries. The trade route to Lyubech offered too great facility for a quick raid on Brahin, like the raids on other Vishnevetsky property, if Boris decided to resort to such measures. Zalozhtsy, the residence of Adam's cousin, Konstantin Vishnevetsky, well over three hundred miles to the west, would be much less vulnerable.

Although it is not known just when Prince Adam set out on this journey, summer must already have turned to autumn, and alarming news was beginning to circulate in the capital city of Kraków, nearly a thousand miles away. Those declared *hostes patriae* called the Cossacks — those "enemies of the fatherland" — were gathering once again, perhaps even accompanied by some of their own mortal enemies, the Tatars, to march on Poland's sacred soil. Though the Cossack ataman Nalivayko, leader of the latest Cossack uprising, was dead — some said barbarously roasted in a hollow brazen bull by order of the Polish Diet — Cossack forays recommenced.[1]

Prince Adam was not unaware of what was talked about in Kraków. Nor was he unaware that it was high time for him to inform the Polish government officially of Dimitry's arrival. Accordingly, on October 7, he sent a letter to the Great Chancellor and Field Hetman of the Republic, John Zamoyski, the brother-in-law of his cousin Prince Konstantin. It was couched in the formally humble terms which were considered proper.

A man had chanced to appear at his home, he wrote, who confided in him that he was the son of Ivan the Dread. This man wanted to call upon His Majesty the King for help in regaining the capital of his country. Because the Great Chancellor not only was the devoted guardian of the Republic but also loved the House of Vishnevetsky well, Prince Adam dared "to ask for advice as to what to do with him." He would have written sooner, but he had been in doubt himself. Now, "more than a score have come running to him from Moscow," swearing that that realm belonged *jure naturali* to this man; and furthermore, the *starosta* (prefect) of the border-town of Ostyor testified on his behalf. Prince Adam therefore enclosed digests of "a couple of letters," and once more asked what to do in the matter.

Meanwhile, very disturbing details were reaching King Sigismund's ears. Cossack atamans were thronging into Poland already, to join this "Pretender," swear him allegiance, march with him to Moscow, and crown him with the ancient Crown of Monomakh — the legendary gift of the Byzantine Emperor Constantine IX "Monomachus" which had become the symbol of anointed sovereignty in Moscow.

King Sigismund had not long since signed a twenty-year peace treaty with Tsar Boris Godunov. He had just lost a war in Sweden. He was entangled in Austrian politics. He was at odds with the almost omnipotent Great Chancellor, and his influence in the Republic of which he was the head was at low ebb. Under such circumstances he could not risk any violation of the treaty. Peace with Moscow must be kept.

The King accordingly sent a letter to Prince Adam, asking for full information and commanding him to see that the "Pretender" present himself in the Royal Palace on the Wawel at Kraków. About the first of November the answer to this reached the King.

Judging by the transcript later sent to Pope Clement in Rome, which still survives, Vishnevetsky's letter was a long one. This is fortunate, for it contains what amounts to an official account of how Dimitry said he was saved, perhaps dictated by Dimitry himself.

Beginning with a brief history of the life of Ivan IV and the birth of his last child, Dimitry, Prince of Uglich, the communication went into some detail regarding the reign of Fyodor, the plots asserted to have been devised by Boris Godunov, and Boris's reputed attempts to have Dimitry murdered. It was the second of these attempts, that of May 1591, which was popularly supposed to have been fatal. To prove that it was not, however, and lacking real knowledge of what had happened, facts had to be invented for the letter, one of which was palpably at variance with history. Nevertheless, that one point is not positive proof that the whole story is untrue, for memories are fallible. If Dimitry was not murdered, or did not die, the basic fact recited in the letter, that another boy was substituted for Dimitry, was undoubtedly true.

In any case, the letter went on, the outcry after the murder was

such that all Uglich was aroused, and in short order an infuriated
mob cut the assassins to pieces. Not only that, the rioters killed
some thirty children to boot, all of whom were apparently so fero-
ciously slaughtered, including the substitute Dimitry, that their
identity could not be determined. Dimitry's mother could not tell
that it was not her own child.

It is fairly clear that most or all of this, along with a great deal
more, was told to Dimitry by someone whose name is still unknown. This someone was probably the same as the person who
originally told — or reminded — Dimitry that he was the rightful
heir to the throne, and who had either to invent an explanation for
the survival, or clarify what happened for a boy recovering from an
epileptic fit. Some of the details may have been sheer fiction, but
the story has some ring of truth in it — *if* the Tsarevich was saved,
and grew up to be the Dimitry who had come to Brahin.

From then on, the story of Dimitry as recounted in Prince
Adam's letter to the King is in considerable part confirmed by independent historical documents. When his protector died, Dimitry donned the habit of a monk, to lose himself in a vast and virtually anonymous throng. He seems to have been in Moscow in
1600, when King Sigismund's ambassador, Leo Sapieha, arrived for
discussions regarding a peace treaty. It is even remotely possible
that Dimitry made some sort of contact with the Sapieha entourage, if not with the Ambassador personally. His first appearance
in Poland, however, seems to date from 1601 — a date not mentioned in Vishnevetsky's letter, but known from other sources.

While the letter merely states that "he fled into Poland, where
he first stayed secretly with Pan Gabriel Hoyski," other sources,
helped out by later allusions of Dimitry himself, show that he
really went (and logically) first to Kiev, where he appeared in the
garb of a monk or lay-clerk.* How long he remained there is uncertain, but in time he made his way west to Ostrog, the seat of the
Princes Ostrogski, one of whom was the octogenarian Voyvode,
Prince Constantine. There he remained for some months, part of
which he spent in nearby Derman (where Prince Constantine had

* See Appendix D, p. 317.

a monastery) and in Hoshcha, the residence of Pan Gabriel Hoyski.

Although Prince Constantine later denied all knowledge of Dimitry, his son Prince Janusz admitted that he had known him. This admission of course does not explain what Dimitry was doing on the Ostrogski estates, yet it should be stressed that an atmosphere of religious liberty existed at Ostrog, Derman and Hoshcha which was at least in great contrast with the antithesis of liberty which prevailed in Muscovite Orthodox surroundings. Only Catholics, and particularly Jesuits, were not tolerated by the Ostrogski Princes. Any Orthodox (or heterodox) pilgrim was virtually certain of hospitable reception and "entertainment."

It was at this time, and for unknown reasons, that the still fugitive young Dimitry went to Hoshcha, where Gabriel Hoyski lived, twenty-odd miles down the Horyn from Ostrog. Gabriel was assistant to the very Orthodox Prince Constantine at Kiev, and marshall of the court at Ostrog, but this provided no conflict with the Hoyski non-Orthodox leanings. Both Gabriel and his son were ardent proselytizers of the Unitarian branch of Protestantism which had been planted in Poland by Fausto Socini not many years before. The two Hoyskis founded schools at Hoshcha to teach Unitarianism, and to inculcate Polish liberalism in young minds. Dimitry attended one of those schools.

Although details are again wanting, it appears that Dimitry spent his twentieth birthday — that is, the Tsarevich's twentieth birthday — at Hoshcha. He may have worked in the kitchen, as suggested by a Jesuit report, or studied, or both. Whatever he did, he unquestionably had an opportunity there to acquire an education strongly tinged with religious skepticism, along with a carefree spirit of accommodation to circumstances. Then, still waiting for the proper time to "reveal himself," he left. His goal was Brahin.

At Ostrog or Derman, either Dimitry had tried to get the ear of the Ostrogskis and failed, or in the long run had feared to try. Something apparently led him to believe that the wealthy and distinguished Vishnevetskys would hear him more sympathetically.

However it was, his decision to go to Brahin was superlatively fortunate, or well calculated. Within a very few months, an interview with the King of Poland, whose backing he had to have, was not only possible — it was commanded.

For his part, Sigismund properly reserved judgment on the matter of Dimitry until he could talk to him personally. He therefore avoided an open breach with Moscow by having strict orders issued on December 12 prohibiting the Cossacks to assemble into any sort of warlike group or army, and at the same time forbad the free people of the Republic of Poland and Lithuania to sell them arms or ammunition. Whether or not the people obeyed is not known. That the Cossacks would pay little heed should have been a foregone conclusion. Royal edicts unaccompanied by troops were accepted most indifferently by the Cossacks. Although from a philosophical point of view such documents might be admirable, they had no bearing on practical life.

At this juncture, the former ambassador, Leo Sapieha, now Great Chancellor of Lithuania and second only to the Great Chancellor of the Republic in the curiously organized state, took an interest in the affair of Dimitry. Ever since his embassy of 1600–1601 he had been keeping Sigismund informed about famines and troubles in Muscovy and similar welcome news. War with Muscovy was to be avoided, but weaknesses and calamities there were appreciated and carefully watched.

Sapieha either had in his employ, or employed for the purpose, a Livonian (possibly a Latvian) fugitive from Moscow named Petrovsky, who was said to have been a servant of the Tsarevich in Uglich. By command of King Sigismund, Petrovsky was sent to Zalozhtsy about mid-January, 1604, to spy. It is obvious that the King needed some sort of testimony from somebody, but it is equally clear that machinations of one kind or another led to the choice of Petrovsky for the identification-assignment. Hints of motives and their outcome did not delay in showing up, but for the moment it need only be said that Dimitry "recognized" the spy immediately, and challenged him to tell the truth.

Petrovsky thereupon broke down and acknowledged that he was

an agent for the Lithuanian Great Chancellor. But to the amazement and gratification of the cousins Vishnevetsky, Petrovsky did not hesitate to see his "Tsarevich" in the young man before him, and to point out Dimitry's blue eyes and "fiery blond" hair, just like the Tsarevich's. But the climax came when he added that the young man also had a birthmark by his nose, and one of his arms was shorter than the other. Although a dozen years had passed since he had seen the Tsarevich, and the boy of eight and a half had become a man of twenty-one, there could be no doubt in his mind. The young man was Dimitry Ivanovich, Prince of Uglich and rightful Tsar and Great Prince of all Russia.

Other details were perhaps not so convincing, but they were obviously either not noticed or explained away. Dimitry, for instance, was far from a tall man, while Ivan the Dread had been at least six feet three — but Fyodor was not above medium height either, and was pudgy. Then, in contrast to Ivan's originally long, thin face, Dimitry had a large nose, full lips, and a generally broad face, with prominent cheek-bones and little or no beard. (He probably shaved, which would not have been remarkable enough to be mentioned by Polish writers.) His complexion was swarthy, possibly due to life in the open air, though his hands were described as "aristocratically" white. Ivan had had more of the Viking build and had been handsome in his youth. Dimitry could hardly have been called that. Yet Fyodor had been even less well favored, so that it could be said that both sons took after their respective mothers. Actually, in the end, whatever could be said against Dimitry's facial lineaments was submerged in the appearance of the man as a whole, with his Ivan-like broad shoulders, his carriage, and his tremendous vitality, coupled with an uncommon agility such as Ivan had never possessed. His confident grace, on horseback or on foot, brought wild acclaim not only from Prince Adam and Prince Konstantin, but from scores of guests and hundreds of the neighboring magnates.

Indeed, the Polish nobility — and it has been said that one out of every ten Poles was a noble — flocked from near and far to Zalozhtsy to be presented to "the true Tsar of Muscovy." Some volunteered the support of their arms and fortunes in his forthcoming campaign to claim his throne. Others entertained him lavishly, as only Polish noblemen could in those days, vying with one another in the Polish equivalent of big potlatches. A few even chafed over the delay, though it was the dead of winter, and demanded that Dimitry mount horse with them and prance right off to Moscow. But *Królewicz Mróz* (Jack Frost) and prudence won out. Dimitry was persuaded to ride to Kraków instead, to demand (more likely, to beg) men and money of the Polish King. It is not known whether anyone mentioned the royal command.

Dimitry himself unremittingly maintained the dignity mixed with friendliness of royal blood. No Polish noble, however lordly, matched his lordliness; no magnate, however vast his treasure chamber, wore jewels, brocades and sable with more air of habit. Kindness and hospitality he accepted, but only after promises of future recognition and reward. His knowledge of the Polish language was outstanding, and among men more accustomed to wars and frivolities than learning, he wrote letters and dispatches quickly and with a bold command of words. He knew Russian history, which in itself was complicated. But even more wonderful was his knowledge of Polish etiquette. The tangled interests, rivalries and finances of the Polish *szlachta* (nobility) were clear to him, but that was not enough. It was gauche to address a nobleman by family name if that nobleman held any position, even a minor one. All the voyvodes, castellans and starostas should be addressed by title, and there were more than a hundred of the highest, and smallest, category — the starostas were numberless. Dimitry not only met this test, but in addition rode a horse like a Cossack, faced wild beasts on a hunt with only a knife, a spear, or a bow and arrow, and jousted with the strength and dexterity of a hero of the Battle of Tannenberg. As some said, if he indeed were not descended from Rurik the Viking and Vladimir Monomakh, he should have been. For everyone this made him the rightful Tsar.

By then Zalozhtsy had become cramped for so great an entourage. A mob of young nobles milled around Dimitry, urging him toward Kraków or tugging him toward Moscow, jostling, fighting, and above all strutting and boasting. As one contemporary put it, these snobs, these ferocious young embodiments of Mars, "cracked nuts with their eyes, killed flies with their pointed moustaches," and hated flowers because they did not explode or smell like gunpowder. To get Dimitry away from these and other distractions, Prince Konstantin decided it was time to think of obeying King Sigismund.

Nevertheless, he decided on taking a slightly circuitous route, involving a further delay. For a mixture of reasons, he would make a detour beyond Lvov, and stop at the castle of Sambor.

Sambor was the birthplace of Princess Ursula, née Mniszech, Konstantin's illustrious wife. Princess Ursula had a younger sister who was very charming. She was just the right age — about fifteen — for a promising young man such as Dimitry Ivanovich, Prince of Uglich, and rightful heir to the ivory throne of Ivan the Dread. It would be a nice tie for the Vishnevetsky family. Rurik the Viking was one of their ancestors, too.[2]

CHAPTER 2

THE PRICE OF AID

S AMBOR IS ABOUT one hundred and twenty-five miles west of Zalozhtsy, across the Volhynian hills. There Prince Konstantin's father-in-law held court magnificently. This great nobleman was Pan George Mniszech, Palatine (Voyvode) of Sandomierz, Castellan of Radom, and Starosta of Lvov, Sambor, Sokal and Rohatyn, with the title of Superintendent of the Red-Russian Saltworks thrown in for good measure. Pan George — *Pan* was a title comparable to *Don* in Spanish — was the son of Nicholas Mniszech, of Velké Kunčice, Moravia, who migrated to Poland and married the daughter of the Castellan of Sanok. This lady's name was Barbara Kamieniecka.

The marriage brought Nicholas valuable connections, important posts, and two daughters and three sons. George was the youngest son and with his brother Nicholas "the Younger" spent his youth at the court of King Sigismund II Augustus. Sigismund quite unwittingly laid the foundations of George Mniszech's fortune.

During more than twenty years, Sigismund's family life was exceptionally unhappy. This resulted in *affaires de coeur* which cast a scarlet light on an otherwise illustrious reign, and in regard to which, for an unknown length of time, the Mniszech brothers were his confidants. George was both sharp and glib — much more so than Nicholas the younger. He promoted his personal interests with consummate skill. Even the King's favorite palace was his for the taking, so to speak, and when its royal master went to join his ancestors, the contents of Château Knyszyn went to join George Mniszech — table service, silver, jewels, and the kind of cash that takes three or four days to count.

A colossal scandal followed, which mounted up to the very Diet of the Republic. But George and his slower-witted brother were not without supporters. They pleaded that others had also made fair haul of the royal spoils, and the plea told — a kind of reasoning far from unknown today. The final upshot was that, with the aid of the supporters and some of the "others" who had profited, the whole affair became too involved for any one, or even ten, individuals to be directly accused. Gradually the storm subsided and before long vanished, dispelled by the refusal of the late King's sister and heiress to prosecute. This lady, Catherine, wife of King John III of Sweden, be it added, was already the mother of another Sigismund, a boy who was to be crowned King of Poland fifteen years later.

For some little time after, George Mniszech's activities were apparently quite innocent. Henry of Valois was elected King of Poland, only to run away a year later and be succeeded by King Stephen Báthory, Prince of Transylvania. Stephen got involved in a war with Muscovy which he would have won if the Poles had let him. But the "rights of the nobles" stopped the victorious march of the Polish King, giving the enemy all the advantages.

The defeat by default, however, did not interfere with George Mniszech's progress toward financial and social ascendancy. For his part in the campaign, about which almost nothing is known, Pan George was rewarded with the towns of Sanok and Sokal, as mentioned, and later the important castellany of Radom.

About this time, Pan George married Jadwiga Tarłówna, who had valuable family ties, and begat five sons and five daughters. Then, in 1588, just before the birth of his last daughter, Marina, his cousin Bernard Maciejowski, Bishop of Kraków, got the ear of the new King, Sigismund III, and Pan George was put in charge of the royal residence of Sambor, including the management of the royal saltworks, as well as of the finances of the royal estate as a whole. These nominations, to complete what has already been

listed, were followed by his appointment as Palatine of Sandomierz, the fifth palatinate in rank in the Republic. Pan George,
the son of an immigrant of undistinguished provenance, had risen
to be the peer of princes and nobles whose pedigrees rivaled that of
the King.

Since Pan George was an exceedingly devout man, the resources
which had been thrust upon him led him to dedicate himself lavishly to religious foundations and to earn a name for himself
particularly among the Bernardine monks — although the Do-
minicans were not left unnourished by the pabulum of his charity.
Indeed, so great was his affection for the Bernardines that he de-
fended that order personally before a tribunal in Rome and, perhaps because the matter was hardly of grave importance, won his
case. It is therefore not surprising that it was in the Bernardine
church in Sambor that his daughter Ursula married Prince Konstantin Vishnevetsky on January 13, 1603.

But all these grand gestures cost money, even beyond the extraordinary demands always made on a Senator of the Republic.
In addition to his sacred donations, he had to make secular hand-
outs for the entertainment of guests, for maintaining a small private army, and for lavish *fêtes champêtres* such as became a great
Polish magnate. Finally, Her Ladyship Pani Jadwiga demanded
her share of valets, ladies-in-waiting, and guards.

As a result, the congeries of wooden pigeonholes, as a contemporary description calls the buildings, which made up the castle at
Sambor was not equal to the demands made on it for room. Some
of the fancy *hajdúk* (imported soldiers, mostly Hungarian) had to
be quartered in the town. Bitter complaints from the townspeople
resulted. But these were wholly minor irritations compared with
the intense annoyance caused by the inadequacy of Pan George's
resources. His responsibilities had become such by then that, despite his considerable talents and ingenuity, his efforts to increase
his income and to develop and protect local commerce were in
vain. He could not solve his financial problems.

The climax came just when his daughter's wedding had brought
further glorious ties to the house of Mniszech. Pan George was

obliged to inform His Majesty that he was virtually bankrupt. Indeed, the wedding was undoubtedly the immediate cause of the unpleasant admission, for the attendant festivities were as costly as staging a musical comedy on Broadway today, and were far from dissimilar in garishness. The groom's resources would have been more than equal to the emergency; the bride's father's were not. In fact, by then he was unable to remit the royal rents that were already overdue.

Sigismund had long been patient, or more likely apathetic, but these further confessions of shortages were too much. He sent one of his courtiers to Sambor to investigate, and if need be to act. To avoid additional delays, he also supplied the courtier with full powers, signed and sealed.

It was a case of he came, he saw, and if he did not conquer, he at least produced his ultimatum. Pan George flushed scarlet at the prospect of sequestration and the shame of ruin. Begging the agent to hold off any action, he sent another letter to Kraków, not only filled with piety, but even enclosing the cash proceeds of the sale of some of his personal property. Sigismund accepted the piety and the money, and recalled the agent. Mniszech then wrote once more, on September 18, 1603, asking for one year's grace on the balance.

By this time it is far from unreasonable to assume that news of the remarkable apparition of Prince Dimitry of Uglich had reached Sambor. Surely Pan George's son-in-law would not have gone out of his way to conduct his guest to Sambor without prior communication, and it may be that it was at Mniszech's suggestion that Prince Konstantin decided to make a halt there on his slow progress to Kraków. In any event, the speed with which Dimitry made himself at home in Sambor was in sharp contrast to the Vishnevetsky procrastination in setting out.

To be sure, although travel generally was taken for granted in Poland in those days as nowhere else in Europe, princely travel was hampered in reverse proportion. Nothing in the rest of Europe quite matched the showiness or magnificence of a Polish nobleman's journeying — unless it was a matter of royal "progresses," such as Queen Elizabeth's. Depending on the season, there were arabas or sleighs for the prince and his wife and guests, and simpler conveyances for bed-linen, robes and gowns and the infinity of other things needed during and at the end of the journey. There were horses for the servants as well as the guests and relief horses for both riders and carriages. There were court attendants with armor for the prince and other nobles, robes of state, and jewels, and a detachment of private militia for protection.

Such a procession, including the baggage-train, was slow to organize, and slower to move. In a similar instance to that of Dimitry's cavalcade to Kraków (about which nothing specific is known), a princely train advanced in five sections, at one-day intervals, with the musicians two days ahead of the prince. They had to keep out of the way of His Highness's Cossacks, his coach and his court. And this was just an "ordinary" prince.

Konstantin of Vishnevets can scarcely have accorded much less pageantry to his guest, the rightful Tsar of Muscovy. That the ride should have taken three to five days would consequently not be surprising. It could hardly have taken less, although movement by sleigh in the winter was reasonably fast. Under such circumstances, and because the caravan was going on all the way to the capital, the Prince would have had many hours en route to spend unfolding his plans and showing Dimitry how his father-in-law would be of great help. Pan George sat in the Senate and could volubly back Dimitry's request for men and arms — and effectively, too, because he was a Catholic. It was time for Dimitry to realize that the "Russian streak" in him, which envisioned an army of undisciplined Cossacks to march on Moscow, virtually without any well worked-out plans, must yield to sounder tactics and to trained Polish backing.

It is to be taken for granted that Dimitry showed enthusiasm for the proposals, for he clearly followed Polish advice during the next few months. But by the same token, Dimitry was certainly told all about Prince Konstantin's sister-in-law, little Panna ("Señorita") Marina. No fairer or more regal princess could be found to brighten the dark, medieval apartments of the great palace in the Kremlin.

Leaving aside conjectures, however, it is recorded that Dimitry and the Prince arrived at Sambor in February, 1604, probably early in the month. He was received there as the true Tsarevich, with all the honors due that rank. Ostensibly, it was a state visit to a Senator of the Republic, but it was also a family affair. Dimitry met Marina along with other members of the family, and a strong bond developed quickly between them.

Marina was petite. Many called her beautiful, although her high, prominent forehead, long nose, and small mouth probably reflected pride rather than grace. Nevertheless, she was in strong contrast with the heavier Russian girls of the day:

> For the world has no pearls like the sweet Polish girls,
> With soft voices so merrily tinkling;
> Their cheeks are milk-white, lashes black as the night,
> And their eyes are like stars, ever twinkling.

Indeed, it was her eyes which were Marina's real glory. They were large and intelligent, and they gave charm to a face otherwise so chiseled that it seemed of marble. Dimitry was evidently soon caught by their spell.

But if Dimitry was caught by this spell, Pan George was caught by another. With nearly half the period of grace granted by Sigismund gone, and no relief in sight, his situation was little short of desperate. Still, twenty years and more before, Pan George had found his way out of a different sort of trouble by aligning himself with King Stephen in a campaign against Moscow. Now, by the grace of good fortune and an intelligent son-in-law, he had an opportunity to align himself again, not with a King against Moscow, but with the rightful heir to the ivory throne in the Kremlin against a usurper. The reward, if the heir gained the throne, would be far more lavish than anything he had ever obtained from Stephen. It could be hard cash, not offices which brought more trouble than honor. At least, he could try to place himself in a position which would make such cash available. This seems to have been the line of reasoning which led Pan George to his next step.

By this time one of Mniszech's domestic servants came forward

to declare to his master that he had been made prisoner by the
Muscovites at the siege of Pskov the year before Dimitry was born,
and that he was sent to Uglich. There he had often seen the young
Prince, and he had no doubt whatsoever that the resplendent figure which had arrived in Sambor was that same Prince in adult
form. This second identification was received with joyous satisfaction and without any inquiry into such details as the continued
captivity of the servant long after the war was over. Pan George
asked no questions, either of the witness or of the object of his
testimony.[1]

A more important affair had developed: Pan George had noticed
the attraction exerted by his daughter on his guest. With great
inner comfort he observed each little sign that pointed toward further conquest, and before many days had slipped by he was convinced that Dimitry was inextricably caught. Whether Marina's
wiles were innocently or deliberately employed was an academic
question. From Pan George Mniszech's point of view, Dimitry
must be persuaded to dally there a little longer while he could lay
plans.

Marina, true daughter of her father, was a devout girl. She had
been raised in the bosom of the Bernardine church, and the Bernardine fathers were as much her friends as they were Pan George's
debtors. Pan George soon began talking rather pointedly to some
of the more discreet Bernardines. In answer, through a fog of indi-
rection born of an urge to say the right thing, the impression was
conveyed to Pan George that the budding romance was generally
approved. Specifically, however, Dimitry had a grave shortcoming;
he was a schismatic, an Orthodox strayed lamb. If the romance was
not to be broken off for the sake of the soul of Marina, Dimitry
must be brought into the Fold.

The undelayed upshot was that a plot was devised, which undoubtedly deserves the label "pious," in which the Bernardine
Abbot, Francis Pomaski, who was also curé of Sambor and a royal
secretary, and Father Anserinus (or Gonsiorek), an accomplished
theologian, joined Pan George in a religious assault on the unsus-
pecting former monk or lay-clerk of Orthodox monasteries, Dimitry.

Dimitry was ill-equipped to combat so determined a trio, even had he sincerely wanted to. His theological luggage was light, as one historian has put it. By nature he did not like verbal controversy, and he had no reason to love monks — Catholic, Orthodox, or otherwise. On the other hand, his life at Hoshcha had bred in him a mixture of skepticism and opportunism — if that is not too strong a word — which enabled him to evade issues which were difficult to avoid. Thanks to this training, when Father Anserinus came to the direct point of proposing that he abjure his errors and find forgiveness in the Church of Rome, Dimitry neither said yes nor no, but satisfied the devout triumvirate by "foreseeing a happy outcome to their talks."

Dimitry had advanced another step toward Polish help without seriously compromising himself. Mniszech was convinced that all was well. And Abbot Pomaski was felicitated in due time by no less than Pope Paul V for his "victory" over Dimitry.

With an atmosphere of saintly blessedness warming the icy blasts of late February, Dimitry felt that the time had come. His nature was fiery as his hair, and impetuous. The passion of youth had caught him, irrevocably, and would not be quieted until satisfied. He suddenly demanded the hand of Marina in marriage from a startled but unquestionably transported Pan George Mniszech.

Pan George was not so easily bowled over as Dimitry. There was probably nothing he wanted more at the moment than the rightful Tsar of Russia for a son-in-law. He would risk all to see Dimitry crowned. But before any agreement was reached Pan George wanted terms. He wanted to know precisely what profit the wedding would bring him, personally, as well as what Marina would get out of it. Of course, she would be Tsaritsa, but there must be no doubt about her right to worship as her forefathers had, and she must have property of her own for her fitting, independent state. All of this, Pan George evidently decided, could be taken care of in a marriage contract, the terms of which were surely beginning to spell themselves out already in Pan George's mind.

How far Dimitry committed himself to his potential father-in-law at this time is not known. But circumstantial evidence points to no little degree of clarity between them. The signs are these.

By the time Dimitry reached Kraków, his attitude toward his future
had changed materially. No longer was he a waif with pretensions
to the Muscovite throne and a hare-brained dream of grabbing it
with the help of a band of hare-brained Cossacks. He had become
in the eyes of the Vishnevetskys and of Mniszech and their kith and
kin a rightful monarch with a just cause, soliciting the effective
cooperation of a great Republic, and the approval of a great King.
By dethroning Boris Godunov, Dimitry would also dethrone the
Asiatic torpor and isolation of contemporary Russia and restore
the ancient ties with western Europe which had once placed Russian princesses on the thrones of France, the Holy Roman Empire
and Hungary, and German and Polish princesses on that of Russia.
By reuniting Russia with the modernizing stream of European
civilization, Dimitry would create an invincible barrier against
further Ottoman expansion, and perhaps point the way to a united
Christian Europe. Such a concept, Dimitry undoubtedly realized,
even though it came from a schismatic, could not but interest the
Pope as well as many secular rulers in the West.

By this time, Dimitry's presence in Poland began to take on
more significance for the Great Chancellor than Prince Adam's
letter had at first inspired. After ignoring the letter, Zamoyski now
announced his wish to interview the "Balkan princeling," as he
called Dimitry, with a hint that the man was unimportant but
might stir up trouble. Dimitry's stories did not impress him at all,
he said; on the contrary, to him they were highly suspect. He knew
men well, he added, and he would like to peer into Dimitry's
mind — a human lie-detector three centuries ahead of time. He
would see if there were anything to all this tale.

Whether there was any direct connection or not, Prince Konstantin and Pan George just then decided that it was time to obey
King Sigismund's command. Order was given for assembling the
necessary arabas, wagons, horses, supplies and people, and about
leap-year day 1604 a vast caravan lumbered out of Sambor. Kraków
was nearly two hundred miles away.

If the long delay was intentional, as seems likely, it was not to
show disrespect to the King, but rather designed to permit the ba-

cilli bred by Pan George in Dimitry's cause to infect the suscepti-
ble Polono-Lithuanian body politic. To the great contentment of
Sambor, they had already reproduced marvelously. Whereas the
Dimitry fever had so far attacked mainly the young, restless petty-
nobility, by the end of February it had set grave but highly inflammable senators at odds amongst themselves. Kraków awaited the
impending visit in a turmoil of intrigue and partisanship of the
kind then often described in Biblical language as a tohu and bohu.

The nobility and governing classes of the hybrid Republic,
which formed essentially one group, were ardently individualistic,
inordinately proud, jealous of their prerogatives, and ebullient.
These classes had chosen for their ruler, in parliamentary election,
Sigismund III Vasa, son of King John III of Sweden and Catherine
Jagellonica, sister of Sigismund II Augustus of Poland. Sigismund
III was virtually devoid of Polish blood, being in the sixth generation of descent from the Polish Princess Elizabeth, who married
Charles Robert of Anjou, elected King of Hungary. Thus from
the middle of the fourteenth century the influences which formed
Sigismund's character were Swedish or otherwise non-Polish, and
the King was taciturn and cold, in contrast with his vivacious subjects. His reign of forty-five years, only sixteen of which had
slipped by when Dimitry was in Brahin, was already showing signs
of exacerbation of the feelings of mutual suspicion and mistrust
with which it may be said, for all practical purposes, to have begun.

It was therefore to be expected that the reaction of Sigismund's
most reliable advisers to the appearance of Dimitry and his cause
would differ greatly, if not totally, from that of Sigismund himself.
Hardly had Vishnevetsky's letters to Zamoyski and to the King
been received than doubts as to Dimitry's identity began to be expressed, largely by the Zamoyski faction, which threw members of
the opposing faction onto Dimitry's side. Sigismund was caught in
the middle, but his antipathy for Zamoyski may have influenced
him toward Dimitry at the start. Nevertheless there were good reasons for careful and cautious inquiry.

Students of European history will recall — and Dimitry's contemporaries well remembered — that the crusading King of Portu-

gal, Sebastian, had been killed in Africa in 1578. His body was buried on the spot and doubts quickly arose as to whether it *was* his body. As a result at least four different individuals appeared in Europe who, in rapid succession, claimed to be the deceased monarch. The latest of these, Marco Tullio Catironi, had only in those very days, so to speak, been turned over to the interested authorities. The young man from Moscow, Dimitry, might well be another example of such imposture.

Insistent voices were nonetheless raised on Dimitry's behalf, and where six doubted or outright denied, half a dozen trumpeted his authenticity. When, then, it appeared that Prince Konstantin Vishnevetsky was going to bring Dimitry, "in state" of course, to Kraków, the excitement boiled up again. In fact, as early as January 6, 1604, Sigismund Myszkowski, Great Marshal of the Court for the Kingdom of Poland, began writing letters to friends in Italy, stating that Dimitry had been examined by envoys from certain boyars in Moscow who were convinced that he was the true son of Ivan the Dread.

In addition, Myszkowski — who enjoyed flourishing an all but baseless title, "Marquess of Mirow" — predicted that Tsar Boris Godunov would not last another year. The boyars, he wrote, would tell Boris of the "coming" of the Tsarevich, and Boris would deny it with insulting language. The boyars would then draw their swords and do away with the man who now was for them only a usurper.

This flight of imagination is a reflection of what people were gossiping about in Kraków early in 1604 — and not mere "ordinary people." Myszkowski was one of King Sigismund's confidants. Along with the Royal Vice-Chamberlain, the Bishop of Kraków, and the Governess of the Royal Household, Myszkowski had a voice in the King's Council of far more authority than the position or judgment of any of them justified.

Other monarchs also consulted the wrong people, but that did not alter the outcome in the case of Poland. That Myszkowski wrote more than one letter predicting the early assassination of Godunov *because Dimitry was genuine* shows what was being talked about in Sigismund's camarilla. It also shows that Mniszech well knew how to reach the King's ear and influence people through such intermediaries as the Bishop of Kraków.

Between early November and early January, then, enough word had spread from Sambor to the royal palace on the Wawel for the Great Marshal to circulate — practically to broadcast — the news. Two of those to whom he is known to have sent details were Pietro Cardinal Aldobrandini, son of Pope Clement's brother, and Vincenzo Gonzaga, Duke of Mantua. Myszkowski's gossip-mongering was followed, only eleven days later, by a letter from the Papal Nuncio in Kraków to Pope Clement which informed the Holy Father of the mission of Petrovsky to Zalozhtsy. In this, he added an important detail: "From Moscow there is word that the people's detestation of the Grand Duke [Boris] there continues." Although it is certain that there was unrest in Muscovy, such letters from Poland reflect a shocking amount of hope for the worst for Moscow and Boris alike.

Disturbed meanwhile by reports, and by the delay in Dimitry's arrival in Kraków, Sigismund wrote again — this time to Prince Janusz Ostrogski, Castellan of Kraków and premier secular peer of the Republic. He commanded that Dimitry be dissuaded and prohibited from his move to enlist Cossack support, since it was "evidently dangerous to trust to the aid of those people." And Dimitry was to be urged again to visit His Majesty. Further evidence of Sigismund's real impotence as a ruler is hardly needed.

The letter to Prince Janusz was sent shortly before February 7. It was followed within a fortnight by a circular letter from the King to all members of the Diet. Calling Dimitry's appearance in Poland "a matter of no little importance," which was to prove one of the understatements of the century, Sigismund outlined Dimitry's story briefly, closing with summaries of reports that Tsar Boris was alarmed and was taking military precautions along the border with the Republic. Then, in what amounted to a postscript, Sigismund explained that Sapieha's spy had recognized Dimitry as the true Tsarevich, and added: "Several members of Our Council have pointed out to Us that a great occasion presents itself to Us for the good, the honor and the enlargement of the boundaries of the Republic, because if this Dimitry were elevated to the [Muscovite] empire with Our help, then much could be gained thereby."

More specifically, but obviously to be veiled over, what would be gained would be gained for Sigismund personally. To put the points briefly, at the time he was elected King of Poland, Sigismund was heir to the Swedish throne. On his father's death, that throne as well as the Polish should have been his, but religious fanaticism combined with other troubles (principally having to do with Livonia, torn between Sweden and Poland) never permitted Sigismund to avail himself *de facto* of his succession. Indeed, an attempted reconciliation with the Swedish people had only resulted in his deposition in 1599, in favor of his uncle Charles, declared "hereditary ruling Prince."

These historical factors underlay Sigismund's pretensions that "Sweden could be freed more quickly [from his uncle], Livonia pacified [under himself], and power [Sigismund's] strengthened against any enemy [Muscovy?]." Nevertheless, he had to admit that at the same time there was the question of "breaking the peace and the loosing of burdens on the Republic, and not on us." Since there were advantages and disadvantages in the matter of supporting Dimitry, Sigismund asked the members of the Diet to communicate with him, after considering "all sides."

There can be little doubt as to which way Sigismund was leaning. Whether Dimitry was indeed the son of Ivan IV was of so little consequence to him that the word of a single, untested witness virtually established that identification for him. What was really important was the question, should the Republic avail itself of a beautiful opportunity to intervene in Muscovy. Although he may not have been entirely "persuaded" yet, the letter shows that Sigismund hoped the senators would help persuade him. Ten days or so after he sent the letter, Dimitry arrived in person.[2]

The calvalcade conveying Dimitry from Sambor reached the Mniszech town-house in Kraków about March 5. While the answers to the King's letters began arriving at the palace, word of mouth perquisitions and conclusions proliferated. And the cause of Dimitry prospered.

With his name already known from Gdańsk to Kiev, from Finland to the Beskid Mountains, and in all directions beyond, Dimitry's arrival could not but attract enormous popular attention in the captial. He did not disappoint expectations. Lodged as a prince should be, Pan George's guest was continuously accompanied by an escort of thirty gaily bedight gentlemen and nobles. The Muscovites in his train swore he was their prince, the Cossacks of the Don protected him, Polish magnates opened their homes to him, the ordinary citizens of Kraków flocked to see him in the streets, and the Bishop of Kraków received him in audience.

All of this except the audience was spontaneous. That, coming within a day or two of his arrival, merely testified to the preparations Pan George Mniszech had made beforehand. At the same time, it gave Dimitry the opportunity to assure the Bishop that if he were given ten thousand men to help him break through the Muscovite border he had no doubt that the whole country would give itself over to him. And word brought from the heart of that country just then by one Ivan Poroshin seemed to confirm the claim.

Within the following week, Mniszech, who had no intention of letting the iron cool, struck again. A royal audience was imminent, the outcome of which could determine Dimitry's, and consequently Mniszech's, future. It must not end in the irresolution and indecision which usually characterized Sigismund.

To that end, the royal ears must be influenced in advance — but not directly by Mniszech. For example, an ostentatious banquet for his senatorial colleagues, with Dimitry present but tactfully kept in the background, could supply other voices to speak in his favor. Such banquets, where the Polish magnates could gorge themselves in an atmosphere of outrageous glitter, offered the pomp and circumstance so beloved by them, to use words penned in those very days by William Shakespeare. How better win a few champions in the Diet?

So, about March 12, a week after their arrival, the Mniszech residence sparkled and glowed with the cream of Poland's governing class, arrayed in all the solemn finery for which the court at Kraków was famous. Dimitry dined, as inconspicuously as if he were just another young noble, amongst bishops and palatines, castellans and prefects, all these to see him, but not to notice him. It was a clever plan.

Monsignore Claudio Rangoni, Prince-bishop of Reggio in Emilia and Papal Nuncio in Poland, was one of the guests of honor. In his dispatch of March 13 to Pope Clement VIII he described the scene in these words:

> The Palatine of Sandomierz gave a banquet for the Senators, and since he expressed particular desire for me to attend, I went; and there that Dimitry who says he is the Grand Duke of Muscovy sat at another table in the same room with a few others, almost as if incognito, so that I had a chance to see him, study him, and hear the various arguments and opinions expressed. He is a young man of good presence, brown of complexion, with a large birth-mark on his nose by his right eye, with long, white hands, so shaped as to indicate noble extraction. He is spirited in speech, and in his behavior and manner of treating others he has true grandeur.

The Great Chancellor, Rangoni went on to write, said that he had visited Dimitry in his residence, and that he was not entirely satisfied with his answers, while the Vice-Chancellor [Peter Tylicki], without having spoken with him, could not but think of past pretenders, notably the pretended King Sebastians. Nor did the Castellan of Kraków, Prince Janusz Ostrogski, believe the story.

On the other hand, said Rangoni, the majority of those present believed him to be the true heir of the deceased "Grand Duke" [Tsar Fyodor], and these included not only the Livonian, who was not at the banquet, but another Pole who had been a prisoner in Moscow and the Chief Notary of Lithuania, Woyna, along with the Chancellor, Sapieha, who were. In addition, both the Bishop and the Palatine of Kraków expressed their conviction that Dimitry was genuine, and the former particularly made friends with him, giving him a book which espoused the cause of the "Ruthene Union" — a sugar-coated way of referring to the return of the Orthodox Church to the Catholic fold. The Bishop, it should not be forgotten, had already talked with Dimitry.

This is the first hint that the Catholic circles in Kraków were interesting themselves in converting Dimitry. Indeed, as perhaps was to be expected, Rangoni stressed even more the advantage to the Church of seeing Dimitry's wild red hair confined by the Crown of Monomakh than he did the value of his friendship, once on the throne, for Poland. But Dimitry had already seen to it that word should reach the Nuncio's ears of his interest in a secret meeting — secret, because his Muscovite supporters would regard with more than mere disfavor any intimacy between the true heir to the Tsardom and the representative of the feared and detested occupant of the Chair of Saint Peter. The letter therefore concluded with a cautious suggestion that Rangoni would see Dimitry if the King approved, but that the King's approval would in some measure depend on the Archbishop Primate of Poland and the Diet of the Republic.

Whether this was an informed guess or a logical supposition, Dimitry was "admitted to kiss the King's hand" the following Monday, March 15, 1604. Those present were Vice-Chancellor Tylicki, Marshal Myszkowski and Grand Secretary Rudnicki, all representing Poland, along with the Chief Notary, Woyna, for Lithuania. It is significant that all of these high officers were predisposed to believe, and therefore to favor, Dimitry. The audience was otherwise strictly private, and *in camera.*

Dimitry stood before the impassive descendant of Emperors of the Holy Roman Empire, Kings of Poland, Sweden and Hungary, and Great Princes or Grand Dukes of Lithuania and even Muscovy, and declared that

it was with him as it had been with the son of Croesus, who was dumb and had never spoken, but when stricken with the overwhelming grief of seeing his father placed in great danger by Cyrus suddenly found his voice; so he, Dimitry, also had not been able to speak before. But recalling the dangers through which he had passed and his miserable present state, and the suffering of his fatherland, occupied, not by a great Prince such as Cyrus, but by a low, vile person, his own subject — such was his grief that he could not but summon a voice with which to pray His Majesty to

take pity on him, and lend him aid to get back his legitimate dominions.

He then reminded the King that other great Princes had
suffered similar wrongs and had been aided by other Kings, particularly the Kings of Poland. He had turned to Sigismund because
he well knew his power, goodness, and piety. If Sigismund would
take up his cause, Dimitry promised true gratitude. Indeed, he
perorated, perhaps God had willed, through his hour of need, to
extend a great token of favor to the King, the Kingdom, and all
Christianity.

The Image of Royalty sat as mute as the son of Croesus while the
Vice-Chancellor replied for him, in purely protocolary style, with
words of compassion and love. The audience was over.

Dimitry retired to an antechamber, where he seems to have been
met by the Marshal of the Court, Myszkowski. Accounts are far
from clear, but either Myszkowski or another royal attendant gave
him some sort of a royal promise to pay part of his expenses while
he remained in Kraków, and either then or at the time of his departure offered Dimitry brocades, furs, and other such customary
gifts, along with a gold chain and medal, the latter bearing a like-
ness of King Sigismund. Dimitry also received a pension of four
thousand florins, but again it is not certain whether this was provided right after the first audience, or at the time Dimitry made
his congé. Whatever the date, King Sigismund did extend some
sort of courtesies to Dimitry, but it is more important to know
that on March 15 it was whispered in the young man's ear that
Sigismund was personally favorable to his suit, as the sworn enemy of Boris Godunov. Just what did Sigismund hold against the
Tsar?

Slowly the inclination of Dimitry toward Poland and the West
became more and more evident. Slowly Sigismund inclined more
and more toward Dimitry. Backstage, Mniszech and his party labored. And in the coulisses, Rangoni oscillated uncertainly — now
Seraph, now Lilith — between devotion and opportunism. Yet it
may justly be said of Rangoni that the motive of self-aggrandize-

ment appears to have been all but submerged in the sea of his devotion to his Church. The prospect of welcoming Muscovy into the Papal flock through the young man who called himself Dimitry was enticing to Rangoni. It soon flashed into an obsession.

Four days after the royal audience, Dimitry accompanied Mniszech and the Palatine of Kraków, Zebrzydowski, to the Friday sermon and exercises in the Franciscan oratory, after which he took part, lighted candle in hand, in the procession of the Holy Sacrament and in the benediction pronounced in the Church of Saint Francis. Crowds jostled around the Prince and the two Senators, filling the church beyond the capacity of its ancient Gothic walls. Dimitry radiated pleasure at the offerings of self and purse on his behalf by many who were there.

Later, still followed by great crowds, Dimitry rode up to the Nuncio's palace, craving an audience with him "who represented the person of the Great Father in that Kingdom." Zebrzydowski had returned home, but the presence of Pan George hints that the visit was prearranged. The superficial spontaneity was for the benefit of those who might question the propriety of a visit by a pillar of Orthodoxy to the Pope's representative.

Characteristically, once he was received, Dimitry did not delay or hedge about the purpose of his visit. Not only did he want to assure Rangoni of his "offices and services," but also to explain his position in person and beg him to send friendly words to the Holy Father, the Universal Shepherd. He asked for the Pope's protection and his help in the eyes of the King of Poland. And he assured Nuncio, Pope, and King that the restitution of his throne would bring advantages to the Kingdom and to Christianity. Then he concluded shortly with an innuendo that all this would work to the confusion of the enemy of the Holy Cross. The Sultan did not have to be named.

Meanwhile, Sigismund tried another tactic. In a letter to Zamoyski dated March 23, he proposed initiating secret preparations for backing Dimitry after obtaining permission from the Diet and Zamoyski himself, and then, when all was ready, openly appearing in Dimitry's defense as the rightful heir to the Tsardom — or

"Grand Duchy," as King Sigismund and the Polish Government persisted in calling it.

Far from winning Zamoyski over, this communication prompted only a more elaborate explanation of why he was opposed. Even if the "little Prince" reached Moscow and were crowned, said the Great Chancellor, he doubted if the Republic would receive any advantages. He stood adamantly in defense of the *Republic.* That defense did not envision any support for Dimitry.

Dimitry, however, in great measure nullified Zamoyski's determination to stand in his way. The King, he seems to have known, was already captivated by a dream of drawing Muscovy into the Polish sphere of influence. King Stephen, a generation before, had attempted to reduce the Muscovite danger by dismembering the state as much as the Poles would let him. Sigismund proposed to eliminate it through Dimitry, and by absorption. Dimitry appears to have been ready and willing to be absorbed, politically — at least until he was crowned in Moscow. How sincerely he intended then to requite Sigismund may be doubted, as Zamoyski doubted it. But Sigismund, *pari passu,* was himself none too altruistic about the help he seemed to be on the verge of giving. As a result, politically Dimitry's cause at the moment was on what is mechanically called dead-center.

At that point, before the end of March, 1604, Father Pomaski arrived in Kraków, undoubtedly summoned from Sambor by Pan George Mniszech. Simultaneously a mantle of secrecy was thrown over chapels and council-chambers, hiding everything but a few names: Matthew Woyna, Francis Pomaski, Father Frederick Bartsch (the King's Confessor), and of course the Mniszech clan. What these apostles of Dimitry's cause in reality did remains unknowable, but the spotlight of history soon swept over the outcome. While Sigismund's fundamental indifference relaxed again in Lenten inactivity, hushed perseverance had prepared a telling blow.[3]

CHAPTER 3

PAYMENT

On Sunday, April 4, Dimitry visited the Royal Chapel on the Wawel incognito and sent a Polish gentleman to find the Nuncio. He wanted to tell him something. Rangoni, this time apparently unforewarned, gladly agreed to listen. Thereupon, according to Rangoni's report to the Holy See, Dimitry begged him literally to "turn on the heat" for his expedition, "explaining in various ways how important speed was, and openly promised of his own accord to promote the Union [of the Churches], if God granted that he regain his father's throne."

On the heels of this, without waiting for an answer, Dimitry baldly asked if he could go to confession on Easter Sunday, two weeks later. He was ready to become a Catholic, and he required only that this should remain an absolute secret and that the instruments of his conversion should be the Jesuit fathers. Yet Father Pomaski, with whom he had first discussed the matter, was a Bernardine.

Perhaps Dimitry's choice was prompted by the fact that Sigismund's confessor, Father Bartsch, was a Jesuit. If so, the conversion was surely not to be kept secret from the King. No, that sort of secrecy was even to be avoided. Had Pan George, then, extended a helping hand, putting Pomaski in touch with the Jesuits? Or was the deciding factor Father Gaspar Sawicki, also a Jesuit, who had visited Dimitry the last day of March, possibly at the instigation of Father Bartsch? However it was, someone had put ideas into Dimitry's receptive head, and that someone apparently was a

Jesuit. The organization of the ideas was more likely Dimitry's own.

In any event, Rangoni did not hesitate. His mind was trained to act quickly, and secrecy of this sort not only appealed to him by nature, but in this case was conspicuously for the greater glory of God and His Church. Before many minutes had passed, Dimitry "accepted an invitation" to the palace of the Palatine of Kraków, Nicholas Zebrzydowski — a violent and unscrupulous man on whom Dimitry had clearly made a great and favorable impression.

Moving with a speed inconceivable to King Sigismund, Dimitry visited the Palatine three days later, after allowing time for all arrangements to be made. Leaving his Muscovite companions in an antechamber, he entered Zebrzydowski's private chambers, where Sawicki, the Jesuit of a week before, was waiting with his colleague, Father Stanislas Grodzicki. Zebrzydowski imperiously urged Dimitry to speak frankly, but to weigh his remarks.

There is something strikingly reminiscent in this clandestine encounter of what took place but eleven years before in Paris, when Henry IV discussed his conversion with the Abbé du Perron and others, attended and encouraged by Sully. Both Henry and Sully realized that peace in France and Henry's crown materially depended on Henry's becoming a Catholic. Dimitry had decided for himself that *his* crown depended on Polish aid, and that the way to that was the same.

A second discussion was held on Holy Thursday, April 15, in the Bernardine convent. Since Dimitry's mind was by then made up, this meeting was merely a sort of ratification that he was to be received into the Catholic Church. But the next day the real test came.

Dimitry faced Father Bartsch and the renowned Jesuit, Father Peter Skarga, preacher of the King, and king of preachers. Someone, possibly Pan George, had called them in to help provide a solution to the only major problem still confronting the eager convert: he must remain a cryptocatholic, a secret communicant, at all costs. If his Muscovite supporters mistrusted his Orthodoxy, his cause was still-born. But it was, perhaps logically, Zebrzydowski who knavishly provided the means for his abjuration of Orthodoxy in total and effective concealment.

Some time before, Father Skarga had founded a confraternity of Brothers of Mercy, after the Spanish or Italian pattern. This group wandered through the streets in Holy Week, robed in black with hoods or masks over their faces, as do the *cofradías* in Seville today, begging alms for the poor. The social elite was drawn on for the confraternity, and Zebrzydowski was a member. As he would start his rounds the morning of Holy Saturday, he suggested that Dimitry robe and mask himself and come along. No-one would recognize him, and nothing could interfere with his doings.

Dimitry understood. A plan of action was quickly worked out, and advance notice was sent to Father Sawicki, whom Dimitry had chosen as his confessor. Then the Prince and the Palatine set out. Stopping first at the royal palace and the nunciature, the two detoured through back streets until they skirted the great market place, the Rynek, and arrived at Saint Barbara's, the church given to the Jesuits by King Stephen in 1583. Zebrzydowski led Dimitry to Sawicki's confessional and retired.

Like Shakespeare's Richard III, Dimitry had set his life upon a cast; he must now stand the hazard of the die. Sawicki had heard the rumors that Dimitry was not the real son of Ivan, not the real heir to the Crown of Monomakh. Before he could accept the abjuration of a man who acted in the name of Dimitry Ivanovich, he must know the truth. Pointedly, he reminded the confessant that God's aid is given only to those who are sincere. Who thinks to sham beneath God's gaze imperils his soul. Dimitry caught the hint, and hesitated. Then, imploring the protection of divine providence, he protested before God and man his absolute sincerity. Sawicki, satisfied, received his abjuration. The confession began.

The next day, Easter Sunday, Dimitry had wanted to attend service in one of the churches. Although most men could easily be swallowed up in the vast throngs of Easter worshipers, this was not the case with him. He stood out too prominently. Furthermore, 1604 was one of those years when Easter was the same day for Catholic and Orthodox alike. Dimitry's appearance in a Catholic church, while his Muscovite compatriots were celebrating the religious festival *par excellence* of Orthodoxy, would arouse grave suspicion. Therefore, Dimitry attended no service at all, but devoted his time Easter Sunday to drawing up a letter to Pope Clement VIII. Sawicki stood by, to guide his hand in Polish, and to translate into Latin.

Pope Clement had been skeptical of Dimitry's story, and Dimitry conceivably knew this. So, to strengthen his position, he opened his letter piously, submissively. After brief mention of how he escaped death and came to Poland, he wrote that all he wanted was to repent his past errors (religious, of course), and rest in the peace of the Catholic fold. God's will he would serve, were that even that he should renounce the crown his ancestors had worn. But if God willed to aid him, his cause was not lost. Then, suddenly swerving from almost abject humility to a flight of impassioned oratory, he concluded with a direct appeal to His Holiness:

> Father of all the lambs of Christ, the Lord God can be making use of me, unworthy [as I am], to spread abroad His glory by the regeneration of strayed souls, and the uniting of great nations to His Church. Who knows to what end He has thus preserved me, and bound and reunited me to His flock? Kissing the feet of Your Holiness as those of Christ Himself, with humble and profound greeting I declare before Your Holiness, supreme Pastor and Father of all Christianity, my obedience and my submission. I do this secretly, and I humbly pray Your Holiness for weighty reasons to guard the secret. Executed at Kraków the 24th of April of the year 1604.
>
> Your Holiness' most humble servant,
>
> > DIMITRY IVANOVICH
> > TSAREVICH OF GREAT RUSSIA AND
> > HEIR TO THE STATES OF THE MUSCOVITE MONARCHY

The Pope who had received Henry IV into the Church, who had broken the Spanish hold on Papal diplomacy, and who clearly saw that the destruction of the Ottoman threat was indispensable for the freedom of Christian Europe, was not a man to repulse a convert who might indeed bring millions of souls with him. Dimitry was not unaware of this.

Although this letter was written on Easter, which was April 18, it was not signed until the following Saturday, April 24, when Dimitry called at the nunciature, as will be seen. The day before this call, he took leave of Sigismund, for it was time to return to Sambor. He appears to have received presents, but as has been mentioned there is confusion as to what he received on each of his two audiences. The matter is unimportant.

More to be noted is Sigismund's habitual chilliness, contrasted with Dimitry's self-confident vivacity and eloquence. Whatever traces of uncertainty he may have evinced during his earlier presentation to the King seem to have disappeared. Dimitry now had the manner of a man who has made his decision and is content therewith.

Nevertheless, rumor had it that the senators had already expressed the opinion that nothing should be done for Dimitry until the entire matter had been discussed in the Diet, and this may explain the King's reticence. The King was known to have mentioned to Rangoni privately that Zamoyski refused to go along with any proposal to help the "little Prince" at least until then, even if the delay would damage his cause. Since Zamoyski was Supreme Marshal of the Republic as well as Great Chancellor, that meant that he would not authorize any troops that might help Dimitry. Consequently Dimitry, as Pretender to the throne, would have to lead the troops himself. If he undertook this, and any Polish troops were involved, it could be only with Sigismund's aid, and unofficial, secret aid at that. No reference to any of this was made at the leave-taking.

Meanwhile, Dimitry had called Father Sawicki to his residence and indicated that he wanted to take holy communion while he was in Kraków. This was arranged, and on the day after his visit to the royal palace Dimitry presented himself at the nunciature, ostensibly to take leave of Rangoni. The visit was open, public, as far as the gate. Within the building it was private, in the absolute sense. Dimitry was to receive communion in the Catholic rite from the hands of the Papal Nuncio.

Confirmation followed communion, after which most cordial greetings were exchanged. Dimitry vowed to work for the union of the Muscovite Orthodox Church with the Catholic, so soon as God permitted him to reach Moscow and assume the crown. It would take time then, he admitted, but eventually even his Moslem and pagan subjects would embrace the True Faith. This he promised, not in his personal interest nor as a ruse to gain support, but out of his loyal and sincere conviction.

Seemingly overcome by his ardor, Dimitry attempted to throw himself at the Nuncio's feet, crying that since he could not kiss the feet of His Holiness, he wished to kiss those of his representative. Rangoni gently raised him from the floor. Recovering himself, Dimitry took out his letter to Pope Clement, signed and dated it, and handed it to Rangoni, asking that it be dispatched by the next post.

Rangoni took the letter with such evidence of affectionate pleasure at Dimitry's piety that the latter then went on to say that he would like to have a priest attached to his person. But since difficulties might always arise, he added that the Nuncio could write to the Jesuit Provincial proposing that one of that order be sent to Prince Konstantin Vishnevetsky, with secret instructions to attend Dimitry. He also asked that he receive a dispensation regarding fasting, on the stated grounds that his health suffered, but clearly meaning that conflicts between Orthodox and Catholic practice would be noticed.

All was granted, with Rangoni only requiring time to communicate with His Holiness about certain problems with Dimitry's coronation in Moscow, when that happy event came to pass. All in all, the significant aspect of the conversation was the fact that Dimitry of his own volition offered so many concessions. It was all one-sided. Not a hint was there of a mutual agreement — a contract, so to speak. In this, as almost always, Dimitry exhibited extraordinary foresight, in that he did not lay himself open to the possibility of demands, to be made later. The most the Church ever could do would be tactfully to remind him of promises made.

Yet there can be no doubt of Dimitry's basic sincerity at the time. He had loathed the Orthodox monks whom he had known. He had tasted their almost universal ignorance, superstition, and at times physical incontinence. Among the Jesuits he found sharp minds; among the Bernardines, intelligent piety. In Poland there was light, while in and over Muscovy a pall of stagnation seemed to hang, dense, persistent. So he had chosen the bright faith of the Poles, his benefactors, of the Pope, symbol of union with Europe, and, not least, of Marina, his love.

Once upon a time, centuries before, Russia too had been a part of Europe. Then came the hordes from the East, destroying, cutting all links, engendering suspicion and fear. It had taken four generations to pull Russia herself together again. Now it was time to bring her back into the European world of freedom and progress.

Jumbled thoughts of this sort unquestionably jostled, collided, in Dimitry's impulsive brain. The rapidity with which he passed from one subject to another, from plan to plan, as recorded in letters and contemporary records, shows quick decisions, spur-of-the-moment answers. His was a character of great contrasts. Because of that the major question remained, had Dimitry by then a planned strategy at all? On the chess-board of his coming struggle with Moscow, would he know how to defend his opening gambit?[1]

Taking leave of Rangoni, Dimitry returned to Mniszech's townhouse. Preparations had already been made for the return to Sambor, since all objectives in Kraków had been met and, at least in greater part, conquered. It was not merely that the Muscovites in Dimitry's entourage were bridling with impatience, not untinged with suspicion over so many pourparlers with the papal "instruments" at Court. Time was of the essence. *Anything* might happen now in Muscovy.

In Dimitry's mind, Marina was perhaps uppermost. He was bursting to tell her of his new-found faith. Pan George, also, was ready — for more reasons than one. Keen knower of his fellow Poles, and of his fellow senators, he was satisfied with his stay in

Kraków. Chill Sigismund had leaned perceptibly toward Dimitry's cause. The Mniszech clan and its hangers-on could sustain it
in the capital, and there were hopes that even the arch-conserva-
tive, constitution-thumping Great Chancellor and his "confeder-
ate," Janusz Ostrogski, would either be bent or balked.

Trumpets blaring and drums rattling, Dimitry's cavalcade
pranced and lumbered out of Kraków after mass on Sunday, April
25, 1604. Yet, despite the fanfare, only one detail of the return
journey to Sambor is attested. Dimitry and Pan George were
present at a legal action in the municipal courts of Sanok on May
4. Prince Konstantin Vishnevetsky was not with them. Pan
George probably made a logical halt there because it was the residence of his son Stanislas, the new Starosta of the town. On this
occasion, the leading nobility of the region had assembled for the
regular and inevitable lawsuits involving property rights, or some
such thing, and this provided an excellent opportunity to present
Dimitry in full panoply of state. Pan George knew that local support was needed to supply men for Dimitry's army.

Since "pride, pomp and circumstance" beat the cadence for Dimitry's glittering cortège, it had taken eight or nine days to cover
the hundred and thirty miles to Sanok. No matter. The reception
was as theatrical as Pan George could make it. All Sanok turned
out to greet the hero, whom Pan George eloquently styled in
pompous Latin *Illustrissimus ac Invictissimus Demetrius Ivanovich, Imperator Maioris Russiae, uhlecensis, dmitroviensis, grode-
censis Princeps, omniumque ditionum monarchiae Moschovi-
tarum subjectarum dominus et haeres* — Most Illustrious and Most
Undefeated Dimitry Ivanovich, Emperor of Great Russia, Prince
of Uglich, Dmitrov and Grodek, and of all countries subject to the
Muscovite monarchy Lord and Heir. It all sounded very important.

But to impress the magnates at Sanok who were being invited to
Sambor, it had to sound important. Sambor itself was filled with
important-sounding things, with its Great House for His Majesty
the King, Royal Lodging of His Highness, Lofty House, Great
Royal Dining Rooms, and so on — names of wooden buildings scat-

tered in abandoned profusion within the wooden palisades and walls, gay with red shingles and little gilded onion-bulb domes. And all this importance rapidly became the Mecca of the Tarłow and Vishnevetsky families, Pan George's in-laws, and the vain and generally low-principled Stadnickis of the early 1600's. These were soon joined by a score or more neighbors of great distinction, among whom were Stanislas Borsza and John and Stanislas Buczyński, all three of whom joined Dimitry's expedition.

Both Dimitry and Pan George had written Zamoyski, again urging him to unsheathe his sword for justice and the restitution of the Crown of Monomakh to its proper owner. That was just before leaving Kraków. Two weeks later, after they reached Sambor, Pan George sent a more detailed letter, mentioning the enormous support he had throughout that region. But the prematurely old Great Chancellor, only in his early sixties, was obdurate. He did not even bother to reply.

At the same time, Pan George wrote to Prince Janusz and his father Prince Constantine Ostrogski. The latter, half a generation older than Zamoyski, remained unconvinced by anything Mniszech wrote, and his son went even further. He bluntly stated that Dimitry's "gang" would not reach the border of the Republic, hinting that he proposed to interfere.

Dimitry in the meantime was making love and planning his campaign. At least, the conclusion of his biographers of then and now is that love was not forgotten. (Of the military preparations there is recorded evidence.) Marina is still a totally obscure figure at this crucial period in Dimitry's career, but there can be no doubt that she was pulling the threads of her net ever tighter around the glamorous Prince. She may have had doubts about his real identity before he went to Kraków, and these may not have been entirely stilled even after his return. But the steady assembling of soldiers, slow as it was, the aid granted by the King, meagre as it was, and the prospects that Dimitry might indeed fight through to Moscow, all began to give clear lines and color to the shadowy picture of herself as Tsaritsa of Muscovy which was gradually emerging in her mind. It may even have won some measure of tender feeling toward Dimitry, although a sober study of history insinuates that the love between the two was extremely one-sided. Perhaps there is truth in the words imagined by Aleksandr Pushkin for Marina's reply to Dimitry's declaration of love:

> . . . as God is my witness, till your feet
> Are resting on the dais of the throne,
> Till Godunov is overthrown by you,
> I will not hear more monologues on love.

Love entered little into Pan George's thoughts either. He was determined to reap lavish rewards for his support of Dimitry. Nevertheless, to prevent the cup from slipping on its way to the lip, he must put Marina first and himself second. Pan George therefore now found time to draw up a wedding contract. It was to be the keystone of the lofty arch of Pan George's ambitions.

This preposterous document was apparently originally written in Polish, perhaps by Pan George himself, and translated into Russian. The high-flown style and total neglect of the most elementary application of modesty in the use of titles were characteristic of Polish and Russian intercourse generally in those days. Consequently, the daughter of an insignificant, bankrupt Pole of petty-noble birth is swathed in titles equalling in number, if not in rank, those of the immortal Queen Elizabeth I. The nobleman himself is of course equally emblazoned. Yet there is curious restraint regarding Dimitry. He is modestly referred to as Tsarevich of Great Russia, Uglich and Dmitrov only, with an etcetera and a few generalities.

This modesty is counterbalanced, however, by the lavishness of his gifts. In the words of a recent historian, in that contract Dimitry "did as he liked with the empire and the thousands of millions [of rubles] which were not yet his." He disposed as Mniszech proposed.

After brief, but costly, mention of Pan George, Dimitry specified gifts to the Most Illustrious Lady Marina Mniszchówna of Velké Končice, Voyvodess of Sandomierz, Captainess of Lvov, Sambor and Medenitsa, and so on, daughter of the Most Illustrious Lord

George Mniszech, etc., in order that the latter would grant him the hand of the former in marriage, as follows:

> As soon as I enter into the inheritance of our realm of Muscovy, I will give to His Grace [her] Lord father ten hundred thousand Polish zlotys, for His Grace himself for hastening the departure, and for the payment of debts, and for bringing to us [in Moscow] the Lady Marina, our future wife; from our treasury in Moscow, I will give for her attire the most precious regalia, and in like manner table silver; in case her Lord father himself is not present for any reason whatsoever, I will without delay give as stated above to such messengers as His Grace may send, or as we may dispatch, on which I give my word of promise as Tsar.
>
> Second, upon our mounting the imperial throne of our father, we shall immediately send out ambassadors to the Most Excellent King of Poland informing him and doing him obeisance, to the effect that our agreement be known to him and be allowed us without prejudice.
>
> Third, to the above-mentioned Lady our wife, we give two great realms, Novgorod the Great and Pskov, with all districts, members of the councils, noblemen, boyars'-sons, and priests, and with all revenues and suburbs and towns and villages, with all the authority and freedom and all that we and our father possessed and directed with regard to these realms . . .

And in this same legalistic style, on rolled the phrases providing for Marina after marriage, if they had no children, and guaranteeing her religious freedom to worship according to the Catholic faith, with Catholic priests, and the privilege of establishing Catholic schools. Dimitry furthermore agreed to work toward the introduction of Catholicism in Muscovy, and to lead the country into union with Rome. But if God did not grant that he might accomplish so much within a year, both Pan George and Panna Marina are free to separate from him and go their own way — whatever that may have meant. However, a renewal period of an additional year was hopefully provided.

This document was endorsed on May 25, 1604, by "Dymitr Carewicz, with his own hand," under the Polish text, and "Tsarevich Uglitsky" under the Russian.

A fortnight later, Dimitry signed a contract with Pan George, again filled with high-sounding titles and dripping with gifts. Out of "love, kindness, good-will and inclination," Dimitry gave him and his heirs and assigns forever the principalities of Smolensk and Seversk of the realm of Muscovy, "with all that pertains to those principalities, with towns, forts, villages," and so on, ending with a legal flourish. But, he added, for "known and weighty reasons," out of love and goodwill for the King of Poland and the entire Kingdom, in testimony to the concord and peace between the Polish and Muscovite peoples then existing, he gave half of the Smolensk lands, etc., to Sigismund — with detailed explanation of how the halves were to be split.

Along with this further gift, he "bequeathed" to the King and the Polish Republic six cities in Seversk, with the usual etceteras. Indeed, the whole donation ends in a whirl of geographical verbiage which leads the reader to wonder if there was any thought of fulfilment at all. However, it was written on parchment, signed by Dimitry in Sambor, June 12, and, like the marriage contract, tied up with blue ribbon with a red seal affixed. Pan George possibly thought that he had Dimitry tied with something stronger than ribbon.

About the same date, a messenger brought a letter from Michael Ratomski, Starosta of Ostyor, a Polish outpost on the Desna River north of Kiev. Ratomski, in the clearest of Latin, urged "His Celsitude" Dimitry to attend to his affairs more diligently, for "they could easily cool off." Nevertheless, even with Dimitry's documents in his pocket, Pan George did not dare move. There was still danger that Zamoyski and the Ostrogskis would stop Dimitry's army, such as it was.

It was probably about this time that Mniszech went to and returned from Kraków on a jaunt to plead Dimitry's cause once more with Prince Janusz, with a very long detour through Zamość, to see Zamoyski. In vain, and worse. By this time the Palatine of Volhynia had also joined the Ostrogski-Zamoyski camp, because of a distant tie to the Ostrogskis.

All this time, Dimitry was not guarded, in any literal sense of the word. He was surrounded by friends and backers, and this was apparently considered enough. Still, there were those who did not wish him so well. One of these, a monk or priest named Varlaam Yatsky, of disputed status and residence, turned up at Court and presented a story to the King and a number of magnates to the effect that Dimitry was not the Tsarevich, but a monk or laybrother from the Monastery of the Miracle in Moscow, who had fled with him and the Chorister Misail Povadin to Kiev, Ostrog and Derman. Varlaam had lost sight of him in the autumn of 1602, but was sure it was the same man. Since neither the King nor the magnates believed what he said, he was sent to Sambor to tell his tale to Pan George, and to Dimitry himself if he wanted. That was early in August, 1604.

At this point it seems that one Yakov Pyhachov, a boyars'-son of obscure background, joined Varlaam, and the two arrived in Sambor together. While accounts differ in detail, as is usually the case, according to Pan George they were sent by Boris Godunov to murder Dimitry. To be specific, festivities in connection with the impending departure of Dimitry's army for Moscow were in progress, and on the occasion of an unusually late carousal so many of his informal bodyguards were inflamed with wine, brandy, vodka, and what not, that the two thought their opportunity had arrived. Yakov apparently decided that he would go to Dimitry's bedroom, armed wtih a "huge and sharp knife," while Varlaam went to the public pasture outside the castle walls and harnessed a couple of horses for a quick getaway.

Yakov then uneventfully penetrated the royal bedchamber and waited. Varlaam, equally uneventfully, made his way out of the rambling castle. But the pasture slept in Stygian darkness. To find mounts for his *tovarishch* and himself he had to strike a light, a torch. This frightened the entire drove of horses and cattle into a nervous frenzy of galloping round and round the area, and their hoof-beats quickly attracted the town guard, who smelled horse-thievery in the air. In the confusion, Varlaam neither saw nor heard the guard, and was caught red-handed.

What he said by way of explanation is not mentioned in the

delation he later came to write under much altered circumstances. Other sources relate that he was threatened with torture and that he implicated Tsar Boris in his misadventures. The truth is far from clear. Nevertheless, whatever Varlaam revealed saved his life, while his less persuasive companion, seized by Dimitry's guard, was condemned to death the next morning. Dimitry and Mniszech, who judged the case, then ordered Varlaam to prison, from which, for completely unknown reasons, the Lady Jadwiga Mniszech and her daughter Marina had him released five months later — with or without Pan George's knowledge. Whatever the facts of the outcome, from then on Dimitry was strictly guarded, even when among those of Muscovite origin who seemed to be his friends and followers.[2]

Meanwhile, the results of cautious steps taken some time before in Kraków began to materialize. Dimitry had let it be known to Father Striveri, Provincial for the Society of Jesus in Poland, that he wanted a Jesuit chaplain to accompany him on his march to Moscow. There were the usual complications about keeping the matter secret from the Russians in his army. Nevertheless the Jesuits were not long in finding a convincing explanation. Since there were many Catholics enrolled as well as Orthodox, a Catholic chaplain was as proper as he was necessary. And in a burst of generosity not unmixed with proselytism not one but two Jesuit fathers were sent from the College at Jarosław, fifty-odd miles to the west. The senior of these was Father Nicholas Czyrzowski, occasional Governor of one or another college, while the junior partner in this religious exercise was Father Andrew Lawicki, whose youthful body longed to be rent in fiery martyrdom in the tropics but whose ardent mind was willing to exchange refrigeration for incineration. They arrived at Sambor for an interview with Dimitry on the eve of the Feast of the Assumption.

Both sides were charmed by their respective personalities. Dimitry won the fathers to himself, just as they won him to their religious zeal. Almost breathlessly, Dimitry outlined his plans for converting Muscovy to the True Faith, while Mniszech stood ready to second his words when language seemed to fail. This proved hardly necessary, but his real purpose soon became clear. When a lull came, Pan George suggested that Dimitry take communion from the hands of the Jesuits the next day, August 15. He was putting Dimitry's sincerity to the test.

Again, secrecy must be preserved. Still, in the sprawling castle at Sambor this could not be a problem. Dimitry confessed himself then and there, in a secluded spot, and the next day attended the Bernardine Church with Pan George after clandestinely taking communion from the Jesuits. Shortly after, Father Czyrzowski and Father Lawicki returned, bursting with enthusiasm to Jarosław. Their mission in Russia would be hard, no doubt, but oh how important.

The neighboring city of Lvov had been chosen a little while before as the assembly point for Dimitry's troops. Already, streams of otherwise unoccupied Poles were swarming to the ancient city. Although it had been ravaged by fire in 1527, Lvov was greater and more prosperous than ever, and the inhabitants were far from happy at the influx of unruly volunteers for a madcap adventure. Of course, the greater the influx, the greater grew the town's concern. Before long, official complaints were lodged with the King, including protests even from Moscow over the massing of troops so near the frontier. Characteristically, His Majesty took action — in time.

Summer was already on the wane, by then, and Dimitry's plans had taken shape. The interview with the Jesuits had been highly satisfactory to him, and they would join him as soon as they could complete their preparations. Within ten days Dimitry had completed his, however, and there was no further reason to wait. And then, only then, the royal command for the "quelling of certain wrongs occurring in those regions" was borne to Lvov by the Castellans of Poznań and Lvov, to be published on August 31. A week later, a second document, of broader scope and of the kind called a "universal," was sent out from Kraków. It commanded those "not resident to disperse, and to desist from committing violences, murders, and wrongs," and provided suitable penalties for infractions. Somehow it took the officer charged with delivering this thirteen days to ride a little over two hundred miles. But even had he sped on the fleetest horse, he would have arrived too late.

By the date on which Sigismund endorsed the universal, Dimitry had not only taken his leave of Marina and departed from Sambor, but had even moved his troops from Lvov. The March on Moscow had begun.

CHAPTER 4

MEANWHILE IN MOSCOW

A THOUSAND MILES to the northeast, in the Tsar's great palace in the Kremlin, a spectre walked. Beyond all men's belief, the long-dead youngest son of dread Ivan — so it was whispered — had come again to life. The only element that now could threaten Boris's grip on the supreme power welled up inexorably from the very soil of his realm, and the nameless voices of the multitudes stole on the Tsar's ear, babbling softly: "Dimitry is arisen."

Strangely, the superb executive who had ruled for the Angelic Tsar had lost his magic once his own head bore the crown. Yet his reign had begun under the most auspicious circumstances, so far as Muscovy's external security was concerned. Sweden and Poland, neighbors to the west, were at one another's throats in 1598. This provided the possibility of peace with both, along with an opportunity to strike a bargain with one of them to the detriment of the other — always a pleasant prospect for rulers looking for territorial and other advantages.

At this juncture, Poland had made the mistake of sending to Moscow an ambassador furnished with totally unacceptable proposals for an elective dynastic union between the two nations, which would nullify Boris's determination to found a "Godunov dynasty." This move nudged him toward Stockholm, if it had any effect at all, as any sensible or informed Pole must have known it would. At the same time, Boris had no intention of going so far as a military alliance with Sweden, since that would be contrary to his determination to maintain peace. Not even a faint hope of profit-

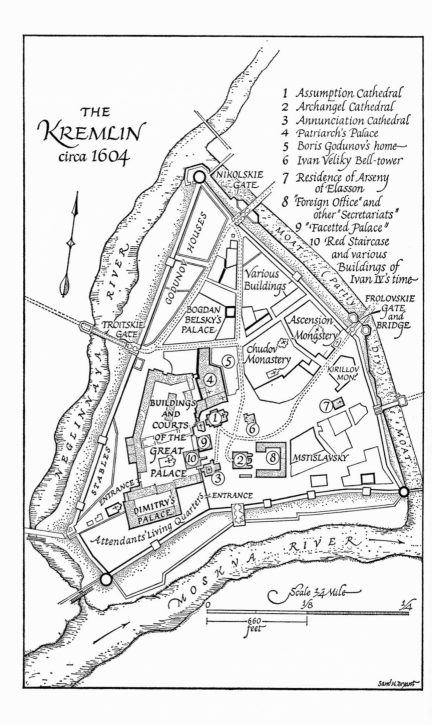

THE
KREMLIN
circa 1604

1 Assumption Cathedral
2 Archangel Cathedral
3 Annunciation Cathedral
4 Patriarch's Palace
5 Boris Godunov's home—
6 Ivan Veliky Bell-tower
7 Residence of Arseny
  of Elasson
8 "Foreign Office" and
  other "Secretariats"
9 "Facetted Palace"
10 Red Staircase
  and various
  Buildings of
  Ivan IV's time—

NIKOLSKIE GATE

GODUNOV HOUSES

Various Buildings

BOGDAN BELSKY'S PALACE

Ascension Monastery

Chudov Monastery

KIRILLOV MON.

FROLOVSKIE GATE and BRIDGE

MOAT (partly)

DRY

TROITSKIE GATE

NEGLINNAYA RIVER

5
4
BUILDINGS AND COURTS OF THE GREAT PALACE
9
1
10
6
3
2
8
7
MSTISLAVSKY

STABLES

ENTRANCE

DIMITRY'S PALACE

ENTRANCE

Attendants' Living Quarters

MOSKVA RIVER

Scale ¼ Mile
1/8   ¼
0
660 feet

Sam! H. Bryant

ing by the Polish-Swedish conflict in the way of attempting to recover the port of Narva, Estonia, lost by Ivan to the Swedes in 1581, would move him to take sides. No. He had a better way to win some advantage.

Boris's eldest surviving child was his daughter Ksenia, universally recognized as an intelligent girl of striking beauty. "She was rosy and white of face," wrote Sergey Kubasov, who knew her, "and her black eyes sparkled . . . Her body was perfectly formed, and so white that one could believe it was molded of milk." She was still in her teens.

Since princesses and princes were generally tools of nationalism or dynastic preservation in more than one sense, the first fiancé chosen for Ksenia was logically a Swede, and a potential bearer of territorial gifts. He was Gustav Eriksson, heir to the deposed Erik XIV, uncle of King Sigismund of Poland, long since dead of poison administered because he was insane. Prince Gustav, at least a dozen years older than Ksenia, might conceivably provide Boris Godunov with some claim on Livonia, including Estonia, or at least on Narva. In addition, Gustav was called Paracelsus the Second because of his exceptional mental gifts, in short supply in Muscovy in 1600. But regrettably he had defects of character and habit which were not overslow in manifesting themselves.

Within months of his arrival in Moscow, with oriental fanfare, Gustav imported his mistress of some years' standing, along with a handful of offspring who had not had the benefit of clergy, as the saying goes, but who promptly disappeared from the historical scene. A few excursions of Prince Gustav and his odalisque around the capital of Holy Russia in a coach drawn by four white steeds were enough to convince the Tsar that this scion of the House of Vasa would benefit neither Muscovy nor the House of Godunov. He shipped the unneeded lady back to Gdańsk, whence she had come, and presented Gustav with the town of Uglich in fief. Perhaps it might prove as unhealthy for Gustav as it had for the Tsarevich Dimitry. In any case, he was "safe" there.

By this time the first rumors that Dimitry was not dead began to circulate openly enough to be heard all over. Boris suspected the boyars from the start, particularly the Romanov family, but delayed action until he found a ruse to rid himself of an even larger thorn, in the person of a far from unassuming old crony of Ivan IV named Bogdan Yakovlevich Belsky. This arrogant connection of the Nagoys (and therefore of the dead Tsarevich) had at one time been considered, along with Fyodor Romanov and Fyodor Mstislavsky, a more likely successor to Fyodor, the Angelic Tsar, than had Boris himself. Now that Boris was Tsar, however, Moscow was too small to provide Belsky with a suitable arena for his boundless energy. He was therefore "honored" by being entrusted with the foundation of a fortified settlement nearly six hundred miles to the south, astride the Tatar road (track would be more accurate) over which the Crimeans had ridden in raids on Moscow more than once. The place was to be named *Tsaryov-Borisov,* or Tsar-Boris-town.

Belsky carried out his task quickly and with regal ostentation. Before long word reached Moscow that Belsky was boasting that Boris might be Tsar in Moscow, but he was Tsar in Borisov, which could be twisted into a hint that he thought he was Tsar over Boris too. Boris retaliated in time, after still further provocation on Belsky's part. He commanded a Scottish surgeon to pull Belsky's luxuriant beard out, hair by hair. A greater insult to Orthodox dignity could hardly have been imagined. Belsky's raw cuticle eventually healed, but deep within him venom seethed.

Boris's racking and humiliating punishment for a trivial impertinence reflects his growing sensitiveness and suspicion. Moscow now seemed to him to be swarming with plotters, mischief-makers; and as his uneasiness grew, so did his steps to protect himself. Soon, as a contemporary chronicler phrased it, the devil put it into Boris's head to want to know everything. This led to such wholesale spying as had not been known even in the days of Ivan the Dread. And the evil thus started brought more evil in its train.

Before long, an informer brought word of a plot hatching among the Romanov family, Boris's next target after the deportation of Belsky. Under the circumstances, the truth of the information may honestly be doubted. Yet such a delation could only lead to further spying, and to the "discovery" (to be doubted) of alleged poisonous herbs in Aleksandr Romanov's storehouse. Since Aleksandr was one of the nephews of Ivan IV's first wife, the entire family was brought to trial, in June, 1601, before the Council of Boyars, a body in some senses similar to England's Court of Star Chamber.

The verdict, possibly influenced by suggestions from the Tsar, and certainly contorted by his family connections, was exile for all the Romanovs and for their leading relatives: four princely families and two of great nobility. In addition, Fyodor Romanov, Aleksandr's eldest brother and head of the clan, was shorn a monk by imperial command, under the name of Filaret. Boris was sparing of human blood, in contrast to Ivan, but he did not shrink from political murder.

The sequence of events hints that the judgment was not passed on these prominent magnates for "plotting" against the life of the Tsar, with poison or otherwise. Their plot, if any, was against his rule, against his assumption of autocratic authority over the rightful heirs of the many-branched descendance of Rurik the Viking and his band of mercantile rovers and robbers. Possibly for that reason surviving records do not suggest what evidence was actually found, or with what specific variety of lèse majesté the guilty were charged. At the same time, not too vivid an imagination is needed to see that the rumor of Dimitry's survival was what really disturbed Boris. As has been mentioned, Boris strongly suspected Romanov connivance in the Dimitry rumor, but the rumor grew louder after the Romanovs were removed. And it began to annoy Boris exceedingly. Indeed, the poet Aleksandr Pushkin was undoubtedly not far from the truth when he put these words in Boris's mouth:

> Who is the foe? An empty name, a shadow —
> Can a mere shadow tear the purple from me?

But by then a greater foe than Dimitry's "empty name" or the cabal of the nobles had borne down upon Muscovy. Nature first blessed, then cursed the countryside with rain — continuous, unmitigated rain. The grain could not ripen but stood green as grass, green as rice in the autumn monsoon. Then on Assumption Day (August 15) came a killing frost. Wheat, rye and oats withered on the stalk. Poverty, hunger and death began to harrow the land.

Boris poured money out of the coffers where Ivan had so rapaciously stored it. The warehouses of the realm were opened, and food distributed. None but the hateful could have said anything of Boris but that he was the living personification of generosity and sympathy, and fatherly care. Nevertheless, in his need to protect and help his people, he had to take measures which brought curses on his name and on all his acts. Peasants and tillers of the soil swarmed toward the capital in search of charity, only to leave their fields untended, and by improvidence even to bring about instances of cannibalism along the rain-soaked, frosty roads.

To halt this insane flight, the Tsar issued an *ukaze* on November 20, 1601, prohibiting the "removing" of the body of farm labor and otherwise providing against further disorder and tragedy. The details are far too complicated for discussion here, but the general salutary intent of the moves was negated, as often happens, by the unwillingness of the people to understand and the refusal of those who were better off to comply, loyally. Prejudice and dishonesty joined hands to thwart a conscientious, if imperfect, design. The inevitable followed.

With the 1601 crops destroyed, the farmers who remained in the fields unfortunately sowed new grain, which was rotten, and nothing sprouted either in the autumn or the next spring. Even greater famine followed, until it was estimated that half a million people died, out of a total population of perhaps four and a half million. Then brigandage came to waste the tortured state. The situation was so bad that a national uprising did not take place only because the people were not strong enough. This meant that repressive measures had to be taken which were both contrary to the Tsar's principles of government and provocative of still further unrest.

In the midst of so much national suffering and agitation, Boris's

private life was largely dedicated to the attempt to found a Godunov Dynasty, to succeed the dynasty of Rurik and of Ivan Kalita,
extinguished by the death of Fyodor the Angelic. In 1600, Boris
had sent an ambassador to England to announce his accession to
the throne and to discuss commercial matters, as well as to look
into dynastic ties with relatives of Queen Elizabeth. Nothing came
of the last quest.

Tactful soundings in the same direction then followed in Aus-
tria, but the results were equally negative. Meanwhile the political flirtation with Prince Gustav had fizzled out and was followed
by an inquiry in Denmark. This proved more fruitful.

Young King Christian IV of Denmark let it be known, through
Boris's envoy, that he was nothing loath to see his youngest
brother, Duke John, wed the daughter of the Tsar. For Ksenia the
nineteen-year-old Dane must surely have seemed a thrilling groom,
with his inevitable breath of western freedom in the musty atmosphere of Muscovite tradition. From Boris's point of view, it was a
superb match. Duke John was also the brother of Anne, Queen of
Scots, who unquestionably would be crowned Queen Consort of
England, with her husband James VI of Scotland, someday in the
not too distant future. Pathetically, the dashing young prince
died, apparently a victim of too much hospitality, on October 28,
1602, very likely even before Muscovite tradition permitted him to
see his future bride.

Yet not even this tragedy turned Boris away from his determination to bring Russia closer to the rest of Europe. If the Mongol-
Tatar invasion of 1236–1240 had clamped down an iron curtain to
shut Muscovy off from the West, Boris had many a precedent of
pre-invasion times to justify his open-mindedness. Through a
daughter of the great prince Yaroslav I, a trace of the blood of the
Viking Rurik flowed in the veins of Queen Elizabeth and James,
King of Scots, as well as in those of Henry IV of France. More
recently, Ivan III had imported Italian architects to help him
build and rebuild Moscow.

With these thoughts in the back of his technically illiterate
mind, Boris then sent a number of young Muscovites westward to

learn science and foreign languages. Four left for London in 1602, and five went to Lübeck the following year. It was a kind of foresightedness that should have been rewarded. But in 1603 the wind which had been sown by dread Ivan had become a whirlwind for Boris to reap.[1]

Ivan had seen that the southern part of Muscovy, the region known as the Ukraine, or "borderland," had remained somewhat depopulated since 1240, to the extent that it offered a temptation to lawless bands, and to Tatars and Cossacks, to roam at will. It was a breeding-ground for raids on Muscovy proper.

Without second thoughts, Ivan initiated a policy of sending any and all who were "fit for things martial" to occupy the land. No matter if they were criminals, colonists (as we should call them today) who were willing to establish themselves in the northern parts of the Ukraine were encouraged, even driven, to settle there. (The south was already occupied by Poles and Cossacks.) In theory, these colonists were to protect the border; in practice, they formed unruly gangs which in time became the greatest menace to the border they were supposed to guard.

Fomented by the atmosphere of this region, which had been well prepared by Ivan's policy, a struggle broke out between the peasants — serfs who had become virtual slaves — and the dregs of the town-dwellers against the established feudal lords, princes and magnates. Hastened by the tragic years of 1601 and 1602, the first armed revolt came in 1603. A numerous band of what were then described as "robbers," with one Hlopko Kosolap as its *ataman,* or gang-leader, appeared under the very walls of Moscow. On September 9, 1603, Boris sent an army under Ivan Fyodorovich Basmanov to the encounter. Hlopko was wounded, taken prisoner, and executed. Basmanov, son of a handsome favorite of Ivan the Dread, was killed. The survivors, denying that they were in the wrong, fled southward, to the Ukraine. And, according to a contemporary historian, not long afterwards more than twenty thousand men capable of bearing arms were assembled there.

So the year 1603 saw the first stage of the peasant war against the State. Although the power-struggle among the boyars had not yet reached its climax, and was far from its end, the peasants and serfs had stepped over the brink of revolution. The struggle lasted, now flaming, now smouldering, until 1917.

On the heels of Basmanov's victory and death, the never-still voice of the people, which is the voice of nobody and yet of everybody, began ever more confidently to murmur that in truth the Tsarevich Dimitry was not dead. He had been saved and had fled to Poland. And as the year wore on, it was impossible for Boris Godunov not to take the murmurs seriously. Semyon Godunov, Boris's cousin and chief of his secret police, then flung spies throughout the land, and many suspects were arrested and interrogated. But there was no sign of the man who pretended he was the Tsarevich Dimitry.

Meanwhile, on September 27, 1603, Boris's sister, the widow of Tsar Fyodor the Angelic, was buried. Many said that her death was only the result of her unhappiness over the troubled state of the empire and the behavior of her brother. The same voices also said that her devotion to Boris was what kept him on a steady course, and that with her death he would fall under the influence of his less kindly and less pious wife, the daughter of Malyuta Skuratov. All Moscow wept the loss of the Tsaritsa-nun, good-angel of Tsar Boris.

Even before this, however, Boris had sent his secret messenger to Prince Vishnevetsky, as has been mentioned, and as early as October 20 it is known that he had begun replacing the captains of border forts with men he considered more loyal to himself. Then, in what seems like despair, he closed the frontier. Fear of "contagion" was his excuse, but the poet Pushkin has phrased his commands, with poetic license, in words that surely reflect his thoughts more honestly:

> Take steps this very instant
> To fence our Russia off from Lithuania
> With barriers, so that not a single soul
> May pass the line; that not even a hare
> Can scurry here from Poland; that no raven
> Can come winging its way from Kraków.

But the iron curtain was of little use. The control of rumor is as difficult as the control of thought. Trickles of reports seeped through a hundred fistulas in the police-dam that ran from Estonia to the Dnyeper River, while rivulets of moral erosion attacked the citadel of government from the unprotected steppes of the Ukraine. And there the Tsar had to protect his flank against men as well as tales. Cossacks and Tatars were more prone to bandy sword-thrusts than words. Yet he must get at his enemy.

Boris now took a step that would have been inconceivable during the lifetime of his sister. He sent for the mother of the Tsarevich Dimitry, the nun Marfa who had been Tsaritsa Maria Nagaya. Personally he questioned her closely, while his wife, daughter of Ivan's former executioner in fact if not in title, watched. Perhaps *she* could tell if Marfa was lying.

In the words of a young Dutch merchant then in Moscow, Isaac Abrahamszoon Massa, Boris and his wife

> subjected the unhappy woman to severe cross-questioning, to know what she thought about the existence of her son. Straightway she said that she did not know whether he was dead or alive. Then Boris's wife, carried away by rage, said to her: "Don't hide from us what you very well know, you whore!" and thrusting a lighted torch into her eyes would certainly have blinded her, had not the Tsar protected her with his own body. Then the Tsaritsa Marfa did not hesitate to answer that her son was alive, that he had been conducted secretly out of the country, [and] that it had been done without her knowledge; but that some people, since dead, had reported it to her.

It must be said that Massa is the only contemporary who supplies the details, that he is consistently prejudiced against both Boris and his wife, and that he was obviously not an eye-witness. Nevertheless, Mikhail Ratomsky of Ostyor reported independently that Marfa at least was questioned by Boris, and gave the date: April 7, 1604 (old style), the day before Easter.*

After this "interview," Marfa was sent back to the monastery where she was exiled. Then, trusting in the untrustworthy, Boris

* Easter, 1604, was on April 8, old style, and April 18, new style — the same day.

sent for Prince Vasily Ivanovich Shuysky, a member of the Commission which he had sent to Uglich in 1591. Of him the Tsar demanded an oath that he had in reality seen the Tsarevich dead and that he had been present at his funeral — that, in short, the Tsarevich had been buried. He was assured that this was true. But in spite of all assurances, there were times when Boris seems still to have wondered if the young man in Poland were not the real Dimitry.

All this while, the chief of Boris's secret police was pursuing his quest. Perhaps through his investigations, perhaps on Boris's own initiative, the Patriarch of Moscow, Iov [Job], Archbishop of Rostov, was next summoned to the palace. Iov owed his patriarchate to Boris, although Fyodor had been Tsar when he was invested with that new rank. He might be trusted, on grounds of sacred duty mixed with gratitude. *Who is this impostor?* Boris asked.

In time, and not too great a time, between Iov and Semyon Godunov, a culprit was produced. Evidence had been found, Boris was told, that enemies among the boyars had connived and broght to Moscow the son of a *syn boyarsky* ("boyars'-son," petty nobleman) by the name of Yury Otrepyev. His family came from Galich, at least a week's ride to the north.

Yury had lived as a serf of one of the Romanov brothers and later of Prince Boris Cherkassky, a brother-in-law of one of that unloved clan. Although Yury was noted for his knowledge of reading and writing (in an age in Russia when few could wield a pen), he was "already known to the Tsar as a suspect person." When misfortune threatened him, in the form of the long arm of the law, Yury fled to a monastery, to be tonsured as a monk. Immune in this way from all civil actions, the youth wandered from cloister to cloister until he turned up in the Chudov Monastery ("of the Miracle") in the Kremlin, where he even worked for the Patriarch himself. As a monk, Yury took the name of Grigory, or Grishka for short.

Grishka apparently was either a fool, despite his penmanship, or the tool of powerful agents. He soon let it be known that he would someday "be Tsar in Moscow." This remarkable assertion was not long in reaching the ears of the Metropolitan of Rostov, Iona, who reported it to Iov. Iov paid little heed, so Iona went directly to Tsar Boris. The latter, who is reported to have called a number of meetings to find out what he apparently already knew, then located an uncle of Grishka among his petty nobles, one Smirnoy-Vasilyev Otrepyev, and told him to place Grishka under tight security guard in the Kirillov Monastery at Belozersk, in the far north. Someone — people said it was the devil in person — whispered in Grishka's ear, and before the guard arrived Grishka hurriedly left for his home town of Galich.

After more wandering, according to the discoveries of the Patriarch and the police chief, Grishka returned to Moscow about 1601 or 1602, where he ran across a monk by the name of Varlaam Yatsky. Between them, there was much talk of this and that until Grishka finally came around to saying that he had in mind leaving Muscovy to go — for purely religious reasons — to Kiev, to the great Pechersky Monastery, and then perhaps even to Jerusalem. Would Varlaam go with him?

Varlaam objected that it was hard to get across the border, past the guards, into another country. Grishka rejoined that times were harder in Muscovy than in the Polish Republic, and furthermore the Tsar had signed a treaty with King Sigismund. These weighty considerations were enough for Varlaam, who agreed to meet Grishka the next day and start on the long, long trek to Kiev. To show his enthusiasm, Varlaam added another monk to their consortium, Friar Misail, whose real name was Mikhail Povadin and whom Varlaam had met on the estate of Prince Ivan Petrovich Shuysky, long since deceased. So far, Grishka was identified, without particulars as to when he and his friends reached the free soil of Poland.

By this time, an ambassador had arrived in Moscow from the Holy Roman Emperor, Rudolf II, in the person of Heinrich von Logau. It was mid-July and von Logau had been en route for two months only from Wolgast, then a port of some consequence in Pomerania whose fame was eclipsed three hundred and forty years later by the notoriety of Peenemünde, half a dozen miles away.

Von Logau gave details about Dimitry in Poland which were then unknown in Moscow.

Boris, however, not to be put in the shade by an Austrian ambassador, quickly countered that the "fake" was a recognized traitor and impostor, and that with one finger he, Boris, would flip him out of the way — or chuck him into jail. After the audience, the ambassador was showered with food and gifts, while Boris lost no time in dispatching a messenger to Lithuania (and Poland) to tell Dimitry's supporters that he was not Ivan's son, but just a smart humbug.

In the meantime, Semyon Godunov's best efforts went to assemble facts to prove the identity of the young man who had turned up in Brahin. Part of what he assembled can be called into serious question, although the amount of pure invention is impossible to know. At the same time, Grigory (Grishka), Varlaam and Misail were three living monks, and some of their activities are independently provable. It could therefore be that the points where their story as told by the Muscovite authorities seems least well attested are those which were added to make it *possible* for the Dimitry in Poland to be the monk Grigory who had fled from Muscovy.

By then the details were unimportant to Moscow. Boris Godunov and the Patriarch, with the aid of Semyon the secret-service man and Prince Vasily Shuysky (a distant cousin of Prince Ivan's), at last had a man of flesh and blood to catch. The ghost had been exorcized. Boris's practical mind could turn away from phantoms to problems of government.

In a mood of complete confidence, Smirnoy Otrepyev was carefully groomed for a special embassy to the Polish Republic, equipped with snares and traps for his "nephew Grishka." That he would succeed in his mission seemed foreordained, since he had every advantage authority and international courtesies could give him. Dimitry's only defense lay in the simple fact that he knew who he was. His so-called uncle, Smirnoy, was far from sure.[2]

CHAPTER 5

THE MARCH

On July 30, Dimitry sent to Monsignore Rangoni a pious bu eloquent letter addressed to His Holiness, Clement VIII, to be for warded. In it he thanked the Pope for an apostolic letter just re ceived and informed him that "within a few weeks, with the aid c God and the benediction of Your Holiness and the grace of Hi Majesty of Poland, and the help of several Senators of the King dom, with what few forces I have, I shall take the road towar those confines [of Muscovy] to present myself before those who ar waiting for me." Such at least is the wording of an Italian transla tion of the original, now apparently lost. To what extent, if any Rangoni edited it, cannot be known.

Nevertheless, the Pope's letter to him must have lifted Dimitry spirits. There was no hint in it of Clement's former skepticism although the salutation was limited to the vague phrase, "dear so and noble lord." But if there was no reference to Dimitry's offer to "all Christianity" and other grandiloquent verbiage, the gat was open, and the strayed lamb was received into the fold. No ma. as serious and cautious as Pope Clement could have done more.

Early in August, Smirnoy Otrepyev arrived in Lithuania. H had traveled six hundred miles in two weeks or less, which is som indication that he did not dally by the wayside. Yet, despite thi bit of haste and the urgency Boris placed on identifying and if po: sible seizing Dimitry, he came strangely equipped for his task.

In the first place, his letters of accreditation were not issued b the Tsar, but by certain boyars of the Council, and addressed t

Leo Sapieha, Great Chancellor of Lithuania, and Christopher Radziwiłł, Palatine of Vilnius (Vilna), who had been dead since the year before. In addition, the bearer was not named — quite contrary to custom — and the documents he bore merely listed complaints: complaints about inspections of the boundary, complaints about border-marauding, complaints about new tolls. There was no mention of Dimitry.

These matters were discussed at some length in the weighty and generally meaningless language of protocol, in public session. Then, when the meeting was adjourned, Smirnoy asked for a private interview with Leo Sapieha. This was again contrary to custom, and Sapieha had no intention of compromising himself. His colleagues, even though junior in rank, were also representatives of the King, he intimated. He could not discuss, or so much as listen to, messages sent for his ears alone.

Smirnoy was pleased to comply with Polish, or Lithuanian, custom, and in a few minutes the boundary commissioners — for were not boundaries the subject? — were startled to learn that Smirnoy's real object was to meet Dimitry and talk to him. Not only that. This curious messenger from the Kremlin, now that he had admitted the truth, went on to say that he believed Dimitry to be his nephew. If this was the case, he wanted to turn him from a road that would prove both fatal for him and dangerous for his country. But if, on the other hand, Dimitry really was the son of Ivan the Dread, then he averred that he would subject himself to his authority, and "personally help him mount the throne."

While Smirnoy's clumsy tactics can today be attributed in part to clumsy instructions from Moscow, the staid and ceremonious commission which he faced straightway reached two conclusions: Smirnoy was not an ambassador, but a spy; and neither Boris nor his boyars really knew who Dimitry was. Jointly and severally, their refusal to permit any interview with Dimitry was quick, polite and final.

Once this business had been concluded, however, the commissioners privately agreed that some danger might arise on account of Dimitry, and Lithuania must exercise great caution. Sapieha re-

ported all this to the King, with a suggestion that it might perhaps
be well to delay Dimitry's moves until the Diet of the Republic
had convened and studied the entire affair.

As if to confirm the impression that Moscow did not know who
Dimitry was, the Patriarch, Iov, then sent one Afanasy Palchikov
on his own behalf to Prince Constantine Ostrogski, in Kiev, asking
him to arrest and punish Dimitry for "heresy and black magic" —
in the name of the Orthodox Church. Prince Constantine kept
this courier a while, only to send him back without an answer.
After that, Iov and the clergy jointly entrusted another messenger, Andrey Bunakov, with a mission to the Polish clergy, to exhort
them not to befriend sedition, in the person of Dimitry. Bunakov
was halted at the border town of Orsha, five hundred and fifty
miles as the crow flies short of Kraków.

But by this time Dimitry had left Sambor, with the core of his
army. On Wednesday, August 25, 1604, they rode and marched as
far as Zupnowice, spent the next night at Lubień, and encamped at
Sokolniki, two or three miles south of Lvov, Friday night. The
village "belonged" to Pan George Mniszech, who was also Starosta
of Lvov. They had advanced forty-nine miles toward Moscow.

On Sunday Dimitry went to Lvov to hear mass in the cathedral.
Father Czyrzowski and Father Lawicki had left Jarosław on August 28 to join Dimitry at Sokolniki, but they could not have arrived in time to accompany him to Lvov. It was reserved for the
preacher of the day, a Jesuit by the name of Father Adrian Radzi-
miński, to greet Dimitry in the name of the Jesuit college. Dimitry
received him warmly and took the opportunity to repeat his devotion to the Holy See and his affection for the Society of Jesus.
These religious protestations could be made in safety because the
army and its Orthodox Russian members were encamped outside
the city.

Confusion rather than what today might be called "organiza-
tional problems" probably caused the delay of well over a week
which held them in Sokolniki. It was Tuesday, September 7, before the undermanned and undersupplied force moved on to Gaye,
only a few miles beyond. Two days later they reached Glinyany, a

no-place another miserable dozen miles on towards the Muscovite frontier. Economic history says of Glinyany that it was on the trade route from Lvov to Moscow; the history of Dimitry can add that an unexpected embassy awaited him there.

Some time before, Tsar Boris had sent Pyotr Khrushchov, who was probably the same as the boyars'-son of that family who had lived with the Don Cossacks back in the 1590's, to harangue the unruly inhabitants of the Ukraine and dispose them against "Grishka Otrepyev" — Dimitry. At the same time, Boris dispatched two voyvodes south to Livny, with troops, to "prevent a possible foray by the Crimean Tatars." The voyvodes met Khrushchov, and during a festive dinner, accompanied by the usual bowls of heady mead and vodka, suggested that they thought their real errand had nothing to do with Tatars at all. It was hard, they added mysteriously, "to raise their hands against the legitimate Tsar."

After a pause to let their meaning sink in, they went on to say, "Boris is not well. His legs are so weak he can hardly walk, and he is thinking of secretly sending the State treasure to Astrakhan, and into Persia." On and on they babbled about the Tsar, mostly unfavorably, until one of them realized the danger of talking so openly. Then all three swore eternal secrecy before the ikon of the Most Holy Mother of God. In time, Khrushchov voyaged on to the Cossacks of the Don.

His arrival among them could not have been more ill-timed. Just then the Cossacks were assembling a force to send to aid Dimitry. Because they thought it proper, they therefore pounced on the luckless petty-nobleman, chained him securely, and in a day or two sent him off to Dimitry, accompanied by a small escort. This is the group which was waiting for him when he galloped up to Glinyany in the midst of a bustle of spruce, dashing Polish nobles, well-armed soldiers, horsemen and lancers.

Boisterous Cossacks, resplendent in a bizarre riot of color, wheeled and pranced their mounts around a groveling, chained figure as Dimitry approached. Then, as soon as they recognized their "Tsarevich" they flung themselves to the ground, pushing their leaders to the front, and dragging their prisoner with them. A shout rang through the air as Dimitry, glittering in bejeweled armor, stood to greet them. And Pyotr Khrushchov was literally thrown at his feet, his chains clanking in the dust.

Dimitry demanded who this was, and why he was chained. Khrushchov struggled onto his knees, pouring tears and beating his forehead on the ground. He begged forgiveness. He had been a fool, he burbled, like so many. He had believed the story of the murder of the Tsarevich Dimitry. But now he recognized him. He knew that his natural lord stood before him. He saw "the true image of his father, Ivan," in Dimitry's lineaments. And again he abjectly beat his head at Dimitry's feet. Dimitry, overcome with pleasure and sympathy, ordered the chains struck from Khrushchov. Then, surrounded by his Polish and Muscovite friends and the Cossack envoys, he chatted with him for some time.

The story of Khrushchov's meeting with the two voyvodes, and the tales he told of the "true conditions" in Moscow (based on a five-day stay there) were heard with transport. Clearly, all Russia only awaited the return of her rightful Prince. Their conquest of Muscovy would be but a march of triumph.

The following day there was a review of all the troops. Then the Polish knights made a ring, Cossack fashion, and voted certain articles of general comportment during the coming campaign. They would maintain discipline, and they would behave like gentlemen and soldiers in camp, on the march, and in the presence of the enemy. This accomplished, they elected as *Hetman,* or commander, Pan George Mniszech, along with Pan Adam Zulicki, Pan Stanislas Gogoliński, and Pan Adam Dworzicki as colonels under the Hetman. And with the calling of the muster roll, the day's business was finished.

At Glinyany, the whole strength of Dimitry's army comprised five hundred and eighty Polish and Muscovite hussars, five hundred infantry, and fourteen hundred and twenty Cossacks and "light-horse" (*pietyhorcy*). With these two thousand five hundred men, Dimitry set out to conquer gigantic Muscovy.

The weekend was spent in Glinyany, to permit Sunday services for Catholic and Orthodox alike. And on Monday morning, September 13, the gallant force rode off, banners flying, drums beating, and Cossacks shouting. Mniszech took the bulk of the army by one route eastwards, while four hundred infantry and three bands of hussars accompanied Dimitry. His own troop carried a red banner with a black eagle on a gold field. The other two, with their banners, rode under the command of Jan Fredro and young Stanislas Mniszech. Despite their warlike splendor, they moved slowly and cautiously.

The cause of the caution virtually marched with them. Prince Janusz Ostrogski, Castellan of Kraków, son of the Palatine of Kiev, had maintained a skepticism regarding Dimitry which amounted to hostility. Prince Janusz and his father had the redoubtable Great Chancellor, Zamoyski, on their side. They also had command of not inconsiderable troops — troops which Pan George had attempted to obtain for Dimitry, with no success. These troops now escorted Pan George's army across the rolling highlands of Volhynia and Podolia. The leaders feared some show of resistance or hindrance daily, although Prince Janusz had apparently given strict orders only to watch Dimitry. They therefore placed strong guards around the camps each night, kept the horses saddled, and slept on the *qui vive*. In this way they could move on with a minimum of delay.

Yet, despite these overfriendly hostile troops, volunteers began to join Dimitry as his men marched on. Two days out of Glinyany they reached Zborov, beautifully situated by a lake, between hills. In two more days they skirted around Tarnopol, a fort founded by Prince Janusz's grandfather, the Hetman Jan Amore Tarnowski, and after one more day reached Skałat, where Pan George apparently felt he could pitch camp for a couple of days of rest. They were then some three hundred miles from Kiev.

From Skałat Pan George dispatched an eloquent Latin letter to his revered friend, "the Most Illustrious and Most Reverend Prince," Monsignore Claudio Rangoni. It was dated September 18, a Saturday, and it conveyed the first news of the attempt on Dimitry's life by two *sicarii* ("dagger-men"), as well as the capture of Khrushchov, whom he did not name, and the latter's meeting with the two voyvodes. He also described briefly their form of march.

In conclusion, Pan George wrote enthusiastically about the ten thousand Don Cossacks who had enlisted and were joining them, and the promises brought by an envoy from the Zaporozhtsy, the famous Cossacks of "below the Falls" (of the Dnyeper), the intrepid horsemen of Gogol's novel *Taras Bulba*. All these details he gave so that Rangoni would know that Dimitry was not without strength, and that he was relying on Rangoni for further spiritual support now that the benediction of the Holy See had cast a most resplendent light over Dimitry's entire enterprise.

The first weekend in October was spent at Strzyzow, a few miles north of the potentially dangerous fortified town of Vinnitsa. Then, after three-day rests in or near Wierzchownia and Wasiłkow, the courageous little army reached the holy city of Kiev, at that time a provincial capital in the Polish Republic.

Although Kiev had been destroyed on several occasions since its founding by the legendary Prince Kiy, a period of great prosperity had begun over a century before Dimitry's arrival, when the municipality was granted the so-called *Magdeburg Law* by the Polish Diet. This guaranteed self-government for the city, with its own courts of law, its own custom-house and trade administration, and even its own mint. The hoary Voyvode, Prince Constantine Ostrogski, whose beard was so long he carried it in a sack hung from his belt, was purely a military chief, with no governmental authority over the conduct of municipal affairs.

It was therefore possible and proper for the Mayor, Mitkowicz, to entertain Dimitry and lodge him in his own home. It was also possible for various groups of merchants to welcome the army as they saw fit. Prince Ostrogski could do nothing, despite his conviction that Dimitry was an impostor.

One group of visiting merchants, from the city of Mogilyov (three hundred-odd miles up the Dnyeper) called Dimitry "little Tsar," and rejoiced that he had come to Kiev, *konno, zbrojno i strojno* — mounted, armed and finely arrayed — with his army of

hussars, cossacks and infantry, twenty thousand of them. Other
merchants lavished attentions on Dimitry, too. And in gratitude,
the bounteously welcomed Tsarevich, by special privilege before
he left, freed all these merchants of tolls and customs duties
throughout the whole of Muscovy.

It had been many a year since so much noble finery had been
seen in Kiev. Dimitry, the center of it all, was a shining knight
straight from the legends of ancient Kiev. With him rode the
pompous dignity that was Pan George Mniszech, arrayed in all the
bravery of a Hetman. But others who were also there were hardly
outspangled by Dimitry or Pan George. There was Prince Konstantin Vishnevetsky, who had been joined by Prince George Czar-
toryski, the husband of Prince Konstantin's cousin Aleksandra, and
a prince named Ruziński. Pan Michael Ratomski also seems to
have been there, although it may have been his brother. Pan Michael was from Ostyor, where he held the chief post, but his
brother accompanied Dimitry into Russia. And there were many
others. All of these notabilities made for a lively three-day stop in
Kiev.[1]

When the time came for their departure, however, the swank
and swagger dissolved in a chilling paralysis. The watchful-waiting
policy of Prince Janusz had turned into action, and on their arrival
on the banks of the deep, wide Dnyeper River, Dimitry and Pan
George discovered that all the ferry-boats which normally plied
across from the town of Wyszogrod, twelve miles above Kiev, had
been ordered removed. Not so much as a wherry tugged at anchor
on the cold, gray-brown waters.

There, facing the river, they halted for "several days," according
to Stanislas Borsza, who wrote a detailed account of their march on
Moscow, "until some ferry-boats came up, and by the grace of God
we were conveyed across the Dnyeper without scathe." Had the
Almighty not helped them, it is to be wondered how they would
have helped themselves. As it was, but one comrade was lost — a
Pole who was suffering from a fever and in despair jumped in the
river and was drowned.

The transit apparently took up the weekend, and it was Monday, October 26, before the army was again in marching order and able to proceed. Following the Desna River now, a big tributary of the Dnyeper, they kept to its right bank, reaching the Polish village of Żukin on the 27th. The following morning, before they set out, a Russian delegation arrived to assure Dimitry that the Muscovite fortified town of Moravsk would surrender to him. Dimitry then delayed one day longer in Żukin, and moved on to Połczow, more or less opposite Ostyor, the last Polish fort and on the other side of the river.

At Połczow Muscovite subjects advanced to meet Dimitry, bearing the traditional bread-and-salt of capitulation and homage, from Moravsk. But that the town authorities had been inclined to resist was shown by another oblation of doubtful spontaneity. Tsar Boris's voyvodes stationed at Moravsk were presented to Dimitry, trussed up with ropes and thongs.

As Hetman, Pan George had sent on ahead "a few Cossack regiments," which meant two thousand Ukrainians. This hint of power, Borsza thought, frightened the Muscovites so that they took council among themselves, and, as another account adds, overpowered and bound the voyvodes. Only then did the small favor-currying embassy march out to welcome Dimitry.

Dimitry had already prepared a proclamation for the occasion. For, as the classic Russian historian Karamzin wrote, he "went with a sword and a manifesto" — not the last invader to do so. No sooner had he crossed the border and entered the outpost of Moravsk than he sent messengers to spread the glad tidings that, thanks to the benevolent dispensation of Providence, he had been saved from Godunov's henchmen, and was at last on his way to Moscow to sit on the ivory throne of his father.

At the same time, Dimitry sent a letter to Boris, which he apparently was so negligent as not to seal. Indeed, since it is not known that Boris ever received the letter, its contents may have been intended to reach him only by hearsay. Whatever the truth, the missive is a masterpiece of invective, molded with a sharp sense of propaganda-values. "It grieves us," he wrote, that Boris is endangering the salvation of his soul by his deeds. Does he not know that he is mortal?

Then, coming to the point, Dimitry scolded:

You, Boris, should have been content with what the Lord God
gave; but contrary to the will of God, although you are our subject, you have stolen our realm, with the aid of the devil. Your
sister, the wife of our brother, gave over to you the administration
of the whole state, and you took advantage of the fact that our
brother for the most part occupied himself in the service of
God . . .

Next, he listed in detail Boris's many misdeeds, culminating in
the attempted murder of himself, Dimitry, after which, lapsing
into sarcasm, he said that the princely families of Romanov, Cherkassky and Shuysky knew Boris's "kindness" — for everyone knew
that they had been exiled or even slyly murdered. But if Boris
repented, Dimitry promised in the end:

Give us what is ours, and we for God's sake will forgive you all
your wrongdoings, and assign you a quiet place [to live in]. It is
better for you to suffer something on this earth than forever to
burn in hell for the Oh-so-many souls you have destroyed.

With these psychological moves off his mind, Dimitry put a reliable man in charge of Moravsk and metaphorically set sail for
greater things on the first day of the first week of the new month,
Monday, November 1, 1604. His goal was the ancient fort and
trading center of Chernigov. For nearly seven hundred years, Chernigov had been the capital, or at least the leading city, of a principality. In 1604 much of its independence had been lost; none,
however, of its pride.

For three days the swarming, unopposed army pushed through
thick woods and across marshy land. The distance was but forty
miles or so, yet their rate of advance was not exceptionally slow.
Caution was still needed. That was shown by a report — a rumor
— of potential sedition among Dimitry's Muscovite troops, which
was contributed by a boyars'-son the day after they left Moravsk,
and by the capture of a spy. Then, one day later, eighty Muscovite
horsemen galloped up. This was hardly dangerous to an army
which numbered in the thousands, yet the eighty might have been
a scouting party from much larger forces. Pan George's jumpiness

was relieved when he learned that the group merely wanted to join the liberating army of the Tsarevich.

At last, on Thursday came the halt. Pan George jotted down in what may be called his diary that they were then three Polish miles from their goal, and that they pitched camp at that spot. In modern terms, and allowing for Pan George's rough estimate, the distance was eight to ten miles, which was unquestionably a suitable distance from so strong a fort. If Chernigov did not spontaneously yield, as Moravsk more or less had, it was better to be well out of the reach of the cannon which threatened from the slopes of Mount Boldina. A squadron of Cossacks was sent under one of the Buczyńskis to demand surrender. That same Buczyński had succeeded at Moravsk. It may have been thought that he had some magic which would work again.

The first reaction from Chernigov was a volley of shot which ended the careers of many of the Cossacks. But somehow a leather-lunged partisan of Dimitry's conveyed the information that Moravsk had already opened its gates to the rightful lord of Muscovy. Thereupon the volatile citizens called a meeting that had religious overtones. Indeed, the townspeople intoned a sort of litany in which one group led with acclamations of "Prince Dimitry Ivanovich, our resplendent sun [*krásnoye sólnyshko*]," while others fervently responded, "God has returned us our sovereign. May his holy name be blessed!"

A vote to surrender formed the emotional *Amen* which closed the meeting. Nevertheless, the chief Voyvode, Prince Ivan Andreyevich Tatyev, refused to violate his oath of loyalty to the Tsar, despite his strong personal disaffection for Boris. In short order, the populace tied Prince Tatyev up in some of the excellent rope for which Russia had been noted for half a century in western Europe, and delivered him like a parcel to Dimitry's camp.

All would have been well had the town's defenders not killed any Cossacks. Such behavior was a declaration of war, and the Cossacks meant to make the most of it. Ignoring both the embassy that brought Prince Tatyev through the lines and the orders of their commander, Buczyński, the Cossacks stormed the fort and captured it. Plunder was what they wanted — a sort of mass wergeld due them for the loss of their companions, plus any obtainable excess for their personal enrichment.

The Chernigovians protested, begging Dimitry to call off his men. Dimitry, sympathizing, sent a detachment under Stanislas Borsza (who wrote an account of the happenings) and a nobleman named Przeradowski with orders to the Cossacks to desist. But by then Chernigov had been despoiled. The houses were as empty as the boxes that lay scattered in front of them.

Official rules of conduct had been drawn up before the army left Glinyany, but these could hardly be considered applicable to the Cossacks who had joined since. Dimitry, uncertain as to the identity of the marauders, made no reference to what had been decided before. But when he saw the extent of the wanton destruction, he angrily sent word to the Cossack camp that everything which had been taken must be returned, forthwith. "Otherwise," Borsza wrote, "the Tsar would ride against them with troops."

The Cossacks, feeling that right and essential strength were both on their side (for numerically they were the strongest body in the army), devotedly justified their action. They had no mind to rebel, or disobey, they said, any more than they privately had a mind to let go of the wergeld. So they protested through a well-instructed embassy that the Tsar should be pleased to remember how many of them had been killed and wounded by the Chernigovians when they took the town, "only" to serve him. "We were afraid," they ventured to plead, "that the Muscovites would be reinforced, and be stronger than ourselves."

Dimitry, caught between the need to conciliate the townspeople and yet not alienate his followers, played Fabius-Cunctator for a day or two, and then ordered the Cossacks in any case to restore "reprisals." The restoration followed, in part only and only with all the deliberate speed of unwarmed virgin-honey on a gentle slope. Yet, once the flow had started, "Tsar" Dimitry casually found it convenient to snail down — he was in no hurry, either — to the Cossack village. With him went the Hetman, Pan George Mniszech, for unknown motives. Thus Dimitry avoided a brush with his Cossacks. They evaded the shadow of an insurrection by truly sparing restitution. In short, the bond between Dimitry and his wild-reared partisans was too strong and at the same time too flexible to be so easily broken.

Other bonds were not so sure for the claimant to the Muscovite crown. Trouble began with the Polish *rycerstwo,* the body of dashing young (and not so young) knights, as soon as the thievish prowess of the Cossacks became known. The knights peppered Dimitry with demands for money with which to obtain "clothing and provisions." Such articles were of course obtainable in such a trading center as Chernigov, and by the same token there was money in Chernigov with which to buy them. Dimitry, instead of robbing the inhabitants, as the Cossacks had done, took possession of the treasury in Chernigov Fort, and divided ten thousand of the fifty-five thousand *zloty** thus acquired among the knights.

The knights seemed contented therewith, and the next seven or eight days were spent resting. Prince Tatyev delayed only a respectable time before changing sides in the matter of loyalties. Dimitry thereupon attached him temporarily to his staff and placed Pan John Zaporski in charge at Chernigov as Voyvode. Then he started for Novgorod Seversky, nearly one hundred and fifty miles away by whatever road was open. This most southern "Novgorod" (there were two others of importance) was called "the Northern" (*sever,* "north") after the Slavic tribe that moved north (and east) from the region of Kiev even before the time of Rurik (before 862 A.D.). Novgorod Seversky was less of a city than Chernigov, but it stood squarely in the way of Dimitry's route to Moscow.

During the stay in Chernigov not a day passed but what new volunteers arrived to augment Dimitry's forces. Usually it was a trickle of a few hundred a day, but on November 12, nine thousand Don Cossacks rode up, to the immeasurable joy of all. It was not only a matter of numbers. The new arrivals testified to the growing support Dimitry found in his own land. His army now

---

* *Zloty* were then worth a little less than three to the pound sterling, and a little less than two to the ruble. In terms of modern purchasing power, ten thousand *zloty* may be compared very roughly with $200,000 to $250,000.

numbered thirty-eight thousand, according to letters sent to Poland by Prince Tatyev. Even by Muscovite standards it was a force not to be despised.[2]

CHAPTER 6

VICTORY AND DEFEAT

Leaving Chernigov on Sunday, November 14, Dimitry's army reached the little river Snov the next day. Although the region was thickly forested and often swampy, a bridge enabled them to get across and bivouac near a village on Tuesday. Then, for the rest of the week they plodded slowly along the commercial beaten-track through the woods, camping at night by the wayside.

Pan George's comments in his laconic "diary" are too brief to indicate what route the army followed, and Pan George himself may not have known. But by Sunday, one week after leaving Chernigov, the strong fortress of Novgorod Seversky loomed up before them, perched on a hill above the Desna.

Four hundred and twenty years before, Prince Igor Svyatosla-vich had sallied forth from Novgorod to fight the Polovtsy Tatars, and had inspired the greatest monument of ancient Russian litera-ture — not to mention Borodin's famous opera, *Prince Igor*. Nov-gorod Seversky was a city of character, of history, and it was well fortified. Its *Dyetinets,* or Inner Citadel, had been known to resist attack even after the outer bastions had fallen. If Dimitry and Pan George were not aware of this, the Commander of the Fort, Pyotr Fyodorovich Basmanov, was.

Basmanov was the grandson of the Boyar Aleksey Danilovich Pleshcheyev "Basmanov" — one of the outstanding Russian war-lords of the sixteenth century, and a close associate and willing tool of Ivan the Dread. Aleksey's bravery was little short of legendary, as was his masculine comeliness. His mental make-up was perhaps not so beautiful. His son Fyodor, however, the father of the Commander of Novgorod Seversky, had been even more handsome and even more closely associated with Ivan, who preferred this sort of audacious and vigorous company to that of the tradition-bound scions of the "old families."

For ten years or more Fyodor Alekseyevich Basmanov slept in the same room with Ivan, called the Dread, even when the Tsar's wife was with him. Such attachment gave rise to malicious talk and, in the case of the exiled Prince Kurbsky, to direct accusation of unnatural behavior. Whatever the truth, in 1569 Fyodor was made a voyvode. Then, in strange thanks for such favors, he sided with his father in an obscure plot to rid Muscovy of Ivan. The plot was uncovered, and Fyodor won Ivan's forgiveness by acting as executioner for his own father in 1570. In less than a year, Ivan completed his vengeance on the family by commanding the extirpation of such an unnatural son. Only little Pyotr and his baby brother, Ivan, survived. Their mother, still a very young woman, married an illustrious prince, as will be seen later, and the two infants were brought up in the peace and tranquillity so often longed for by Russian nobles in those troubled days.

With the coming to power of Boris Godunov, the two Basmanov lads were brought back to Moscow from a country estate, and by 1601 Pyotr was made a junior courtier. Two years later his brother, Ivan, was killed in the rebellion of Hlopko Kosolap; Pyotr then became a most-favored soldier in the eyes of the Tsar, for wholly obscure reasons. No-one has accused Tsar Boris of favoring Pyotr because of his inherited good-looks and nothing else.

For whatever reason it may have been, then, Pyotr Fyodorovich Basmanov was sent with Prince Nikita Romanovich Trubetskoy to stop Dimitry at Chernigov. Ten miles or more before the two military leaders got there, however, they heard of the surrender of that bastion. They therefore retired to Novgorod Seversky, determined to resist the "impostor" there. In that determination, Pyotr Basmanov clearly outshone Prince Nikita, largely because Tsar Boris had promoted him in defiance of the ancient and all but inviolable "Book of Nobility" (*Razryádnaya Kníga*), which provided for the dispensation of offices strictly by precedence in birth. Basmanov, promoted over the heads of many who were above him in the sacrosanct Book, was grateful to Boris in his stubborn way.

When, therefore, Dimitry sent couriers to Novgorod to demand surrender, Basmanov took the peculiarly Russian measure of setting fire to the whole of the city outside the inner walls, dispersing the ordinary population (who never counted), and shutting the upper-crust of the bourgeoisie along with himself and five hundred *streltsy* in the fort proper, under the ponderous primacy of the First Voyvode, Prince Nikita. This accomplished, with Basmanov completely behind them, the town's defenders bellowed from the walls to Dimitry's assaulting forces that they would not yield. "Whoresons," they cried, "you only came with a thief [Dimitry] to steal our money!"

At this rebuff, Dimitry and Pan George set up camp by the river, somewhat more than a mile from the smoking ruins of the outer city and suburbs. Pan George then ordered trenches dug near the partly burned palisade, while some of the men plaited heavy protective "baskets" of wickerwork to cover soldiers and diggers alike. At the same time, eight medium-sized field-guns were mounted, supplemented by six falconets, with which the gunners soon began to harass the fort proper.

Under the protection of the bombardment a small body of hussars galloped forward in an attempt to storm the inner walls, but were repulsed twice. In a third attempt, that night, the men mounted wooden turrets on sleds and pushed them forward, while three hundred sappers tried to place straw and brushwood in the ditch before the walls and set it on fire. But the defenders were not asleep, and they drove the attacking force off, with no little damage. This attempt, in bitter cold weather, lasted until dawn. One of the Polish volunteers, John Zabczyc, described it in verse:

> The walls were coated by the rain with ropy glair,
>   And on the snow, now frosted by the bitter air,
> Many a body lay struck down by hail of lead,
>   Their onetime stalwart legs and hands now stilled
>   and dead.

When the news of this failure reached Dimitry, he ate his heart out with grief and vexation. This first real obstacle since the day he revealed himself to Prince Adam Vishnevetsky abruptly deadened his impetuosity, and more than one Pole noted that he seemed stunned. Then, with slowly rising anger, he grumbled, "I had a better opinion of the Poles, but now I see that they are just people like everybody else."

The Polish knights, always inflammable, shot back: "Don't throw mud on our reputation! The world knows that it is no news for Poles to capture mighty forts. But it is not our task to scale walls. Even so, to keep the fame of our ancestors bright we have not refused even that, and will not refuse! Order a breach made, and you will see, gracious Tsar, true Polish manliness and valor, which you so little understand just now."

Dimitry seems to have refrained from saying anything further at the time, and any possible prolongation of the dispute was halted the next day. "Thanks to Almighty God," Borsza wrote, "there came the welcome news that envoys from the town of Putivl, fifteen miles from Novgorod [actually sixty modern statute miles as the crow flies], had arrived with word that Putivl had surrendered."

In this instance, the intervention of the Almighty was specifically influenced by a group of Dimitry's Muscovite halberdiers who had gone to Putivl for supplies. They had been arrested on arrival and questioned. In answer, a spokesman declared, "We are your brothers, who are going to the Fatherland with our natural lord, Dimitry Ivanovich."

The excitable Putivlyans wanted to put them to the torture, but the spokesman went on: "Our life is in your hands. Do what you will with us. But we cannot tell you anything other than what we know. We have told you the truth. Dimitry Ivanovich is the true heir, and we advise you to swear allegiance to him."

A characteristic town-meeting was promptly held, the inhabitants discussed the matter, and in very little time marched to the castle, seized the voyvodes stationed there, bound them, and shipped them to Dimitry's camp at Novgorod.

This favorable event was all the more enheartening to Dimitry since a deputation from Kromy, a third of the way to Moscow, arrived at almost the same time, with the same sort of news. And three or four days later, further emissaries came, announcing the submission of other strong-points in the district of Komarichi, on the way to Kromy, from nearby Rylsk and Sevsk, from Kursk to the east, and from Oryol, twenty-five miles beyond Kromy.

All these defections from Tsar Boris did not, however, bring about the surrender of Novgorod Seversky. Basmanov stood fast to his oath of loyalty, even after the Putivlyans brought up five siege-guns and five smaller pieces. The first day after they were mounted in the trenches, Basmanov lost some sixty men, but after that more precautions were taken. Furthermore, there was no need to risk lives so openly.

News came through that Tsar Boris had at last collected a big army at Bryansk (though some said it was at Kaluga), and it was marching on Novgorod. According to rumors, it numbered two hundred thousand men and was under the supreme command of the premier boyar, Prince Fyodor Ivanovich Mstislavsky, grandson of a first cousin of Tsar Ivan IV. Prince Fyodor has been described as totally unpossessed of knowledge of the art of war, and of superior faculties of any sort as well. For aides, he had four princes, including a brother of Prince Vasily Shuysky, and a number of *okolnichi* (gentlemen of the privy chamber), including a cousin of the Tsar.

Dimitry promptly sent out a group of no more than eight hundred volunteers, including native Russian guides, to reconnoitre. Prince Fyodor, cautious for all the reputed immensity of his army, did likewise, but chose to send several thousand Tatars, who were not acquainted with the terrain. Dimitry's partisans ran across the unwary Tatars one night and gave them battle. The Tatars, startled and perhaps unsure, quickly gave way and were driven into one of the swamps along the Desna, where many of them were drowned. Others were taken prisoner, to the number of "several dozen," Borsza wrote, "who on the rack gave us proper information about their army, and intimated that it was very large." The

truth was that whatever its original or planned size not over forty
to fifty thousand reached Novgorod, due to bad organization at the
beginning and later defections.

Meanwhile, Christmas had come and gone (Polish Christmas,
that is), and Pan George had received a letter from Tsar Boris's
voyvodes urging him to return to Poland without delay, leaving
the "unfrocked monk," Dimitry, to the fate he deserved — a letter
which he did not bother to acknowledge. He had also seen three
suns on December 26, which was a matter highly worth recording.
Then, on December 28, Boris's whole army arrived, passed within
a Polish mile of Dimitry's camp, and exchanged shots. Two boyars
deserted to Dimitry as they passed.

The next day, one boyars'-son went over to Dimitry, but otherwise nothing happened. The leaders of both sides were apparently
sizing up their opponents. The day after that there was a sharp
preliminary skirmish between the armies, which Pan George laconically described as resulting in "some scores of dead." Borsza
adds that Prince Fyodor drew so near that night that his men were
almost up to the Polish camp, and the sentinel gave the alarm: a
huge army was attacking. Pan George, unperturbed, "sent a fresh
sentinel with orders to watch the enemy until the Lord God
granted day." [1]

So, on the last day of 1604, according to the Polish calendar,
Dimitry was at length face to face with the might of the Russian
State. He had tried before, through emissaries and negotiations, to
persuade the troops to surrender voluntarily. Their ears had been
deaf. Now as the chill December sun rose, the die was cast.

Dimitry calmly but vigorously addressed his followers, exhorting
them to be courageous. It was a leader's standard bit of oratory
before a battle. With that terminated, however, he stretched his
hands toward heaven, and raised a loud, clear voice in prayer: "Almighty God, Thou gazest deep into my soul! If I take up my sword
contrary to justice and the law, cut me down with Thy heavenly
bolt. But if my soul is clean and pure, give invincible strength to
my hand in battle. And Thou, Mother of God, be a shield for our
men!"

No sooner had the opposing troops lined up in battle array than Nieborski's left-wing company of two hundred attacked the Muscovites under Prince Dimitry Ivanovich Shuysky and Prince Mikhaylo Kashin. Nieborski was driven back, only to reorganize his men, add two more squadrons, and fly at the Muscovites again. Pan Adam Dworzicki came up with his light-horse, followed by Stanislas Mniszech, John Fredro and others, and mingled savagely in the fray.

When Dimitry's own company of two hundred horse also struck, the huge opposing army seemed shaken. For some reason, Prince Fyodor's streltsy (literally "archers" — crack troops) remained in the valley, below Novgorod, doing nothing, until the Polish infantry discovered them and drove them away. In such manner, and almost incomprehensibly, Tsar Boris's horde retreated two Polish miles from the battle-scene and surrounded itself with an abatis and ditches in the forest. Dimitry's men captured the Russians' gold standard, of great value — the banner for the entire army. This capture symbolized their victory.

The next day Dimitry ordered the bodies of the dead Muscovites buried in three huge tombs erected on the site. Borsza estimated the casualties at six thousand, adding the detail that when the Tsarevich rode up with his troops and saw so many of his people slain, "he was sorely grieved, and wept."

The Polish losses, including not more than twenty noblemen, were some six score all told. The "élite" were buried near a small church around which their camp had been built; the common people found their last rest in a little tomb near the Russians.

As for the wounded, only one needs special mention. This was Prince Fyodor Mstislavsky himself, cut down with fifteen wounds early in the fight, and barely saved from capture by a squad of streltsy. Borsza commented, in slangy terms, "he was all hashed up."

Captain Jacques Margeret, a French mercenary in the Tsar's army, summed up the action from the professional point of view, saying that if the Polish companies had been backed by an additional hundred horse, there is no doubt that four companies would have defeated the Emperor's entire army . . . In fact, one would have said that the Russians had no arms to strike with, although there were forty or fifty thousand of them.

Reporting this, the Russian historian Karamzin added, "the foreigners who witnessed their cowardly flight wrote that . . . all they had was legs" — to run with.

But Dimitry himself had little to be happy about. The unruly Polish knights, having won an extraordinary battle, immediately turned on him, complaining that they and their men suffered from dearth of everything, to which some few subjoined their fear that still greater misfortune was waiting for them. Money, however, would do a great deal toward dispelling such feelings. "If you don't give us money," they announced, "we'll go right back to Poland."

Dimitry begged them to be patient about the money, and to take advantage of the enemy's confusion to finish the struggle then and there. But it was a repetition, in principle, of King Stephen Báthory's experience when he tried to bring his Russian campaign to a successful conclusion twenty-odd years before. The knights would not even let Dimitry finish. "To Poland we go if you don't give us money," they cried.

At that, Dimitry called a consultation with some of the leaders. Admitting that he did not have enough money for all of them, he asked their advice. Although no advice was forthcoming right away, a handful of John Fredro's company later took him aside and whispered: "If Your Grace will give us money without letting anybody know, we will stay. The other companies watch us closely, and follow what we do. If we stay, all will stay." Dimitry, duped, agreed.

But no sooner had Fredro's men gotten their money than all the others heard about it, and forthwith revolted. At the same time, Pan George Mniszech took it into his head to return to Poland himself, claiming that he was sick, and that he had to attend the meeting of the Diet in Warsaw. On behalf of Pan George be it said that, although these motives — these excuses — entered into his actions, his real reason for leaving was that he saw that more men and more funds were needed, and he had to get both. He was too deeply involved in Dimitry's cause to give any thought at all to deserting it.

All these things added to Dimitry's perplexity and vexation. And when Pan George left, accompanied by a large section of the Polish knights, some of these behaved most outrageously, adding to the bitterness of — remarkable to relate! — his *victory*. They seized the great Muscovite banner from his hands and even forcibly appropriated a sable *feryaz*, or long robe, which the Russians had just ransomed for three hundred zloty. Heaping insult on injury, some of the knights (who were supposed to be gentlemen) addressed him in shameful language, one going so far as to jeer: "By God, you'll be on a stick!" meaning that the Tsar would capture him and have him impaled. Dimitry smacked the rowdy in the mouth.

Yet even with all this shabby treatment, Dimitry went from company to company, begging the knights and their followers to stay with him. He exhorted and implored in vain. Only a few volunteers from this and that company agreed to remain; in all, not more than fifteen hundred Poles.

Even so, an old, old saying goes, "when need is highest, help is nighest." Hardly had the last turncoat disappeared into the forest to the south than the advance guard of a strapping Cossack brigade emerged from it. The all but empty camp soon filled again, until it overflowed with twelve thousand new and blindly zealous troops, dragging with them a dozen or more cannon. Soon Dimitry had reorganized his forces, called for the election of a new Hetman (Adam Dworzicki, a neighbor of the Mniszechs), and moved from the siege of Novgorod east to temporary winter-quarters near Sevsk, in the Komarichi district. The uncourageous Russian army meanwhile had retreated north to Starodub. Basmanov the brave remained in peace, surrounded by the blackened ruins of his town, the icy shores of the Desna valley, and the new mounds covering the dead that slowly faded into the great white waste. A cheerless Russian Christmas had come and gone, and the Polish calendar soon said it was mid-January, 1605.

Meanwhile Boris had heard of the disgraceful behavior of his troops, as well as of Prince Mstislavsky's condition. In less than a fortnight he completed his plans for renewing the attack and sent Prince Vasily Ivanovich Shuysky to Novgorod to take command, under the wounded generalissimo. At the same time he sent doctors and other help to the army, and an escort to bring Voyvode Basmanov to Moscow to receive stupendous rewards for his gallantry. In addition, by way of personal precaution, he also dispatched his cousin Semyon Godunov to size up and keep an eye on the situation. The Tsar's fear of "Dimitry the False" had not been allayed by the events of the last days of 1604.

As January wore on, Boris's army received reinforcements almost daily, until toward the end of the month it numbered between seventy and eighty thousand men. Prince Vasily and his brother then decided it was time to seek out "that vagabond named Dimitry" and finish him. Neither of the Shuyskys was any more capable as a commander than Mstislavsky, but it might be hoped that still another general, the boyar Fyodor Ivanovich Sheremetyev, would be more inspired. Sheremetyev received a special commission to invest Kromy, one of the fortresses which had declared for Dimitry.

At last, after dawdling around in the forest for a couple of weeks, Boris's army was led up to confront Dimitry. When it reached the village of Dobrynichi, a dozen miles northwest of Sevsk, camp was pitched for the night. Dimitry had word of this and called a council to discuss plans. Hetman Dworzicki and other Polish officers strongly recommended waiting for the enemy in Sevsk, starting negotiations again, and only in the end brushing with them, after a place could be found which would give the advantage to Dimitry.

Although this seemed excellent advice to many of the leaders, the Cossacks disagreed vigorously. The chief Cossack Ataman, backed by others, urged an immediate attack. Since the Cossacks were now the backbone of his army, Dimitry could do little but ask for further details.

The Cossacks pointed out that Mstislavsky's men were very crowded in the village where they were, and that a surprise move

to set fire to their quarters and tents would throw them into complete confusion. Thereupon the Cossacks would attack, and the
day would be theirs. Under strong pressure from the atamans, Dimitry yielded.

The night of January 30, a handful of dare-devil peasants
slipped up to Dobrynichi with incendiary material. But the older
Shuysky, Vasily, was sly even if not a born army-officer, and he had
scouts who quickly discovered the peasants. They were caught and
put to death. Thus, when Dimitry's forces arrived at the village,
there stood the Muscovites in battle-array. Twenty thousand
Tatars formed their right wing, among whom were a few Muscovite divisions and companies of foreign mercenaries. The left wing
was "pure Muscovites," thirty thousand of them. And the remaining twenty thousand or more were congregated in the center.

Facing this formidable foe, Dimitry placed his Polish mercenaries in the center, with the newly arrived Zaporozhtsy Cossacks
on the right, and the artillery, infantry, and Muscovite regiments
on the left. Dimitry's Muscovites wore white shirts over their
armor to distinguish them from Boris's.

How the battle was fought is best described by Captain Margeret, who took part on the Tsar's side:

> The armies converged, and after some skirmishing, with cannon
> play on both sides, Dimitry sent his main cavalry along a small val-
> ley to try to cut between the village and the army. Mstislavsky,
> noticing this, sent his right wing forward, with two foreign com-
> panies. The Poles, seeing that they had been forestalled, played
> for double or nothing, and charged [our] right wing in a body of
> ten cavalry companies with such fury that, after some resistance by
> the foreigners, all turned heel except for the main body of the
> army. This stood as if in ecstasy, as motionless as if paralyzed.
> The Poles headed straight for the village, but ran into the greater
> part of the infantry and some cannon.
>
> The infantry, seeing the Poles so near, let fly ten or twelve thou-
> sand rounds of harquebus-shots, which so frightened the Poles that
> they reined back in great confusion. Meanwhile the rest of their
> cavalry and infantry were coming up as quickly as they could,

thinking that the field was theirs. But on seeing their companions wheel about in such confusion, they too began to run away, and were pursued by five or six thousand horse for more than seven or eight versts.*

Stanislas Borsza, speaking for the Poles, blamed the rout on the Cossacks, who took fright, he said, at the clouds of smoke from the harquebus attack mentioned by Margeret. The Poles begged the Cossacks to turn back and help hold the line, but in vain. On the whole, this explanation seems logical, although the secret of the defeat seems to have lain in the lack of coordination and discipline. If anything was more unruly than the Polish nobility it was, of course, the Cossacks.

In any event, the battle resulted in a disastrous defeat for Dimitry. He lost fifteen banners and thirteen pieces of artillery, and five to six thousand were killed, in addition to those taken prisoner. Those of the survivors who were Russians were hanged immediately by the army. The rest were paraded in Moscow in triumph, along with the banners and other paraphernalia of war.

Dimitry and his followers first fled to Rylsk, which had just declared itself for him. Followed closely by scattered groups of the enemy, Dimitry himself had a horse killed under him, and only the quick action of Prince Vasily Mikhaylovich Mosalsky-Rubets saved him from capture. Prince Vasily, Voyvode of loyal Putivl, gave him his own horse and mounted his groom's nag instead.

When the sound of the chase died down, the remnants of the army slept in the woods. Russia's poet Pushkin supplies a colorful picture of the scene — where Dimitry lies down, puts the saddle of his dead horse under his head, and falls asleep with the words, "Good night to you!" His companion murmurs:

> And pleasant dreams, Tsarevich!
> Though smashed to bits, and saved only by flight,
> He's just as carefree as a foolish child.
> Providence certainly keeps watch on him . . .

* One *verstá* equalled 500 *sázheni*, or 3,500 English feet.

Indeed, Providence did seem to provide for Dimitry. Boris's army moved so slowly in pursuit that he could rest two days in Rylsk before he found himself again in danger. By that time, Rylsk prepared to resist the Tsar's attack and hold the army there while Dimitry fled on toward the south, toward the nearest Polish frontier.

Boris soon got reports of all these glorious happenings. He even heard that Dimitry was no longer of this world, and that the whole rebellion was stamped out. His foreign captains, Jacques Margeret and Walter Rosen, he thanked in the most profuse language for their loyalty and courage. And all participants were showered with gifts. Peace seemed at last to have come.

Unhappily for Boris, in stone-walled Putivl, but thirty-five miles from Prince Vishnevetsky's fort at Romny, the man called Dimitry still lived.[2]

CHAPTER 7

FROM THE ASHES,

A PHOENIX

THE BATTLE AT DOBRYNICHI had been fought on a Monday. By the following Saturday, Dimitry was safe inside the towering ramparts of Putivl, clustered on a rocky height above the marshes bordering the river Seym. Ever since the Tatars had besieged it in vain in the twelfth century, its inhabitants had been known for their bravery. Their ancient semi-independence of Chernigov had nurtured this. In 1605 they were ready to fight for the man they believed to be their rightful Tsar.

Before that, the Zaporozhtsy Cossacks had swarmed together again and appeared before Dimitry in Rylsk, but he would not let them in the town. Cowardly poltroons, he called them, and traitors. So the Cossacks turned back to their homes, shamed and chagrined. Fortunately for Dimitry the Tsar's army was busy near Dobrynichi, punishing and killing, indulging their human thirst for blood and screams and the glassy eyes of the dead. Dimitry reached Putivl without incident.

Such was his own chagrin, however, that his first reaction was to flee farther from the scene of the calamity. Somewhere between Putivl and the Vishnevetsky fort of Romny an ill-defined border was stretched between the realm of Muscovy and the Polish Republic. In Romny he could have real safety, along with an opportunity to beg for further help from Poland.

But Dimitry's despair lasted, as usual, less time than an April shower. His followers surrounded him, crying: "We have sacrificed everything for you, and you care only for your own miserable life. You want to hand us over to Boris's vengeance. But we'll save ourselves instead; we'll turn *you* over to Boris . . ." Then, less angrily, for they were not sure that he was serious, they persuaded him that his life and fortune were in the hands of those who believed in him, whether they were in the villages and towns, or even in Boris's own regiments. They would protect him.

So too would the Cossacks of the Don, another four thousand of whom had just pranced up to Putivl. And Dimitry willy-nilly embraced their enthusiasm. Had he not originally, long before, intended to conquer his country with the help of his fellow-countrymen? Now that most of the Poles had deserted him, was it not indeed his Muscovites and Cossacks who would win him the crown?

The Battle of Dobrynichi was as good as forgotten. Dimitry called a council again, entrusted Prince Tatyev with a mission to King Sigismund to obtain immediate help, went to work to strengthen the fortifications of Putivl, and drew up another manifesto for distribution. It was far more eloquent than the first, and far more elaborate. Since the Russians had not yet heard just how he had been saved, and how the Hand of God was working for him, all this was explained — not without subtle exaggeration and a suitable quantity of the pepper and spice of convenient invention.

Oddly, Boris stepped in to help Dimitry sell himself to the Russian people. When, between rumors and copies of manifestos, Dimitry's cause began to reach the ears of all Muscovy, so did reports of the behavior of Boris's troops at Dobrynichi. While Moscow was treated to the spectacle of a barbaric triumphal procession of prisoners and captured souvenirs of victory, hundreds of voices cried out that the farmers and common people of the Komarichi District were being tortured and murdered, as mercilessly as thoughtlessly. The army accused these people of treachery, of sedition, or even of nothing at all but happening to be there. This was unjust, and hatred of Boris mounted throughout southern Russia. Even the elaborate rewards heaped on Basmanov's head only served to augment the dislike for everything the Tsar did and increase the longing of the Muscovite people for Dimitry.

It was not merely the lower class of people who welcomed the young "Pretender" to the throne. They had long dreamed of a "good Tsar," a virtuous prince who would rule by love and not by passion. Dimitry would be this sort of monarch, they thought. But the upper classes, indeed the highest class, also saw something in Dimitry, even though in a sense it was negative. The boyars of princely birth resented Boris, an elected Tsar of far less natural dignity than themselves. He was of lowly origin, and a Tatar to boot. They, the great boyars, were often descended from Rurik — at least, from the almost legendary Lithuanian ruler, Gedimin. If Dimitry were genuine, he would deserve the throne. If he were not, as seemed likely to many of them, he would still be a different kind of coin from Boris. He was very young. One or another of the princely boyars could handle him — one way or another.

While the chances of rapprochement between Boris and his people were flickering out, the former was taking drastic steps to remove what had become the epitome of his troubles: the "name," the "shadow," against which he was pitted.

When Smirnoy Otrepyev had failed in his attempt to see and hopefully to seize the person of Dimitry, Tsar Boris found an abler envoy in the person of Posnik Ogaryov, a petty courtier otherwise unknown. Dimitry had not much more than left Glinyany, back in September, 1604, when Ogaryov set out from Moscow by the common route to Warsaw, through Smolensk and Minsk. His westward passage lay nearly three hundred miles north of Dimitry's eastward one, but he knew of Dimitry's spies in the Ukraine, of Ratomski's activities in the province of Seversk, and of the contacts with Cossacks and possibly the Crimean Khan. In short, he was better prepared than Smirnoy.

But when he reached the Polish border, before Dimitry crossed the Dnyeper, the Polish guards took him into custody, with little explanation, and quarantined him so long that when he at last appeared in Warsaw Dimitry had already sought refuge in Putivl. All protocol properly complied with, it was February 10, 1605, when Posnik Ogaryov first appeared before the Polish Diet. Different from Otrepyev, Ogaryov bore a letter to King Sigismund. It was presented with full panoply of diplomacy.

But this letter was, if anything, even more extraordinary than the evasive document borne by Otrepyev. It stated, categorically and at some length, that a rogue and ex-monk had turned up in Poland under the false name of Dimitry, and that this rogue had disobeyed his father, had fallen into heresy (Catholics were heretics in Russia), and had run wild — stealing, gambling, drinking, and finally becoming a monk to elude the police. But even as a monk he had not abandoned his vices, and he had practiced black-magic and called up the spirits of evil. At last his rascalities were discovered, Boris wrote, and

> the Patriarch and the Holy Council [of the Church] condemned him to everlasting prison in the Monastery of Kirillov Belozersky; but he and his companions the priest Varlaam and the chorister Misail Povadin fled to Lithuania. And We are astounded at the way such a rogue has been received and believed in your [King Sigismund's] realms, without sending to Us for the true facts. Even if this rogue actually were Prince Dimitry of Uglich, risen from the dead, he would not be of legitimate birth, since he was born of the seventh wife [of Ivan the Dread].

Tsar Boris's demand that Dimitry be turned over to Ogaryov was politely answered with the statement that he was not receiving any aid from the King of the Polish Republic, and that those who did help him would be punished, with the implication that none were known. But nothing happened.

Although there was a vast amount of discussion, Boris again defeated his own aim. He should above all not have admitted the possibility that Dimitry was genuine. The reference to the Tsarevich's illegitimacy was absurd to Polish ears. Everybody knew that Ivan had married the Tsaritsa Maria. That she was his seventh wife made no difference.

Ogaryov possibly did not know that Dimitry had been discussed in the Diet before his own appearance there. On February 1, John Zamoyski had voiced his doubts about Dimitry's genuineness so passionately that he ended his speech in a torrent of tears. Swept by Zamoyski's oratory, Leo Sapieha, possessed of a weather-vane's constancy, changed sides and himself attacked Dimitry. Then both of them condemned Dimitry's "foolhardy expedition," and called attention to the Peace Treaty with Russia which his moves had imperilled. Had Ogaryov not appeared, it is conceivable that, after settling a few other matters such as King Sigismund's forthcoming marriage to a sister of his deceased wife (highly unpopular), some sort of condemnation of aid to Dimitry might have been voiced. Ogaryov succeeded masterfully in defeating his own ends.

As soon as he was accorded the privilege of speaking, Ogaryov began to plead the very same points mentioned by Zamoyski and Sapieha with the same heartfelt eloquence. Before long, the senators who had not yet taken sides began to be disturbed by an attitude which seemed to make him, Ogaryov, another Polish senator, not a visiting diplomat. Nevertheless, they listened while the envoy cried that Dimitry must be disowned and denied, and those guilty of supporting him punished. Otherwise, the treaty was clearly infringed, Polish honor sullied, the King's word profaned, and a cause for war clearly indicated. Indeed, if Poland were faithless to her sacred word, she would be denounced before all Europe, to be scorned by the whole of Christendom.

This was a good deal for the Diet to swallow. The senators had no intention of airing their differences before outsiders, and especially before a Muscovite ambassador. They therefore recessed, to have an opportunity to go over the matter behind closed doors. Meanwhile, Pan George Mniszech had arrived in Warsaw. What he said is not recorded, but some influence of Mniszech origin may be felt in the ensuing meeting of February 26, when the duty of answering Ogaryov was entrusted to Leo Sapieha. By then, weirdly, Ogaryov himself had undermined his case to some extent by contradicting previous charges and stating that the "rogue" was not an Otrepyev, of the petty nobility, but the son of a peasant. It was now up to Sapieha.

The speech which followed, possibly delivered in Russian for the better understanding of the visiting ambassador, was truly a model of inaccuracy, evasiveness and irony. Virtually denying everything that had been said before, Sapieha summed up the situation in some such language as this:

As for Dimitry, His Majesty sent no soldiers to bring him, but when he arrived wanted to know everything he had to say so as to inform the Grand Duke [Boris], and find out from him whether the young man was really of the ducal family. When Dimitry learned this, he fled to the Zaporozhtsy Cossacks, with whose help he is said to have made a few sorties into Muscovy. He [His Majesty] said he did not *know;* and just as the Grand Duke of Muscovy is unable to keep the Cossacks of the Don in line, so His Majesty cannot restrain the Zaporozhtsy either. But he has commanded that those who go to his aid be punished, and [adds] that if Dimitry is found in the kingdom again he will be arrested, and the fact reported to his [Ogaryov's] Master, who, being so powerful, can catch him and his followers if he is in Muscovy.

It only needs to be added that, if Sapieha demonstrated how pliant he could be, the Diet showed remarkable consistency in not revealing diplomatic probity. Ogaryov left Poland as had Otrepyev before him: unanswered, and not permitted to verify anything for himself. Nevertheless, his appearance in Warsaw is important, as showing that Moscow and the Tsar were far from being sure who Dimitry was. Although Ogaryov's letter said that Dimitry was Grishka Otrepyev, his own words denied it. And in the end these words were so uncontrolled that the senators lost interest in trying to understand. The representative from Moscow heaped accusations and slander on Dimitry without regard even to the compatibility or consistency of the charges.[1]

Ambassador Posnik Ogaryov could not have been far on the road of return to Moscow when a strange figure was conducted before Dimitry at Putivl. According to the two Jesuit chaplains, Czyrzowski and Lawicki, shortly before March 8, 1605,

a dangerous sorcerer has been brought, Grishka Otrepyev, famous throughout Muscovy, whom Godunov has made pass among his people as the prince who came from Poland with the Poles and was trying to seize the throne of Moscow. In this way it was obvious to the Muscovites [in Putivl] that Grishka Otrepyev was one person, and Dimitry Ivanovich another.

Tsar and Great Prince Boris Fyodorovich [Godunov]. A "portrait," not from life, from the "Titulary" of the seventeenth century. Courtesy of the State Historical Museum, Moscow.

SERENISS. ET INVICTISS. SIGISMVNDO III. REGI POLONIAE, MAGNO DVCI LITHVA·
NIAE, RVSSIAE, PRVSSIAE, MAS. SAMOGITIAE, LIVONIAE, SEVERIAE. ETC. HAEREDITARIO REGI
SVETIAE, GOTHIAE, VANDALIAE, MAG. DVCI FINLANDIAE, TRIVMPHATORI MOSCOVIAE AC
OMNIVM SEPTENTRIONVM REGIONVM.

Sigismund III, King of Poland, Grand Duke of Lithuania, and so
on, by Abraham Hogenberg. Note that Sigismund here has the
title *Invictiss*[*imus*], "Most Undefeated," which Dimitry was called
blasphemous for using. Note also that Sigismund has "triumphed
over Moscow and all the Northern Regions." Sigismund had no
intention of letting modesty ruin him. Courtesy of the Trustees of
the British Museum, London.

Ierzy (George) Mniszech, of Velké Končice, Voyvode of Sandomierz. Reproduced from D. A. Rovinsky's second edition of Grochowski's Wedding Brochure, 1605. Courtesy of the Trustees of the British Museum, London.

Bernard Maciejowski, Cardinal of the Holy Roman Church, Bishop of Kraków. Reproduced from D. A. Rovinsky's second edition of Grochowski's Wedding Brochure, 1605. Courtesy of the Trustees of the British Museum, London.

MOSCVA
ad Architypum Foedori Boriſſou

35 40 45

A. Kremelena-gorod, Aula Imperatoris
B. Kitay-gorod urbs media
D. Skorodom, urbs exterior
C. Tzar-gorod urbs Cæsarea
E. Streletska sloboda, vel
   Vicus militaris.
a. Curia
b. Patriarcheion
c. Templum D. Michaelis
   Imperat. sepultura
d. Podium Ecclesiasticorum
   in supplicationibus Odæo
   proclamationibus Imper-
   atoriis destinatum
e. Tabernæ mercatoriæ
f. Tribunalia urbana
g. Fusorium ærnmento-
   rum
h. Forum equarium
i. Balneæ publicæ
k. Forum lignarium
l. Viridarium Imperat-
   oris
m. Equile

Occidens
Meridies
Septentrio
suno

An adaptation of Tsar Fyodor Godunov's drawing of the Kremlin, forming part of the
map of Russia attributed to him, but undoubtedly redrawn, or modified, by western
hands. Courtesy of the Trustees of the British Museum, London.

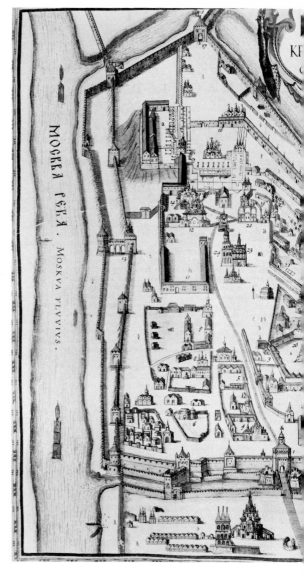

Bird's-eye view of the Kremlin, Moscow, drawn by Joan Blaeu of Amsterdam, "as
the time of Tsar and Great Prince Boris Fyodorovich [Godunov]," but dedicated
Tsar Aleksey Mikhaylovich (crowned in 1645). This drawing was undoubtedly bas
on young Tsar Fyodor Godunov's cartographical sketches, which had been availa
to Blaeu's father, Willem Janszoon, by 1614. The long buildings of the "New Cour
upper left, can hardly represent either Boris's or Dimitry's palace accurately. Nev
theless, the sketch is valuable as showing how basically *empty* the Kremlin then was

nany small buildings enclosed within walled courtyards. The three cathedrals clearly appear below and to the right of the "New Court," while Boris's old palace is the argest building to the right of, and below, the bell-tower of Ivan the Great with its adjoining building. At the very bottom, a horseshoe represents the Place of the Skull, with "St. Basil's Cathedral" immediately to the left. (The exotic architecture of that amous building was apparently too much for Joan Blaeu's pen.) Courtesy of the Trustees of the British Museum, London.

Russian Armor of the sixteenth century, drawn by Fyodor Grigoryevich Solntsev (1801–1892), artist and archaeologist. From a collection which belonged to Tsar Nicholas II. Courtesy of the Rare Book Division, the New York Public Library.

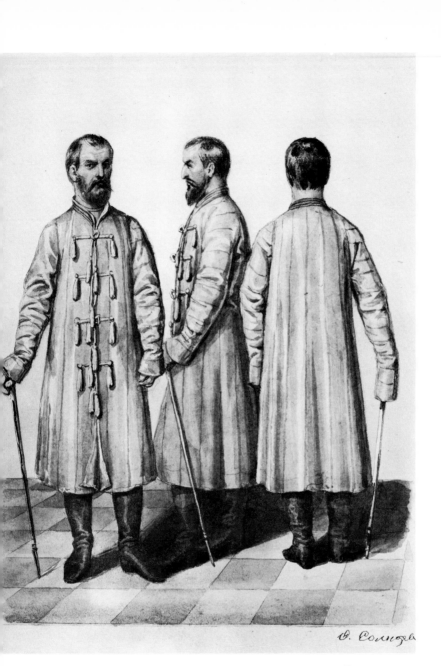

Silk Kaftan of Tsar Ivan Vasilyevich IV, the Dread. From the same collection. Dress of this type was very slow to change in Muscovy.

Boyars' attire of the seventeenth century. From the same collection, based on drawings made by Adam Olschläger (Olearius) in Muscovy, 1634–1636.

One of the Russian Streltsy or Musketeers. From the same collection, also based on Olschläger. For fire-arms they habitually carried harquebuses or muskets, despite their name of "archers."

Anonymous woodcut of Dimitry, published in a brochure by Grochowski in honor of Marina's marriage-by-proxy in Kraków, November 22, 1605. This is the basic engraving on which those of Sniadecki and Kilian were based, but was apparently produced independently of the aquarelle sketch of Dimitry which was sent to Darmstadt. This reproduction is from D. A. Rovinsky's photolithograph of the second edition (1606), the first edition being entirely lost. (For details, see D. A. Rovinsky, *Materialy*, listed in the Bibliography.) Courtesy of the Trustees of the British Museum, London.

Marina Mniszchówna, of Velké Končice, Great Tsaritsa of Muscovy. From Rovinsky, Grochowski's Wedding Brochure, 1605. Courtesy of the Trustees of the British Museum, London.

The French mercenary Captain, Margeret, also heard about this later and added the detail that Grishka was thirty-five to thirty-eight years old and much addicted to drunkenness. Dimitry kept him for a few days, said Margeret, and then sent him off to Yaroslavl (one hundred and seventy miles north of Moscow), where he was still living a year or more later.

Outside of the arrival, probably involuntary, of the individual said to be Grishka Otrepyev, life in Putivl beat with the slow pulse of winter. The Seym River was undoubtedly frozen over throughout its lazy, meandering course until late in March or early April. Prince-Boyar-Voyvode Mstislavsky offered no further threat, for he had commanded his troops to invest not Putivl but the insignificant fort of Kromy, where, in the words of Captain Margeret, who was one of them, they lingered "without doing anything even worth laughing at."

Curiously, despite his ruinous defeat, Dimitry was master of the province of Seversk. With Kromy holding out against Mstislavsky, as his advance-post, Dimitry could rest at ease in an unassailable position. Indeed, no Muscovite army went so far as to attempt to threaten or surprise him. Yet it was Dimitry himself whom Tsar Boris must conquer to stifle the insidious and stubborn threat to his throne.

Of real activity, then, there was little. An *ex post facto* examination of the causes of Dimitry's defeat produced some curious suggestions from the pious chaplains, who excused the Cossacks as neither the chief nor the only responsible elements. On the contrary, a single soldier had called down the wrath of heaven by brutalizing a Muscovite woman, publicly. The act cried for vengeance. "There," said the chaplains, "you have the secret cause of your misfortune. The sins of man bring down the wrath of God." Dimitry agreed in principle, but went on to ask if that meant that he should renounce his campaign. The chaplains shrugged off the detail; that was a matter for soldiers. As for themselves, they had full confidence in God, Lord and Master of life and death.

Dimitry did not go to the soldiers for advice, for he kept his politico-military plans pretty well to himself. On the contrary, he continued to charm and intrigue the chaplains with general, all-encompassing projects. And for the chaplains there could be no doubt that he was the rightful heir to the throne, since the people as a whole were wildly for Dimitry. *Vox populi, vox Dei,* and God punished traitors through the *populus*. The people cut down on the spot two voyvodes who were only *suspected* of conniving with the Tsar's forces. Such "enthusiasm" proved who Dimitry was.

Naturally, no-one dared disclose the close contact that existed between Dimitry and the Catholic chaplains. In the eyes of the Muscovite masses, Dimitry must be a pillar of Orthodoxy. For, was he not the Orthodox Tsar? Thus, too, Boris's accusations and the anathemas of Iov fell on deaf ears. The people saw in Dimitry their true ruler. No doubts whatsoever assailed their hearts.

Knowing this, Dimitry kept his conversion to Catholicism a sacred secret in which only the Jesuits shared, even though many Poles must have at least suspected the truth. This secret drew him and his chaplains together from the beginning, and the ties were cemented a few days before the victory at Novgorod.

Meeting one of the Jesuits by chance, Dimitry stopped him and said, "I have made a vow that if God blesses my labors I will erect a church in Moscow in honor of the Holy Virgin, and I expect to place it in your hands." The chaplain was so charmed by this that he took advantage of the opportunity to mention a precious relic he had just received from Poland for Dimitry. It was a bit of the True Cross. Dimitry urgently asked for it then and there, and hung it around his neck in a locket. When the battle was won, he credited the relic with the victory, and proclaimed himself as much favored by Heaven as Constantine had been when he saw a Flaming Cross with the legend: *By this, conquer!*

With a mind thus devoutly inclined to belief in the supernatural, Dimitry found great encouragement in Putivl when the miraculous Image of the Virgin of Kursk was brought to him there. It was framed in gold and silver and adorned with pearls and had been found intact in the ashes of a church which had been burned to the ground. Dimitry marched at the head of a procession of Orthodox priests and Muscovites in general conveying this ikon into the Putivl castle. Since the Catholic feast-day of the Annunciation, March 25, was at hand too, Dimitry had another image of the Virgin given to the Jesuits and the Poles — a very ancient one, likewise framed in gilded silver, with pearls and precious stones.

Good Friday came two weeks later, and, as in 1604, it fell on the same day for both Catholics and Orthodox. Dimitry's Hetman, Adam Dworzicki, got permission to celebrate the night from Holy Saturday to Easter Sunday after the Polish fashion, with cannon-fire before the altar set up for Catholic services outside the city walls. Dimitry gave this permission, however, only after warning the Muscovites not to be alarmed over the unusual Polish way of celebrating the Resurrection.

This done, at the appointed time bedlam broke out in Putivl and the surrounding countryside. Cannon roared and boomed, Orthodox bells pealed wildly, Catholic trumpets brayed and drums rumbled and rattled, while lusty Polish throats bellowed hymns in Gregorian chant. The Muscovites, one Catholic reported, were at first startled. Nevertheless, "they rested quite enlightened and satisfied with the piety and ceremonies of the Catholics."

During these days of enforced idleness, although winter was breaking up, Dimitry occupied himself largely with self-education. He knew how to read and write, it is true, and that was an accomplishment which graced few of his Muscovite associates. But his reading was limited almost exclusively to the Bible, particularly the New Testament, and his knowledge of history and geography was sketchy and romantic rather than scientific. With the help of the Jesuits, he was able to make great progress toward sounder knowledge. His presumptive father, Ivan IV, had been a well-educated man for his day.

Then, too, although the traitor Boris was little better than illiterate, he was enlightened, and his son, Fyodor, could have been called erudite, for all his sixteen years. Fyodor was working in those very days on the finest map of Russia yet attempted by Russian hands. Dimitry probably knew of Fyodor's studies, and of the Russian youths Boris had sent abroad to study. If so, and it seems all but certain, Dimitry intended to continue and expand the initiative. Boris was a reformer on a small scale; Dimitry would work out colossal changes — changes which even Peter the Great found difficult a century later. He would found schools and colleges, send more young men abroad, and bring from abroad teachers and scholars capable of scattering the darkness and backwardness which enveloped the land of the Tsars. Putivl gave Dimitry a chance to work on his plans.

During this time, Boris's army was sitting aimlessly in front of Rylsk. Then five thousand Cossacks from Putivl slipped through their lines to bring supplies to the defenders. This so discouraged the Tsar's troops that they retired toward Novgorod, and it was suggested that they disband, at least for the winter. When Boris heard of this, however, he expressly forbade any discharging of soldiers whatsoever. So when the army was rested (from doing nothing!), Mstislavsky, now well again, and Prince Vasily Shuysky, sent from Moscow to help, led the troops to Kromy, where a detachment had already been placed right after Dimitry's defeat.

Kromy was a little town, protected only by a single wooden palisade. Boris's two generals consequently thought they could take it without trouble. But Dimitry had a loyal friend acting as voyvode there, supported by a force of six hundred Don Cossacks under their ataman, Andrey Korela.

Korela had the reputation of being a sorcerer, and his success in warding off the imperial army with six hundred men would seem to justify it. By digging tunnels through the frozen ground under the palisade, and out into the fields near the enemy camp, Korela was able to take advantage of any carelessness of the soldiers. Time after time Cossacks would appear out of nowhere to cut the throats of the Muscovites, only to disappear before they were caught. As one historian put it, the besieging army was more besieged than the fort they sought to take.

Dimitry's strength now began to grow almost like the grass that was springing up under the warm April sun. Soon it would be time to take the initiative. Boris himself, however, took an initiative of sorts first. He sent a trio of monks to Putivl with secret letters for the inhabitants, against Dimitry. "He is a heretic and a renegade," these said, "and his real name is Grishka Otrepyev. We were his superiors [in the convent]. We have often punished him for his black-magic and other evil practices."

But the people of Putivl were loyal to Dimitry. No sooner had the monks begun to whisper such things than they were arrested. Put to the torture, two of them refused to speak despite the pain inflicted on them, but the third broke down and confessed. They had a poison with them, he said, which was to be given to two boyars to burn with the incense in the church Dimitry attended. "Anyone who breathes this poisonous vapor," the monk told Dimitry, "will swell up and die within ten days. These are the instructions which Boris sends to the traitors who surround you." Then he named the boyars chosen for the deed.

The boyars were tied to stakes and tortured to death by arrows and harquebus-shots carefully aimed at non-vital parts of their bodies to prolong their agony. The monk who talked was rewarded. The other two were only imprisoned, since it was not proper to execute any sort of clergy. Dimitry then sent letters to Boris and the Patriarch telling them "to recognize Dimitry as the legitimate Prince, and to persuade the [Muscovite] magnates not to rebel *contra jus et fas* [against the laws of man and God]."

Early in May Dimitry was attacked by a virulent fever, against which he had neither medicine nor physician. Not knowing which way to turn, he called in the chaplains, who suggested a bezoar-stone as an antidote. Dimitry had apparently never heard of this concretion found in the stomachs of Persian wild goats, but gladly accepted the offer since the chaplains had come provided with so miraculous a remedy. The stone was brought, a bit of it cut off and put in a glass of water, and the chaplains and other attendants knelt before the feverish patient. Making the sign of the Cross and mumbling the Lord's Prayer, Dimitry swallowed the medicine. Since the virtues of faith are great, Dimitry's recovery was swift and sure.

By this time, Dimitry's activities in the politico-military arena had burgeoned with the snowdrops and birch-buds. He kept in close touch with Poland, even though his envoy, Tatyev, was not permitted to attend the meeting of the Diet at which unkind things were said about himself. But, while displaying vast confidence in the efficacy of Polish help, which had failed him despite royal insistence that without it he was lost, Dimitry now turned back to his original plan of conquering his throne with the aid of Muscovites, Cossacks, and Tatars. Yet it was a revised plan which he adopted — a plan of truly colossal proportions.

As the snow began to melt in the Ukraine, Dimitry's messengers scoured not only the valleys of the Dnyeper and the Don, but even the slopes of the Urals, a thousand miles to the east, and the realm of Ghazi II Giray, Khan of the Crimea. Cossacks and Tatars were called to take up arms and meet at designated points. There they would be organized and deployed toward Moscow, but with orders to bypass all fortified posts while occupying the countryside. In this way, Tsar Boris would find himself attacked without hope of help or provision from the provinces. It was a bold plan, which revealed uncommon knowledge of the terrain, the people, and the Tsar. Dimitry's trust in its practicability was soon justified.

The Don Cossacks had already responded to Dimitry's appeals with numerous horsemen. Now they added a political stroke of genius. On the southern undefined borders of Muscovy the remnants of the great Golden Horde that once was master of Moscow still roamed the steppes beyond the Volga. These were the Nogay Tatars, who took their name from the great-great-grandson of Genghis Khan. Although most of their past glory was gone, they were still a powerful people. Boris therefore had already attempted to confine them to the wilderness north of the Caspian Sea, under a ruler who would be a vassal of Moscow. This ruler was Ishterek Mirza. He received a valuable sabre from Tsar Boris, with an oracular monition that it was for the enemies of Russia or for those who did not know how to use it (meaning those who did not defend Boris). At the same time, Boris sent presents to a rival Tatar prince, thinking perhaps to guarantee loyalty the better.

Ishterek, however, smelled something redolent of danger, perhaps treachery. He "complied" with Boris's monition by collecting some seventy other Tatar princes and declaring himself for Dimitry, although he is not known to have returned the sabre. Then he summoned the Don Cossacks, who undoubtedly had inspired his move, and gave his solemn oath of loyalty to Dimitry, in token of which he surrendered to the Cossacks several of his children for them to send to Putivl as hostages. When news of this reached Dimitry on April 30, he responded with a note of copious thanks and an order to Ishterek to commence his long journey to Moscow as soon as convenient.

Three days later, about the time Dimitry was miraculously cured by the bezoar-stone, the Crimean Tatars received evidence of Dimitry's friendship in the form of presents hardly to be expected from so unimportant a town as Putivl. The presents were persuasive. These nearer Tatars began to appreciate the value of Dimitry's claim on the ivory throne of Ivan the Dread.

By then the following important posts in southern Muscovy were in Dimitry's hands, or held by avowed partisans: Voronezh, Oskol, Belgorod, Valuyki, Borisgorod, Yelets and Livny. They were scattered along the Muscovite "great wall" (a palisade) protecting the empire from the untamed hordes that swept the *Dikoye Pole,* the "Wilderness." Yelets and Livny were the nearest to Moscow, and the latter was chosen as an assembly-point for Dimitry's forces.

Two days passed, and a bolt from paradise fell on Putivl. On Thursday, May 5, Avraamy Bakhmetyev galloped up from Moscow. He came in all haste to offer his services to the Tsar and Great Prince of all Russia. Boris Godunov, the usurper, was dead.

Dimitry could hardly contain himself for joy. Just as he was about to set in motion his plan for vanquishing his enemy, the enemy had vanished — unexpectedly and almost beyond hoping for, as Dimitry wrote to Rangoni. So excited was he by the news that he recorded the date incorrectly. But then doubts assailed him. What if it were not true? While still writing the letter, he changed his tone and concluded by calling the news a rumor. And to be triply safe, he put off sending the letter until May 13.

By then there was no doubt. Other messengers arrived, and there were letters from Livny, only three hundred and thirty-odd miles from Moscow. In the long run, what was most surprising was the time it took the news to reach Putivl. Perhaps Dimitry's own troops and partisan town-officials had delayed the messengers and couriers.

According to the message from the Voyvode of Livny, supplemented and corrected from other sources, despite Boris's ill health for a year or more, no-one suspected that he was near death. On Saturday morning, April 13 (according to the Muscovite calendar, but April 23 by that used so far in Dimitry's story), Boris had risen in excellent spirits and health. Accounts of what he did after rising are conflicting, but in the words of John Merick, an English merchant then residing in Moscow,

> his death was very sudden, and as it was in itself, very strange: for within some two hours after dinner, having (as he usually had) his Doctors with him, who left him in their judgments in health, as the good meal he made could witness, for he dined well, and fed plentifully, though presently after as may be thought, feeding overmuch, he felt himself not only heavy, but also pained in his stomach: presently went into his chamber, sent for his Doctors (which always speeded) yet before they came, he was past [help], being speechless and soon after dying.

Before his death, however, there was time for Boris to be shorn a monk, as had become customary for Tsars at the time of their death, and he gave himself the name of Bogolep. Furthermore, according to Merick, it was reported that

> some of his Councillors and Nobility demanded if he would not swear them anew to the Prince [Fyodor], and whether he should not be their Emperor [and], his answer was, "as it pleased God, and the Commons:" thereby presuming of the sufficiency of their former oaths . . .

The suddenness and symptoms of Boris's death led to conjectures that he had died of poison, perhaps even self-administered. Certainly, suicide is hardly to be considered. Yet that Boris may have been murdered by poison is far from impossible. The English agents in Moscow thought that he had been. Then, as has been mentioned, King Sigismund's Great Marshal, Myszkowski, had baldly predicted that he would be. If there was talk of doing away with Boris early in 1604, and of poison when he died in 1605, it must remain an open question whether there was any connection, at least until firm evidence can be found. Moscow at that time was as dark and toxic as the Rome of the Borgias. Anything evil could happen.

Boris Godunov had loved Russia and had dedicated himself to her advancement and weal. But perhaps he had loved his family more. And the unconquerable urge to see his young son on the throne, to be followed by a Godunov dynasty, contributed not a little to his final failure as a ruler. He died unmourned, outside of his family.

The Tsar's death was announced to Moscow and the whole of Russia the next day. Then began the slow, peaceful, even apathetic, trickle of citizens, walking up to "kiss the cross" (swear fealty) to "their sovereign lady the Tsaritsa and Great Princess Maria Grigoryevna of all Russia, and her children the sovereign lord Tsar and Great Prince Fyodor Borisovich of all Russia, and the sovereign lady of Tsarevna Ksenia Borisovna."

The oath they took was the same as that administered when Boris had acceded to the throne, even to the by then absurd affirmation that they would not have for Tsar that unhappy Tatar Prince, Semyon Bekbulatovich, whom Ivan the Dread had set up as fictitious Tsar over himself thirty years before and had been blinded (people said by Boris) in 1593. Then they swore also that they "would not have any other ruler over the Muscovite State," and "would not side with the *vor* who calls himself Prince Dimitry Ivanovich, nor appeal to him or his Councillors . . . nor want to see that *vor* who calls himself Prince Dimitry [rule] over the Muscovite State . . ."

There was nothing remarkable about swearing loyalty to the whole family, mother, son, and daughter, and there was nothing remarkable about placing the mother's name first. What did seem remarkable was that the Patriarch and boyars who prepared the oath should have abandoned the name Grishka Otrepyev for Dimitry, after the Patriarch's own statement that such was the "Pretender's" true name. The reasons, which probably involved the danger of confusion, may have been logically sound. But they were far from convincing to the people at large.

Dimitry had been called a runaway monk, heretic, necromancer, and so on, and the story of his life had been lavishly circulated in great detail. Now all this was omitted. He was merely a "rogue who called himself Dimitry." For many, this was an admission that the whole story about Dimitry was a deliberate lie.

For Dimitry, however Boris had met his death, there was now but a boy on the throne, acting under a regent (his mother) who could inspire no love among the people. No matter what they might think of young Fyodor, Maria Godunova was still the daughter of the hated Malyuta Skuratov. Knowing that he faced inexperience guided by an abomination, Dimitry made rapid plans for an attack. He was certain as never before of his success. From the ashes of defeat, Dimitry soared on the wings of confidence toward his goal.[2]

CHAPTER 8

VISITING THE INIQUITY
OF THE FATHER ON THE SON

T HE TRADITION OF SUCCESSION from father to son on the Muscovite throne was relatively new. Although accident had made it a practice for a long time, the theory had been established for less than two centuries when Fyodor Godunov took up the reins dropped by Tsar Boris. At sixteen, he was in the flower of youth, with the added charm of being strikingly handsome and strong in body and spirit, firm yet kind, and — most remarkable of all — outstandingly well educated.

Furthermore, Boris had associated the youth with himself in the Council of State and in public audiences, where he had sat on a smaller throne just below his father, and there Fyodor had learned both the administration of the law and the exercise of mercy. On all counts, he was the most promising Tsar since Ivan III mounted the throne at the age of twenty-two in 1462. If all Russia did not welcome him with extravagant love, it was only because the reign of Boris still rankled in the people's hearts.

Fyodor was more mature than a modern boy of his age, and it could be said that he was ready to rule. Still, although Ivan the Dread had taken matters into his own hands before he was seventeen, Fyodor's mother considered him too young. Undoubtedly under the influence of some of the boyars, she immediately sent for Prince Mstislavsky and the two brothers Shuysky, Princes Vasily and Dimitry, informing them of Boris's death and asking them to leave the army and return to Moscow.

Mstislavsky, it will be remembered, was the premier boyar of the realm, and the Shuyskys were not only descendants of Rurik and distant cousins of the dynasty that had been extinguished by the death of Fyodor Ivanovich, but also were considered by some to be entitled to the throne, even above Mstislavsky. These three rivals for the supreme power were, amazingly, asked by the Tsaritsa to govern in the young Tsar's name, while that ancient trouble-maker, Bogdan Belsky, was invited back to Moscow and again granted his liberty, honor, and property. That the Tsaritsa, who was not known for artlessness, should have brought such a quad-rumvirate together for the purpose of *helping* her son seems in-credible. Did she not know that gossip had it that Boris had exiled Belsky permanently because the latter told a priest that he had poi-soned both Ivan IV and Tsar Fyodor the Angelic by order of the same Boris?

Next, the Tsaritsa replaced Prince Mstislavsky at the front by Prince Ivan Mikhaylovich Katyrev-Rostovsky, a man noted for his goodness, and for weakness. He was to be First Voyvode. To offset these shortcomings, however, she called to the Kremlin Pyotr Fyo-dorovich Basmanov, newly created boyar and commander, and gave him the highest rank permitted by the rules of precedence, second only to the Commander-in-Chief. A more able and reliable man could not be found, people said.

When Basmanov appeared in the great palace and knelt before Tsar Fyodor Borisovich, in the presence of his mother, Fyodor ad-dressed him with great emotion: "Serve us [my mother and me] as you served my father!" Basmanov, ambition swelling mightily in his breast, swore to die for the Tsar and the Tsaritsa-mother.

After this ceremony, Basmanov joined Katyrev-Rostovsky, and the two generals, accompanied by Isidor, Metropolitan of Novgo-rod the Great, left Moscow to take the army's oath of loyalty to the young Tsar. The three rode with a small guard, a body of priests, and all the urgency which the circumstances seemed to require. No-one, except possibly the Tsaritsa-mother, can have failed to recognize that it was over Fyodor's head, not Dimitry's, that Damo-cles's sword hung. The question, not decided even today, was whether an army could defeat "an empty name, a shadow" — as Pushkin put it — or a hope.

The young Dutch merchant, Isaac Massa, has left a vivid description of the turmoil which broke out in Moscow at the time. Mobs billowed up to the palace, demanding the recall of nobles exiled by Boris. Some even called for the return of the Tsaritsa-nun Marfa, to learn from her whether the Tsarevich was alive or not. Fyodor's mother was adamant on this point, but more flexible on others. Still, there was contention among the boyars as well as the common people, and it was not until Prince Vasily Shuysky reached Moscow and addressed the crowd that some semblance of order returned.

Shuysky roundly denied the legitimacy of Dimitry, spread out his hands before the people crying that with them he had placed the Tsarevich in his coffin in Uglich, and adjured the people of Moscow to be faithful to the new Tsar. It was the third time he had borne testimony that the Tsarevich was dead. Yet the calm that followed was tense. Restless days passed inside the ancient Kremlin walls.

By then, the Prince, the Voyvode, and the Metropolitan, since joined by Ivan Ivanovich Godunov and others, had reached the walls of Kromy, nearly three hundred miles away. Somewhat to their surprise, they found that Mstislavsky and the two Shuyskys had already left for Moscow. It seemed impossible that they should not at least have met en route, but the bald fact is that not an officer of rank remained to control a large and agitated army.

Yet, strangely, the Prince is not mentioned in the records as having acted. It was Basmanov who called the troops together under their colors, Muscovites and foreigners, officers and other ranks, and on April 17/27,* 1605, informed them of the accession of Fyodor, and read them his proclamation. After brief mention of the death of Boris, the young Tsar promised splendid rewards to his loyal, zealous army as soon as the period of mourning was over. Some wept at the news, fearing for Russia's future. Others scarcely concealed their hateful joy. But the army, like Moscow, swore loyalty to Fyodor. Basmanov himself reported this to the Metropolitan, and Isidor was soon on his way back to Moscow, his mission accomplished.

---

* Previous dates have generally been given according to the new style, or Gregorian calendar. Russian dates are all old style (ten days behind), hence the double-date.

About this time word reached Dimitry that the object of Ivan Godunov's presence with the Tsar's army was to burn Kromy to the ground. Whether it was true or not, this prompted Dimitry to send his own forces to succor his allies, shut up inside the walls, and at the same time to endeavor to find out the private attitude of Fyodor's army toward himself. The main body of Dimitry's forces could move only rather slowly, with its two thousand or so Poles and perhaps ten thousand Muscovites and others, but John Zaporski had orders to hurry ahead with two hundred lancers and one hundred infantry. The balance would join him as quickly as possible.

The Kromyans meanwhile had already learned that Tsar Fyodor's army was far from completely loyal. So as soon as Zaporski arrived at a nearby cover beyond Basmanov they got in touch with him, and contrived a plan to confuse the enemy completely. Conniving with malcontents among Basmanov's troops as well as with Zaporski, the Cossacks under the ubiquitous Ataman Korela made a sortie. Basmanov sent a brigade to attack them. The brigade had been carefully infiltrated by men secretly in favor of Dimitry, and as soon as the attack came these turned tail and ran, leaving the rest at the mercy of the Cossacks. There was great carnage before Basmanov could send reinforcements, and by that time the Cossacks had retired.

But the plot was far from fulfilled as yet. Zaporski next called up a peasant named Boris Bilzoma, gave him a ruble, and asked him to deliver a letter to Kromy. Although Basmanov's troops were right in his way, the peasant went stolidly on, only to be captured. He was of course searched, and the letter was promptly found. It contained the "news" that forty thousand Polish light-horse were on their way, and would fight to lift the siege the next day.

The peasant had naturally seen Zaporski's companies, and by then advance bodies of Dimitry's ten thousand Russians were beginning to show up. Consequently, when he was put to the torture, as was invariably done, he did not have to be hurt very much before he cried out that there was a big Polish army only a league away. That was enough. Basmanov's men took such fright that it was with great difficulty that he assembled them all in camp again.

How Zaporski timed his movements is not known, but the result of that timing was almost unbelievable. A day or so after the affair with Korela and the peasant, Basmanov, having discovered that the forty-thousand-man army was at best a gross exaggeration, sent two companies of a hundred soldiers each, followed by a regiment of two thousand men, to attack Zaporski. Behind these, he lined up the main body of his army. Here is the account of what happened, as narrated in a letter of the Jesuit Father Andrew Lawicki:

> Our men started to fight. There was a hullabaloo on both sides. Boris's Muscovites, when they had seen our lances and our sentries coming suddenly out of hiding to attack them sharply, persuaded that our army was very numerous and that they had no hope of victory, spontaneously surrendered. Thereupon Basmanov, who had made so much trouble for us at Novgorod, sprang from the center of a few soldiers, and in the presence of the whole army, acclaimed Dimitry his Most Serene Lord and heir to [the throne of] Muscovy. Swearing an oath of loyalty, he gave himself into our hands, and, as the Russians say, he kissed the Cross to His Most Serene [Highness] Dimitry.

It was May 17, 1605. Three weeks and two days had elapsed since Basmanov had vowed before God to die for Tsar Fyodor, the young.

There can be some doubt as to the exactness of the Polish story in all its details. Some sort of negotiations seem to have been held between the Polish leaders and the Muscovites. Dimitry always relied a great deal on advance negotiations and had won over a number of towns and forts that way. It would therefore be hard to believe that he did not negotiate at Kromy, where stood the only loyal army opposing him when Tsar Boris died. Boris's death had put all the trumps in his hand.

But with or without negotiations, the reasons for Basmanov's tempestuous *volte face* are not far to seek. Boris had showered him with gifts. One gift, however, he could not grant. Basmanov's place on the established order of rank was not far from the bottom.

Nothing Boris could do, legally, would advance Basmanov higher than the military rank he had won by loyalty and merit.

With Boris gone, Tsar Fyodor could certainly do even less. He was inexperienced — always that same unconquerable defect — and he was too good, too intelligent, too human, to pounce on Power as Ivan IV had. Fyodor at sixteen could not arrest a man of his own free will, with murderous intent, as Ivan had arrested Prince Andrey Shuysky, had him murdered, and his body thrown to the palace dogs in their kennels when *he* was twelve. Nor would he murder Basmanov, as Ivan had murdered Basmanov's father. So, from Tsar Fyodor, Basmanov could expect love and trust, but only such advancement as was legal. And Basmanov was ambitious.

There is nothing to indicate that Basmanov really believed that Dimitry was the son of dread Ivan. At the same time, there is nothing to hint that he actively thought he was not. Basmanov saw in Dimitry a young, vigorous leader, in whom the bulk of the soldiery had faith, and who inspired military leaders with confidence. All Muscovy loathed the Godunov family. Neither Fyodor's personality and intelligence nor the still unproven claims of Dimitry made much difference with the people. Anything at all was better than a Godunov for Tsar.

In fact, Dimitry had not yet won the trust of the common people. He had become a national hero of sorts, not because he had won one battle and lost the other, but because he shed an aura that betokened a "good Tsar." That was what they longed for. The story went that this strong young man was the son of "the Dread," and that he had been snatched from the murderous knives of Boris's hired assassins by a Providence that loved Holy Russia. Fate, then, had sanctified Dimitry. Dimitry himself believed this, moreover, and it was the secret of his success.

Pyotr Basmanov was not one to fight against such conviction. Furthermore, to support a cause that was doubtful and for himself not clearly profitable was ruin. Therefore, as the Russian historian Sergey Solovyov has written, not wanting to fall a victim to his oath, Basmanov decided to call an end to the matter.

He was not alone. The princely brothers, Vasily and Ivan Golitsyn joined him, along with the boyar Mikhail Glebovich Saltykov-Morozov. These three were present at Kromy as army officers. The two voyvodes, however, refused: Prince Katyrev-Rostovsky and Prince Andrey Andreyevich Telyatevsky. They fled to Moscow.

Promptly the rebellious leaders chose Prince Ivan Golitsyn to ride to Putivl to report to Dimitry that the army at Kromy had wheeled about in its allegiance and joined forces with him. Basmanov remained behind, to attempt to re-establish discipline and halt what was by then a mutiny in reverse. Whereas the original mutineers had consisted of the elements in favor of Dimitry (or merely opposed to Godunov), by no means all the army was wholeheartedly behind him after the switch. Not a few now became rebels against the rebels, without really being in favor of the boy Tsar, Fyodor Borisovich.

Meanwhile, Ivan Godunov had been captured attempting to flee. He was trussed up in traditional style, in accordance with the vow the Muscovites made in the presence of Zaporski: "The great army does obeisance to you [Dimitry], and we will shackle all who are traitors to you." Golitsyn took Ivan along to Putivl.

There he was cast before Dimitry, no longer "Tsarevich" but seated on a throne as Tsar, while Golitsyn himself touched his forehead humbly to the ground, declaiming: "Son of Ioann [Ivan]! The army places the realm of Muscovy in your hands, and awaits your complaisance. Misled by Boris, we have long stood up against our rightful Tsar. But now, knowing the truth, we all with one mind and heart have pledged ourselves to you. Come to the throne of your forefathers, and reign long and happily! Your enemies, Boris's minions, are in fetters. If Moscow dares to show resistance, we will subdue her. Come with us to the capital and receive your crown!"

Golitsyn's speech needed only the hand of a Shakespeare to make it noble. Perhaps the spirit of nobility was wanting in the speaker. Others present murmured more heartfelt words: "God has heard the prayers of our priests. He has humbled the hearts of our enemies, and brought them into obedience to Prince Dimitry."

When the little ceremony was over, Dimitry retired to consult his aides, not the least of whom were the two Jesuit fathers. To them, he hastened to say: "Behold what you predicted, my Fathers, after that sad day at Novgorod. I understand now. As our Lord brought me great affliction, so He would bring me greater consolation. I must not lose hope for a perfect victory."

This evidence of Divine aid, however, did not lull Dimitry into rash faith. He had already seen to it that "his" towns were fortified properly, with arms and supplies. Now he undertook to protect his right flank by sending an embassy, with gifts, to Ghazi Giray in the Crimea, asking for an alliance. Then he wrote Pan George Mniszech that victory was virtually his. (Letters of the same time to Stanislas Mniszech and his wife to this effect still exist.) And he started his army on the march to Moscow.

Dimitry himself left Putivl on May 19/29, with some six hundred Poles, the Don Cossacks, and the Russians who had been with him from the start. It was over one hundred and fifty miles to Kromy by the shortest possible route — Dimitry's route is not known — and it was somewhat out of the way. But regardless of this, Dimitry had to stop at that valiant fort. Its garrison deserved his sincerest thanks. Had not Kromy resisted Boris's army when Dimitry fled to Putivl, who knows what might have happened.

At Kromy itself scenes that beggar description had taken place. Terror-stricken Muscovites rushed there from the capital, or out of there to the capital, according to the inclination of their loyalties — if any. Fresh mobs reached Kromy, replacing the mobs which had fled or were fleeing.

In one instance, a swarm of Dimitry's adherents attacked a body of his opponents just outside the walls, where a bridge had been thrown across the marshes around the fort. As they did, three or four Orthodox priests were advancing on Kromy chanting and bearing crosses to be kissed in token of loyalty to the Tsar; it is not clear which Tsar. The mobs collided right on the bridge, a shaky one at best, and bridge, people, priests and all fell into the river, swollen by spring rains and possibly melting snow. Men on horseback struggled with their mounts, while those on foot swam or fought madly to find a foothold, a ford. A great many were drowned.

In short, as Isaac Massa wrote, it was such an "affray" that it seemed that it was the end of the world. Some fled home, some fled to Moscow, some fled into the forest. None knew whither or why. But they killed one another while fleeing, with sword or gun, "like animals seized with rage." Not pausing to explain just how animals use swords and guns, Massa raced on to add: "One cried, 'Long live Dimitry!'; another, 'Long live Fyodor Borisovich!'; a third, 'Long live the one that grabs the throne!' "

In the end, the great bulk of the army sided with Dimitry, while the rest scattered in mad confusion, urged by stark terror — terror that turned bushes and shadows into relentless enemies hot on their trail. Carts and wagons were abandoned where there were roads, so that the horses could be unharnessed and used for mounts. A witness wrote that these fugitive soldiers scurried through Moscow for three whole days. Asked what they were afraid of, they did not know. And when persons in authority demanded an answer, they only cried: "Go see for yourselves!"

Such a commotion had far from a calming influence on the citizens of Moscow. A popular outburst, without any clear goal whatever, threatened. But the infinitesimal additional stimulus that would have loosed it never came.

In the palace the young Tsar smarted with a nameless and helpless pain. Seventy German mercenaries who had left Kromy to bring their unshakable loyalty to Fyodor reached there and were received. Fyodor thanked them with tears in his eyes, while manfully acknowledging the misfortunes that harried him. It was said that some nobles laughed up their sleeves at Fyodor's words, but he and his mother and sister presented figures that were far from derisible. Ignoring any and all threats and mockery, they faced their future, and death itself, with unconquerable dignity, never forgetting to provide generously for the poor.

By this time, Dimitry and his followers had reached Kromy. The post was calm again, and order had been restored. He inspected the walls and the legendary tunnels, not sparing his words of praise for Korela and the mettlesome Cossacks who had devised and maintained these outworks. He recalled, he said, that for six weeks they had stood against seventy or eighty thousand or more men, backed by seventy great cannon, and had kept them in a state of enforced harmlessness and inactivity — beyond futile, though uninterrupted, bombarding of the fort. For these men, he could not express his amazement. For the mercy and favor of Heaven he gave heartfelt thanks.

Outside Kromy an illustrious quartet was waiting for Dimitry, to accompany him to Moscow. Basmanov was there, and with him Saltykov-Morozov. Behind came Prince Vasily Vasilyevich Golitsyn, brother of the Prince Ivan who had brought the glad tidings to Putivl, and the boyar Pyotr Nikitich Sheremetyev. Pyotr Nikitich was a cousin of Elena Ivanovna, the third and last wife of Tsarevich Ivan, murdered by his father Ivan the Dread one month after the birth of Tsarevich Dimitry. He was also remotely related to the Romanov family, all of whom had been exiled by Boris. The four solemnly averred that it was "hard to fight against a natural sovereign" — "him whom heaven created for thy ruler," as Shakespeare put it.

In the meantime, the bulk of the army had been waiting at Oryol, twenty-five miles on toward Moscow. Since a portion of the troops had already been sent home with discharges or on furlough, the others were now transferred to Tula and Kaluga, both about halfway to Moscow, to make way for Dimitry. He then entered Oryol, accompanied by a Polish and Russian guard of two or three thousand. One hundred of the Poles formed a special bodyguard for him, night and day. Caution is the half of safety, goes the Russian proverb.

Oryol distinguished itself in its own way by producing a handful of irredeemable anti-Dimitrists. Nothing would persuade them to "forsake the law," they said. They were soon thrown in jail to think over the vicissitudes of fortune, which in their case were not sweet.

By way of balance, a delegation arrived in Oryol at about the same time from Astrakhan, bearing the struggling body of Mikhail

Saburov, local voyvode, and cousin of both Tsar Boris and Tsare-vich Ivan's first wife. Oryol was festive indeed, then. It is recorded that there a great paean of joy went up to God and to Dimitry such as never had been accorded to the Dimitry who overthrew the Tatars at Kulikovo or the Ivan (the Dread) who had captured Kazan. Oryol went out *en masse* to crowd around Dimitry's horse and kiss his feet. It was not out of flattery or fear, the classic histor-ian Karamzin snorts, for to him Dimitry was the personification of imposture. It was out of willing love.

From Oryol, Dimitry moved on to Tula, a great fortress and a budding center of weapon-manufacture, where he tarried. He had surmised that his letters demanding the surrender of the capital had not reached there — they had, but the bearers had been put to death — and he did not want to fight his way in, if he could avoid it. Indeed, he had fought but twice since he crossed the Dnyeper, and then he had wept over the needless slaughter of his own people. He wanted Moscow to give herself to him, to welcome him as her lawful and beloved master and lord. So at Tula he penned another message to the people of Moscow.

Nearly as long as the American Declaration of Independence, this *Gramota* (communication) is addressed: "From the Tsar and Great Prince Dimitry Ivanovich of all Russia, to our Boyars, Prince Fyodor Ivanovich Mstislavsky, and Prince Vasily and Prince Dimitry Ivanovich Shuysky, and all Boyars, and *Oprichniki*," and so on, according to rank, down to ". . . and all commoners."

After reminding them of their oath to his father and the abuse he himself had suffered from Boris, he touched on his salvation at Uglich. In that connection, he accused the boyars, the army, and the people of swearing loyalty to Boris, "a shady character," while in ignorance they thought Dimitry had been killed by assassins.

He then continued with an expression of hope that he might enter Moscow without bloodshed. He had great backing, he wrote, and many towns had offered troops to help him. These offers he had rejected, despite the senseless and cruel killing of innocent people in the Seversky district by order of Maria Godunova and her son Fyodor. Therefore, he concluded:

We, a Christian lord, not wanting to see Christian blood spilled, write you . . . that, remembering God and the Orthodox Church, and your own souls, and in the blessed memory of our father . . . you kiss the cross [in token of fealty] to us his son, and do obeisance to us, your rightful Lord Tsar and Great Prince Dimitry Ivanovich of all Russia . . . and we will welcome you all into our grace according to the custom of the Tsars; and we will honor you, the Boyars, in your rank, and confirm your patrimonial estates, and grant further increase [in them], and hold you in honor; and you, members of our court and public servants, we wish to hold in our grace; and to you, foreign and local merchants throughout the realm of Muscovy, [favors are granted] . . . and we wish all Orthodox Christianity to live in quiet and peace and blessedness. But should you not do obeisance to our Person as Tsar, and come to ask us our grace, then you may know that you will answer for this on the day of God's righteous judgment, when each shall be rewarded according to his deeds, and none shall escape God's just wrath, or the grasp of the hands of your Tsar. Come, then, if God wills, to us, the great lord of the realms justly his.

Considering the inflated style of the day, Dimitry's letter was open, kindly, and persuasive. It is a far cry from the murderous documents occasionally signed by the dread man he called his father.

Dimitry entrusted this message to Naum Pleshcheyev, of a military family, and Gavrila Grigoryevich Pushkin, a member of Boris's Council who had decided to support Dimitry. Both of them were as daring as they were artful.

The two circled around Moscow to the suburb of Krasnoye Selo, outside the walls to the northeast, where they arrived on Saturday, June 1/11. This village was chosen because many rich merchants and tradesmen lived there, and it is known that in general they were not friendly to Tsar Boris. One of the two messengers read the proclamation to a sympathetic audience. The effect was amazing. The people of Krasnoye Selo swept Pleshcheyev and Pushkin up and marched them in a noisy procession right into the heart of Moscow.

Someone sent a band of streltsy to stop the throng of invaders, but the sight of such a concourse of people frightened them away. Dimitry's message-bearers were propelled straight into Red Square and to the circular platform called the Place of the Skull, after Golgotha in Jerusalem. Here it was that the decrees of the Tsars had been read since the days of Ivan the Dread's babyhood, and that church announcements were made, and executions effected. Mounting this stage, with its historic associations, one of the two intoned the rolling sentences with all the majesty innate in the Russian language. Mark Antony's triple appeal to the Roman mob in Shakespeare's drama could not have kindled a greater fire. The people ran mad.

Several boyars sprinted to the Patriarch's palace in the center of the Kremlin, crying "Mutiny!" But that dignitary did not think of investing his holy chasuble, taking his cross as his shield, and advancing to Golgotha with a blessing for the loyal and anathema for all traitors. Instead, bursting into tears, he told the boyars to go and do something with the people. The boyars listened respectfully, took his advice, returned to the Place of the Skull and did precisely nothing.

The crowd spotted Prince Vasily Shuysky, however, although his presence in the square at the time is not explained. Some of the leaders hurried up to him and gathered around him calling for quiet. Then they asked him point-blank to tell them the truth. Six weeks before, Prince Shuysky had stretched out his hands toward them, saying that with those hands he had buried the Tsarevich Dimitry. Was that true? the crowd shouted.

Prince Shuysky quickly answered: "The Tsarevich was saved from his murderers; a priest's son was buried in his stead." Three times — when he returned from Uglich, when Dimitry first appeared, and right after Boris's death — Shuysky had vowed that the Tsarevich was dead. Now, with Dimitry's messengers standing in Red Square, he forswore his oath. Upon his head, then, must fall much of the blame for the consequences of his faithlessness.

Through the open gates of the Kremlin, the people whose name was legion rampaged up the slopes to the great palace, seized the helpless Tsar who had sought safety on the throne itself, and his mother and sister, and dragged and carried them to Boris's earlier home as a boyar. Someone seems to have protected them from the mob's fury, and they were safely shut up inside. A guard was placed around the building.

Other members of the Godunov family were no better off. Present or absent, their property was ransacked, while a few of their houses outside the Kremlin were torn down before anyone stopped the marauders.

Not too strangely, perhaps, the man who did step in to halt the uproar was Bogdan Belsky — the same whose beard had been pulled out by order of Boris Godunov. He was said to have been the Tsarevich's godfather and could be expected to know something about the matter. By then, too, he had no living enemies, for his enemies had been put away by *their* enemies, but he had enemies of his own invention. That is, there were people whom he hated, namely the Germans who worked for Boris and who carried out Boris's orders.

Belsky did not stand in pompous silliness before the mob to harangue them. Characteristically, he stood right among them, gently talking, almost whispering. "Boris's evil advisers," he said, were "the German doctors, who got rich through their foul counsel. Their wealth is huge, and their cellars are filled with wines of all kinds . . ." Off went the mob to ravish the German winecellars. Without mentioning Dimitry directly, Belsky had become one of his best backers.

Two days later, a group of those unidentifiable individuals usually referred to as "they" sent Prince Ivan Mikhaylovich Vorotynsky, Prince Andrey Telyatevsky, Pyotr Sheremetyev, and the Dyak Vlasyev from Moscow to Dimitry with full powers to present the regrets and apologies of the capital. (Telyatevsky, it will be remembered, was one of the officers who fled from Kromy at the time of Basmanov's "revolt.") Almost simultaneously, new emissaries from the Don Cossacks arrived in Tula. Dimitry already knew of the success of Pleshcheyev and Pushkin and availed himself of the opportunity to press a point.

From the day of his emergence from nothingness, Dimitry had

shown a spirit of freedom uncommon in any sphere in those days. Among the freedom-loving Poles, he was the most free. Among the regimented Muscovites, he dared breathe and exhale a whiff of liberty. Among the Cossacks he was at home. Like the *Gaucho*, Martín Fierro, of another continent and another century, Dimitry could have sung:

> My glory is to live as free
> As any bird in heaven . . .

This spirit prompted him, when the Muscovite dignitaries arrived, to take the rude horsemen of the Wilderness by the hand and lead them before the punctilious, long-robed princes of the realm. There, in so bluff an atmosphere, Dimitry berated the capital and its inhabitants for their long and heated opposition to their rightful sovereign. The Cossacks, entranced, heaped additional scorn on the envoys, and all but cudgeled Telyatevsky for his support of the "impostor" Godunov. It is only necessary to conjure up a vision of the immense stiffness, golden drabness, and hieratic conservatism of the Muscovite princes of 1605 to sense the everlasting poison Dimitry's action injected into those representatives of the body politic.

But even before Moscow had officially humbled herself through the envoys to Tula, indeed the moment they heard of the oath sworn to Dimitry by the people of Moscow, a handful of hatred's brood took off to wreak vengeance on the Godunov clan and all its appurtenances. Dimitry undoubtedly gave them orders to arrest and jail, but whether detailed instructions were added is not clear. It is even doubtful.

The hard core of this group consisted of Prince Vasily Golitsyn and Prince Mosalsky-Rubets, already mentioned, along with a Dyak by the name of Bogdan Sutupov. Their first target was Iov, Patriarch of Moscow, whose position as pillar of Orthodoxy implied also that he was the pillar of the loathed reigning family. They pounced upon him in defiance of God and propriety in the middle of a service in the cathedral and tore his robes from his back.

For once, Iov recovered his dignity and his courage. Removing the medallion which was the emblem of his ecclesiastical rank from his breast, he laid it before the ikon of the Virgin of Vladimir and loudly declaimed: "Here before this image I was invested with the title of Archbishop, and for nineteen years I have protected the Faith. Now I behold the desolation of the Church and the victory of deceit and heresy. Mother of God, preserve Orthodoxy!" Iov was given a simple monk's robe and was dragged out and sent off to the Staritsky Monastery. No-one was so bold as to halt the sacrilege.

From the cathedral, the unholy trio turned to the Godunovs and their relatives. One only did they think to do away with — perhaps there were orders in this case — and that was Semyon Nikitich Godunov, the hated and feared chief of Boris's secret service. An executioner was sent to catch him in Pereyaslavl and garrotte him. In Moscow, many others were sent off to prison. All that was left of the family was Boris's widow with her two children, immured in the ancient home of the Godunovs, but still safe.

On June 10/20, Golitsyn and Mosalsky-Rubets gathered up a courtier of obscure background and one Sherefedinov, along with three streltsy, and marched to the attack. Previously, as has been mentioned, Fyodor had tried to stop the rebels in the royal palace by sitting on the throne, in full regalia. In better days, he had seen the respect, the fear, that the crown, the jeweled tippet called *bármy,* and the sceptre and orb had inspired when his father wore them. But such puppetry had been less than noticed. Now that these symbols had been taken from him, he could only sit, in company with his mother and sister, and attend the will of God.

The quartet with their trio of streltsy entered the palace, found the family, and took them to a private room, even as the Tsar and his family were taken three centuries later in a town by the Ural Mountains. There in similar fashion executioners were ordered to do their work. Not with guns, but with silent hangman's ropes they were to kill. And before anyone thought even to cry for help, the Tsaritsa-mother was strangled and left dying on the floor.

But when the streltsy turned to Fyodor himself, far from frightened, the husky youth grappled with them. Struggling and kicking with all the force of a sturdy young body, he screamed for aid at the top of his lungs. Fyodor was fighting for his life, but the object of his assailants was extermination, and they gave no quarter. When the three streltsy were not enough to subdue him, one of the princes joined the fray, reached up under his robe, and seized him foully, with the grip of hands hardened to the use of battle-axes.

Fyodor roared with the excruciating pain, tearing at the torturing hands, then, failing, begged them to kill him and end the agony. One of them raised "a great stick and smote him about the shoulders."

Outside, a crowd gathered at the piercing cries, but no-one ventured in. For people fear to go to the aid of victims of barbarism. At last, all was still.

Then the wooden doors opened, and the two princes emerged, bloodied and disheveled. "The Tsaritsa Maria and her son Fyodor," they announced with princely stiffness, "have taken poison because they were afraid. They are dead."

The crowd gazed at the figures before them, and was silent.

CHAPTER 9

THE PRIZE OF

FAITH AND FORTUNE

THERE IS EVERY INDICATION that Dimitry was aware beforehand that the death of Fyodor and his mother was well-nigh a political necessity. But whereas Boris had perhaps ardently hoped for the death of the Tsarevich in 1591, Dimitry seems to have regarded the idea of assassination with thorough dislike. It is reported, too, that the people still had respect for Fyodor and the Tsaritsa-mother, despite the universal hatred of Boris, because of the mystique of the name of Tsar. Furthermore, Fyodor was free of any guilt of any kind.

Many Russians are said to have hoped that Dimitry would exercise clemency and grant Fyodor and his mother their lives. Indeed, a convent would be the place for them. There were other ex-Tsaritsas already in convents, still living — among them the nun Marfa, Ivan's seventh wife and theoretically the mother of Dimitry. An ex-Tsar would be more of a novelty, but Dimitry was known for his kindness.

In his tent at Tula, Dimitry apparently discussed the matter with his advisers. The historian Karamzin specifies that Basmanov warned Dimitry that he would not be safe on the throne with Fyodor living — that no wilderness was wide enough to hide a deposed young Tsar from Russian sympathy. Yet Basmanov himself would take no part in any move to murder either the son or the mother. And it would be well within the character of Dimitry as evinced by history to have seen the need to rid himself of the danger presented by Fyodor, yet to have refused, like Basmanov, to take any part in it.

Poets understand such situations better than historians. So, in a somewhat similar instance, the words of Bolingbroke in the last scene of *King Richard II* could well have fallen from Dimitry's lips, "They love not poison that do poison need." And once the assassins, who distrusted Dimitry's impassioned clemency, returned to Dimitry with the report, "Fyodor and his mother are dead, by their own hands, by poison," Dimitry may be imagined to have greeted them also with Bolingbroke's words:

> though I did wish him dead,
> I hate the murderer, love him murdered.

But in whatever mood Dimitry did receive the news, his horror mixed with relief could not last. He was volatile by nature. What event, then, could in all his life have more quickly blotted out all other feelings than the advent of the knowledge that he was without rival to the throne?

Within a few days, on June 25 according to the Polish calendar, Dimitry could write to Pan George Mniszech that there had arrived before him, "from the capital city of Moscow, the entire senate, both spiritual and temporal, the nobility, the merchants, and the common people," presenting their submission, imploring his grace, and begging him to condone their faults. And he could add a (not entirely correct) report of the death of Fyodor and his mother, and the near-death of the Tsarevna Ksenia, whose fate will be explained shortly. From that date, then, it can be said that Dimitry took up the sceptre of government. The tragic end of the Godunov dynasty had faded from his mind, to be recorded in the untrustworthy pages of often-tampered-with history.

Someone in Moscow had already set to work, if not to tamper, at least to speed the fading. Tsar Boris was removed from his tomb in the Cathedral of the Archangel Michael. The corpses of his wife and his son were put in plain wooden boxes and joined with the Tsar's coffin. Then all three were smuggled out of the Kremlin to a little monastery a mile or so away, near the outer wall of the district known as the White City, and not far from the Neglinnaya River. There, in the yard of the Varsonofyevsky monastery, without song or service, the three were put into the earth. Suitably, the place was popularly known as the Beggars' Cloister.

Boris's daughter Ksenia was somehow saved during the massacre of her mother and brother. Accounts are conflicting, but it seems that Mosalsky-Rubets had commanded that she be not harmed. Some reports say that he was lecherously keeping her to bestow on Dimitry, to curry favor. These reports add that Mosalsky-Rubets took her to his own house. Others, equally credible, discreetly say that Ksenia was kept in safety in the "Maidens' Cloister," the Novodyevichy monastery, by the river, far from Moscow's moiling, turmoiling multitudes.

By then a ground-swell of collective hatred came bursting up through the body politic of the city. Entrenched against all movement toward greater freedom and decent living for the common folk stood the boyars, the nobility and the magnates. Yet this domineering class had been split by its own petty ambitions even under the iron hand of Ivan the Dread. It could present no common front to the masses, any more than they themselves could as yet offer any coordinated protest. They could but fight, rebel or flee, or put on masks of content.

Over this ferment Ivan and Boris had spread an incrustation, the handiwork of repressive police, through which tiny vents of censure puffed, like sulphuric vapors blistering through the cooling surface of a volcanic lake. God's holy idiots, the naked crazed yuródivye, heaped their scorn, all unmolested, on both the hereditary Tsar and the parvenu Tsar without distinction. Now that Tsar Ivan and parvenu Boris were gone, and the axe of political necessity had struck down the beardless student-prince, an empire without loyalty or order, and cursed with self-seeking and chicanery, came to rest on the knees of the man called Dimitry.

He could expect no quarter from his enemies, no unselfish aid from his partisans. Yet, happily for him, his sanguine temperament failed to see this. He received the cankered state with all the joy of a young father lifting the miracle of a new-born son with loving, caring hands toward Fate.

As soon as Dimitry received word of Moscow's capitulation to his representatives (and even before he heard of Fyodor's death), he began sending out letters to all the cities, towns, villages and hamlets, appointing noblemen, boyars'-sons or local magnates to take the oath of fealty to himself from all inhabitants. And at the same time he began to demand information regarding the government and affairs of the realm.

In this way, Dimitry heard that the ambassador from the King of England, Sir Thomas Smythe, had only recently obtained new privileges from Boris Godunov, and had just left the capital to return to England. Dimitry called his secretary *instanter* to prepare a letter to the Moscow agent of the Russia Company, John "the son of William" Merick (or Meyrick), commanding him to appear as soon as possible, "to behold our clear and princely eyes" — so ran the diplomatic formula in Russian. To facilitate Merick's quickest possible appearance, the new Tsar authorized his use of the imperial post-horses and instructed him to present himself to the "Chancellor," Afanasy Ivanovich Vlasyev. The letter was sent on June 8/18, 1605.

Merick accordingly picked up William Russell, another employee of the Russia Company and married to his sister-in-law, called on Vlasyev, and all together they went to Tula. There, offering suitable gifts to Dimitry, Merick delivered himself of a speech in Russian, in which he said, among other things,

> That whereas it had pleased God so miraculously to preserve him, and so gloriously to establish him on the throne of his Ancestors [he trusted that]: it would please him to look upon the English merchants with the same eyes as they [the ancestors] have done; in doing which, he should not only merit their loves, but no nation would be more thankful unto him . . .

Dimitry responded graciously and invited the Englishmen to attend a dinner which had already been planned in his luxurious tent for Smaga Chertensky and his companions, newly arrived Cossacks from the Don.

By virtue of a natural coincidence — the general recognition of Dimitry as Tsar — Prince Ivan Mikhaylovich Vorotynsky and Prince Andrey Andreyevich Telyatevsky arrived at the same time.

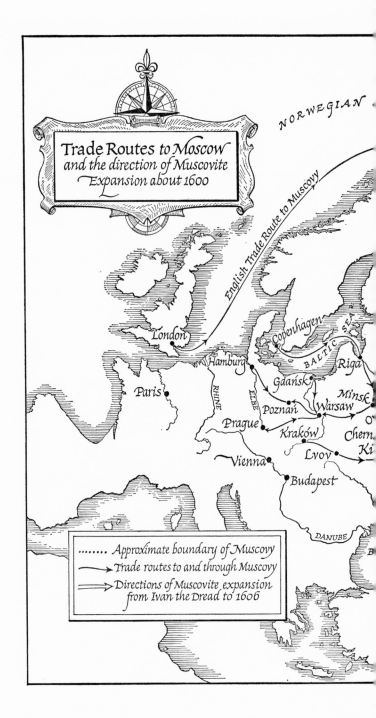

NORWEGIAN

Trade Routes to Moscow
and the direction of Muscovite
Expansion about 1600

English Trade Route to Muscovy

London

Copenhagen

BALTIC SEA

Riga

Hamburg

Gdańsk

RHINE

ELBE

Minsk

Paris

Poznań

Warsaw

Prague

Kraków

O'

Chern.

Ki

Vienna

Lvov

Budapest

DANUBE

B

.... Approximate boundary of Muscovy
⟶ Trade routes to and through Muscovy
⟹ Directions of Muscovite expansion
from Ivan the Dread to 1606

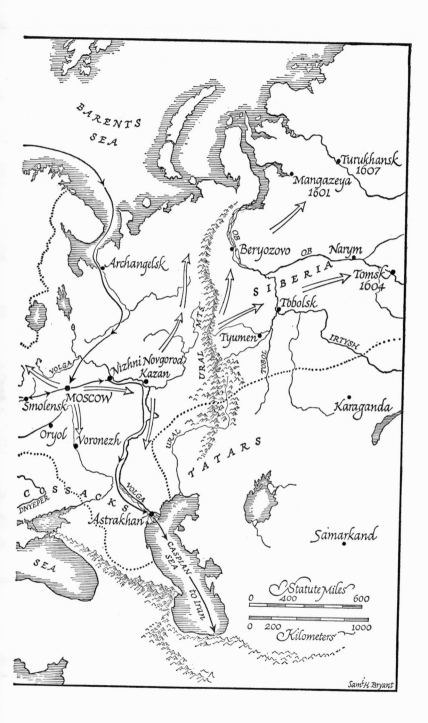

BARENTS SEA

Turukhansk
1007

Mangazeya
1601

Archangelsk

OB

Beryozovo   OB   Narym

SIBERIA

Tomsk
1604

Tobolsk

VOLGA   Tyumen

IRTYSH

Nizhni Novgorod
Kazan

URAL MTS.

Smolensk

MOSCOW

TOBOL

Oryol   Voronezh

Karaganda

URAL

TATARS

VOLGA

C O S S A C K S

DNYEPER

Astrakhan

Samarkand

SEA

CASPIAN
SEA

to Iran

Statute Miles
0   400   600

0   200   1000
Kilometers

Sam¹ H. Bryant

The latter was the one who had fled to Moscow when Basmanov shifted his allegiance to Dimitry, while the former was descended from a first cousin of Vladimir Monomakh and was related to the Vishnevetskys as well. These grave ambassadors who bore the penitence and submission of Moscow to Dimitry were given second place, after the Don Cossacks, and humiliated by an excoriating speech from Dimitry for their opposition to him, their "legitimate ruler." John Merick intruded into this planned discrediting of a Prince of the Blood at the psychological moment for Dimitry. He was entrusted with conveying Dimitry's true friendship to the King of England.

Merick's report of the meeting, finally sent to King James half a year later, described Dimitry as "the indubitable son of the old Emperor Ivan Vasilyevich and now the sole heir of all those great kingdoms." He also took pains to add that Dimitry first inquired for King James's health, as was proper, and then went on to say to the boyars and others present that "the world affordeth not so learned a Prince as is our most renowned King, saying also that himself had seen an especial[ly] learned book set forth by His Majesty, with divers other princely speeches."

That Dimitry should have known of King James's flair for writing is remarkable in itself, although he may have acquired the information in Poland. That he should have interested himself in increasing trade with England can be called natural, since both Ivan and Boris backed such trade. But that Dimitry should so strongly have advanced further relations with the west of Europe is most remarkable. In Merick's words:

> The Emperor's Majesty is very desirous to have divers artificers sent out of England, promising not only entertainment [wages, maintenance], according to their merits, but their choice also to stay or return.

Previously, only "Western" doctors or physicians and soldiers had been welcome in Muscovy. (The merchants were of course self-supporting.) Boris had groped warily toward opening Moscow's gates to foreigners. Dimitry, however, intended to fling them wide.

Merick left Tula without delay. So, apparently, did Dimitry. Accounts, as often, are not in agreement, but it is evident that Dimitry heard of the murder of Fyodor within two or three days, either in Tula or in Serpukhov, the latter less than sixty miles from Moscow. Again, although there is some confusion as to details, it appears all but certain that he arrived at Kolomenskoye, today a short autobus trip from the capital, on June 16/26. There a great tent sent out from Moscow was erected for him. It must have been a welcome sight after riding one hundred and twenty-five miles in a little over twenty-four hours.

According to Stanislas Borsza, whose account is a little confused, this tent (or group of tents) was "very costly and big . . . [with] four gates and four turrets. It all looked like a stone fortress." There were inner tents or "rooms" in the ensemble, after the manner of a Turkish or Tatar pavilion, which were "very valuably decorated with gold embroidery, especially the throne room where the Tsar entertained us and the boyars. Five hundred men could sit there."

All this sounds so much like the description of the tents put up for the King of Fez written a century before by Leo Africanus, that Borsza could almost be suspected of quoting, without acknowledgment. Nevertheless, the minutiae he supplies regarding the cooks, housekeepers and other servants, all of whom came from Moscow, contribute valuable bits of color. In fact, everything needed was supplied from Moscow, including two hundred of the five hundred horses in the imperial stables, along with several handsomely decorated coaches equipped with correspondingly handsome and decorated coachmen. And every day boyars came to greet the Tsar, bearing gifts of sables and silver and gold.

By this time, Dimitry had chosen a new Patriarch of Moscow, to replace Iov, high-handedly deposed a few days before. While he was in Tula, the Archbishop of Ryazan had visited Dimitry for the ecclesiastical reason that Tula lay within his diocese. The Archbishop was a Greek named Ignaty who had been Bishop of Hierissos in Thessaly, and after that Archbishop of Cyprus. When the Turks conquered that island in 1570–1571, Ignaty had fled to

Rome, where he lived for several years. Then about 1590, or a year or so before or after, he went to Moscow, where he "found favor in the sight of the king," to apply the Biblical Esther's remark to Boris Godunov. It was about this same time that Boris had persuaded the Patriarch of Constantinople, Jeremy, to consecrate Moscow's first Patriarch, Iov, and Boris had been happy to give Ignaty, the Greek, the archbishopric of Ryazan.

Ignaty's motive in going to Dimitry's headquarters remains unknown, of course. It could even have been an odd demonstration of loyalty to Boris Godunov: If the Dimitry at Tula was the Tsarevich, the Tsarevich was still living and Boris could not have murdered him. However it was, Ignaty came to Tula and found favor once more. Dimitry chose him to succeed the Patriarch from whose lips so many anathemas had been thundered against himself. And Ignaty let it be known that he would stand ready to place the Crown of Monomakh on the brow of the true son of Ivan Vasilyevich, the Dread.

It seemed that no detail had been overlooked by the "inexperienced" young man who had so often been called the son of nobody, or worse. The arms of Moscow were stretched out to embrace him. The boyars, whatever they might think, were robed and ready for his triumph, Roman style. Even the moon had reached her full. All through the brief but brilliant midsummer night, monks and merchants, beggars and boyars, courtiers and commons, loosened the invisible tethers that held Dimitry fast. Then dawned the day of June 20/30.[1]

For the Orthodox, June 20 was of no outstanding religious significance. But for the Catholics, June 30 was the Feast of the Commemoration of Saint Paul. The Lord had said: *"Ecce ego vos mitto sicut oves in medio luporum"* ("Behold I send you forth as sheep in the midst of wolves"). And the zealous Jesuit father, Lawicki, associated that mandate with Saint Paul. It also seemed somehow to fit their arrival in Moscow. Perhaps it was even this mistaken association of doctrine that led, coupled with the full moon and (Muscovite) midsummer-day, to Dimitry's decision to enter his capital on June 20/30.

Whatever astrological, mythological or religious influence may or may not have been in play, no better day, meteorologically, could have been found. Now, as Dimitry's goal was reached, a bright sun shone from a virtually cloudless sky, and the warmth of summer was mitigated by gusts of pleasant breeze. As Borsza tersely wrote, "By the grace of God, we reached the capital on a beautiful day."

From Kolomenskoye it was seven miles or so to the outer wooden palisade that surrounded Moscow. On the morning of that solemn day a fresh whirlpool of humanity eddied up to Dimitry's pavilion. Boyars of the Council brought robes of velvet and of silk, embroidered with gold thread and studded with pearls and precious stones, to offer to the Tsar. Nearly three centuries before, Ivan I had been called "Money-bag" from his acquisitive and preservative instincts in financial matters. Seven generations later, Ivan IV had still gathered treasure. He was proudly displaying his gold and jewels on the day he died — showing foreigners his wealth. Small wonder it was, then, that the boyars of the Council carried from the Kremlin to Kolomenskoye a few tokens of the known contents of Ivan's and Fyodor's and Boris's Croesus-like hoard. (There is a tradition that Ivan's treasure has never been found, and is still lying hidden in vaults under the Great Kremlin Palace.)

The boyars brought these trifles as if Dimitry needed some inducement, some tangible bewitchment, to move him to enter the capital. With deep genuflections they displayed their gifts — from the Tsar's own coffers! — while with one voice they implored him to sit on the throne of his forefathers and reign long and happily over them. The traitors had been rooted out, they said, and Moscow's time of distress had come to an end.

Behind the boyars marched a sturdy band of German mercenaries. Lining up before their lord, vaguely like the pilgrims in *Tannhäuser,* with justice and inspiration on their side, they presented a letter in which they reverently apologized for fighting against the true Tsar at the battle of Dobrynichi. It was their duty, they formally set forth, to obey, and to be true to their oath to the late Tsar. But that Tsar was dead. In the future, if the living

Tsar willed, they would serve him equally truly and obediently.

Their straightforwardness, their manly admission of error, and the patent sincerity of their stand impressed Dimitry. They had not knelt, to plead. They had stood and excused themselves like men. Dmitry's Russian soul (*shirókaya dushá*) expanded, unrestrained by any metaphorical jeweled kaftan. Their valor at Dobrynichi was admirable, he understated, and their refusal to take his side at Kromy, when almost the entire army revolted, was exemplary. Most of all, their loyal return to Moscow at that time to continue serving Boris Godunov was peerless. "If you will serve me," he concluded, "as faithfully as you have served my betrayers and enemies, I will trust you even more than my Muscovites."

After a pause, he added, "Who is your banneret, your standard-bearer?" Walter Rosen stepped forward. Dimitry patted him on the head. "You scared me with your standard. You were so close [with it] that you could hurt my horse badly. Somehow, he carried me, anyway. — If you had caught me, would you Germans have killed me, too?"

The Pilgrims' Chorus answered, bowing from the waist: "It is better that Your Majesty escaped without injury. God be thanked for it. May He protect Your Majesty still!"

Outside, miles beyond Dimitry's tent, Moscow prepared to bow at the waist, also — Muscovite style. In contrast to the formal, trained bearing of the German mercenaries, the vast populace of Moscow, by nature always fluctuating between anarchy and angelolatry of the Tsar, agglomerated outward from the city toward the approaching personification of good (or bad) rule — the monarch whose mystic, ancient, inherited power would provide security while permitting a maximum of popular fermentation.

The southern exposure of Moscow was peculiarly suited to the staging of a triumphal welcome. A bend in the Moskva River accommodated a bell-shaped suburb called the Earthen City after the embankment that protected it, in which thousands upon thousands of "ordinary people" lived — working people of all kinds. The houses were of wood, roofed with wood, and over and onto embankment, walls, houses and all, the populace scrambled, climbed and perched.

The procession was slowly formed at Kolomenskoye. At its head were the Poles, prancing in glittering finery on their thoroughbreds, with trumpets, shawms and kettledrums sounding. Behind them a body of Muscovites marched, armed with *esclopettes* (primitive carbines), surrounding gaily decorated coaches from the royal stables and more thoroughbreds caparisoned with bridles of gold decorated with precious stones and led by grooms. Then a body of Muscovite cavalry appeared, followed by innumerable priests escorting religious banners and ikons of the Virgin Mary and Saint Nicholas, glowing with gold and jewels. With these, enclosed in a forest of banners with holy images or brief texts from the Scriptures, the newly appointed Patriarch of Moscow hove into sight, resplendent in his archiepiscopal vestments and towering, crown-like mitre. Dimitry himself followed immediately after, riding a white horse, and conspicuous for his youth and the blinding glory of his uniform. He came uncrowned, of course, for he was on his way to receive that final highest sacrament. Sixty boyars and princes attended him as he rode. And, finally, his Polish bodyguard and a mass of Germans, Cossacks, streltsy, and Muscovites in general brought up the rear.

As Dimitry passed through the wooden gate in the earthworks, the advance guard of Poles was already coming into the open space called the Balchug, just across the river from the red brick-and-stone walls of the Kremlin and the Chinese City, as the core of industrial Moscow was named — no-one could remember quite why. A floating bridge crossed from the Balchug to the main gate into the Chinese City, to the left of which rose the higher walls of the Kremlin. Above these, raised by the low hill on which they stood, loomed the white stone masses of the three cathedrals, with their golden cupolas, and the new slender bell-tower of Ivan Veliky, also crowned with gold, like an immense episcopal mitre. Still farther to the left, and behind, was the lower, darker hulk of the Tsar's palace. Scattered beneath, not clearly visible behind the walls, were the wooden dwellings of the princes and leading clergy. The

Chinese City to the right was nothing but a chaos of low buildings, almost all of wood, surrounded by the crescent of more dispersed habitations which comprised the White City, or Tsar's City, also built of wood.

Moscow had long since boasted of being the Third Rome and had certainly far passed the original Rome in population. By 1605 it most likely also had more churches than the Eternal City, although some of them were very tiny. All of these had suitable bells for summoning the faithful, and for warning of fires and other dangers. Upon the appearance of Dimitry's advance guard of Poles, the bells of every church in the capital burst into a jangle of tireless, wild pealing. Such was the clangor and reverberation that Father Lawicki wrote that he was almost deafened. Konrad Bussow, also present, had a different opinion, but he had lived in Moscow a long time. He said that all the bells in the "castle" (the Kremlin) rang and everything "took place so magnificently that by their standards it could not be better" — an ill-concealed disparagement in any case.

"The great wide streets of the Earthen City were so crowded," Bussow added, "that you could not see a hand's breadth of bare earth, and the roofs of the houses, and of the churches, towers and shops, were so full of people that anyone looking on it from a distance would have said it was a bee-hive."

As Dimitry rode through, countless bystanders fell on their faces before him, crying, "God keep you, lord! He Who has miraculously preserved you, may He guard you on your way. You are the sun that shines on Russia!" And Dimitry called back, "May God keep my people, too! Rise, and pray for me!"

Hardly could he have expected to need those prayers so soon. According to Bussow, he had scarcely crossed the floating bridge and reached the Water Gate that led into the Chinese City than an unusually violent gust twisted into a whirlwind that scooped up sand and dust in a blinding cloud. For a few moments, no-one could see.

Needless to say, this was taken for no good omen by the superstitious Muscovites. They beat their foreheads and breasts with the

sign of the cross, and cried: *"Pomíluy nas Bǫg, pomíluy nas Bog!"*
— God have mercy on us! At the same time, since only Bussow has
mentioned this occurrence, its impact must have been limited to a
small area. Obviously, neither Dimitry nor the Poles were
alarmed.

All through the weltering mob, Dimitry rode on, up the hill,
smiling, gesturing — the image of a true Tsar. In a few moments
he reached that vast rectangular waste at the summit called "Red
Square" then and now, and paused near the Temple of the Inter-
cession of the Mother of God.

This newest of the great Moscow "cathedrals," which is the emblem of Moscow today as the Eiffel Tower is the symbol of Paris,
had been erected under Ivan the Dread. Later a chapel was ordered built in it by Tsar Fyodor the Angelic for the tomb of God's
holy idiot, Basil, who "would take it upon himself to reprove the
old emperor [Ivan] for all his cruelty and oppressions done towards his people." So goes an account written by the Englishman,
Giles Fletcher. In any event, Basil, who was amazingly allowed to
die a natural death, was reputed to work many miracles from his
tomb, and by this token the church came to be called the Cathedral
of Basil the Blessed, as it is known today.

There, gazing at the walls of the Kremlin, at the exuberant
towers of the temple, and above all at the sea of faces before him,
Dimitry's eyes once more filled with tears. Snatching his flashy cap
off, he stopped his horse and bowed his head in prayer. The
people went wild, many bursting into torrents of tears. And just at
that moment Ignaty came up to him on foot, carrying a priceless
ikon of the Mother of God.

Dimitry dismounted, cap in hand, to kiss the ikon. The Russian
clergy began to intone a chant, their rich voices alternating with
high-piping tenors. Thereupon the Polish mercenaries struck up a
musical bedlam with their trumpets and drums. Slowly the procession advanced to the Frolovskie Gate, the main entrance to the
Kremlin. Crossing the bridge over the half-dry moat which then
protected its eastern walls, Dimitry soon passed from sight.

Already the universal transport was tainted. A few monks, look-

ing for the slightest deviation from monolithic Orthodox recti-
tude, noticed or thought they noticed that Dimitry did not kiss the
ikon according to Muscovite custom. They watched him intently,
so intently that they may have seen what was not there. But they
began to whisper, "He cannot be the son of Ivan." Other malcontents caught up the censure. It was sacrilege to drown out the holy
songs with blaring brass and beating drums. Poison mounted
again into the medieval air. Ivan the Dread's unspeakable mockery of religious worship at Aleksandrovskaya Sloboda was wiped
out by an imperceptible error in Dimitry's overwrought reverence
to an ikon. *That* was sacrilege.

And sacrilege followed upon sacrilege. Muscovite Orthodoxy
proscribed contact with infidels, such as Catholics, for Orthodoxy
was a closed society. Ivan and Fyodor and Boris all had kept a
basin handy when receiving foreign ambassadors at court, to wash
the befoulment symbolically from their hands. Roman Catholics,
Lutherans and Unitarians were treated without distinction in the
impenetrable sanctity of Holy Russia.

But Dimitry entered the Kremlin surrounded by such infidels
as the two Jesuit priests and the Lutheran Private Secretary to the
Tsar, Buczyński. Such a thing had never happened before. And
now these unholy outlanders, as foreigners were called, strode
along the Kremlin's wooden "pavements," past the Monastery of
the Ascension and the great bell-tower into the Cathedral of the
Assumption. A Christian wearing boots into the Mosque of the
Holy Wisdom (Saint Sophia) in Istanbul could hardly have caused
greater repugnance. That their Tsar should permit such desecra-
tion was incomprehensible.

The Cathedral of the Assumption, the largest in the Kremlin
but small indeed to western European eyes, was Westminster
Abbey or the Cathedral of Reims for Muscovy. It was the coronation cathedral. There, Dimitry stood in company with many who
had marched with him from Poland, to hear a thanksgiving service
conducted by Ignaty and the clergy. Next, crossing Cathedral
Square to the Cathedral of the Archangel Michael, Dimitry entered to pay his respects to the tombs of his predecessors, all gathered there in plain caskets by the walls.

Seeking out the tomb of Ivan the Dread, Dimitry bowed, and said softly: "My beloved father! You left me a persecuted orphan, but by your sainted prayers I have survived to reign."

A minute's walk away, he came to the third cathedral, that of the Annunciation. This tiny church was in reality the private chapel of the Tsars, and in it the Protopope, or Archpriest, Terenty, presented a curious allocution. Hinting strongly, but with Delphic obscurity, that in Moscow things might not be as they seemed, he said: "Do not listen to people who whisper in your ear to arouse your anger. If someone is an enemy to you, God is your friend. God sanctified you in your mother's womb, protected you, raised you to the throne . . . Who can shake you? Turn your eyes in kindness upon us, have mercy, and turn aside from us your righteous wrath!"

Shadows were lengthening over the walls when Dimitry was solemnly led through a private entrance into the Tsar's Palace. The accounts are not entirely clear, but it seems that he went along the elevated platform at the top of the "Red Stairs" to the "Facetted Palace," where the throne-room for formal audiences occupied the upper story. In any case, in that room he mounted Ivan IV's ivory throne, and before him, according to ancient custom, the boyars of the Council knelt, hailing him as their new Tsar.

Outside, the crowd, informed of what was taking place, screamed and howled in discordant polyphony with the clanging of score upon score of bells.

Dimitry then withdrew, while Bogdan Belsky gathered a group of illustrious princes and boyars and went to Red Square, still crowded with people. Marching straight up to the Place of the Skull, Belsky took a medallion with the image of Saint Nicholas from his bosom, put it to his lips, and vowed before all Moscow that the new Tsar was the son of Ivan the Dread, saved from death for them by that same Saint, the Thaumaturge or Worker of Miracles. He urged them to love the Prince who was loved of God, and to serve him.

In response, the mob shouted, "Long live, long live, our sovereign lord Dimitry! Death to his enemies!" Then they pushed and crowded out of the square. For in the Moscow of 1605, people seemed to have little to do beyond crowding into, or out of, or up to, somewhere; or just crowding about. Such is the impression left by contemporary chroniclers. In both Polish and Russian sources, the phrase "innumerable crowds" appears with the frequency of "ox-eyed Hera" in the *Iliad*.

Nevertheless, in time the crowds disbanded. Then, far into the midsummer night, the Tsar in the Kremlin, with his nobles and his clergy, feasted and drank, while in the homes of the common people each man with his family celebrated the unforgettable day as his resources would permit.[2]

Meanwhile, Prince Vasily Ivanovich Shuysky again began the sinuous chicanery which seldom failed to occupy his thoughts. During Boris's lifetime, he had proclaimed loud and long the falsity of Dimitry's claims. Yet when young Tsar Fyodor succeeded to the throne his tongue was silent. When the Godunovs needed his support most, his tongue was silent. When Pleshcheyev and Pushkin read Dimitry's letter in Red Square he even retracted what he had said before. He swore that Dimitry was genuine, and that another boy had been slain in his stead. Not a finger did he lift to aid the hapless Fyodor then, and by not lifting a finger drew upon himself no small part of the blame for Fyodor's scurvy end. Now that Dimitry sat on the throne of Ivan, Shuysky once more found his tongue. Choosing a merchant and a physician, both of them of the meaner sort, the very noble prince poured pestilence into their ears, murmuring that the new Tsar was a fraud, and suggesting that they secretly spread the information among the people. For the fifth time Prince Vasily swore his unreliable oath, first this way and then that, about Dimitry called the Pretender and about Dimitry the supposedly dead Tsarevich.

But the stolid burghers of Moscow did not know how to pass news on, secretly. Pyotr Basmanov, who had ways of informing himself and was intensely loyal to his new master, soon heard the slander and was not long in finding out its source. Furthermore, someone discovered that there was a plot to set fire to the crowded Polish barracks (some said, the churches) and in the confusion stage a revolt in which Dimitry and many Poles would be killed.

Between Basmanov and a Polish Secretary named Stanislas

Słoński, Dimitry learned all there was to be known, along with a good deal of invention, no doubt. Since he had already been warned in a vague way by Terenty a day or two before, for once Dimitry took stern measures. Several arrests were made, culminating with that of Shuysky. Shuysky was merely put in prison; several others were subjected to the customary "questioning," aided by mild application of the rack. The "others" confessed without appreciable delay, throwing the basic blame on Shuysky as instigator of the plot.

Dimitry did not want to judge Shuysky and his accomplices himself. He therefore called a meeting, some say on Monday, June 24, of members of the Council of Boyars and the clergy and a group of what we should call civil servants today. Some reports even deny that Shuysky was arrested but say that he was called as a member of this jury, unaware of why.

Whichever way it was, Dimitry opened the proceedings with the usual long speech — speeches were always long in Moscow, even as today — in which he recalled misdeeds committed against his predecessors on the throne, with particular reference to those of the Shuysky family. Then, becoming more specific, he gradually got around to stating that, in his own case, certain members of that family had given him their oaths of obedience and loyalty, and then without hesitation had turned around and, like Saint Peter, denied their lord. They had gone so far, in fact, as to make an attempt on his life, as well as the lives of his Polish friends. These would-be assassins were the brothers, Princes Vasily, Ivan and Dimitry Shuysky, sons of Ivan Andreyevich, and therefore grandsons of that Prince Andrey Shuysky whom Ivan the Dread had had thrown to the palace dogs for his misdeeds.

"Because of this," Dimitry concluded, "although it is within our power, we do not want to be judge in this matter. We demand of you that you say what should be done." Characteristically, he did not even mention punishment.

The Shuyskys fell on their knees, imploring mercy, and Prince Vasily, sensing or knowing that he was regarded as the chief culprit and therefore in danger of being tortured to death, found voice enough to cry: "I am guilty before you, Great Prince Dimitry

Ivanovich, Tsar and Lord of all Russia, but take pity on me and
forgive my blundering folly. And you, Holy Patriarch, illustrious
Metropolitans, God-fearing Bishops, and all of you Princes and
Boyars of the Council — have pity on me, afflicted that I am! Inter-
cede for me, unhappy that I am, for I have offended my sovereign,
and in his person have offended God." The blue-blooded prince
could not make an appeal to the commoners present.

His words had little effect. The commoners to a man declared
him guilty, and their opinion was quickly echoed by Ignaty and
the clergy, and the boyars. What was decreed regarding the other
Shuysky princes was lost sight of in the face of the death sentence
imposed on Prince Vasily. The following day was set for his execution, the day planned by Shuysky for carrying out his murderous
coup.

Early in the morning, suspecting that there might be disorder in
Red Square, Dimitry sent a battalion of eight hundred streltsy
there, under Basmanov. Vast throngs of people gathered around
the Place of the Skull so as to get a good view as Shuysky's princely
gray head and beard came tumbling off, all gory. But many members of the Shuysky family were there, too, accompanied by partisans, followers, and hirelings.

Basmanov noticed that the populace as a whole felt great sympathy for Prince Vasily, perhaps stirred up by the evident grief of
the Shuysky clan. He therefore rode quietly among the groups of
people, stopping here and there to explain. "Our Tsar," he was
heard to say, "is in truth clement. He will execute only those who
doubly deserve death." But even he knew that his words were
none too persuasive. The people seemed but to sympathize the
more.

The executioner arrived. Walking up to the block, on which his
axe already lay, he turned to Shuysky, who stood there in silence,
his short, pudgy figure glittering in a robe of cloth-of-gold and
pearls. The headsman asked him to remove it, not only because
that was customary, but because he would like to have it. It was
very valuable.

Shuysky refused. Some who claimed to have heard him said that
he protested, "I will not appear before my Maker improperly

clothed." Others said that he delivered an oration, and still others that he was completely mute. But in any case, there were a few moments of waiting, also customary, to see if a reprieve would come from the palace. Basmanov was impatient and so were many others who regarded Prince Vasily as a menace to Dimitry's reign.

By then a secretary came jog-trotting through the great gate across the bridge, toward the Place of the Skull. He was in no hurry, for despite the message he carried he hoped to arrive too late. He was of a mind with Basmanov — the only good Shuysky was a dead Shuysky. Nevertheless, the executioner saw him coming, and he was not too late. In a few moments he was standing on the platform next to Prince Vasily, bellowing that Dimitry had signed a pardon.

While the Prince was being led back to the Kremlin, still under arrest, the people shouted and wept for joy, and Pyotr Fyodorovich Basmanov again rode through Red Square, crying: "How gracious a sovereign Heaven has granted us. Behold! He has pardoned the very traitors who have sought to murder him."

Reports are again conflicting as to who persuaded Dimitry to take this step. Some say that John Buczyński, perhaps Dimitry's most trusted adviser, intervened in Shuysky's favor. Others claim that Buczyński was a firm opponent of forgiveness. The truth of the matter probably is that Dimitry himself had determined to pardon Shuysky from the day of the trial, but allowed the trial to take its course up to the last minute for political reasons.

But the pardon unquestionably won over the hearts of the people, if they needed such winning. And Dimitry's action is best summed up in the words he is said to have spoken on signing the reprieve: "I have vowed to God to keep from shedding the blood of my subjects, and I intend to fulfill that vow."

This statement recalls the incident after the battle of Novgorod Seversky, when Dimitry wept at the sight of those killed, even though in a sense their death had brought him victory. It makes the possibility of Dimitry's direct responsibility in the murder of young Tsar Fyodor remote indeed.

Even before the Shuysky affair claimed his attention, however, indeed before he left Tula, Dimitry had thought of the ex-Tsaritsa Maria, now a nun under the name of Marfa, who, if he was the son of Ivan the Dread, must be his mother. She, he was certain, would remove all doubts as to his identity. He therefore associated her name with his in a number of documents he signed on June 11/21, and he would not be crowned until she appeared at his side in Moscow. It was not right, no matter what happened, that his mother should be exiled far from the capital, in a nunnery lost in the vast lake-region north of Uglich, where it was said that he himself had died in 1591.

Now that he had arrived in Moscow, and to the end of bringing Marfa there, Dimitry cast about in the Kremlin for a suitable messenger, one who could ride over three hundred miles speedily, and who was also noble and presumably trustworthy. Before long he found such an individual in the person of Prince Mikhaylo Vasilyevich Skopin-Shuysky, a third cousin of Prince Vasily the Shifty, to give him an unauthorized title, but much younger.

At eighteen, with a round, open and almost "wondering" face, and some reputation for courage and tact, Mikhaylo was ideally suited in appearance for nomination as Port-Glaive for the Tsar, which gave him an official position, and at the same time worthy of appointment as special ambassador charged with carrying out a difficult and confidential mission. Dimitry, doubtless on sound recommendations, elected Mikhaylo to travel into the northern wastes to bring the royal nun, Marfa, back to such sunlight of freedom and civilization as Moscow offered.

Some said that Dimitry delayed too long in sending for his mother. Others claimed that he ought to be crowned immediately, whether she was there or not — would not young Fyodor have sat more firmly on the throne if he had been crowned? But Dimitry held his own counsel. And Prince Mikhaylo, accompanied by an escort, rode as fast as horses would take him, ever northwards.

It seemed odd to some Russians that Dimitry should have picked a scion of the Shuysky family, conspicuous as it was for ingrained if not overt hostility to him. Yet it must have been clear to them that no great love was lost between the young prince and his much older cousin, Vasily, and Vasily was the core of the resistance, if not burning hatred, shown to Dimitry. Indeed, the bald facts of the case are that Prince Mikhaylo was willing to carry out missions for Dimitry. The others were not.

One detail, however, remains unknowable. It hardly required a consummate diplomat to persuade Marfa, still a comparatively young woman, to forsake the joyless life of a cenobite for the excitement of the capital. Marfa had not *wanted* to become a nun. She was made one by command of someone in Moscow — evidently Boris Godunov. Now, fourteen years later, she was to recover all her honors, her dignity, and her rank as dowager Tsaritsa. This much was obvious, and Prince Mikhaylo was authorized to tell it to her. The riddle is left: Was he to add that the price for this was recognition of Dimitry as her son?

In truth, Marfa must have had more than grave doubts about the identity of the young man who claimed to be the Tsarevich Dimitry Ivanovich, risen from the grave. She had seen her son, bleeding to death, on the lap of his nurse, Irina Tuchkova. At least, she is said to have sworn that it was her son. Therefore, the new Tsar must be an impostor. Nevertheless, it would be nice to be Tsaritsa again. Could she perhaps have all the benefits, and then deny him who offered them? If she did, what then?

Or did Dimitry so convince Prince Mikhaylo of *his* story of the happenings, both at Uglich and after, that his mother would be persuaded that she herself was wrong? She had been hysterical, that is known. Perhaps she knew it, too. Yet it is difficult to believe that a young mother, no matter what the circumstances, could really have mistaken another boy for her own child — unless she knew that the child was not hers and feigned hysteria to save her real son's life. In that case, she must have firmly believed that the boy did not hurt himself but was the object of a deliberate attempt at murder.

Or did Prince Mikhaylo have secret instructions to make certain that Marfa would recognize Dimitry as her boy immediately upon her arrival in Moscow? But Dimitry must have been convinced of this before, when he included her name in his decrees and circulars. Still, what certainty could Dimitry have had, or what instructions could Prince Mikhaylo have received, that would have prevented her from disavowing her recognition of Dimitry as soon as she could safely do so?

In fact, Marfa's brothers were already back in Moscow or on their way. The same was the case with her cousins. All of them had been in exile since 1591. She need not fear to tell the truth once she was surrounded by the Nagoys and their allies and friends. The people would back them against an impostor. Even Prince Vasily Shuysky would have to throw his weight with her, for he had been a member of the Commission sent to Uglich. She, not Dimitry, had the upper hand there.

On the face of it, then, for Dimitry to have woven a web to catch the woman he called his mother and compel her to side with him, and to have entrusted this web to a prince of a family not particularly notable for loyal habits, seems impossible. The idea of a web must consequently be discarded, and the answer to the enigma of Dimitry's action can be found in Dimitry's confidence in himself. In his own mind, he *was* the Tsarevich. Therefore it was not the shadow of fear that sent Prince Mikhaylo to Vyksinsky Monastery, but the love of a son who longed for reunion with his mother.

During the following three or four weeks, while the special embassy was away, Dimitry had time to think of establishing a government. He would not rule as had Boris Godunov, through a family clique, nor as had his erratic father, whose governmental vagaries cannot be explained in a history of Dimitry. He wanted rather to establish a more democratic government, under a council of state, after the model of the Polish Seym, or Diet, about which he had heard so much, and which not long before had been arguing feverishly about himself without his knowing it. To accomplish this, he apparently called on John Buczyński for help.

Buczyński, perhaps his closest personal secretary, worked then with Dimitry on a list of those who should sit in the Council, judging by the surviving list of its members written by Buczyński's hand. The idea of such a body was not new to Moscow, although the term "senator," which the Poles sometimes used, was unheard of. On the other hand, there were several innovations — always anathema in Moscow — in the composition of the group, which Buczyński called *Rada* in Polish (equivalent to Russian *Sovyet*).

Following the Polish pattern, Dimitry added a few bishops to the customary lords spiritual. Then, for personal reasons of affection and gratitude, several "commoners" had seats alongside princes of the blood and noted boyars. There were fourteen members of the clergy, headed by the Patriarch Ignaty, thirty-six boyars of the first class, including the "commoner" Basmanov in the eighteenth place, seventeen boyars of the second class, and six *dvoryane,* or gentlemen-pensioners as they would have been called in England.

Prince Mstislavsky maintained his place as premier prince of the empire, followed by Princes Vasily and Dimitry Shuysky (soon to be recalled to Moscow) and Prince Vorotynsky — all descendants of the House of Rurik. Then came Mikhaylo Fyodorovich Nagoy, brother of the Tsaritsa-nun Marfa, who was appointed Great Master of the Horse, the title held by Boris Godunov during the reign of Tsar Fyodor the Angelic. A number of princes followed, along with other members of the Nagoy family, and toward the bottom came Bogdan Yakovlevich Belsky, honored with the title of Great Master of the Armory. Prince Mikhaylo Skopin-Shuysky's name was the last.

Among the boyars of the second class was a handful of princes, along with several secretaries (*dyaki*), such as the Shchelkalov who announced the election of Boris Godunov, Bogdan Sutupov, Master of the Press and Great Secretary, and Afanasy Vlasyev, Master of the Royal Household and Great Secretary. Pleshcheyev and Pushkin, who had brought Dimitry's manifesto to Moscow, became respectively a second-class boyar and a gentleman-pensioner with the title of Great Bodyguard of the Tsar. Some of these titles, imported from Poland, were as difficult to render in Russian as they are in English.

Four weeks to the day from Dimitry's triumphal entrance into Moscow, on Thursday, July 18/28, another entrance, no less triumphant, took place. Prince Skopin-Shuysky had arrived the day before at the village of Tayninskoye, a few miles north of the outer walls of the capital. With him was the ex-Tsaritsa Marfa. Dimitry rode out at the head of a group of boyars to meet her, surrounded by Poles and a swarm of Muscovites of all descriptions. As she entered the village, he dismounted.

The two embraced and kissed, her dull robe and headdress contrasting soberly with his radiant tunic. And with that embrace all doubt vanished into the summer air. The mob again burst into tears.

The Tsar and ex-Tsaritsa spent the night in an "imperial residence" (otherwise undescribed), where a joyous banquet lasted until midnight. Then, the next morning, when Dimitry led his mother to the great coach awaiting her, the atmosphere was once again charged with the electricity of human emotion.

Despite Marfa's visible invitation for him to sit beside her, Dimitry shook his head. Instead, he walked beside the door, talking undisturbedly in the clouds of dust raised by the lumbering coach. At a respectful distance behind, held there in part by Prince Mikhaylo and the boyars, the populace that had marched from Moscow marched back again. It had indeed been a remarkable experience for everyone.

At the gate by the Sretensky Monastery, Dimitry bade his mother temporary farewell. Summoning a groom to bring up his mount, Dimitry hopped into the saddle and galloped virtually alone down the street called Nikolskaya (it is now October 25th Street) to Red Square and the main gate to the Kremlin. A few paces inside, he stopped and got off. There, before the Kirillov Monastery, he waited. And when the coach came up, he personally conducted the Tsaritsa-nun to quarters specially prepared for her by his command.

In the memory of even the oldest inhabitants of Moscow, no Tsar had ever before mounted or dismounted from a horse unaided, nor ridden alone, nor galloped, nor attended without ceremony a Tsaritsa in a monastery. A true Tsar was grave, hieratic, unapproachable.[3]

CHAPTER 10

DIMITRY,

TSAR AND GREAT PRINCE

FROM THAT THURSDAY ON, Dimitry visited the Tsaritsa-nun daily, saw that she was served from his own table, and assigned revenues to maintain her in the dignity of the mother of the Tsar. In the face of this, it seemed impossible that anyone could raise a voice against the legitimacy of Dimitry's claim to the throne.

Then the claim became reality three days later. Workmen had long since been occupied with repairing the roads within the Kremlin — the *derevyánnye mostovýe,* pavements of wooden planks laid side by each. Yard upon yard of scarlet cloth was brought out to drape over doorways, from balconies, and eventually even over the roads. Priceless Persian damasks embroidered in gold decorated the cathedrals. Floors were cleaned and candles supplied for the ceremony. All the pomp and religious splendor of the coronation of a Tsar inundated the inner sanctums of the ancient fort. Dimitry Ivanovich would receive the venerable Crown of Monomakh from the hands of the Most Holy Patriarch. Chosen by Dimitry in Tula, Ignaty had been properly elected at the end of June by a clergy that was generally eager to please.

Dimitry came out of the palace early in the morning of Sunday, July 21, 1605, preceded by a priest who asperged the Tsar's route with holy water. Behind stalked and shuffled the clergy, carrying banners, ikons, censers with incense, and other appurtenances of such ceremonies, all chanting. The procession entered the Cathedral of the Assumption, in the midst of which the ivory throne of Ivan the Dread had been placed. Before it, Dimitry's gem-studded tunic was replaced by long robes of extraordinary value and magnificence.

Thereupon, thus clad, Dimitry stood before the altar and delivered a lengthy speech — an act without known precedent in Russian history. He mentioned his descent from the illustrious line of his ancestors. He spoke with pride of Ivan the Dread. And he referred to his adversities when he was young, glancing now and then at the Tsaritsa-nun, for whom an elevated seat had been prepared.

He then took the sacrament at the altar and was touched with holy oil. After this, he turned toward the throne and was ceremoniously seated upon it. Ignaty placed the crown on his head, while in his hands were put his jewel-studded sceptre and orb, after which he was given the sword of justice, also encrusted with gems. Crowns representing the tsardoms of Vladimir, Moscow, Novgorod the Great, Kazan, and Astrakhan were set before him. All was infinitely stately, infinitely slow, and infinitely rich in the gold-walled chancel of the cathedral before the austere saints of the iconostasis.

At last the Patriarch took up a sacred work and read from it at considerable length, concluding with an exhortation to Dimitry to minister justice, and enjoy the crown of his ancestors with tranquillity. A prayer followed. Then Ignaty blessed the new Tsar and laid his cross upon him. The coronation was over.

Thirty years before, the Emperor Maximilian's ambassador had written, "Never in my life have I seen more priceless or more beautiful things," than Tsar Ivan had shown him. Ten years after that, the English factor in Moscow, Jerome Horsey, had observed that the coronation robes of Fyodor the Angelic weighed two hundred pounds and had to be carried in part by the princes and boyars. There is no reason to believe that Dimitry was more modest.

Whatever the particulars, Dimitry stepped out of the cathedral to a deafening bedlam of bells, cannonading, and human hullabaloo. The customary "bridge" had been built across a corner of Cathedral Square from the coronation cathedral to that of the

Archangel Michael. This was a yard or so above the ground and perhaps twelve to fourteen feet wide. Cloth-of-gold was spread under the Tsar's feet as he emerged, which gave way to scarlet cloth before he reached the end of the bridge.

As he walked, the boyars threw small specially coined gold pieces to the mob. And when he had passed, the mob surged up behind him to hack the cloth-of-gold to bits, for souvenirs — or to sell. Within the memory of no man had such a demonstration taken place, for nearly sixty years had run their turbid course since Ivan, not yet called "the Dread," had been crowned the first Tsar, to heartfelt public acclamation. Fyodor the Angelic and Boris Godunov had been enthroned with magnificence and solemnity, but hardly with fervor.

From Saint Michael's Cathedral to that of the Annunciation was but a short passage. Here, as the great portals closed behind him, shutting out both popular dementia and the stark sobriety of a summer sun, Dimitry faced the mystique of Orthodox iconography. This smallest of the cathedrals breathed Orthodox tradition and unchangeability. And this, of the three, was *his* cathedral, his private chapel almost. Yet he whose it was had been trained in the most liberal Church in Europe, the Unitarian, and had taken Holy Communion from the fingers of the representative of the Roman Pontiff, considered by the Orthodox to be their arch-enemy.

Shut off now from his jubilant subjects, Dimitry tarried shortly among his inscrutable Byzantine saints and then entered the palace, where a feast had been prepared. Poles and even Jesuits jostled with the stiff-robed Muscovites in the anterooms, but soon all were admitted to the Tsar's presence. There a Latin priest stood not far from that personification of Orthodoxy and pronounced an unintelligible invocation.

To the Muscovites it was an evil sign. But to the throng in the Kremlin who were acclaiming red-haired Dimitry as their buoyant monarch, such omens presaged little. Why, the Tsar himself translated the tiresome speech the black-frocked "heretic" had made. It was nothing — just congratulations to the Tsar on his accession to the throne. "Long live the Tsar!" was the response.

And so festivities were the order of the day in Moscow. After that first banquet, more feasts were given on Monday and Tuesday. Holiday humor had seized Moscow.

But before long, as the capital began to settle down to a more normal routine of life and work, Dimitry's often difficult Poles stirred up their first petty squall. If there had not been the matter of the excitement of the coronation, perhaps the trouble would not have been delayed even those five weeks.

Whatever the actual cause, the Russian police had arrested a member of the *szlachta,* the nobility, and had condemned him to be publicly whipped with that notorious instrument called the knout. (The Russians borrowed both the article and the name from the Scandinavians, but they made them very much their own.) The punishment was severe for a fault which was said to be unimportant, but it was not so much the obvious injustice as the insult to the Polish nation which caused the trouble. The offender's compatriots could not see a nobleman being led through the streets by a common hangman, and they buzzed out in his defense like a swarm of wrought-up hornets. The resultant casualties were high, on both sides.

Dimitry was quickly informed of the fracas. Hot-tempered as he was, he promptly sent word to the Polish barracks that those responsible for the bloody interference with the carrying out of the law must be surrendered to the police immediately. This was understandably resisted by the Poles, with the result that Dimitry sent a still sterner note, to the effect that he would "command that guns be brought to level the building [where they lived] and its occupants, without sparing even little children" — surely a figure of speech, since there is no reason to suspect that there might have been any such among the Polish troops.

The Poles responded with like emotion, sending to the Tsar a message couched more or less in these terms:

> Is this what awaits us in thanks for the blood we have spilled on behalf of the Tsar? We are not afraid. Let us be martyred! His Royal Highness shall hear about it — King Sigismund — and our brothers in Poland, too. Meanwhile, we want to die as befits Pol-

lish knights. But before we die, we shall work much evil [in Moscow].

And in token of this suicidal decision, they planned to attack the Russians, obviously far superior in numbers, and summoned a priest to hear their confession before facing certain death.

Had the hotheads been anything but Polish knights of the year 1605 or thereabouts, the message could have been passed off as the composition of a madman. Taking into consideration who they were, however, Dimitry quickly changed tactics, and sent yet another message to the mutineers. He insisted that they turn over the culprits, but at the same time promised that no harm should come to them. It was imperative, he said, that they make a show of obedience to calm the Russians (whose laws were broken and whose Tsar was defied).

The Polish knights thereupon retreated from their peppery stand, and on condition that their companions were not to be punished, on the word of the Tsar, they gave over three *tovarishchi*, one of whom was from Stanislas Borsza's company. It is to him, presumably, that the recorded account of what happened can be attributed:

> They were not guilty, for we were all in the brawl. They were given over only to please the Tsar, who promised to return them unharmed. But they were in terrible fear, because they were put in a tower where it was impossible not to be afraid. In that tower there were narrow benches around the walls, and below these were various hooks, scythes and iron bars. If anybody fell asleep, he would pay for it with his life.[1]

Fortunately the frightened heroes were held only for a day and a night. Unfortunately, Dimitry's obstinate clemency could be taken as a sign of weakness.

Clemency was not Dimitry's only shortcoming, in the eyes of his subjects. As the historian Karamzin wrote, in the 1820's, Dimitry's greatest enemy was himself,[2] for from the Russian point of view he was imprudent and hasty by nature, bluff, proud, thoughtless, and rash. To Karamzin he was, of course, an impostor, and impostors to the mind of a scholar of the 1820's were necessarily possessed of evil characteristics. Nevertheless, the description in a sense is tailored to Dimitry's character. It was a measure of these qualities mixed with others not mentioned by Karamzin which brought Dimitry to the throne. Yet once on the throne he should have discarded them. He should have been a Tsar of standard and time-honored mold. His contemporaries in Moscow saw things the way Karamzin did, two centuries later.

Dimitry had given a foretaste of what he was like to the inhabitants of the capital the day he rode off ahead of the Tsaritsa-nun to be on hand to welcome her back to the Kremlin. Now that the festivities were over, his un-Tsarlike and even un-Russian behavior almost exploded before the astonished city.

Ivan IV's grandfather, Ivan III, had married Zoe Palaeologue, niece of the last Emperor of Byzantium, and granddaughter of the Emperor Manuel II. Zoe had changed her name to Sophia upon marrying Ivan III, but in recompense she altered the "tradition" of Muscovite rule.

Although she had been but five when the Turks dealt the death-blow to the dying relic of Ancient Rome, the hieratic character of the Byzantine court was already stamped on her personality. Her wedding gift to her craggy but eager Slavic spouse was the sense of Empire, and its sanctity. It was therefore not long before a priest came up with the title "The Third Rome" to confirm Sophia's idea: Ancient Rome was long since dead (though Papal Rome lived); Constantinople-Byzantium, the Second Rome, had just been destroyed; now it was Moscow, and there would be no Fourth Rome. Ivan III, "the Great," gloriously accepted all this and handed both the idea and the practice down to his descendants, Vasily III and Ivan IV . In this way, during the century between the death of Ivan III and the arrival of Dimitry in Moscow, tsardom and Byzantine mummery had become almost synonymous in the Muscovite mind.

Dimitry's offenses were therefore conterminous with his violations of the sacrosanct imported custom. Still, in the eyes of the people these aberrations were offensive only when he began to disregard age-old religious observances. Rumor had it that the Tsar did not cross himself regularly and properly before the countless ikons, and that he dispensed with having his table blessed and sprinkled with holy water before all meals. What was worse, he sat down to dinner, not with a prayer, but with cheerful music, and sometimes forgot to lave his hands ceremoniously when he had finished eating.

Whether word got around generally that Dimitry ate veal on occasion — a horror and an abomination according to the more conservative Orthodox — is not certain, but it is recorded that he got into a serious altercation with one of the princes over the matter. On the other hand, it was probably well known that he did not frequent the baths, a cross between the Finnish sauna and Turkish baths, which had been a part of Russian life since long before Finns and Turks had ever been heard of, so to say. Neither did he take a "siesta" every day, as had all Russians from time immemorial, regardless of social status. Instead of sleeping, he went for a walk.

The Tsar's walks were another violation of sanctified custom, and for that reason potentially displeasing to the people. No Tsar, within memory, had ever moved from one room to another, not to say appeared in public, without an escort of kaftan-clad eminences, who stalked with Byzantine solemnity. Dimitry, if he did not go on an inspection tour, to the Treasury say, slipped out of the palace while the guards were taking *their* naps, alone or at most with one or two companions, and walked briskly (the Russians said he "ran") around the shops and stalls in the Chinese City, talking to such people as artisans, goldsmiths, apothecaries, and so on. If all Moscow was asleep at this hour, according to tradition, it can only be guessed that someone told these people that the Tsar was coming. However it was, his courtiers would awake to find their lord gone. Then they too ran around the Chinese City, or elsewhere, until they found him.

Even more disconcerting was Dimitry's physical vigor. He enjoyed nothing more than riding an untamed stallion, and breaking it in, in full view of his subjects. Naturally a man of his make-up would not be contented with being just a spectator at the usual amusements of the day. Therefore, when a bear-fight (the Russian equivalent of a Spanish bull-fight) was arranged at Tayninskoye, Dimitry could not sit still and enjoy it, as Tsar Fyodor the Angelic had loved to do, but had to clamber into the arena himself. Then he ordered everybody else out, and killed the bear with a spear, himself. Perhaps he had heard of the feats of the Emperor Commodus and wanted to imitate them, but the Russians did not like the idea any more than the Romans had, so many centuries before.

More constructively, and most of Dimitry's innovations were intended to bear progressive fruit, he tried out new cannon, manufactured in the great foundry (*Púshechny Dvor*) established in the reign of Ivan III by the Neglinnaya River just north of the White City walls, about where the famous Moscow Circus now is. But whereas Ivan IV had had his ordnance taken to a field beyond the city and there formally inspected it once a year, Dimitry frequented the foundry itself.[3] And whereas Ivan had ridden a horse "garnished with gold and silver abundantly," Dimitry used an everyday saddle. And whereas Ivan had worn a "gown of rich tissue, and a cap of scarlet," set with pearls and precious stones, and had been accompanied by five thousand harquebusiers and a swarm of noblemen, Dimitry rode alone or with one or two, and was dressed simply. And finally, whereas Ivan had taken up a post "where he might see all the ordnance discharged," Dimitry tried out new cannon himself, and displayed rare marksmanship. If old Andrey Chokhov was still there — he had been master of the foundry since 1569 — Dimitry must indeed have left him speechless.

In short, Tsars had for centuries been stately, haughty, rigid in their gem-encrusted kaftans. Grooms had to lift them onto their horses, and all their movements were slow and majestic. Dimitry, on the other hand, rode bareback at times, fought alongside his soldiers, and flew into a passion, reprimanded, or even struck the most distinguished officers for the slightest infraction of discipline. A century before Peter the Great, Dimitry plunged resolutely toward revolutionizing the Russian way of life.

But if Dimitry's military frowardness was startling to the soldiers, his behavior in meetings of the Council of State was appalling. The Russian name for this body had always been the *Duma*, a name borrowed long since from a Germanic language much as English had borrowed the word *Parliament* from French. But as *Parliament* basically meant to talk, *Duma* meant to think, mediate, deem. Since the character of the council reflected its name, it was far from an active body. It counseled the Tsar, with due solemnity, but was usually as resistant to action as any body summoned to *think* or *deem* probably should be. It was not idly that the fiats of the Muscovite government were couched in the formula: *The Sovereign has directed (decreed) and the Boyars have given their consent.* In other words, the Tsar acted, even before Dimitry's day, and his council thought about it.

Since by custom and habit the Duma reflected or thought slowly and gravely about all matters, Dimitry amazed it by his quick comprehension of even the most complicated affairs of state, and by the general keenness of his mind. In fact, this quickness of wit was none too welcome in so stolid a body, and his raillery at their lack of knowledge of the outside world offended the councillors. His praise of Poland and all things Polish particularly provoked them, somewhat naturally, because the Poles had acquired considerable bits of former Muscovite territory well within the memory of all but the youngest boyars. Then, Boris Godunov, the hated, had sent a small group of youths, less than a score, westward to study; now, Dimitry wanted everybody to travel, so it seemed. They should see foreign countries, he intimated, observe carefully, educate themselves, and earn the name of *men*. The implications were not flattering. Yet the Duma was of his own choosing, with minor concessions to custom, and was in theory the cream of Muscovite political intelligence.

Dimitry had no true model to go by, for his knowledge of the Polish Diet was by hearsay only. Yet it is apparent in his broadening of the Duma to include bishops and what can be called "upper class" commoners that he was endeavoring to introduce some sort of leaven in the heavy, doughy conservatism of the former ruling cliques. Still, additional clergy of whatever rank would only in-

crease the anti-productive power of the Church, while the commoners introduced self-seeking opportunities for themselves and
were patently despised by their associates, the princes and boyars.
Peter the Great, to recall again the inevitable comparison, succeeded in forming a useful and intelligent council only after many
years of reign.

But along with these assorted varieties of irritation to the Russians, high and low, Dimitry swept virtually the entire country
back into his arms by frequent gestures of the kind they liked.
Since he preferred riding horseback, even to church, he preserved
and added to the Tsar's stables, without neglecting the coach-
houses. In addition to the elaborate coach which had been the gift
of Queen Elizabeth of England to Boris Godunov,[4] Dimitry had
other coaches decorated with silver-work and draped with velvet
and sables. Matching these wheeled vehicles, there were sleighs for
winter use. The horses for both were high-bred Asiatics, whose
stirrups, bridles and saddles gleamed and glistened with gold, sapphires, emeralds and rubies. And the drivers and equerries were
dressed to match, at least in value. Indeed, when Dimitry went out
in full array, it was a sight to bring enthusiasm of the wildest sort
from those who complained that he lacked the majesty of a Tsar.

This remarkable young man, warrior, statesman and at times religious controversialist, also showed at least an elementary interest
in artistic matters. Kings, princes and dukes in Western Europe
already had small orchestras attached to their courts — groups of
instruments, including strings of all kinds, flutes, recorders, trumpets, drums and cymbals. In Muscovy such forms of entertainment
were unknown, and undoubtedly highly suspect. Dimitry brought
a score or more instrumentalists with him in an attempt to introduce a little gaiety into the somber court.

Furthermore, immediately upon his arrival he went to work on
the architectural and decorative shortcomings of the imperial palace in the Kremlin. The early stone structure of Ivan III had been
partially rebuilt by Boris Godunov as a long, narrow building, parallel to the Kremlin walls along the Moskva River, two stories
high, with the ancient cellar beneath and with a wooden super-

structure containing eight large apartments.[5] These were all but bare inside, and dismal even in the bright sunshine of summer and autumn. Dimitry had the superstructure torn down and a new wooden building, a double-palace, erected on the old stone foundations. Half of this was for himself, the other half being designed for his bride, Marina Mniszech. The interiors of both, divided according to his own taste, were bright with colored Dutch-style heating-stoves, and the walls were hung with Persian silks. All trimmings, such as hinges, door-locks, and the like, were silver and gilt. In a word, it was all livable, cheerful. And it no longer exhaled any lingering aura of the hateful family of Godunov.

Rumor had it that workmen, cleaning out the cellars beneath the new palace, found a statue in a vault which had been devised by one of Boris's sorcerers, all of whom were noted for their ingenuity and evil works. This statue was made with a lamp in its hand, which was filled with oil. Once the lamp was lighted, after a given time an ingenious mechanism would break the spout off and drop the burning wick onto a large deposit of gunpowder carefully piled up around the statue. Then, God willing, Dimitry and his entire court would be blown sky-high as soon as he came to occupy the palace. Absurd as the story is, it is extraordinary that it should have been invented almost at the same time that Guy Fawkes and his fellow-conspirators were seeding the cellars of the Houses of Parliament in distant London with equally combustible material. The difference is that the Gunpowder Plot, discovered on November 5, 1605, was a fact. Godunov's statue was a figment of an imagination overheated by the events in the capital of Muscovy.

Dimitry himself, however, may have contributed to the firing of popular fantasy, as will be seen shortly. His imperial eyrie was exotic enough, to Muscovite eyes, to cause comment, and abuse. From the outside, it had more of the warmth and simple dignity of a Polish country mansion than the orientalized homes of the boyars with their elaborate woodwork. (It was a Pole who said it was the most beautiful building in the Kremlin.)[6] But it was not the beauty of the place which fired Muscovite imagination and started tales of statues.

As has been mentioned, Dimitry was intensely interested in things military. Somehow a nameless German artisan apparently got his ear with a plan for a wooden and bronze "fort" built in the form of a "Trojan horse," or movable statue, which could be pushed up against enemy troops, to frighten men and horses — particularly the latter. It was painted in gaudy colors, had mechanical doors through which figures appeared in a volcanic display of fire and smoke, and before it was a "life-size" representation of the three-headed guardian of Hades, Cerberus, which let out a terrifying roar when touched.

The purpose of this may have been purely theatrical, although it seems more likely that it was a highly embellished model for a secret weapon to be used against the Tatars in an already vaguely planned campaign. But whatever it really was, to the superstitious Muscovites such a guardian — for Dimitry had it temporarily set up outside the entrance of his new palace — meant that a sorcerer or an accomplice of the Evil One lived there. One horrified chronicler-monk even wrote that the contraption portrayed the future abode of the Tsar in eternity: hell and its flames.

Other folk, less literate but probably still more imaginative, soon began to people Dimitry's "pleasure dome" with dozens and hundreds of odalisques or concubines, with whom their lascivious young sovereign spent his days and nights in unspeakable dalliance. Rumors flew wildly throughout the capital, until certain master minds, monks or princes of the blood, to cap it all, reported that the daughter of Boris Godunov, the lovely Ksenia, had been secretly removed from the nunnery where she was living and was occupying one of the Tsar's apartments. The fire under all this smoke was almost certainly the simple fact that Dimitry, aged twenty-three, liked to have a good time and was certainly not averse to feminine charms.

Indeed, Dimitry had already begun the tedious process of importing, so to speak, his bride Marina from the Polish Republic. Therefore, to put a stop to the unworthy rumors, he ordered that the unfortunate girl be forced to take the vows of a nun. To modern minds, this is shocking. But Ksenia in the Muscovy of 1605 was only the disgraced daughter of a disgraced family, despite her charm, intelligence, and beauty. Such "deposed" nobility, and indeed deposed royalty, invariably ended in monasteries. Ksenia became the nun Olga.

That Dimitry, who enormously admired that "great gallant," Henry IV of France, may have had, or did have, relations with young women in his palace is by no means out of the question. That he seduced Ksenia is attested only in the same chronicles which made him a rival of that Great Prince and Saint, Vladimir I of Kiev, who "entertained" three hundred concubines in Vyshgorod, another three hundred in Belgorod, and two hundred in Berestovo. The rumored affair with Ksenia seems completely out of keeping with his character.

During all this time, and later, Dimitry was walking a religious tightrope. He had joined the Roman Catholic Church in Kraków a year and a few months before. He had with him two zealous Jesuits priests and perhaps other members of the clergy. He also had several companies of Polish soldiers who were Catholics. All these people were looked upon with fanatical suspicion by the Orthodox citizens of the capital.

Yet somehow, even in the very days when the new Pope, Paul V, was beginning to look hopefully indeed on the prospects of adding Muscovy to the widespread spiritual dominions of the Church, the Jesuits in Moscow understood Dimitry's problem, and were patient. Surprisingly, the Polish mercenaries — after their one brush with the local police — also were willing to subside into temporary oblivion. It is known that Jesuits and Roman Catholic laymen alike were always welcome in the eyes of the Tsar, and frequently took advantage of this welcome. For the time being, however, Dimitry studiously eschewed open or frequent contact with his unpopular "heretics" and "enemy aliens." Their occupations therefore can be told only in general terms, although one highlight is worth mentioning.

Since the early 1580's some three thousand Poles had been living in Moscow and the neighboring countryside. Most of them were former prisoners of war, from King Stephen Báthory's campaigns.

Some of them had kept their Catholic faith, even in the capital of Orthodoxy; others had found it easier to be rebaptized. Almost to the man, these homesick exiles now turned to the Jesuits for religious and even patriotic solace. They were anything but denied. And that gave the Jesuits additional cause for pleading for the construction of the promised Catholic church in Moscow. In other places, even in other times, similar requests have been shelved. Dimitry wisely demurred.

The Jesuits, with comparable wisdom, did not insist. They turned their attention to an Italian physician, Erasmo Birischi, who had been sent by the Emperor Rudolf II to Boris Godunov. He had been an acquaintance, if not a friend, of Edmund Campion, the English Jesuit martyr of twenty-odd years before. Undeterred by any language barrier, he soon became a friend of the Poles, and gave them a copy of Livy's history, most likely in Latin. Grateful though he may have been for this addition to their small library, Father Andrew Lawicki still dreamed of being the Saint Patrick of the Slavs, and dedicated himself to mastering the complexities of Russian.

While unimportant events were occurring on the surface, and very little happened to which a definite date or term can be given, there is no question that the ground-swell of discontent in Moscow had not subsided. Although Moscow as a whole was enjoying the beginnings of a rebirth of prosperity, a pestilential virus grew there, difficult to identify and, when discovered, virtually impossible to reach.

As far back as people could remember, Russia had been a land favorable for the breeding of "blessed idiots," yuródivye.[7] As Giles Fletcher described them,

> [the Russians] have certain eremites (whom they call holy men) . . . [who] go stark naked, save a clout about their middle, with their hair hanging long and wildly about their shoulders, and many of them with an iron collar or chain about their necks or middles, even in the very extremity of winter. These they take as prophets and men of great holiness, giving them a liberty to speak what they list without any controlment, though it be of the very highest himself . . .

These pitiable madmen were outlets for popular feeling in oppressed Moscow, much as was the statue of Pasquino (or Pasquillo) in Rome, with a vast difference. Pasquino was but a pillar on which written invectives were pasted. Pasquino was "literate." The yuródivy was illiterate, and vociferous. And he lived in the ubiquitous sanctuary of "blessed idiocy" — or in Fletcher's words:

> This maketh the people to like very well of them, because they are as Pasquils, to note their great men's faults that no man else dare speak of.

Dimitry's religious "infringements" could not but stir up the rhetoric of these "fools in Christ." Boris Godunov was said to have made away with some of them. Dimitry, tolerantly but illadvisedly, allowed them to poison the air, freely. This they did, with religious prejudice.

The idiots were far from the only people who raised the intolerant banner of Orthodoxy in Muscovy. For religion was surely Dimitry's greatest weakness as a Muscovite ruler. In fact, what sort of religion dwelled in his heart is impossible to say. It is fairly evident that his sympathies were far from being Orthodox — at least in the form in which Orthodoxy was then believed in and practiced in Russia. It is known that he embraced Catholicism, but it is not clear to what extent that was purely a political move. As for Unitarianism and Lutheranism, his favorite secretaries were Lutherans, and he had attended a Unitarian school, but these details do not prove any leaning toward either branch of Protestantism. Only one thing is certain. He was ardently Christian, conceivably "early Christian" of the second-century type, before the splintering began. But there was a touch of pagan tolerance about him, lacking in the early Christians. Typical of this was his answer to a Muscovite nobleman who asked him directly if he was planning to build a church for the Poles in Moscow: "Why not? They are Christians, and they have rendered me faithful services. You have already allowed heretics [Lutherans] to build a church and a school."

Nevertheless, there was a powerful tug on his religious convictions, whatever they were, by Catholicism. Pope Paul V, reversing the chill aloofness of Clement VIII, was eager for him to convert Russia, or at least unite it with Rome. Then, Rangoni exerted all the influence he could. Pan George Mniszech, that pillar of Vatican policy, also threw his weight into the struggle, and the Jesuits by their piety and learning — especially the latter — were almost constantly personal reminders of the Catholic Church. But the strongest magnet of all, the overpowering one, was the imperious lady of his heart, Panna Marina Mniszech.

Between the time of his costly victory followed by his defeat and then his entry into Moscow there seems to have been little communication between him and the Mniszechs. Between him and Marina there does not seem to have been any, perhaps because it was not felt proper under the circumstances. Now, with his coronation celebrated, and his rule auspiciously begun, his love for Marina swelled within him. As the hapless Earl of Surrey had written in the days when dread Ivan was young, "The farther off, the more desired." A month of all-consuming activity had already slipped by — four Sundays of sterile attendance at the empty form of the solemn Orthodox mass of those days. The fifth Sunday after his coronation ushered in a new month, September.

Despite the many distractions which came from continuous reports of local magpies and other offspring of Ananias, with tales which ranged from idle inventions to virtual sedition, Dimitry at last got around to planning his first embassy to King Sigismund, and planned it well. No longer a suppliant before the Polish throne, but at last a crowned monarch, richer if not more powerful than the royal head of the Polish Republic, Dimitry showed consummate tact in his behavior.

Tact, however, is perhaps less appropriate a word than realism. Sigismund, before whom he had properly bowed a year before, was ardently Catholic. He was also frigidly proud, as well as ambitious in a curiously apathetic way. He had married a distant cousin, the daughter of Archduke Charles of Styria, who had died, and he was about to marry her sister, with the aid of a dispensation from the Vatican.[8] Both of these ladies were first cousins of the Emperor Rudolf II, who had been at war with Turkey since 1593.

In 1605, Rudolf was hoping for peace, since the old Sultan had died and Ahmed I, a boy of fifteen, had become "God of the Earth and Governor of the Whole World."

Ahmed had inherited a war with the Iranian King of Kings, Shah Abbas I, as well as with the Holy Roman Emperor. The Shah in turn had made himself a friend of Tsar Boris Godunov and presented him with a silver- and gold-leaf throne studded with gems. Dimitry, heir to tradition regardless of the interloper Boris, quickly spotted a chance to overthrow the vile Moslem Sultan Ahmed by supporting that most noble lord, the Shah (also a Moslem), with the aid of all Christian Princes, including Sigismund III (whose interest was tepid) and Rudolf II (who wanted peace but was also mildly insane). It would be a Holy War, led by the Tsar, designed forever to eradicate the threat of the heathen followers of Muhammad to the tranquillity and well-being of the pious followers of Christ. Under Dimitry, all Christianity would join in the utter destruction of the Ottoman hordes. His war-cry amounted to *Istanbul delenda est*.[9]

Dimitry used this war-cry and a former ambassador from Boris Godunov to Rudolf II as a combined tactic in soliciting the permission of King Sigismund for a Polish lady, daughter of a Senator of the Republic, to leave her home and to voyage in foreign lands and become the Empress of Muscovy — a lady named Marina Mniszech. He had no intention of appearing as a suppliant again, yet the King's permission was needed before Marina could leave the country in the style befitting an Empress.

Therefore, Dimitry overshadowed his immediate request with a vision of greater glory for Sigismund and the Republic through the leadership of Dimitry in a crusade. The Emperor himself would approve the idea. (Six months later, the Habsburg archdukes declared Rudolf incapable of ruling.)

The former ambassador of Godunov who was chosen for the mission to Sigismund was Afanasy Ivanovich Vlasyev, Dyak (Secretary) of what can be called the Foreign Office, along with other important charges. Such a position in Moscow in 1605 was essentially stultifying, but Vlasyev could be counted on to behave precisely as an Ambassador Extraordinary for the Tsar should behave.

To attest to the solemnity of his charge, Vlasyev was assigned suitable ostentation in the form of attendants, both civilian and military, and bore with him elaborate gifts for King Sigismund, Pan George Mniszech, and above all the Tsar's bride, Marina. Indeed, the greatest honor devolving on the Ambassador was that of marrying Marina in the name of his master. Dimitry wanted her to enter Russia with all the pomp due a Tsaritsa. Marina supposedly was not averse.

But if Afanasy Ivanovich could be counted on to perform his duties punctiliously, perhaps even over-scrupulously, there were matters of high diplomacy which could hardly be entrusted to him. Although Dimitry could not have known that Boris's ambassador to Queen Elizabeth a few years before had amused London by his pomposity mixed with courtliness — as John Chamberlain put it, "The Muscovy ambassador took his leave like a dancing bear" — there was no doubt in his mind that a Pole could deal with tact where that was more important than protocol. The question of religion called for just that.

Dimitry knew that Moscow was already unhappy over the thought of a Tsaritsa who to them was a heathen. Marina must be cautioned to follow Orthodox practice within the bounds of possibility, and to go to almost all lengths not to rouse religious antagonism. He himself would take care of the problems of her remaining faithful to the Catholic Church after her arrival in Moscow.

This delicate mission was entrusted before long to John Buczyński, a neighbor of the Mniszechs, perhaps because he was neither Orthodox nor Roman Catholic. It would take a Lutheran to walk the difficult path between the Greek Church and the Latin in those days, when all Muscovy knew of the efforts of Rome to bring about a Union between them. (Of the Patriarchs of the East, his Beatitude of Moscow was the most truly irrevocably opposed to such sacrilege.) And there were other matters for Buczyński to investigate, which will be seen shortly.

Meanwhile, instructions had been issued to Vlasyev to cover all foreseeable eventualities, gifts had been prepared, and a thousand delicate details attended to. Then, sometime in September, the embassy left Moscow. Although it is astounding that under the circumstances the exact date should have slipped from sight, it is known that King Sigismund had sent an embassy to Dimitry on August 23, and it had not arrived when Vlasyev moved with solemn pageantry down the Arbat Road and crossed the Moskva River. Kraków was a thousand monotonous miles away.

CHAPTER 11

A MARRIAGE
DAINTILY TO BE DEALT WITH [1]

THE POLISH DIET had come to a stormy conclusion on March 3, 1605. From the outset, the King and his Great Chancellor, Zamoyski, had faced one another on many questions, with the latter usually holding his ground. Zamoyski was determined to keep Poland in her traditional state of liberty, which was sinking under his very eyes into license and anarchy, while Sigismund insisted on his second unpopular marriage (with a Habsburg Archduchess), tried to abolish the universal right of veto,* and leaned ever more toward supporting Dimitry. All three questions were opposed strongly by Zamoyski.

On the matter of the marriage, Zamoyski had been so outspoken that Sigismund at one point started up from the throne, his hand on his sword. *"Rex, ne move gladium!"* the Chancellor is said to have cried in Latin. "Don't touch your sword! Let not the future call you Caesar and us Brutus . . ." And he went on to remind the King that he was an elected monarch, and that Poland was a Republic.

Sigismund had to yield. He had to retreat also before Zamoyski's attack on his attempt to curb the power of the senators. But on the subject of Dimitry, the King kept his peace, after presenting his point of view. As had been mentioned, Boris's Ambassador Posnik Ogaryov was examined on the heels of Smirnoy Otrepyev's appearance, and Zamoyski had been able to win over a few senators originally inclined to favor Dimitry. Not even when Leo Sapieha, that

* Any member of the Diet could veto any legislation.

political chameleon, changed sides and joined Zamoyski in opposing help for Dimitry did Sigismund raise any outward question. But the real effect of their stand was not quite what that group expected. Sigismund, coldly angry, privately became more determined to support those who supported Dimitry.

Three months passed, in comparative quiet. Word came of Dimitry's defeat, and hibernation in Putivl — or "somewhere." Then the winds of Providence began to turn in his favor. On June 3, Zamoyski suddenly died. Oddly, the very next day the new Pope, Paul V, dictated a dispatch in Rome asking his Nuncio, Rangoni, to supply him with full information on Dimitry and his claim on the Russian throne. It was almost the first piece of "foreign" business of his pontificate.

Dimitry had acquired his most influential supporter before his most impenitent opponent was lowered into the grave. It would be many days, of course, before the effect of these events became entirely clear, but that could not diminish their significance.

Word of the death of Boris Godunov had already reached Kraków, stirring up a vast amount of prophesying. Then Dimitry's special envoy arrived — Tatyev, who had spent some time at Sambor. Tatyev was followed by another emissary, one Shulesh Bulgakov, who brought word "from the princes and boyars, from the castles and towns such as Putivl and so on, and from the clergy and the laity," that all recognized Dimitry as their Tsarevich.

The cause of Dimitry was soaring into exultant triumph, while a new surprise was in preparation in Rome. Hardly had word reached the Vatican that night had fallen on the reign of Boris Godunov than Pope Paul himself addressed a letter, dated July 12 (new style), to: *Dilectissimo filio Demetrio, Domino Russiae, Magno Duci Moscoviae, Noveguardiae, Smolentiae, Wlodimiriae, Domino Casani et Astracani, multarum Provinciarum Principe Magno,* or "Most beloved son Dimitry, Lord of Russia, Great Duke of Moscow, etc." [2]

In this communication, Pope Paul expressed his happiness that Dimitry had been recalled to his ancient realm, now that the tyrant was dead, and in a great many words tactfully reminded him

of his Catholic duties. But the most important feature of the letter
is the title, given without restraint, and certainly given before the
death of young Fyodor was known. Paul V's hand was not held
back by the doubts which had assailed Pope Clement VIII.

The Cardinal Secretary of State, to give him his modern title,
was more cautious when he wrote to the Nuncio in Poland four
days later. Repeating that the death of Boris was confirmed, he
pointed to the "prodigious" success of Dimitry, and asked Rangoni, *if* Muscovy recognized the "new sovereign," what steps
should be taken to confirm him in the Catholic faith and to preserve his affection for the Holy See. It was an urgent matter.

Rangoni meanwhile had prepared an answer to the Pope's letter
of June 4 which covered twenty-seven manuscript pages, and sent
it off on July 2.[3] It reached Rome before the end of the month,
apparently by "ordinary post." In it Rangoni recounted all that
he knew about Dimitry as far back as October, 1603, and added
various bits of news. One partially accurate item, received only
three days before, was that Boris's widow was dead, and that his son
(Fyodor) had sent ambassadors to swear allegiance to Dimitry.
(This rumor was fairly frequent.) Although another report had
it that Fyodor had won out and defeated Dimitry, Rangoni dis-
counted this version of the story, largely for the following reason:
it came through Gdańsk, a notorious hotbed of heretics opposed to
all causes that might advance the glory of the Catholic Church. In
any event, Rangoni suspected that opposition to Dimitry was a
thing of the past.

Having thus dismissed Russian opposition to Dimitry, Rangoni
went on to point out that the Palatine of Kraków and the majority
of the nobility were in favor of considering Dimitry the legal heir
to the Russian throne. The King furthermore had given Dimitry
many presents, generally favored his cause, indicated that he would
receive ambassadors from him, and even offered him armed help in
case of need.

Did that mean that the King regarded Dimitry as the true heir?
Rangoni vaguely hinted that the answer was *yes*. But what came
most pellucidly from his pen was his tribute to the nobility, piety

and zeal of the young sovereign. Dimitry, he asserted, was ready to march against the Turks, and he "is determined" to reunite the severed Churches.

This was sufficient for Rome. The Pope envisioned a Tsar devoted to the Holy See and an ardent Catholic, on good terms with Poland and bellicosely inclined against the Ottoman Empire. This led to plans for an exchange of ambassadors directly between the Eternal City and the Russian capital, and less than two weeks after sending a letter of thanks and admiration to Rangoni, the Vatican launched an epistolary attack in three directions at once: the King, Cardinal Maciejowski, and the Palatine of Sandomierz.

It was the Pope's desire, said the triple communication, that Dimitry be aided, as an instrument supplied by Providence to establish the Church in Russia. The King was asked to give full support to Dimitry, the Cardinal to fan the fire of his piety, and the Palatine to coordinate — although that is not quite the word used. Most important of all, the whole thing was the Pope's own idea. Even to the tentative appointment of the Nuncio's nephew, Count Alessandro Rangoni, as special Papal envoy to Moscow!

The elder Rangoni was so exhilarated by this coronation of his efforts to win the Church to Dimitry as well as to win Dimitry to the Church (Pope Clement it will be remembered had hardly been enthusiastic), that he anticipated the embassy planned for his nephew by sending his private secretary, the Abbé Luigi Pratissoli, on ahead. Pratissoli always had the advantage that he would be less conspicuous in his black robe than Count Alessandro in the splendor of contemporary Italian dress, and undoubtedly could enter the Kremlin all but unnoticed. This move reflects wise caution on Rangoni's part.

For credentials the Abbé carried an informal letter — Rangoni's first since he had heard of Dimitry's coronation. He also took a few pious presents to the new Tsar. The presents were symbolic rather than of great value, and the letter was tactful. It barely went beyond the gentlest of reminders of the project of Union (of the Churches), and a mild call for friendship with Poland. Finally, there was a suggestion that Dimitry place himself in the paternal hands of the Pope, whose succession to the chair of Saint Peter he simultaneously announced. Rangoni was never wanting in finesse.

Sigismund however, apparently in ignorance of Rangoni's private ambassador to Dimitry, decided to make an open diplomatic overture in that direction, independently. His choice for this mission was Alexander Korwin Gosiewski, starosta of the frontier town of Velizh and a connection by marriage of Prince Konstantin Vishnevetsky. His reason for such unusual precipitation, since he customarily was lethargic, was apparently the official silence which had followed Dimitry's coronation. More than three weeks had passed without any word, and if he had not actively suspected Dimitry of forgetfulness in the matter of his promises, the "opposition" in Poland may have hinted that, as Tsar, Dimitry would ignore them.

Sigismund signed Gosiewski's letters of credence on August 21. Overtly, the envoy was instructed to congratulate the Tsar on his coronation and to invite him to attend the King's marriage to the Archduchess Constance. Secretly, he was to sound Dimitry out on the subject of Sweden. Sigismund had lost the Swedish throne a few years before, it will be remembered, mostly because of his burning Catholicism, but he had not lost hopes of regaining it. Boris Godunov would not help him. Dimitry might.

The pretext chosen for presenting the Swedish matter to Dimitry was devious in the extreme. A shady nobody of unknown nationality had turned up in Kraków with a story that Boris was not really dead, but had buried a "double," while himself escaping with a vast treasure to England. Sorcerers, of whom Boris was known (or imagined) to have had many, had predicted that he would save the Empire of Muscovy in that way, and would soon return to power. Dimitry's life and crown were thus in danger, but Sigismund would send spies (meaning assassins) to London, and close his borders effectively against Boris's passage if he got out of England. Supposedly this would throw Dimitry into King Sigismund's arms and into a war to restore him to his Swedish throne — out of gratitude. But before Gosiewski reached Moscow on this remarkable errand, which he was by nature and training totally unfit to carry out, Dimitry's Envoy Extraordinary was already well on his way to Kraków.

It was November 9 by the Polish calendar before Vlasyev arrived at his destination, accompanied by Dimitry's personal secretary Słoński and an entourage of three hundred. Nothing quite like it had ever been seen in the ancient Polish capital — a fact underlined by Vlasyev's gesture two days after his arrival.

Advance notice had reached Pan George Mniszech, so that he was on hand to welcome the Ambassador. Vlasyev thereupon, and with great ceremony, presented the Palatine with half a million rubles, a black dappled steed whose harness sparkled with gold and precious stones, a suit of finely wrought armor, some *objets d'art*, several Oriental tapestries and other precious stuffs, a live sable, and three gerfalcons with golden leg-bells and caps embroidered with pearls. Many an insolvent noble cast avaricious eyes on these munificences.

Three days later Vlasyev was presented to the King, and after a stately banquet offered by Pan George, there was a royal audience on the Wawel, on November 18, with a handful of senators in attendance. Vlasyev made a formal statement of his mission. He desired to inform His Majesty of the coronation of Dimitry by the Patriarch of Moscow, Ignaty, and of the new Tsar's assurances of continued friendship with the Polish Republic. He called the attention of His Majesty to the dangers presented by the continuous pressure of Turkish arms, and Dimitry's projects for a Christian union to remove it. And in the name of the Tsar he requested royal assent to the marriage of Marina, at the same time that he extended an invitation to His Majesty to the wedding.[4]

Sigismund was pleased to be informed of the Tsar's coronation and his Turkish plans, and graciously granted his permission for Marina to become the bride of the Tsar. The audience was over. Somewhat astoundingly, Marina arrived from Sambor within twenty-four hours, yet without benefit of any sort of internal combustion engine. She was accompanied by her mother, who was ill.

Half a week later, on Tuesday, November 22, the élite of

Kraków began to invade the Great Market Place about noon. There, among the town residences of several great magnates, stood the homes of the Firlej, Mniszech, and Montelupi families, all in a row. (Pan George's eldest brother had married Jadwiga Firlej.) Between these mansions, portions of walls had been broken through to provide passageways to permit the circulation of the guests at a fabulous wedding. Due to Orthodox sensitivities it was impossible to have a church ceremony, but even in the face of this bit of realism, many Muscovites complained that the locale was not worthy.[5]

King Sigismund honored the festivities in person, accompanied by his sister Anne, Princess of Sweden, and his son, ten-year-old Wladislaus. The Papal Nuncio, Rangoni, and the Ambassadors of Venice and Florence attended, while a numerous throng of court dignitaries and relatives and friends of Pan George filled the three houses. As one modern historian has written, one could have believed that Dimitry had been recognized as the resurrected Tsarevich, that Sigismund had denied his doubts, and that the Polish Diet had renounced its opposition to the new Tsar.

One room in the Firlej mansion was converted into a chapel, which the King entered directly from the square. About the same time, Ambassador Vlasyev arrived at the Montelupi mansion with a guard of two hundred horse. He too went straight to the improvised chapel, where Sigismund barely acknowledged his presence, to Vlasyev's irritation. Cardinal Maciejowski took his place at the altar, accompanied by the clergy. Then, when all was ready, Marina entered, supported by two senators.

Her wedding-gown of white brocade was studded with pearls and sapphires, while from a diamond crown her dark hair fell over her shoulders, sparkling brilliantly with jewels under a gauze veil. Excitement had given her the radiance of a storybook princess — of Titania, Queen of the Fairies.

Nearby, Dimitry's proxy had by then virtually taken root. His dazed eyes, puffy cheeks and luxuriant beard emerged above a carapace of cloth-of-gold which hampered what little movement he was inclined to make. He represented the Muscovy of 1605, and he represented it well, almost libelously. Called upon to open the ceremony with a speech, he gravely intoned formalities, without expression, without emotion, even without meaning.

When he had finished, the Palatine of Leńczyc responded in the name of Pan George. He spoke long and enthusiastically, but also without meaning. Then came the turn of the representative of King Sigismund. Leo Sapieha, Great Chancellor of Lithuania, stepped forward. To the amazement of those who had heard his speech in the Diet, less than ten months before, in which he had as much as called Dimitry a fraud, Sapieha radiated contentment with the wedding about to be solemnized. It was a symbol of union between the two countries, he said, and it testified to the favor of Divine Providence. Marina was an emblem of beauty, wisdom and virtue; Dimitry, the embodiment of princeliness and the model of sovereigns. Together they would fulfil a glorious mission. Then, directing his remarks to Marina, he added: "If the honor of wearing a crown is great, it is not too great for a Polish lady. How many queens indeed our Poland has given to all Europe!" On that patriotic note he ended, with meaning, if without sincerity.

Last came a religious address by the Cardinal, who alone among the Poles did not hesitate to name Dimitry *Tsar of Muscovy*. He digressed on theology, morality, the state of Moscow, and other suitable subjects, and in conclusion recounted the many benefits and kindnesses Dimitry had received at the hands of the Poles. Thereupon two Muscovite pages spread a silk carpet before the altar, while the clergy sang *Veni Creator*. All fell to their knees, except for the Princess Anne, who was a Protestant, and the Orthodox Ambassador from Moscow.

After the hymn, Cardinal Maciejowski continued talking, cautioning Marina to forget the house of her forefathers, as is written in the Bible. Dimitry, "a new Abraham," he said, had sent his faithful servant Vlasyev in search of a new Rebecca. And on and on he rambled until Vlasyev was visibly succumbing to a sort of torpor. And at that point, coming to the routine questions of the Catholic marriage service, the Cardinal suddenly asked if the Tsar had been married before. Vlasyev came to, and said that he knew nothing about that at all.

There was a pause while several bystanders tried to explain to him that it was a customary question, and that he had to answer *Yes* or *No*. But Vlasyev refused to speak until at last he thought up an answer which proved satisfactory. "If my master were already married," he said, "he would not have sent me here."

Then, when it came time to present Dimitry's ring, Vlasyev handed it to the Cardinal in a small casket, refusing to touch it even with the tip of his finger. And when he had to take Marina's hand he wanted to take it with his own hand wrapped in a handkerchief. Maciejowski insisted that the ceremony could not proceed until he did take her hand, however, and Valsyev at last agreed, muttering that it was not right for a subject to paw his sovereign. But when he was handed Marina's exchange ring for Dimitry he was adamant. The Cardinal had to put it in the little box himself. And finally, upon the Cardinal's asking him to repeat the marriage vows after himself, Vlasyev told him to keep out of it. "I am to talk with her ladyship," he said determinedly, "not with you. The lady Marina is to marry the Tsar, and I am to marry the lady, for the Tsar."

At last, despite the difficulties, the marriage was effectuated. Vlasyev and his entire retinue bowed to the ground before their new Tsaritsa. And a young courtier dashed from the room, sprang on his horse, and rode off for Moscow at full gallop, with the news.

An orchestra of two score musicians struck up at the arrival of the wedding party in the hall set aside for the banquet. King Sigismund placed Marina and Vlasyev on his right, and Princess Anne and little Wladislaus on his left. Vlasyev promptly refused to sit by the bride, for he was not worthy. Neither the King nor anyone else could persuade him, so when the time came to be seated, several gentlemen sat him there, forcibly.

In this position, he faced Cardinal Maciejowski and Monsignore Rangoni. High court dignitaries served the meal, and the table glittered with polished gold and silver. Marina was too overcome to eat by then, and Vlasyev did not fail to notice it. He, too, refused to eat. Again, Sigismund attempted to persuade him, but to no avail. He contented himself with bread and salt — emblems of hospitality and subservience in Muscovy.

During the banquet, Vlasyev's attendants brought in the gifts for the bride. And as no-one in Poland had ever seen quite the equal of Vlasyev himself, so no-one had ever seen anything quite like the gifts he brought. There were crimson velvets from Venice, satins of all colors, brocades embroidered with gold and silver, necklaces, pendants and bracelets of rubies and emeralds, crosses of sapphires, and bejeweled pieces of statuary.

A pelican of topaz accompanied a Neptune and a Diana. A ship done in pearls swam on a sea of silver waves. A golden ox opened its belly to shower forth a heap of diamonds. And to conclude the spectacle, an elephant of gilded silver was brought in which carried in place of a howdah an elaborate clock, which played music with trumpets and flutes, and presented scenes with people who strolled about. No queen in Poland's history had been so lavishly endowed.

Marina's grandmother, Jadwiga Tarło née Stadnicki, accepted the gifts in the name of her indisposed daughter. Then the Castellan of Małogość, a connection of Mniszech's by marriage, gave suitable thanks to the groom's envoy in Marina's name, and the toasts followed. Beginning with the King, they were drunk in long and formal procession to both Marina and Dimitry. Etiquette required bows of greater or lesser inclination, according to the rank of the person bowing. Vlasyev surpassed all in reverence. Each time Dimitry's name was mentioned his forehead touched the floor.

The music began again, while liveried attendants cleared away the banquet tables. Then King Sigismund led Marina in the *polonaise,* which was already gaining fame in Europe for "its gravity, its sweetness, and its respectfulness," as the French historian Laboureur put it.[6] Other couples followed, but Vlasyev refused point-blank to take part in the ball. This time he was left in peace. He had played his part to perfection, according to Muscovite custom, and if the Poles had found his actions odd, and even laughable, it was only because *they* did not know how to behave. And if a handful of Muscovites were seen to skew slightly on their way out, how many Poles saw four eyes on faces which boasted only two?

Marina danced last with her father, after which both went to kneel before the King. It was reported that Sigismund had words of fatherly affection for Marina, and advice for her future. Treating her as a reigning monarch, he counseled her to carry the glory of God to far regions, but to keep her love for her native land — to work for friendship between the two peoples, and not to forget promises made to Poland, but to remind her husband of his debt to the King. He then wished her happiness in the foreign land to which she was going, and gave her his blessing.

Marina fell on his knees, in sobs. Unable to speak, she motioned for the Cardinal to reply for her. This time he proferred a few words only, which he knew she would have said. She was leaving all that she knew and loved. It was her sacrifice. — For what? That was not spoken.

Afanasy Ivanovich Vlasyev expostulated vigorously over the impropriety of a Tsaritsa of all Russia kneeling at the feet of a King of Poland, to no avail. Marina only retired, accompanied by the Princess Anne as far as her mother's room. She was alone at last with the ailing Lady Mniszech.

The royal party left then, and Vlasyev found it possible to withdraw as well. Night had fallen long before, but the gaiety continued until the shrill trumpets of the Church of Our Lady across the Great Market Place had sounded the hour of two. All evening, talk was of little but Marina and Dimitry, but none of the suspicion and distrust of former days was voiced. Speeches were made, improvised (or prepared) poetry was recited, and the friendship of Poles and Russians exalted and sung. To believe them, as Paul Pierling has put it, the Wawel was fraternizing with the Kremlin, and the Golden Age had arrived for the Slavs. But can myth become reality?

That question arose the very next day after the wedding. Vlasyev was again received in the royal castle, this time in public audience, to hear Sapieha, as Great Chancellor of Lithuania, express the King's content over Dimitry's accession to the throne of his forefathers, and his auguries for close friendship between the countries. He also professed the King's interest in Dimitry's projects for war against the Turks. Then he handed a letter to Vlasyev for transmittal to Dimitry. Vlasyev glanced at it, saw that in place of "Tsar" it read only "Lord and Great Prince of Moscow," and refused to accept it. Appeal was made to a group of senators, but they stood firm in refusing to accord any other title to Dimitry. Vlasyev was equally firm. And there the matter rested. It would come up again shortly.

Of the three diplomatic representatives at the wedding, Rangoni had his usual views and the Venetian, Alvisio Foscarini, offered little comment — perhaps because he was one of Venice's less noteworthy diplomats. The Florentine, Rodrigo Alidosi of Castel del Rio, however, had come to Kraków also to represent the Grand-duke Ferdinand at Sigismund's marriage, to be held in December.[7] Ferdinand was a good businessman, had built up commerce in Florence, and by complete toleration of Jews and Protestants had given his port of Leghorn a new life. In seeking to broaden his commerce, Ferdinand had learned about Dimitry. Through the efforts of Alidosi he wanted to learn more. Mniszech was chosen as the means to learn, and, now that Dimitry was crowned and married (by proxy, but still married), Alidosi pressed Pan George for commercial privileges in Muscovy. Pan George assured him (for a price?) of his aid, and of certain success.

It was not only here, however, that Pan George was the hinge on which matters swung, or could swing, easily. The Pope himself had approved the marriage which was to take a Catholic Pole to be Tsaritsa of Muscovy. Toward this end he relied largely on Bernard Cardinal Maciejowski, and the latter, in response to an inquiry, wrote a sterling *apologia* for cousin George Mniszech. This had been as long before as the first week in September.

Mniszech was already known in the Vatican as a pillar of the Church. But he had also been a pillar of Dimitry. A little Vatican strengthening for that pillar would be convenient, and so the word was passed from Mniszech through the Cardinal to Rome. Dimitry was conspicuously, and in all truth, the favorite of capricious Fortune (or Providence). He had been crowned Tsar. He had been married to Marina, as he had wanted. A Papal benediction, the Cardinal claimed, was now appropriate. Only God in His infinite wisdom could have brought all these things about.

While this formality was being studied on the banks of the Tiber, opposition to Dimitry on the banks of the Moskva was still as indefatigable as it was now covert. Even among Vlasyev's entourage there was an informer — more appropriately, an agent of the Opposition. Somehow, through someone, Pan George heard what appeared to him to be a factual story of improper relations between Dimitry and the daughter of the late Tsar Boris. In a state of mind between anger and fear, he wrote to Dimitry on Christmas Day stating that "it is known that the daughter of Boris is living with you," and begging him "to take the advice of those who are devoted to you, and send her away . . . People lose respect for their princes on the slightest of grounds." The results of this letter have already been noted.

What Pan George had heard was a preface only. The scene of the machinations of Prince Vasily Shuysky and his clique had been extended to Kraków.

Why?

In Moscow the people all but worshiped their new sovereign, with his youth, his enthusiasm, and his good deeds. Dimitry, the "good Tsar" Dimitry, was moving to help them. There was activity. There was work. Perhaps the Tsar threw money to the winds, with objections from the boyars, but the people knew little of this, and what little they knew they did not quite understand. Cruelty, persecution, exile, unjust laws, and all the unhappy concomitants of the rule of Ivan and Boris were gone, so far as they could see. Rumors had always existed in Moscow. By no means all of them had to be believed. In fact, the people seem to have paid no attention at all to anything brought up against Dimitry.

Therefore the scope of Shuysky's poisonous core of hostility had to be broadened. Where the cabal could find little following, as in Moscow, there would be little activity. But where fresh anti-Dimitry following could be found, there agents could be planted.

The thicket of normal Polish intrigue was certainly worth flushing out for collaborators. No Muscovite in Dimitry's confidence revealed, or perhaps even knew, this. His Polish Secretary, John Buczyński, however, had a keen nose for political odors. Moscow had a definite smell, detected by Buczyński, and it was not a pleasant one. He suddenly decided that he should apply his nose to the atmosphere of Kraków. Was there a similar odor there?

Before the year was out, John Buczyński sought and got permission from Dimitry to go west and join Ambassador Vlasyev.[8] Covering the distance quickly, almost alone and with the help of post-horses, he arrived in Kraków about ten days after Pan George had sent his letter to Dimitry. With two hundred thousand zloty in gold in his saddlebags for Pan George, Buczyński was triply welcome in the Mniszech mansion on the Great Market Place.

As a further mask for his real objective, the secretary also brought specific instructions for Pan George regarding the proper etiquette for Marina as Tsaritsa of all Russia. Since Dimitry's own experience in such matters was necessarily limited, it may be suspected that the court officials in the Kremlin drew up the list. Perhaps the most significant detail was the command that she wear her hair Russian style. Outward appearance was always important to Moscow. Beyond this it was a mere matter of routine: a suitable escort at all times, only her immediate family to dine at the same table with her, and so on.

Some other representative could have handled these matters connected with Pan George's solvency and Marina's way-of-life, obviously. Buczyński simply attended to them first, and then began to look into the activities of the Polish fifth-column of the anti-Dimitry cabal. A little investigation showed that they were even more serious than he had imagined.

From what Buczyński could uncover, a powerful group of boyars was slowly forming a conspiracy to get rid of Dimitry. It was not yet formally organized. The real leaders could be suspected but not precisely identified. Nevertheless, the group was already dangerously active. For the time being its weapon was the anonymous report.

The story of Dimitry and Ksenia was possibly their first shot.[9]

Less specific were continuous rumors of improper conduct in general, and of fickleness in policy. And there were secret messages, which Buczyński did not describe further, sent out by traitors within the Kremlin itself. The traitors were little people, petty clerks, in the employ of magnates who remained unidentified. Regrettably, Dimitry himself added fuel to the fire spreading through the underbrush.

On their way back from Kraków to Sambor the year before, Pan George had presented Dimitry with a grandiloquent title. Dimitry now availed himself of it, brought it up to date with a modification or two, and solemnly used it to open his letter of September 5, given to Vlasyev to deliver personally, in which he informed Sigismund officially of his coronation. Poland knew nothing of Mniszech's contribution of "Emperor," which Dimitry altered to "Caesar," and was aghast.

Emperor, or Caesar, was a sacred name there in 1605. Only one Emperor was recognized, the head of the Holy Roman Empire, and he bore his unique honor by grace of the Pope, or at least of the Church. It was sacrilege for Dimitry to assume such distinction. Indeed, Poland had not yet recognized even the title "Tsar," which Ivan the Dread had instituted as a custom in Muscovy, but without benefit (naturally!) of a Papal blessing. (That it was authorized by the Patriarch of Constantinople did not count, in Poland.) As for "Invictissimus," it was blasphemous. Only God was "Undefeated" — particularly in the superlative degree.

The matter reached dangerous proportions when the Palatine of Poznań discovered in Dimitry's title an insult to the King of Poland, who had befriended him, and went so far as to call on the Muscovites to "unmask" Dimitry before the world. Buczyński looked into the Palatine's call further, only to find that two Muscovites, brothers, had reported to Borsza, Dimitry's former cavalry captain now back in Poland, that the Tsar was reputed to be "false" in Moscow, and that a monster plot was being prepared against him. Buczyński suggested that Borsza be invited back to Moscow, to explain.

While this was going on, another envoy arrived from Dimitry, this time an obscure court-attendant named Ivan Bezobrazov. Bez-obrazov was sent to request official passes for an embassy from Moscow to attend the 1606 session of the Polish Diet, although apparently without specifying why Dimitry wanted to be represented there. Bezobrazov had been recommended to Dimitry, it seemed, by reliable counsellors. But he arrived in Poland with the documents and voice of a diplomat and the heart and tongue of a serpent.

Once the formalities were over, this envoy sought out Leo Sapieha, tested him, and when he thought it safe informed him that he was an agent of the Shuysky and Golitsyn families (both of which had been befriended by Dimitry). These descendants of Rurik wanted it known that King Sigismund had sent them a vile impostor for Tsar, who was cruel, debauched, and a spendthrift to boot, unfit to occupy the throne. They looked for help to rid themselves of this ruffian, and in the event they got it would gladly offer the throne to Sigismund's son, Wladislaus.

Sigismund himself had been remarried in the meantime. The Sunday after Marina's wedding he had ridden out of Kraków to welcome his bride, the Archduchess Constance. Marina had then gracefully retired to a neighboring castle to avoid problems of etiquette, and the wedding had been celebrated on Sunday, December 11. It was characterized by preposterous fanfare, Gargantuan feasting, carousing, and unblushing display.

Thus happily married again, Sigismund's heart was touched by Bezobrazov's message as soon as he heard it. He was as devoted to Wladislaus as Boris had been to young Fyodor, and here indeed was a better way to unite Russia and Poland than through a mere alliance with Dimitry. The Muscovite Empire wanted a Polish King to rule it as well! But perhaps it would be better for Sigismund himself to accept the Crown of Monomakh and only associate the Prince with him until he was of age . . .

However, the uniting of the two peoples would present grave problems, largely financial. Sigismund decided to approach the Pope on the subject. It was unwise, as well as contrary to Sigismund's nature, to hurry. Oddly, judging by a letter he wrote a few years later, it does not seem to have occurred to Sigismund that Shuysky and Golitsyn, being faithless to Dimitry, might be faithless to him as well, or might have wanted Wladislaus because he was only a boy, whom *they* could rule.

Obviously, the exact details of what went on are not known. Yet it is clear that Sigismund once more began to shift and hesitate with regard to Moscow. He is said to have passed word to Bezobrazov that he was sorry to have been duped by Dimitry, that he would take no vital steps for the time being, and that he would trust in Providence — nothing more. Thereupon Bezobrazov, having completed his treachery, re-assumed his rôle of envoy, and refused to accept a royal letter addressed to his master, Dimitry, because it did not include the Tsar's correct title! Clearly, not only in Moscow did mephitic odors rise from the body politic.[10]

This refusal did not disturb Sigismund in the slightest. On November 14, the day Vlasyev was presented to him, he had written to the Bishop of Varmia stating that the coming meeting of the Diet should set up bases for a pact of amity with Muscovy. Nothing Bezobrazov said changed this. He chose two ambassadors to accompany Marina, in what might seem like an excess of courtesy, but they were primarily to bring up with Dimitry the matter of the cession of Muscovite territories to Poland as specified in the marriage contracts of May 24 and June 12, 1604. But this was all part of a plan already worked out before the apparition of Bezobrazov.

The royal instructions to the two ambassadors were countersigned by Leo Sapieha on February 6, 1606. Expediently, they contained nothing specific about the real estate. The ambassadors were merely to suggest that Dimitry send envoys to Kraków to enter into negotiations. In that city, Sigismund expected to intervene personally, for the greatest possible amplification of the Republic's domain.

Sigismund's aim was not expressed in so many words. Yet its compass was as evident as if it were. In 1600 he had sent an embassy to Boris with proposals which amounted to an effort to swallow as much of Muscovy as he could get, and the virtual reduction

of the "Grand-duchy" to the state of the Grand-duchy of Lithuania
— already ingested whole.

Boris's boyars had foiled these plans completely. But with Dimitry on the throne, Sigismund had not only returned to his previous
rapacity, but had sharpened it considerably. Dimitry had suggested an alliance against the Ottoman Turks. Sigismund would
agree to this, in principle. The particulars would require Dimitry
to permit his Polish troops to march across Russia to Finland, to
feed and supply them with money and munitions on the way, and
to help Sigismund regain his father's Swedish throne. This accomplished, Sigismund would receive Dimitry's envoys in the great
palace in Stockholm, and agree to permit Dimitry to take a secondary rôle in the crusade which Dimitry himself had proposed. It was
a glorious plan. But the manner of its implementation was typical
of Sigismund's mentality, which was far from glorious.

Realizing that Dimitry would probably haggle over the territorial cessions to Poland, the King was quite ready to yield a point or
two, so long as he got certain key towns. The rest could wait.
Then, Dimitry's titles offered another point of discussion. Sigismund considered them impudent, but was glad to add them to the
other kinds of grist he was grinding. On that point, the ambassadors were to remonstrate politely, once again mention the King's
generosity, and raise Dimitry's hopes that something would be
done. Then, as in the case of the desired expansion of Polish territory, Dimitry could send envoys to Kraków. The matter would be
"taken under advisement," as we say today, at a future meeting of
the Diet.

At the same time, a strange undercurrent was stirring beneath
the apparently placid waters of the Republic's political life. The
elected King, Sigismund, had never been popular. His heart all
too visibly lay in Sweden, and the assumption of the royal title
there by his uncle Charles had provoked him into even more open
demonstration of interest. Coupled with this was his marriage to
a second (unpopular) Habsburg, along with an attitude toward
the Catholic Church which reminded the Poles of the late unla-
mented fanatic, Philip II of Spain. This religious attitude of

course made it impossible for Sigismund to be tolerant of his Protestant subjects, not to mention the considerable number of Orthodox who had refused to become "Uniates" and recognize the Pope.

In contrast to Sigismund's unpopularity, reports of the activities of the young Tsar were pouring across the border. Dimitry had caught the public fancy in Poland for a number of reasons already outlined. Now that he had been crowned, his appeal grew enormously in certain circles. He was active, well-liked in his own country, tolerant as to religion, a born leader, and an apostle of education and progress. The contrast was as between the fiery sun and the cold moon.

This "sun" had already attracted the attention of the even more fiery Palatine of Kraków, Nicholas Zebrzydowski. Then, since Dimitry's coronation, the almost ferocious Stadnicki trio was scaldingly tempted into action. And before long a group was formed which was determined to dethrone Sigismund and call for the election of a new King. And who was to be chosen? Who else but Dimitry Ivanovich, by whatever title he chose to call himself, Lord of Muscovy.

This covert revolt against Sigismund found emissaries ready to hazard a trip to Moscow and an audience with Dimitry. What precisely was said and done is not recorded, but the upshot of it all was a special envoy from Dimitry to Mniszech — the trusted secretary named Stanislas Słoński.

Słoński was sent to Poland about September 13, at the same time as Vlasyev, as has been mentioned, with instructions to talk to representatives of the discontented group, which by then included Mniszech. Nothing was to be written, and to cover up Słoński's real mission, he was told to attend the royal audience with Vlasyev. It is known that he protested to the King on the sensitive subject of Dimitry's title, but at the same time showed willingness to carry out the King's wishes regarding his cousin, Gustav, the "illegitimate" though legalized son of Sigismund's father's elder half-brother who had gone to Moscow on Boris Godunov's invitation. After the audience, Słoński parted with Vlasyev and took off on his own. Obscure as his later activities have remained, it is reasonably certain that he had a purse of a hundred thousand zlotys available for the embryonic Dimitry-for-King league.

Despite this, it is abundantly clear that at no time did Dimitry involve himself in so shady and venemous a plot as the one which sent Bezobrazov to Kraków. Presumably Dimitry would have accepted the Polish crown if it were made available, but would make no moves of his own in that direction. Consequently a mantle of silence soon covered the whole matter. It was not lifted for many months.

During these weeks of hidden machinations, Afanasy Ivanovich Vlasyev had alternated between letter-writing, patience and self-control, and expostulation. After Sigismund's wedding he had taken off for Słonim, a convenient town in the heart of White Russia. It was there that he had agreed to wait for Pan George and the Tsaritsa Marina.

When a reasonable time had passed and nothing had happened, he wrote to Dimitry that he was "sick at heart and soul because nothing was done as stipulated" between Pan George and himself, and as had been communicated to "His Caesarian Majesty," Dimitry. He was not only worried by the thought that he himself might suffer for it, but also distressed over the long time the boyars and court-attendants were being forced to wait at the border. They were invited, indeed commanded, to welcome Marina on her entry into Muscovy, and all they were doing was "eating up" everything, just feeding their horses and cooling their heels.

Vlasyev's plaint led to further messages from Dimitry, both to himself and to Pan George. To the latter the Tsar sent what amounted to a reproof, even to his Lady, the Tsaritsa, who had not bothered to write him of late. But between delays in the post and other matters, Vlasyev finally decided to go to Sambor himself and try to stir up some activity. A ride of four hundred miles through the snow followed. But by then, whether it was Vlasyev or perhaps Buczyński, or some other kind of prod, Pan George began at last to move toward suspension of inactivity.

On his behalf it may be said that he had other reasons than money and the rumors about his son-in-law's behavior for his endless delaying tactics. Marina was a Catholic. She was going to a schismatic country. Her religion must be protected, and with it the salvation of her soul. Pan George would not leave Sambor until he was certain that Rome would satisfy his inquiries regarding his daughter and his Church.

Finally, after more than three months of preparation, Pan George decided that the imperial cavalcade could set out. Yet by a strange coincidence he chose to leave on Thursday, March 2, 1606, the very day on which the Holy Office in Rome gave a laconic and negative reply to the request for dispensations which Dimitry had long since made regarding Marina's religion. This refusal would raise grave problems in Moscow.

Had Mniszech, Rangoni and Dimitry known of this added complication, Vlasyev might have had many another day to wait before leaving. But only Dimitry knew that he had raised these questions. And Pan George had a feeling that everything would turn out all right.

CHAPTER 12

PANDORA'S BOX

S AINT PAUL STOOD in the midst of the Areopagus and told the people of Athens that they were too superstitious in all things.[1] The charge could well have been made against the people of Moscow in 1605, and for many years before and after.

Had the Patriarch of Moscow denounced their fanaticism it is possible that some might have listened. Even the Tsar might have had some effect if he had addressed all Moscow from the Place of the Skull, as Ivan the Dread had done many years before. But no-one took the trouble to do this. The Patriarch protected the immobility of the Church, the Princes declaimed in private, mostly, on the preservation of the old order. And Dimitry, without explanation, embarked on a course of flaunting the fetishes which custom and ignorance had sanctified. Unrest began to mar a newborn confidence before it really took form.

Dimitry, intensely occupied with establishing his government, knew little or nothing about this. Or, if he knew, perhaps he felt that it was a passing condition. Certainly, the people showed enormous affection for him. Why should he doubt their sincerity? He had graver problems to face.

These problems, as Dimitry saw them, centered on *Poland,* which included Lithuania. Lithuania had long been an enemy of Moscow, despite repeated intermarriages between the ruling dynasty of Russia and the House of Gedimin. But with Lithuania incorporated in the Polish Republic, the Lithuanian enmity had been transformed into enmity for Poland, especially since the days of King Stephen Báthory. No Muscovite could be expected to deal fairly with such an enemy, any more than King Sigismund could be expected to show brotherly affection for Muscovy. As has already been mentioned, it was with some difficulty that a treaty had been drawn up between the two rival "empires" in the days of Boris Godunov.

Poland had put Dimitry on the throne, as the Poles saw it, and in repayment Dimitry had promised a great deal to Poland. But from Dimitry's point of view, the Poles had largely deserted him in his hour of need, their King had vacillated, and it was the Cossacks (rebels against Poland) and certain Muscovite elements which had really made his triumphal entry into Moscow possible. This could be expected to temper Dimitry's enthusiasm for Poland. Nevertheless, he set out to fulfil his promises so far as was at the moment feasible, subject to delays which everyone acquainted with the situation — and this included even King Sigismund — recognized as necessary.

The first disillusionment may have come as early as the arrival of Prince Adam Vishnevetsky in Moscow, on July 30, nine days after Dimitry's coronation.[2] Judging by the date, the Tsar's original protector and sponsor started for Moscow, possibly from his estates on the Russian side of the Dnyeper, as soon as he heard of Dimitry's arrival at the capital, and of his coronation. However it was, Prince Adam arrived, accompanied by a retinue which included his Orthodox clergy. Prince Adam had always been a pillar of Orthodoxy.

What was the consternation of Prince and priests alike, however, when they were refused admission to the Muscovite churches! They did not wear the *skufyá*, a skull-cap of special form used in Russia, and they came with Polish chanters. After argument, and with the exercise of some sartorial ingenuity, this matter was settled. They were admitted. But soon it was discovered that their *zucchettos* (another kind of skull-cap) were not bordered properly, and the singers chanted in heterodox fashion. The entire party was accused of Latinism, and the Patriarch was summoned.

Ignaty had been suspected of Latinism himself, but his behavior on this occasion must have cleared his name. He pronounced anathema against the offending priests, while calling for the imprisonment of a few who were suspected of attempting to perform "heretical" services in an Orthodox church. Prince Adam, after superhuman efforts, poured the oil of harmony on the troubled waters, while the Latin priests denounced the peacemaker as a "schismatic!" The clergy was as usual ready to be shocked.

Although Prince Adam was to have stayed in Moscow until Christmas, it is not certain that he did. Neither is it certain that he obtained all the remunerations and favors which he evidently expected. He is, in fact, said to have left Russia somewhat disappointed, yet the richer for some sort of chicanery at the expense of Sophronius, the Orthodox Patriarch of Jerusalem.

The silly business is of interest only because it brought the blessing of the Patriarch on the head of Dimitry, whose Orthodoxy was so persistently in doubt. Although in fact the new Tsar paid lip-service to Catholicism and Orthodoxy and perhaps Unitarianism, indiscriminately, his generosity at least to the first two hinted that there was some sort of sincerity behind it all.

One instance of this is worth recounting. When the Orthodox community of Lvov wrote him asking for a gift to help them finish a new church, Dimitry came to their aid in some obscure way. King Sigismund was involved, and there is evidence that the representatives of the Orthodox group were in danger of arrest, accused of attacking Catholics. Whatever happened, it is known that the church in Lvov was built and that the incident was closed more or less amicably. Thus Dimitry gained not a little Orthodox backing.

Indeed, during the first months after his coronation Dimitry maintained a remarkable state of calm in religious matters in Moscow. By holding the Jesuits at arm's length, while amusing himself with young people of various sects and at the same time keeping up relations with the zealous Patriarch, Dimitry found a middle path which irritated only such die-hards and convinced enemies as the Shuyskys and a handful of Orthodox clergy of what we should today call "the extreme right." The Jesuits happily bided their time.

They were not alone in this attitude. In Poland, a Corfiote theologian by the name of Peter Arcudius, who had gone to Moscow with Leo Sapieha at the instance of Pope Clement VIII, saw great possibilities of reuniting the Eastern and Western Churches through tact, patience, and a willingness to see what was basically alike instead of what was superficially different. Basing his outspoken opinion on Dimitry's success in Russia, Arcudius showed a good grasp of the situation from the Catholic point of view. But the tragic aspect of the situation lay in the fact that Orthodox "impatience" was unable to see that a situation even existed. To their Orthodox minds, the impatient priests and prelates found little choice betw ɯ the Pope and the Sultan. What choice there was possibly was on the Sultan's side.

On that point, however, Dimitry rose to ennobled heights of vision. To crown his reign with the halo of fame, he looked out across the boundless flat expanse of the Christendom he knew, divided into many and quarreling units, and glimpsed some sort of order which could stand before, resist, and in the end push back the anti-Christian threat summed up in the name, *The Turk*. It was a remarkably penetrating view for the time, and a critical one, for the Turk threatened the destruction of the "European way of life" as Dimitry knew it.

But if the Tsar thought he saw a way to bring about the beginnings of religious tolerance through joint action against the Moslems, he was doomed to disappointment. The flaw in his reasoning was due to the difficulty of a temperament predisposed to tolerance, forgiveness, and loving one's neighbor, in understanding the effects of ineradicable dogmatism. The trumpets of reason will not make such walls "fall down flat." [3]

Word of Dimitry's impending marriage (the one celebrated by the Tsar in person, confirming the earlier ceremony by proxy), soon spread through the land. It was pounced upon post-haste by the sulkily dissatisfied faction — not yet really aroused to defiance by the Shuysky clan. If Dimitry had been accused before of lewd harlotry in the Kremlin, now he was known to be planning something indescribably worse. He was bringing a Pole and a Catholic to rule over Holy Moscow; the Mecca, Medina, Jerusalem and Damascus of Orthodoxy, with the City of Constantine thrown in for good measure.

Fanaticism broke out again. And the love which the ordinary people bore for the new Tsar was troubled by the ceaseless vituperation of monks, and priests, and disaffected boyars, and other Orthodox souls. Now loud, now soft, the chatter knew no end.

In the midst of this ferment of holy hatred, envoys began arriving from Poland — the Abbé Luigi Pratissoli from the Papal Nuncio, the Starosta Alexander Gosiewski from the King. Pratissoli, on several counts, was the lesser evil. Arriving in Moscow during the second week in October, his stay was as inconspicuous as his achievements are obscure. Perhaps he only intended to reconnoitre, and to encourage Dimitry in his friendship for Poland and loyalty to the Catholic Church. If this was the case, he succeeded admirably. The Jesuit fathers were overjoyed at the treatment he received from Dimitry.

Gosiewski followed close upon his heels. Arriving a day or two after October 14/24, he was welcomed with suitable ostentation as a royal ambassador. With him he brought Sigismund's congratulations and the usual gifts: horses, a golden chain, and a great cup, presumably at least of silver-gilt. The chronological nearness of the two arrivals, and the almost furtive character of Pratissoli's visit, led to mistaken conjectures that he was an envoy from the Pope — precisely the impression which up to that time had been studiously avoided. In a city as full of rumor-mongers as Moscow then was, however, any tale could gain credence.

Gosiewski was accorded an audience as quickly as the stiff formality of the Kremlin would permit. According to Russian sources, the audience was held secretly (for reasons already mentioned), yet diplomatic decorum had to be preserved. In any case, despite the secrecy, a Russian translation of Gosiewski's speech to the Tsar has been preserved.[4] The existence of this document, granted the impossibility of concealing anything, hints that Moscow knew a good bit about what went on before long.

Regrettably, Gosiewski was a soldier, not a diplomat. After a minimum of protocolary salutations and good wishes, he burst into a relation of the preposterous story of Boris Godunov in England, after which he turned straight to the matter of Sigismund's uncle, Duke Charles of Södermanland, who had assumed the title of King of Sweden the year before. As already intimated, Sigismund wanted help from Dimitry in regaining his rightful kingdom — a kingdom which had legally dethroned him and chosen Charles in his place. He also wanted Dimitry to seize and send to him any ambassadors who might visit Moscow on behalf of the "usurper" Charles.

A further matter concerning "his" kingdom of Sweden was the presence in Uglich of Gustav, the one-time suitor for the hand of Ksenia Godunov. Gustav had always been treated in Muscovy as of the blood royal. Dimitry was asked to cease this practice. It was also demanded that all Polish mercenary troops in Muscovy be returned to Poland, and that the Poles receive privileges, especially in Smolensk. And there were other details.

A large, if not the greater, portion of this, Dimitry was ready and willing to concede. On the subject of Sweden, however, he was determined to sell his help at a price. He let it be known that he would side with Sigismund in the struggle for power, but only as Emperor (or Caesar) of Russia. Ever since the spontaneous donation of that title to him by Mniszech, Dimitry had apparently been carefully considering the matter. He had now come to the decision to make it the pivot of his diplomacy vis-à-vis the Polish Republic.

The subject was far from a new one in Russia. In ancient times, the Great Prince of Moscow had been considered by the horde of other princes of the blood of Rurik more or less as the *primus inter pares* of the ruling class, somewhat as the Patriarch of Constantinople was (and is) the first among equals among the Eastern Patriarchs. But because of the way he had been bullied as a child Ivan IV had made up his mind before he was seventeen to set himself aside and above all the others.

Utilizing historical distortion, not for the last time in Russian history, Ivan asserted that he was not only the direct and senior descendant of Rurik, but also the direct heir of the Roman Emperor Augustus Caesar. Although his logic was good, his history was bad. But that did not keep him from adopting the title *Tsar*, which had been the Slavic name for the Byzantine Emperor for some five centuries, as well as the title of the ancient emperors of Bulgaria. To this, Ivan added, quite gratuitously, the title *Auto-crat*, to show that he was no longer dependent on the Khan of the Golden Horde for permission to rule.

It is true that Ivan's grandfather had occasionally used these titles, largely at the suggestion of his imperial and imperious wife. But it was Ivan IV who made them part of the official style of the ruler of "all Russia." The importance of his act lay in the fact that he assumed and proclaimed these titles himself. Other, lesser, monarchs such as the Polish King received their titles from the elected Holy Roman Emperor or the Pope. As a modern historian has aptly put it, "Russia's Caesar had chosen and elevated himself." [5]

Dimitry, in his own belief the son of Ivan, not only adopted Ivan's attitude, but perhaps improved on it. Ivan had never been called Tsar by the Poles, and neither had Fyodor or Boris. England had, perhaps with some amusement, extended all the solemn honorifics desired by the Muscovite rulers. Queen Elizabeth, indeed, had once caustically intimated that she was as great a monarch as anybody and was quite content to be merely Queen of England, France and Ireland, and Defender of the Faith, at least part of which must have sounded rather empty to some ears. But the hint did no good, so the ambassadors from London all rolled out the twenty-five required titles whenever the Tsar was addressed. [6] This brought dignity to the person and position of the Russian ruler. And Dimitry saw his chance to bring glory both to Russia and to himself by forcing the issue of the imperial title on the reluctant King of Poland, who included the title of Grand-duke of Russia in his own official style, along with the empty flourish of "King of the Swedes, Goths and Wends."

Nevertheless, all seemed reasonably amicable for the moment. Dimitry made no great issue of the titles with Gosiewski, but invited him to what must remain one of the most extraordinary din-

ners ever held in the Kremlin. The untouchable Emperor and
Great Prince of the hieratic Orthodox realm of Muscovy sat down
to eat with the Ambassador of the King of Poland — unheard-of! —
accompanied by the Envoy of the Papal Nuncio in Poland, and
two Jesuit priests. It is small wonder that the Patriarch of Moscow
before long had to exercise restraint on a brace of Orthodox
bishops.

Gosiewski left for Poland on October 27, which was equivalent
to November 6 on the Polish non-Orthodox calendar. He took
with him letters from Father Nicholas Czyrzowski, with details of
life in Moscow and expressions of the most hopeful piety. He also
possibly carried the conviction that he had won out in the matter
of titles, if nothing else.

Dimitry, however, lost little time in returning to the attack.
Less than a month after giving Vlasyev properly addressed letters
to King Sigismund, he had occasion to write that monarch again.
George, King of Kartlia in the Caucasus, hearing that Dimitry was
the new Tsar, sent congratulations, along with a message asking for
protection. He was in danger of getting caught in the current
struggle between the autocrats of Turkey and Iran. Dimitry took
this to mean that King George offered himself and his kingdom to
Muscovy to rule, and he availed himself of the opportunity to let
Sigismund know of this important development in connection
with his anti-Turkish project. Roguishly, in retaliation for Sigismund's hauteur, he cut that eminence's style down to a mere *Lord
Sigismund III, King of Poland* — nothing else. Three weeks later,
in a better humor, he returned to the usual courtesies.

At about the same time, although it is impossible to establish the
date, Dimitry circulated copies of an epistle he apparently proposed to send to the King of Sweden, that strict, just and honest
uncle of Sigismund whose kingdom but not whose character Sigismund envied. It was written in Latin, and addressed to "Charles,
Duke of Södermanland," and it seems to hide an almost boyish
prank under its formal severity, its virtual impertinence. Yet it is
quite obvious that Dimitry was again playing for his own title, and
that he had no intention of signing and posting the letter until he

had been addressed as Emperor (or Caesar) by "interested" parties such as King Sigismund and Pope Paul V.[7]

The letter is worth a glance, for Dimitry himself shines clearly through the Latin into which it was translated. In the first place, all the verbal pageantry with which he opens other correspondence is missing. He begins, quite simply, "We, the Most Unconquered and Most Serene Monarch Dimitry make known . . . our happy coronation," and so on. Then he accuses Charles of being an enemy to his good friend, the King of Poland and Sweden, and demands that he restore Sweden to the good friend. Failing that, Dimitry has decided to help Sigismund retake Sweden by force. After these points are made clear with excess verbosity, he concludes that God Himself will come to their aid — his and Sigismund's — for He takes care of His Kings and Princes. In short, between God and Dimitry, Duke Charles will be lost. It is obviously difficult to believe that this furbelow of Latinity was ever intended to be sent. Perhaps neither Sigismund nor Pope Paul, both of whom got copies, believed it was serious, either.

By this time, Dimitry had decided to bring the Shuysky princes back from exile, and to confer favors on other illustrious families which had suffered disgrace before his own arrival in Moscow. The restoration of these super-eminences to their kaftaned prerogatives almost inevitably foreshadowed disloyalties, and a tangle of difficulties. Their minds were as rigid as their gold-embroidered tunics whose decorative pearls and rough-cut precious stones matched the hard, cold nuggets of selfish thoughts within them. Dimitry's youth and ambition had neither the perspicacity nor the suspicion needed to see behind the gray-blue and gray-green princely eyes, always lowered in reverence and treachery before his open gaze.

But while the Shuyskys held their peace, at least in Dimitry's presence, two members of the clergy rose in wrath when the Tsar officially informed his Council of his intention to marry Marina, and demanded their consent. Hermogen, Metropolitan of Kazan, and Iosif, Bishop of Kolomna, declared that it would be necessary to rebaptize the bride according to Orthodox rites first. Dimitry, whatever his thoughts in the matter, submitted that it was a purely religious question and left it in the hands of the Patriarch, Ignaty. Ignaty, probably sensing Dimitry's private thoughts, argued the Council into approving the marriage without rebaptism, but the more refractory members, lay as well as clergy, were openly scandalized.

This dispute between the Tsar and his Council was followed by another unpleasantness. Dimitry's patent preparations for war disturbed the tranquillity of the entire realm. It was not just that it was "proclaimed from the belfries" that the Tatars were to be subjected once and for all, which would not be easy. The Swedes were also to be put to flight.

As for the former, in evidence of a planned campaign Dimitry sent an envoy to Ghazi Giray, Crimean Khan, demanding the refund of all the tribute which had been paid by "his ancestors" to the Khans back to the days of Aleksandr Nevsky. To make the point clear, the envoy was commanded to show Ghazi a fur, all the hair of which had been shaved off. "If you refuse," the envoy intimated, "you and your people will be left as bald as this skin." The Khan, nicknamed "The Storm" by the Turks, detained the envoy, permanently.

Dimitry next sent incredible quantities of munitions to Yelets, one of the chief Muscovite border fortresses to the south. By January, 1606 it was estimated that supplies and matériel in general collected at Yelets would be enough for three hundred thousand men, though the authority for this statement is not entirely without suspicion of error.

Not content with badgering the Tatars, Dimitry also sent troops to Ivangorod, the fort built by Ivan III across the river from Swedish-held Narva. Word of this move reached Pan George Mniszech, probably by way of the loquacious merchants of Gdańsk, who included advice on the subject in his long admonitory letter of December 25, 1605. He warned Dimitry not to make any moves which might upset Sigismund's Swedish plans.

Mniszech's advice reflects an increasing fussiness which at that time was not altogether unexplainable. By then the overthrow of

Dimitry spelled disaster for Pan George, and even baseless gossip worried him. Still, it is hard to see that Dimitry's reinforcement of the Russian garrison at Ivangorod could embarrass King Sigismund in any way. The Swedes had been crushed by Sigismund's generals in a battle near Riga as long before as September.

Dimitry's move, for all Pan George's concern, was surely for his own benefit, without thought of Sigismund. Ivangorod was far from the field of Polish interests, but it was precisely where Muscovy almost touched the Baltic Sea. If Narva, across a narrow river, could be captured, Muscovy would have a commercial outlet to the West which had been sought for more than a century, and which would not be hers for another hundred years. Nevertheless, in the face of the opposition of many boyars, and of Pan George, Dimitry rested. It was reserved for Peter called the Great to open the "Window on the Baltic" — at the site now called Leningrad.

The new King of the Swedes, Goths and Wends, Charles IX, soon after these events, himself sent an ambassador to Moscow, one Frederick Tatz. Precisely why he was sent cannot be determined, but among the possible reasons these may be suggested: It would be proper to congratulate a new monarch on his accession; Charles had received what seemed to be irrefutable evidence that Dimitry could not be "genuine," and wanted to explore the matter himself; and Dimitry's responsibility in the matter of the cheeky letter, whether Charles got it or not, ought to be investigated. In the long run, however, it is only known that Tatz reached Moscow and was jailed there by order of Dimitry. Even though there was some threat of sending him to Poland, he was still under arrest in the summer of 1606. It is unlikely that he ever was turned over to the Poles.

Prince Vasily Shuysky meanwhile directly profited by these doings, or adapted them to his objectives. The whispering campaign began afresh, although more surreptitiously. It was the old, old story of Dimitry not being the son of Ivan the Dread, but an impostor and a renegade monk, who surrounded himself in the Palace with foreigners and heretics, loading them with gifts, and who not only did not protect national cutoms, but even insulted the

Orthodox Church. In addition, he was going to marry a heretic
Pole, and even engage in a war which, if it were unsuccessful,
would be calamitous for Moscow.

These of course were charges well calculated to create a maximum of discontent among the people in general. An impostor, an
unfrocked monk, a heretic, a xenophile, a destroyer of national
customs and even of the Church — all these were causes for superstitious mutinies and antagonism in general. The marriage with a
Catholic Pole was all that was needed to put the seal of "Enough!"
to the whole indictment. Prince Shuysky was not a very brave man
on the battlefield, but he was a master-hand at intrigue and trouble-
making.

December passed fairly quietly. A group of Cossacks of the Don
arrived with a captured Turkish *bashi* (captain). The Turks had
ravaged Cossack lands, and punishment was expected of Dimitry.
Shuysky might have made something of this, but Dimitry soon
gave him a better subject. A Pole named Domoracki, who had
come from Poland with Dimitry, was appointed Chief Gentleman
of the Equerry, with the principal assignment of wearing fine
clothes and accompanying the Tsar on his excursions. So far, so
good. But Domoracki was soon joined by a cousin (by marriage)
of Pan George Mniszech named Kazanowski, who came from Poland with youth, good looks and a vast ambition. The chief service
of these two was to provide additional annoyances to the Russians
attached to the Court and further material to Shuysky for his prop-
aganda factory. They were of no real help in an emergency.

An emergency developed when the new year (1606) was but a
week old. Dimitry was in his private apartments one night when a
bold attempt was made on his life. He and two captains of the
guard who were with him at the time had to grab what weapons
they could, and only after a brisk fight in one of the bigger rooms
was the attack warded off. Two or three of the assailants were captured when reinforcements arrived. These were submitted to the
torture, but with true Russian stoicism said they would die sooner
than contribute any information as to the cause or promoters of
the attempt. In the words of Isaac Massa, God indeed protected
Shuysky just then, the brain and the strong arm of all the conspira-

cies. And he added that one of the group was the same Sherefedinov who helped murder Boris's widow and her son, young Tsar Fyodor, presumably for the sake of Dimitry. After that night, Sherefedinov seems to have disappeared from history.

The *attentat* was the first manifestation of Shuysky's return from exile, pardoned by the Tsar whose life he now set himself to destroy. Before long Basmanov reported to Dimitry that there was evidence of treason in the famous Streltsy Guard itself, the eight thousand or so "archers" dedicated to the protection of the Tsar. Some of its members, said Basmanov, openly declared that Dimitry could not be the son of Ivan the Dread.

On hearing this, Grigory Mikulin, head of the Guard and one-time ambassador for Godunov in London,[8] savagely cried: "Permit me, Sire, and I will bite off the heads of these traitors and tear out their entrails with my own teeth."

Thereupon Dimitry decided to turn the disloyal men over to their own company for judgment, much as he had turned the Shuyskys over to the Council of Boyars. Seven reported to have slandered the Tsar were apprehended without the others knowing anything about it. Then early one Sunday morning the entire body was summoned to appear in the palace courtyard, where Dimitry soon came out to meet them. He was accompanied by Mikulin, a few of his bodyguard, some halberdiers, and a handful of dignitaries: Basmanov, Prince Mstislavsky, and one or two of the Nagoys. On his appearance, the entire corps prostrated itself on the ground, Muscovite style, and then remained uncovered to hear what the Tsar had to say.[9]

Dimitry could not repress a laugh. "I would to God," he bawled, "that these bare heads had some brains inside them!" Then he continued, loudly,

> For how long are you going to keep on looking for discord and its unhappy results? Is it not enough for you that the country is gangrened already to the marrow of its bones? Or must it be destroyed in its entirety? After the crimes of the Godunovs, their usurpation of the throne, their tyrannical treatment of the first families of the land, what do you want?
>
> There, in that family, lies the cause of the country's suffering.

But now that God has delivered me from the dangers which surrounded me, and has protected me, you still are not satisfied. You are now looking for excuses for another piece of treachery, and you want to get rid of *me*. What do you accuse me of? Which of you can prove that I am not the son of Tsar Ivan. Let him step out. Right before your eyes I will permit him to strike me down!

When not a man stirred, Dimitry continued:

My mother and all the personages here with me can testify for me. How indeed could anyone have conquered this great empire almost without an army if the justice of his cause had not supported him? Would God have permitted it?

I have exposed my life, not to attain supreme power, but out of pity for you; to free you from the deep misery and outrageous slavery which has been imposed on you by traitors, oppressing the country. Through the inspiration of God, I have accomplished my mission. God's almighty Hand gave me the throne which belonged to me. Why then do you conspire against me? Here I am! Tell me frankly and fearlessly why you do not believe in me.

The streltsy, surprised and ashamed, fell on their knees as one man, bowing their heads to the earth and swearing that they were innocent. They implored the Tsar's clemency. They wept unashamedly. And they begged him to show them the traitors who had so falsely represented them.

Dimitry then commanded Basmanov (where was Mikulin?) to bring forward the seven who had been arrested. "Here are the men," he barked, "who have said that you are plotters, and that you are scheming against your true sovereign and lord." And with that he turned his back on them and led Mstislavsky and the others away.

The streltsy swept forward, snatching the unfortunate seven from their guards. They had been summoned without swords or any other arms, but this did not deter them. With their bare hands they tore arms from their sockets, and ripped fingers from hands. Some of them bit hunks of flesh from the living bodies. One tore an ear off with his teeth and chewed it into small pieces.

At last seven mangled corpses were left lying in the courtyard. A pack of famished wolves could not have left a more horrible sight, but the vindicated streltsy only shook their fists in the air, roaring, "So perish all enemies of the Tsar!"

At this shout Dimitry appeared again. The uproar ceased immediately as he raised his hand to command silence and said again that he was their true Tsar and ordered them back to their barracks. Once more the streltsy fell on their faces, begging the Tsar's mercy. Then they scrambled to their feet and marched off to their billets or homes, their uniforms already stiffening with human blood.

Dimitry, with studied indifference, re-entered the palace. Slowly the courtyard discharged the men and the noise. When all was quiet again, Basmanov sent some of the palace guard with wheelbarrows to pick up the torn bodies and trundle them through the streets of Moscow to an empty place. There the burden was dumped, and left for the ever-present scavenger dogs to devour.

The sight of the wheelbarrows and the tales of what had happened in the palace courtyard frightened Moscow into restless silence. Whispering and rumor-mongering subsided, fitfully. But a handful of fanatics, braving any and all punishment, spread the story that the seven murdered men were guilty of nothing — not even of denying the Tsar's legitimacy. It was not a matter of opinion. Categorically, they were sacrificed to frighten the people of Moscow. No-one asked why. No-one answered. It was merely that those who were paid by Shuysky's cabal would not be silenced.

It was about this time that Dimitry formed a bodyguard of foreign mercenaries for his better protection. There were three companies of them, the first of which was composed of a hundred archers, mostly Swedish and Livonian (Latvian) gentlemen, under the French Captain Jacques Margeret, who has left one of the most reliable accounts of Dimitry's reign. Their uniform was of velvet and gold-cloth and they carried gilded halberds decorated with velvet and silver thread.

The second and third companies, also of one hundred gentlemen each, were halberdiers. The first of these was dressed in violet cloth, trimmed with green velvet, and was under the command of a

Scot whose name seems to have been David Gilbert — reports vary widely — and who had drifted into Russian service under Boris Godunov.[10] The third company, also in violet but with red velvet trimmings, was under the command of Matthew Knutsen, a Dane who had accompanied Prince John on his fateful voyage to Moscow and had remained in Boris's service. All three companies were exceptionally well paid, and the captains also received grants of land and villages, like Polish manorial lords.

The citizens of Moscow regarded these crack-guards with curiosity, and a degree of hostility. Dimitry had retained the usual guard of two or three thousand troops — simple musketeers who attended him on visits outside the Kremlin. Why should he need an additional guard, and why was there so much ceremony about it? Why did the halberdiers go only as far as the gates of the Kremlin, and why did the archers ride with loaded pistols when he visited the various districts of the capital? And then why did he often gallop out of the Kremlin alone, or with only one or two attendants? This was not the way the Tsars of Muscovy behaved. It was all foreign, and undoubtedly heretic. Again, Dimitry gave the Shuyskys and other malcontents the best possible trouble-making material.

These issues bedeviled the restless citizenry of Moscow during the early winter. Yet Dimitry paid no heed and occupied himself with what he considered betterments in the administration and with plans for the greater glory of Muscovy.

With regard to the former, Dimitry wanted to see a change from the Byzantine autocratic form of government to something more like the free and open senate of Poland. To accomplish this, he had to fight the battle both in Council and outside it. That was unavoidable in a state where anarchy was always at work, gaily, under the massive repression of an Ivan or a Boris, like a colony of termites unseen in the substructure of a great wooden palace. To move away from absolute dictatorship has always been difficult.

Although hardly a trace remains of the acts of Dimitry's Council, there are a few surviving records which illustrate his attitude toward the common people and the serfs. Judging by these, he sought to undo much of the rigid control imposed by Boris during the famine years. The peasants had lost their rights and were virtually bound to the soil. Serfdom had made its ugly appearance. Dimitry began to modify the laws, but he still had to reckon with the proprietors. To abolish serfdom in 1605 by a stroke of the pen was more unthinkable than the abolition of slavery in the United States, two and a half centuries later.

Nevertheless, Dimitry was moving in that direction. By one of his decrees, a father could no longer alienate the independence of his children and grandchildren. A man could "sell" himself, but not his offspring. On the other side of the coin, limits were placed on proprietary rights, and owners of serfs had to provide them with food and elementary "comfort." And in case of another famine, an owner who could not feed his peasants lost his ownership of them, and they were free to attach themselves to someone else.

In another field, Dimitry provided for the reduction of unfair or excessive taxation, and profits to "middle-men" were abolished, which was another way of saying that dishonest tax-collectors would be punished. At the same time, Dimitry imposed taxation on the rich monasteries, to counterbalance losses in other revenues. Such an act was almost sacrilege in Muscovy, with dangerous results. Yet the burden on the vast properties belonging to monkish foundations was nothing at all compared with the clean sweep Henry VIII had made in England when Ivan the Dread was a boy. Whether Dimitry would have gone as far as Henry had he lived is of course impossible to know. Still, there can be no doubt that the revolutionary young Tsar was moving in the direction of freedom and justice by taking away from those who had, and giving to those who had not.

Far more appealing to Dimitry, however, than such administrative reforms were his plans for the building of a great military machine which would place Muscovy at the head of all Christian nations. Since the disastrous defeat of Ivan the Dread and the galling Treaty of Zapolski-Yam which ended the Livonian war in 1582, Russia had sunk into military insignificance. That great empire, the largest in Europe, all but trembled at the name of Tatar, although the Golden Horde by then was nothing more than a semi-sedentary and disorganized gathering of horsemen, and the Khan of Crimea was a mere tributary of the Turkish Sultan. So matters stood when Boris died. Russia was respected for its size, not for its might.

Dimitry's attitude toward Crimea has already been mentioned. Neither from there nor from the Tatars to the east did he see any great threat. But Turkey, the Ottoman Empire, still sprawled over the southeast of Europe and all of Asia Minor. *There* lay the enemy of Christianity. *There* Dimitry would make a name for all time to come. For a Muscovy which led Europe to victory over Islam as symbolized by the Grand Signior would be a Muscovy feared by Europe as well as by the vanquished foe.

As early as November 30, 1605, Dimitry played the opening gambit in his military chess-game by sending a letter to Pope Paul V. After a long preamble, in which he recalled his cordial relations with Pope Clement and Monsignore Rangoni, he briefly mentioned his accession to the throne, and quickly launched his plan to unite his forces with those of the Holy Roman Emperor to attack "the monstrous and barbarous enemies of the Holy Cross." To that end, he begged the Pontiff to restrain Rudolf II from concluding the peace treaty with Ahmed I which was already in the air. Beyond this, he announced that his further plans would be explained in person by Father Andrew Lawicki, S. J., a special legate whom he was about to send on his long way to Rome. Although it was a fortnight before Lawicki got his papers, and a month before he actually set out (along with Father Stanislas Kryski), Dimitry's first step had been taken.[11]

To what extent, if any, the people of Moscow were aware of Dimitry's approach to the Pope, is uncertain. It could hardly have had popular support, and surely would have attracted violent opposition from the hereditary princes, the boyars and the clergy. But the steps he took at the same time to open up or improve trade with Poland and the rest of the West were not so universally offensive. Perhaps these covered up the unhallowed dealings with the Anti-Christ in Rome.

Although exact documentation is lacking, it appears that Dimitry saw that past commercial procedures were outdated, and that many abuses had crept in. He consequently commanded that the borders be opened to trade with Poland and Lithuania, and something vaguely anticipating "most favored nation" policies began to emerge: no delays at the frontiers, no inspections en route inside Russia, and no meaningless and irritating formalities. This brought his neighboring states into a position comparable with that of England, which had long enjoyed almost a monopoly in Russia. The time when Dutch and Swedish merchants were to offer serious competition had not yet come.

The month of February, 1606, brought Pope Paul's own Nuncio to Moscow, Count Alessandro Rangoni, nephew of the Nuncio at Kraków. Count Alessandro had received his letters of credence six months before, his uncle had borrowed fifteen hundred Hungarian gold ducats[12] in September, and on October 2 (Polish calendar) the Count had set out, in company with a group of Carmelite missionaries on their way to Iran. Cardinal Borghese, for reasons of his own, had disapproved of Alessandro or of his mission (it is not certain which), and King Sigismund and, for unknown reasons, Pan George Mniszech had also objected. But the Nuncio had not hesitated to send his nephew on anyway, and while Rome was issuing orders and counterorders, Count Alessandro was crossing the snowy wastes of eastern Poland and Lithuania. Fortunately, such formal "progresses" always moved slowly, and when it became imperative to halt him, it could be done at Smolensk, the first important town in Russia on the way from Kraków. There Alessandro relaxed for the winter.

The cause for the delay, as stated in a note from Cardinal Borghese to Monsignore Rangoni, was the Pope's decision "to wait for certain [unequivocal] information regarding Dimitry's affairs." This may refer to the rumors which circulated against Dimitry's legitimacy — rumors which had also contributed to Mniszech's dilatory tactics in starting for Moscow with the Tsaritsa Marina. Apparently the doubts were soon in large measure removed, for the younger Rangoni covered the last two hundred and fifty miles of his journey as Pan George was finishing all preparations for his departure. Count Alessandro was received in audience in the Granovitaya Palata on Sunday, February 9/19, 1606.

Whether the young nobleman from Modena had ever been presented to Dimitry in Kraków may well be doubted. He tended toward a life which has been described as far from austere, and coming as he did from an ancient Italian family he may even have looked down upon the unimpressive figure of the young Muscovite who was seeking help from King Sigismund. However it was, there can be little doubt that he was dumbfounded by the reception accorded him in Moscow.

According to Alessandro's own description of the audience, confirmed in part by Father Czyrzowski, two venerable *pristavy* ("sergeants," according to contemporary English writers) came robed in cloth-of-gold to his quarters, on Dimitry's behalf. The Tsar's own sleigh, covered with velvet and fitted with valuable furs, was waiting for him. His "coachman," dressed in a kaftan of crimson velvet with gold braid, stood behind a magnificent white horse. After the customary formalities, thirty horsemen in gala uniforms trotted off first, followed by the Master of the Horse, mounted and resplendent in a collar of sparkling jewelry. Behind this, three sleighs were lined up abreast, with Count Alessandro's in the middle, and the sergeants' on either side.

As the cavalcade swept over Moscow's snowy streets, people assembled in true Muscovite tradition, until an "innumerable crowd" was gathered at the gate to the Kremlin. Inside, before the palace, two rows of streltsy stood to do the military honors, while a throng of courtiers, richly robed, waited in the entrance-way and antechambers. In the next salon, Count Alessandro found the boyars, seated in state along the walls, as grave as so many Byzantine saints. To complete the picture, the far end of the hall was closed off by a great door, decorated with Byzantine paintings (ikons?) and Persian tapestries.

When he had passed the middle of the long room, the great door was noisily opened, revealing a silver-gilt throne on a dais five steps up from the floor. On the right a large window admitted light to

bring to life the glitter of gowns and furniture, including a pyra-
mid topped by a globe on the left. Two high dignitaries received
Count Alessandro as he entered, and led him *tempo di marcia so-
lenne* toward Dimitry. The Count admitted afterward that he
hardly recognized the young prince he had once or twice seen in
Kraków.

Dimitry sat at ease, robed in cloth-of-silver, with a diamond cross
on his breast and a golden crown on his head — presumably the
Crown of Monomakh, with its jewels, its sable edging, and its
golden cross, tipped with oblong pearls. His be-ringed hand held a
sceptre. On his left, boyars were gathered in disorder; on his right,
the Patriarch and the archbishops and bishops. And at the foot of
the throne stood the four *ryndy,* ceremonial bodyguards, motionless as statues, robed in white satin kaftans trimmed with ermine,
with tall hats, and each bearing a battle-axe of silver.

Count Alessandro mounted the steps to kiss the Tsar's hand,
which was acknowledged by a slight inclination of the head, and
then retired two or three steps from the dais. Having taken position, he delivered a suitable allocution, which was translated by
Buczyński, who then gave the Tsar's reply. In substance he said:

> His Imperial Majesty thanked the Holy Father Paul V, the Sover-
> eign Pontiff, for the augury for prosperity contained in his letters,
> and already voiced by the Carmelite monks. Since the sending of
> an envoy was a still more solemn proof of his good-will, Dimitry
> wished to express equally great gratitude. Nothing was more
> pleasing to him than for the kings and princes who were his
> friends to remind him of God's kindness to him; and as for the
> Papal benediction, he was especially appreciative. "It would not
> be barren," he said, "but salutary and fruitful for him, for his em-
> pire, and for his Christian aims, since it came from the Prince of
> Priests, and Dispenser of Divine Grace." [13]

Then he went on to renew his expressions of gratitude to the
Pope, and of filial love and veneration, which would never diminish. All of this, Buczyński proclaimed in the name of the Tsar.

When Buczyński had finished, Dimitry himself turned to Count
Alessandro and asked if he did not have a letter for him from the

Pope. He was so sure of this that he extended his hand as if to receive it. But one of the secretaries was at hand, and when Alessandro started to hand the Pope's letter to Dimitry, he seized it. Moscow officialdom knew that no communication from a Tsar had ever been delivered directly into the hands of a Pope. A Pope was not to have privileges denied to a Tsar.

At that, Dimitry made a signal for all to rise, and himself rising respectfully inquired for the health of the Pope and his family. This courtesy effectuated, he then said that if the Nuncio had nothing further to communicate he begged him to accept *con animo lieto* (with a happy heart — Alessandro's phrase) the dinner which he would send him from his own table. The audience was over.

Scarcely had he reached his lodging than the Count was visited by some of the highest dignitaries of the Court, bearing a vast profusion of dishes and drinks. There were two hundred "courses" served on gold and silver, and a corresponding number of carafes and urns of silver-gilt, with various kinds of mead and wine. Alessandro, informed of Muscovite custom with regard to dishes sent from the Tsar's table, accepted each platter and each carafe with his own hands. In return, he sent to the Tsar a fine image of the Virgin Mary, brought from Kraków.

Before he was through eating, Count Alessandro received two visitors: Dimitry's secretary, Buczyński, and one of Marina's relatives who was in Moscow. These came to make certain that the Count would not get any incorrect impressions from the reception he had been accorded. Especially, Dimitry did not want him to think that his love for the Pope and loyalty to the Church had undergone any change. Buczyński, a Protestant, and his Catholic companion were to explain that the stiff formality he had to practice was due entirely to the rigidity of Muscovite protocol. Dimitry had had to permit the distortion of the Pope's correct title into a mere *Great Priest of the Roman Church* (the Russian word for "priest" is pronounced *pope*), for he could not antagonize Muscovite sensitivities on this solemn occasion. But he wanted Count Alessandro to know that he was sincerely devoted to the Holy See, and that he had noticed that he had looked sad during the audience. The sadness was conceivably boredom.

Not content with this, he called Father Czyrzowski to the palace the same evening and inquired whether Count Alessandro was satisfied with the audience. Upon Czyrzowski's assurance that he was, Dimitry went on to still greater lengths to express his veneration for Paul V and the Holy See, and his esteem for the Nuncio in Kraków and love for his nephew. And he begged Czyrzowski to convey this information to Count Alessandro, as well as to repeat that Muscovite tradition made it impossible for him to receive him in person at dinner in the palace.

The account Rangoni wrote of his reception by Dimitry leaves no doubt that the young Tsar was old indeed in the ways of handling people. By his care and foresight, he succeeded in gaining the sympathies of two diametrically opposed sides in the religious question. Of course, he did not win over all the Orthodox clergy, nor did all Catholics love him. Yet his success was astounding, in view of the treacherous terrain through which his path lay.

If Count Alessandro came to Moscow with the sole purpose, as seems likely, of showing Dimitry the Pope's interest in him and in his project for ultimate union of the two Churches, he returned to Rome with much weightier diplomatic luggage. Dimitry took advantage of his stay to explain the future he saw for Muscovy, and what was needed to bring that future about.

First of all, Dimitry requested of the Pope, through Count Alessandro, "three or four laymen of good faith, experience and habits, whose services he could use as secretaries or advisers on such matters as the Muscovites, through ignorance, are inept [to handle]." Then turning to his arena of preference, he asked for military experts, practiced in the art of assaulting forts, and inventing, or adapting, petards for breaching walls, artillery in general, and other useful war-machines. At the same time he stipulated that any such specialists should enter his employ in such guise that their contact with the Holy See would remain unknown, and their employment by him would appear to be of their, rather than his, volition.

After reporting this, Count Alessandro added his personal note to the effect that the "fruit to be gathered" by such a mission was so self-evident that it was hardly worthwhile explaining further, were it not for another consideration. Dimitry, he confided, had in his employ a heretic by the name of Buczyński who was doing everything in his power to promote other contacts — say with England — through which the Tsar could obtain all the engineers, advisers, and so on, who might be needed. Indeed, Count Alessandro confided that the English merchants residing in Moscow were promoting these contacts to the best of their ability, with the connivance of the heretic Buczyński, and the intimate chamberlain of the Tsar, Kazanowski, "and many others who are enamored of their [the English merchants'] daughters."

To offset this, Count Alessandro wrote that he had been exceedingly receptive to Dimitry's hints that he would like to send an embassy to Rome, provided it would be welcome. Once he was assured that it would be, Dimitry added that he was also thinking of embassies to France and Spain — a novelty for the Tsars of Muscovy. Between them, the Tsar and the Count agreed that the idea would be investigated, and that the Pope would be asked to use his good offices to advance it.

A further favor to be asked of the Pope was his intervention with the Holy Roman Emperor (once again!) and the King of Spain in favor of Dimitry's anti-Turkish coalition. As for the King of Poland, Dimitry asked the Count to assure the Pope that he would maintain neighborly and even filial good-relations with him, and that he would submit differences which could not otherwise be settled between them to His Holiness for arbitration. (It should not be forgotten that the Pope had been called on to bring peace between Poland and Russia in Ivan the Dread's day.) And in conclusion, Dimitry gave Count Alessandro a secret letter for the Pope, with apologies for its poor wording. In this instance, he said, he had *no-one* whom he could trust for help. If the letter is the Latin one which survives, dated March 5/15, 1606, Ash Wednesday, it can well be wondered who actually wrote it.[14]

This letter is remarkable for its open avowal of Dimitry's attach-

ment to the Catholic Church and his indebtedness to the Holy Father and devotion to the Apostolic See. Had Shuysky or one of his
cabal gotten their hands on it, they would have had all of Russia
behind them in dethroning Dimitry. No minion of Rome could
wear the Orthodox Crown of Monomakh.

Count Alessandro's mission was ended. His orders required him
to report to the Vatican, but the occupation of most of Hungary by
the Ottoman Empire put Kraków on the shortest practicable route
from Moscow. Dimitry therefore availed himself of the Legate to
carry a personal message to King Sigismund. Relations between
Poland and Muscovy had apparently reverted to their normal state
of suspicion tinged with hostility, and Dimitry wanted to hold out
a friendly hand again. At the same time, he could not reflect more
than protocolary "warmth" in external affairs without running
the risk of internal combustion. To obtain Polish support for his
initial moves, he had had to promise much. Now that he was Tsar,
literal compliance with his promises proved impossible.

Dimitry played his cards well. Through Count Alessandro he
assured the ever-hesitant and never-constant King that he would
not forget his help, and would always treat him more as a father
than as a brother monarch. As soon as Sigismund revealed his
plans loyally, Dimitry would prove an ally against "Duke Charles."
But Sigismund must recognize Dimitry's imperial title. Dimitry
may have been vague about manifestations of friendship, but he
was punctilious about his title. He even went so far as to explain
why.

Moscow was full of rumors, he wrote, regarding his relations
with Poland, and particularly about certain cessions of territory to
the Polish Republic. It was necessary to dispel these rumors at all
costs, and nothing would do this more effectively than the recognition of Dimitry's title as Emperor of all Russia. This would prove
that the realm of his forefathers would remain intact.

Clearly, if Muscovy remained "intact," it meant that the lands
which he had promised to cede to Mniszech and Sigismund would
not be ceded. He was therefore breaking a promise, not to mention a written contract. But the contract was with Mniszech, and

Mniszech seemed totally undisturbed by Dimitry's failure to hand over any real estate. As long as he received the much needed hard cash, which he continued to demand, he seems to have lost interest — or to have understood. In the early spring of 1606, before Marina had appeared in Moscow, and before the many problems connected with her Catholicism were solved, it was indeed idle to expect Dimitry to hand over rich provinces that had formed part of Muscovy at least since Ivan III had "assembled" the Russian lands into one great state. Mniszech was evidently willing to wait. Sigismund, legally dependent on Dimitry's contract with Mniszech, would also have to wait. Morally, if Dimitry planned some compensation for going back on his word, or if he hoped eventually to fulfil it, Fate did not give him time.

Meanwhile, a day or two before Dimitry signed the letter to Pope Paul V, he staged a mock-battle in the snow, at a place now called Vyazyomy Bolshiye, some thirty miles west of Moscow, where Boris Godunov had owned an estate. Why this was done during Count Alessandro's stay in Moscow is not clear, for he does not appear to have been present. Nevertheless, Dimitry had walls built of snow near the village, where he assembled a great group of princes and boyars. He wanted them, he explained, to practice attack and defense, and the war-games would end in the storming of the icy fortress. His German bodyguard took part, along with a couple of companies of Polish horse. A body of cavalry was sent a short distance off, where it waited in the snowy fields.

The mock-battle began by the appointment of one of the princes or boyars as voyvode in charge of the fort. Dimitry himself took command of his German bodyguard, and ordered an attack. Although the only weapons permitted on either side were snowballs, a lively fight ensued. Dimitry of course led his men to victory, but not to a bloodless one. For unknown reasons, the Germans had put sand, ice and other hard objects inside their snowballs. Still, Dimitry seemed not to notice, and after the victory, while the voyvode and other boyars were being tied up as "prisoners," he declaimed: "May God grant that I may someday fight my way like this into Azov, in Tartary, and capture the Tatar Khan like this — just as I have captured you."

This signalized the end of the fight. Dimitry released all the prisoners, and had wine, beer, and strong mead brought up, with which they all toasted one another. Then he announced that in a while they would make another practice attack.

At this, one of the boyars came up to him and said quite openly that he should call it off. Many princes and boyars were very angry over the Germans' dangerous snowballs. Furthermore, he said that Dimitry ought to remember that there were many traitors among these noblemen, all of whom carried long sharp knives under their robes. Dimitry and his Germans had no arms, and no armor. A serious accident could happen, if he wanted to call it an accident.[15]

Dimitry took the advice to heart and returned to Moscow. Practice-warfare was postponed for a later season, if not abandoned. And strange confirmation of the boyar's state of loyalty and keenness was not long in reaching the Tsar's ears. He was shortly thereafter informed that a group of princes and boyars had been convinced that his intention had been to murder them during the "practice," and that they showed up fully armed, only waiting for a chance to do away with Dimitry and his bodyguard first. It was further evidence of the tirelessness of the Shuysky cabal.

Count Alessandro, who does not mention the matter at all, evidently left Moscow shortly after receiving his letters and paying final respects to the Tsar. On March 19/29 he is known to have already arrived at the great castle of Mir, fief of the Radziwiłł family, well over five hundred miles from Moscow.

There he met Father Casper Sawicki, the Jesuit who had received Dimitry's abjuration from Orthodoxy. Sawicki was on his way to Moscow with Pan George Mniszech and Dimitry's bride, the Empress Marina. Legate and Jesuit exchanged views, hopes, and perhaps even fears, as is hinted in their reports. But Count Alessandro's ebullient optimism appears to have overridden all else. Marina, he said, was journeying toward a triumph of indescribable glory.

CHAPTER 13

WILLING, UNWILLING WAYFARERS

In Sambor, in the meantime, warmth and brightness had slowly begun to follow the sun northwards, after the physical and mental dullness of winter. Activity had recommenced, as the days of doubt and misgiving passed without fulfillment of any evil presage. Optimistic, confident letters poured from Moscow into Poland, beseeching, adjuring, urging, and at last commanding the appearance of Marina in the Kremlin. Pan George Mniszech, at least superficially confident, made ready to set out. Marina, in an impenetrable state of mind, collected her gowns and jewels toward the same end.

King Sigismund, off on his honeymoon or just returned therefrom, generously suspended any court actions against Pan George, in view of the forthcoming trip to Moscow and the sums undoubtedly available to him there. Considering the lavish presents already received, it is evident that Pan George's debts must indeed have been staggering. And from another viewpoint, had they not been he might have thrown over the entire project when so many adverse rumors came to his ears. This would quite likely have been a great favor to Dimitry, but neither of them saw it that way. So, with imperial fanfare, the caravan started.

Pan George himself, Voyvode of Sandomierz, naturally took charge. The title *voyvode* meant "war-leader," yet this expedition was seen in the light of a gay matrimonial procession, and thoughts of security and military organization seem not to have entered anybody's head. There was neither division of command, nor delegation of authority. With Pan George and his daughter, the Empress of all Russia, there went a shapeless mass of relatives, nobles, priests, gentlemen, and servants.

Close to Pan George were his oldest brother, John, his oldest living son, Stanislas Boniface, his deceased brother's son, Paul, and his son-in-law, Prince Konstantin Vishnevetsky. Then there were his wife's cousins, Sigismund and Paul Tarło, and his sister's connections by marriage, the three Stadnicki brothers, Stanislas, Adam and Martin. Martin was Master of the Court for Marina, while the character of Stanislas may be described by his nickname, "The Devil of Łańcut." A majestic matron, Pani Barbara Kazanowska, née Stadnicka, was Grand Mistress of the Court, while the wives of the two Tarłos and other noblewomen formed part of Marina's retinue.

The clergy was also present in proper proportion, with some seven Bernardines headed by the Curé of Sambor, Francis Pomaski, at the outset, and others added during the voyage. A lay brother called Peter attended in the capacity of expert surgeon. In contrast to these pious, humble, sincere men, Father Sawicki rode in some splendor as representative of the Nuncio, Rangoni, and at the expense of Pope Paul. This does not imply any insincerity, yet there are reports that the Bernardines treated him with a certain degree of un-warmth, as if he were an ornament which could easily have been dispensed with. Yet there was no open friction.

Entertainment was of course indispensable for the szlachta, the Polish nobility. Stanislas Mniszech therefore personally hired a group of twenty musicians, with an Italian buffoon thrown in for good measure. But the overwhelming bulk of the escort was made up of flunkies of every imaginable variety and description. Great lists of people of note who attended Marina have survived, and each of these had to have a colossal entourage of servants of both sexes, for that was customary among Polish magnates — whether they could afford it or not.

The result was that Marina's cavalcade numbered at least two thousand before it left Sambor. After it left, the number of incidents of drunkenness, sexual debauchery, brawls, duels, and murders among the undisciplined varletry can hardly be imagined, in surroundings of such elegance and imperial splendor. Certainly the report of one woman who chopped an unwanted, unhallowed infant in pieces which she threw out of the window, challenges more than the imagination.

Such disagreeable future things were not envisioned when on Thursday, March 2, 1606, the sun rose on the assembly in the court-yard of the King's palace in Sambor. The next day Father Sawicki joined the party as it moved along, probably having ridden down from the Jesuit college at Jarosław.

After covering some hundred and eighty miles in six days, the caravan reached Lublin on March 8. This was the largest city be-tween Warsaw and Smolensk, the seat of another Jesuit college, and the place where the convention of 1569 had determined the union of Poland and Lithuania. A halt was obligatory there espe-cially since the young Jesuit students had prepared a welcome for the Empress Marina: an oration in Latin and a vocal concert with Polish and Latin songs. Despite Afanasy Vlasyev's pressure on Mniszech to move on, the entire expedition remained in Lublin until Tuesday, March 14.

Ten days later the Royal Borough of Słonim was reached, nearly two hundred and fifty miles closer to Moscow. It was Good Friday, according to the Catholic calendar, and Pan George and his daugh-ter stayed there until the following Monday. Father Sawicki made a speech before the entire company after the Easter Sunday service, but the Jesuit records are silent as to his subject. Tuesday or Wednesday the procession in record time reached the Castle of Mir.

This was an imposing, five-towered fortress belonging to the new Palatine of Vilnius, a second cousin of the Palatine already mentioned, and here Father Sawicki informed himself on Musco-vite affairs from the returning Papal Legate, Count Alessandro Rangoni. Whether the unusual speed of seventy miles in not over two days was due to Rangoni's presence or not, the encounter was a profitable one for Sawicki. For Pan George and the Empress Ma-rina it must also have been a happy encounter, for there can be little doubt that Count Alessandro described his impressions of Moscow in glowing terms.

On Thursday after Easter, the entire caravan was received in another castle of the Palatine of Vilnius, at Nieśwież, a short day's ride but somewhat out of their way, to the south. The visit was due to another Jesuit college there, and while Marina and her father were being entertained in lavish style by the civic authorities, Sawicki visited his fellow Jesuits. Shortly after, Marina and Pan George were also invited to the college, where they were received with astonishment. Nothing remotely resembling the pageantry of Marina's escort had ever been seen in the remote and almost isolated settlement, with its cluster of peasants' houses, its castle, its college, and its printing press which had been set up a year or two before Moscow itself had a press. (Russia's first printer was chased out of the country in less than three years as a "heretic and sorcerer.")[1]

For all the Jesuit astonishment, an incident marred the imperial visit and may have reminded Pan George that some Poles still remained who looked with a skeptical eye on Tsar Dimitry. When the time came for the official speeches to be made, only Pan George was asked to be present while one of the students delivered an oration in Latin. Marina was tactfully entertained outside. The reason for this was that a controversy over Marina's titles had arisen at the last moment, and it was thought better not to use them than to seem to recognize them by saying them out loud. It seems that Radziwłł, who was among other things Duke of Nieśwież, was involved in this, although his wife was a first cousin of Prince Konstantin Vishnevetsky, and he had not taken any determined stand on the subject of Dimitry before.

Leaving Nieśwież on Saturday, April 1, the procession reached Minsk, now the capital of the Byelorussian S.S.R., two days later. They had traveled another seventy miles, and their gradual approach to Moscow was becoming evident.

Marina rested in Minsk for two days, which gave Father Sawicki cause and opportunity for recording two incidents involving wine in his diary. On his way to his quarters a drunken soldier attacked

him with his sword and would have killed him had not other soldiers who were not quite so drunk intervened. Then, in the parish
(Catholic) church it was so cold that the wine froze solid in the
chalice, and it was only with difficulty that mass could be concluded.

After this brief stop, the cavalcade moved on to Orsha, one hundred and thirty miles away, which they reached in eight days.
Where they stopped en route is not known except for Smolevichi,
twenty-odd miles from Minsk, where an accidental fire cost Marina
four fine horses. It is to be assumed that on this dreary stretch, as
occasionally before, the little army camped out for the night.

Marina quickly crossed to the left bank of the Dnyeper at Orsha,
while the main body of her escort took two days in the passage.
Since this was the last post of any consequence in the Polish Republic, Father Sawicki felt it incumbent on himself to deliver a
harangue with politico-religious overtones.

For this purpose, on Sunday morning, April 16 by the Polish
calendar, bright and early, he called the company together. They
all should, he said, collect their thoughts and consider the fact that
they were about to enter a strange land, and that they should see to
it that they did not set a bad example for the Muscovites. These
were a barbarous, schismatic people, he explained, who had been
inimical to them, the Poles and presumably the Lithuanians, for
centuries. And the reasons were both nationalistic and religious.
Like many in all ages, the pious Father was too convinced that
right was on his side to realize that good international relations are
hardly based on such talk.

Two days later, on Tuesday, April 18, Pan George Mniszech
conducted his daughter, the Empress of all Russia, across the
wooden bridge that united the Polish Republic and the Muscovite
Empire. The icy stream beneath was not large, but it divided two
worlds, that of Ivan the Dread from that of Nicholas Copernicus;
that of Orthodoxy from that of Catholicism (and Protestantism).
The date was now Tuesday, April 8.[2]

Despite Dimitry's meticulous preparations for the reception of
his bride, Muscovy received her with bad grace. The day of the
crossing was foggy, and the cold was penetrating. The road on the

Muscovite side of the border was ill-kept, and hardly suitable for the passage of coaches. Frequent bridges made it possible to cross the numerous swamps, but not comfortably. Had Pan George Mniszech been clairvoyant he could have pictured Napoleon's army struggling through these same wastes of forest and moor two centuries later. There was even a kind of similarity. Mniszech's cavalcade began to disintegrate while being welcomed into Russia — Napoleon's, while being cast out.

Not far from the bridge, a few silk-robed boyars began to approach, to greet and welcome their Lady, the Empress Marina. Two or three miles beyond, the entourage reached the first Muscovite village, *Wasilewicze* in Father Sawicki's Polish, where four more boyars, "honest men," came up to greet the Empress.

After the usual abject salutations, one of these boyars turned to Father Sawicki and inquired in much detail who he was and where he came from, whether he was a Greek or a Latin monk or priest, whether the Empress had any Greek or Serbian priests with her, and also whether there were any Latin priests with her. Father Sawicki began by answering agreeably, but finally, in spite of his own recommendations of two or three days before, he lost patience with the boyar's curiosity and verbosity, excused himself, and "took to the road," as he put it.

When they entered the village, a Muscovite priest greeted the company, accompanied by many other Russians, saying that they were expecting the Empress, and bringing the traditional offering of bread and salt. This was done in every village through which they passed, and in addition offerings of ikons, mead, wine and such things were brought in the towns and larger places.

Moving on, by nightfall and after traversing two dozen wooden bridges, mostly new, the entire company reached the village of Krasny, the very spot where Napoleon was to suffer a catastrophic defeat on November 6, 1812. Dimitry had commanded that a new, wooden palace be built for Marina and her ladies-in-waiting, but the remaining nineteen hundred and more were quartered in the settlement, "uncomfortably enough." Nevertheless, there was plenty to eat, for both people and horses.

After spending thirty-six hours at Krasny, the company moved on to a village called Lubno. There, the evening of April 10/20, they were received by two dignitaries: Prince Vasily Mikhaylovich Mosalsky-Rubets and Boyar Mikhaylo Nagoy. These special envoys sent to receive the Empress Marina were accompanied by about two thousand soldiers, the whole escort accoutred in magnificent uniforms.

The Prince and the boyar accompanied Marina and her father to the residence assigned to them, where lengthy speeches were made in honor of Pan George Mniszech, to whom Dimitry expressed his gratitude for bringing his bride to Moscow. Marina was then addressed with the customary deluge of grandiloquence by Prince Mosalsky-Rubets, in Russian, and in a costume which some of his audience who did not understand the language spent their time valuing. They guessed that the gold and jewels alone had cost five thousand florins — more than enough to fit out an English two-ship expedition to the North America that was about to be settled.[3]

Pan George responded graciously, extolling Dimitry with proper modesty, and thanking him for his munificent hospitality. The Prince and the boyar then prostrated themselves again before Marina, and placed themselves completely at her orders. This rite concluded, they presented her with thoroughbred horses, and carriages to convey her to Moscow. These were the arabas known in Poland, but far more luxuriously fitted out than any to be seen in that Republic.

Marina's araba was drawn by twelve of the finest white horses. It consisted of a sort of bower on runners, covered with red silk and decorated with silver plaques. Inside, it was padded throughout and upholstered with sables. The side windows were long and narrow, and fitted with glass. And the three charioteers who drove the twelve horses were dressed in Turkish-blue fringed with sables, and they wielded bright red silken whips. Two other arabas were only slightly less pretentious.

Early the following morning, Marina mounted her imperial conveyance, her two thousand companions and servants clambered into or onto their means of transportation, two thousand additional Muscovite troops surrounded them, the Prince and the boyar took their places near Marina, and the astounding cavalcade negotiated the remaining few miles to Smolensk, a city which had traded with Byzantium in the days when Constantine VII Porphyrogenitus was Emperor, before Poland had a King, and had been the capital of a prosperous principality. In 1605 it had a hundred thousand inhabitants.[4]

The city was built almost entirely of wood, on both sides of the Dnyeper, with a great fortress on the left bank surrounded by a fifty-foot wall with two score turrets, built by Boris Godunov. When the great cavalcade swarmed up, however, Pan George and the Empress were amazed to find that the gate of the fortress was not opened to them. And still more astounding, the senior voyvode of the district did not emerge, but sent his junior colleague to greet the Empress and to conduct her and all her escort straight out of the city!

Installed in a suburb, Pan George observed a battalion of archers march up in two files, in bright red uniforms, take positions and remain on guard all the time they were there. The archers were equipped as for a war. Yet no explanation of this curious demonstration was made at the time, nor has any been recorded in surviving documents.

Marina remained in Smolensk until Monday, April 14/24, when the cavalcade renewed its march. They had not gotten far, however, when they were delayed for a day at a point where two "not small rivers" flow into the Dnyeper. The crossing had to be made by ferry, with great difficulty, for the boat was in such shape that some of Mniszech's relatives fell into the water, and a gentleman was drowned. Father Sawicki and a good many others delayed a day in crossing, catching up with Pan George and Marina in Drogobuzh, their next halt. The whole company rested there until April 17/27.

The next day they moved on to Vyazma, fifty miles away, without incident. Then, on Sunday, April 30 according to the Polish calendar, they reached the town of Gzhatsk, forty miles farther on. By Muscovite reckoning it was April 20, and Easter Sunday. For simplicity's sake, the Muscovite calendar will be employed from here on.

Pan George Mniszech, his son Stanislas, Prince Konstantin Vishnevetsky, and Sigismund Tarło left the main party at Gzhatsk, and hurried on to Moscow. Marina and her huge entourage moved more slowly. Father Sawicki loyally stayed with her.

Passing through Borodino, later famous for Napoleon's victory over the Russians, they reached Mozhaysk on April 22.[5] This important commercial center, seventy miles west of Moscow, was then renowned among the Orthodox for a statue of Saint Nicholas of Myra, the Thaumaturge, patron saint of Russia. Father Sawicki heard of this shortly, and expressed a wish to see it.

After some discussion, and a great deal of hesitation, Father Sawicki was finally admitted to the monastery where the image was venerated. He was received by a group of monks, who exchanged greetings with good Christian humility. Courteously invited to refresh himself with cold beer or mead, he accepted a glass "just to be polite," as he explained. While he sipped this, he began to inquire about the customs and rules of the brotherhood there, questions which the ordinary monks had some difficulty in answering.

Sawicki then asked if the abbot were there, and if he could talk to him. To this, one of the monks said: "Our hegumen occupies himself entirely with God, in the inner holy-places of the monastery, and sees only one of the brethren, who attends him and supplies his needs." Sawicki was content with this answer, asked them to greet the abbot for him, and began to talk of other matters.

Just then, a monk with a beatific expression, dressed like the rest, rushed in to greet him. Sawicki bowed, but to his surprise the newcomer was identified as the Abbot himself. Sawicki then extended a more respectful as well as more effusive greeting, to which the other corresponded, but in so doing perceptibly staggered. He also voiced a salutation with an extraordinarily thick tongue. Only then did the Jesuit realize that the Abbot, rather than communing with God, had been communing with his cups.

This discovery was quickly followed by the realization that the apparent simplicity of the monks he had been talking to was in

Ophánás Posel tegoż Cárá Moskiewskiego.

W Łasną twarz Ophánáfá · który w náße strony /
Od Cárá Moskiewskiego postem był po żoney:
Mąż cnotą y rozumem wielkim zárwolány /
Jáki z Moskwy od dawná w polsze był widziány.
Skąd Dimitr Cár wydawa sie w swoiey mądrości /
Ze w spráwách swych posyła ludzie téy biegłości.

Afanasy [Vlasyev], Ambassador of the same Tsar of Muscovy.
From Rovinsky, Grochowski's Wedding Brochure, 1605.
Courtesy of the Trustees of the British Museum, London.

Dimitry receiving the Polish ambassadors. Contemporary oil painting. (The audience chamber of the Facetted Palace. The Patriarch, with members of the clergy behind him, is at Dimitry's right.) Courtesy of the State Historical Museum, Moscow.

The letters visible in the painting:

MARIA M
GEORGII DE M
ÆCH PALATINI S
VXOR VERO DI
MOSCHOZIÆ COR
MOSCHOZIÆ PER
GRECI IN VRBE
PERII MOSCHO
REGIS POLONIA
ANNO D

The Coronation of Marina. A painting by an anonymous (Polish?) artist, of great historical importance. The smaller half shows the wedding procession from the Palace down the Red Stairs and across the raised "bridges" to the Cathedral of the Assumption. Dimitry is accompanied by Pan George Mniszech, in black, and a Muscovite prince (Mstislavsky?). Marina is at the right of Princess Mstislavskaya. The robed figures are boyars. In the background the German and other mercenaries carry banners with the Russian eagle. The larger half depicts the coronation itself, with the Polish

...assadors, Olesnicki and Gosiewski, in ermine-bordered robes in the right fore-
...nd. The dark, bearded figure at the extreme right is Pan George Mniszech, sur-
...ded by Polish nobles (probably authentic likenesses). Dimitry is wearing the
...erial crown, not the Crown of Monomakh, which was used only for coronations.
...identity of other dignitaries and ladies is not known. Reproduced from a photo-
...graph by Rovinsky, from the original in the State Historical Museum, Moscow.
Courtesy of the Trustees of the British Museum, London.

Engraving of the Wawel, Kraków, with the Castle, the Cathedral, and the surrounding area, by Georg Braun of Cologne. Drawn about 1576, it lacks detail, but is probably the best picture available of the city at the time of Dimitry. Courtesy of the Rare Book Division, The New York Public Library.

Des herrn hans wegers sein leger.

Nie

per fluuius.

SCHMO

Des Herrn Winterski

leger vnd Bat   torey

...graving of Smolensk in the year 1611, drawn by Franz Hogenberg. During the ...roubles" following Dimitry's death, the Poles under King Sigismund attacked ...d captured Smolensk, as shown here. Courtesy of Prints Division, The New York Public Library.

Right: Modern view of the three Kremlin cathedrals as seen from the Mosl
River. The street in the foreground is of course modern, and hides a portion of
old Kremlin wall. On the left is Annunciation Cathedral, next to which the up
floor of the Facetted Palace can be seen. Immediately to the right are three cupo
of the Assumption Cathedral, in the background, behind the great brick "Sec
Bastion," so-called from the secret artesian well which it covered. The pres
Bastion was built in 1771–1773, after the plans of the original (of 1485), and
been remodelled in 1862 and 1930. To the right is the Cathedral of the Archan
Michael, built in 1505–1509. Courtesy of the Scandinavian Airlines Syste
London Office.

ft: A procession of the time of Tsar Mikhail Romanov, showing the Golden
lace in the center, with the Red Staircase before it. To the left is the Cathedral of
 Archangel Michael, with that of the Annunciation looming behind it. Right of
ter, the Facetted Palace (*Granovitaya Palata*) is well drawn. The Cathedral of the
sumption is at the extreme right, and in the background are various churches and
er buildings. The scene would have been practically the same in Dimitry's time.
Courtesy of the State Historical Museum, Moscow.

Red Square seen from near the Cathedral of the Blessed Idiot Basil. On the left, the Kremlin wall; in the rear, behind the representative of the armed forces, the State Historical Museum; on the right, the endless façade of the State Universal Store, better known as G.U.M. This view of the square emphasizes its chief characteristics, hugeness and emptiness. By the same token, it is an ideal parade-ground. Courtesy of the Scandinavian Airlines System, London Office.

reality inspired by their heady drinks. In fact, they then began to press him to join them in deeper quaffing. Sawicki thought it time to excuse himself, as politely as he could, but his good manners were wasted. The monks joyously crowded out of the building with him, carrying mugs and drinking-cups overflowing with mead, and calling to him to join them. Sawicki concluded his account of this adventure with the observation that "the vice of inebriety is common among the priests and monks throughout Muscovy."

Father Sawicki ultimately found the famous image of Saint Nicholas in a church dedicated to him. It stood in a chapel, decorated with frescoes depicting miracles and other events of the Saint's life. The statue was of wood, in dark colors, and without a sign of either antiquity or artistic ability. Its expression was hard rather than benign, and it was typically dressed in silken robes and gold and silver trinkets. Although the Jesuit and his companions on that occasion were not particularly impressed, they thanked the custodian and went on to inspect another church. This one was supposed to harbor a naked penitent of great sanctity who had been struggling to attain perfection for thirty or more years. Denied the privilege of seeing the near-saint, the visiting priest and his friends returned to their quarters.

Marina and her escort left Mozhaysk on April 25, and reached the village of Kubinka that night. They were then only forty miles from Moscow. The next halt was at Vyazyomy, where Dimitry had held the war-games a few weeks before. There they were asked to stop for four days, while their solemn entry into the capital was prepared.

Father Sawicki and the Poles generally thus had an opportunity to celebrate the Feast Day of Saint Stanislas of Poland, May 7 (April 27 in Muscovy), in befitting style. This Feast fell on a Sunday in 1606, which was reason enough for a long service in the presence of the new Empress of Muscovy. The celebration of a "national" Polish Saint's Day almost within sight of Holy Moscow was tactless, but nothing came of it, undoubtedly for the reason that the Orthodox calendar was ignorant of the significance of

"Saint Stanislas." Two days later, they moved on a few miles closer to their destination.

During the four-day bivouac at Vyazyomy, Dimitry had commanded the construction of a tent-city for his bride, worthy of the Queen of Sheba awaiting reception by Solomon. When the cavalcade arrived, gay white tents provided comforts they had not had for many, many days. One of these, a large one, was lined with tapestries and hung with banners embroidered with quotations from the Holy Scripture. It was to serve as a chapel, regardless of sect. Other tents adjoined, designed for the rest and recreation of the bride. The most opinionated Pole had to concede that magnificence was not lacking. And the most pious believer saw the hand of friendship in the Twenty-first Psalm, regarded by Catholics as relevant to the conversion of Gentiles, printed or painted for all to see, in Latin, Russian, Syriac, and (Father Sawicki questionably adds) Arabic. In this fitting tent-chapel, the Empress of all Russia heard mass, Latin style, every morning.

Marina and her convoy were now about four or five miles from Moscow, just about the distance at which the bride of Ivan III had been detained when she arrived, also from the West. Ivan's wife was Sophia, the formidable Greek imperial princess who virtually forced her husband to create an empire out of the warring hereditary states, principalities, and one republic which made up Russia. Despite her illustrious and Orthodox descent, Sophia was held at arm's length as she approached the capital, while the Church considered her status, for she had lived in Rome, and a Latin cross was carried before her. In the end, she was admitted after the Latin cross was turned back at the gates of Moscow.

Marina, coming well over a century later, and without a Latin cross militantly borne before her, was also halted while the citadel of Orthodoxy deliberated. And once again Orthodoxy won. Dimitry, for all his self-will mixed with religious skepticism and tolerance, copied his reputed great-grandfather and for once in his life allowed passions to cool.

To this end May 2 was set for Marina's triumphal entry into the capital of Orthodox Russia and the greatest city of the Orthodox

world. Barely had the first gray streaks of a northern dawn appeared over Moscow's golden domes, than Marina sent word to Father Sawicki that she wanted to confess and attend mass, according
to the Latin rite. Father Sawicki hesitated, not for the sensible
reason that such behavior would be an affront to the Faith of the
realm which regarded her as Empress, but because the Bernardines
had theretofore acted as her confessors. The matter was nevertheless settled without difficulty, and Father Sawicki entered Marina's
tent, where an altar had meanwhile been set up.

Realizing that it was his last opportunity freely to offer advice
and counsel to Marina, Sawicki spoke at considerable length on the
importance of maintaining her faith in a schismatic city; on the
duty of Dimitry to the Church he had adopted; and on the eventual
return of the strayed sheep to the Catholic fold. Indeed, he went
so far as to urge her "strenuously" to promote the welfare of the
Church and of the Society of Jesus in Muscovy. And to this Marina
subscribed, "with every indication of goodwill."

After mass, Father Sawicki left the tent and the camp and went
ahead to Moscow, to the quarters Dimitry had established for him.
There, shortly before noon, he found Father Czyrzowski, alone
since the departure of Father Lawicki for Rome. Together they
discussed the problems facing them, in view of the age-old enmity
between the Russian Empire and the Polish Republic.

In the meantime, Marina's procession had been organized.
With a splendor unknown since the entry of the Imperial Greek
Princess Sophia, Dimitry's Empress was to be welcomed to the
Kremlin.[6] Two files of mercenary soldiers lined the road to the
Frolovskie Gate, still the main entrance to the Kremlin. Through
this passage courtiers of the Tsar swarmed, followed by Pan George
Mniszech's brother, son, and nephew, the Stadnicki trio, Stanislas
Niemojewski, and many other members of Marina's cavalcade.
Pan George himself, in resplendent uniform, closed this section of
the pageant, accompanied by an African in a long Persian robe.

Marina had by then mounted into a magnificent coach — probably the "chariot" Sir Thomas Smythe brought from King James I
to Boris Godunov — with a throne-like seat. It was drawn by

twelve (some say eight or ten) Tatar horses. These, however, were not driven by coachmen or ridden by anyone, but were led by six (or four or five) gaudy grooms on foot. Facing the Tsaritsa sat only Pani Barbara Tarłówna née Dulska, widow of the Starosta of Sochaczew. Halberdiers walked at either side, separated from the coach by six footmen in "smooth" green velvet kaftans and wide trousers under red or scarlet mantles. As her coach came up to the gate, a band struck up with Polish music from the open windows of the great tower above.

Behind the Tsaritsa came a second coach, upholstered in red velvet and all decorated with red damask silk or samite, with four seats equally elaborately caparisoned and drawn by eight white horses. The drivers were in Polish uniforms of red satin, and even the harnesses of the horses were of red velvet. But in this coach no-one sat.

The third and last coach was likewise drawn by eight white horses, harnessed with red velvet decorated with silver-gilt, but the drivers wore black velvet kaftans and red satin cloaks. In this carriage rode four of Marina's ladies-in-waiting. Two smaller carriages came along next, also elaborately decorated and padded with silk and satin, after which came simpler conveyances — all occupied by Marina's various ladies, servants, assistants, and the like.

Gaily they rolled over the wooden pavement into the Kremlin, where they halted before the church and monastery of the Ascension of the Lord. Opposite that stood the new convent-building put up expressly for Marfa, the dowager Tsaritsa-nun, mother of the Tsarevich Dimitry.

Marina was ceremoniously helped from her coach. Marfa herself, with impenetrable discipline, received her charge. The Tsaritsa who had been and the Tsaritsa who was to be exchanged a few words. Then Dimitry burst out of the great palace and rushed to greet his bride. Unaccountably, no chronicler has left a description of this first meeting after many months between the ardent lover and the object of his love.

Marina's personal attendants were quickly dispersed to various lodgings. After ten weeks of travel she herself had at last come to rest. At seventeen, she was Empress of a vast land and millions of subjects, but the Oriental splendor around her did not conceal the monastery. The display of wealth did not conceal the religious hostility. The attentiveness of her Muscovite servants did not conceal the inviolable laws of Byzantine protocol, the legacy of Sophia Palaeologue, Tsaritsa and Great Princess of all Russia, Imperial Princess of the Eastern Roman Empire. In the midst of the greatest imaginable satisfaction of peacock vanity and extravagant greed, the little country-girl from Sambor was homesick and annoyed.[7]

CHAPTER 14

PRIDE AND CONTENTION

K<small>ING</small> S<small>IGISMUND</small> III appears to have reached the conclusion during the winter of 1605–1606 that he was at last in a position to rule as well as to reign. Encouraged by his victory over the Swedes in September (and the prospect of Austrian help through his second Austrian marriage in December), he was ready to submit demands to the Polish Diet, when it met in March 1606, for a reform in the Constitution which would give him a freer hand to carry out a bold policy with Sweden.

Pan George Mniszech's expedition to Moscow therefore came at an opportune moment. The coronation of Marina provided a pretext for an embassy, and her huge entourage a partly concealing frame.[1] Thus, after some consideration, King Sigismund chose two ambassadors to go to Moscow with Pan George, and Swedish affairs ranked high on their agenda.

There can be little question that Sigismund's plans for the Republic of Poland itself were in the main sound. Nevertheless, he was unable to persuade the Polish Diet to endorse them. By the same token, his idea of making certain the cooperation of Dimitry and the Muscovite Empire in his Swedish project was accompanied by an approach which could not have guaranteed failure more successfully if failure had been his object.

The young man on the ivory throne of Ivan the Dread still had to command a maximum of respect within his own country if he was not to lose what he had just gained. The matter of title — title to his empire — was therefore vital. Yet as ambassadors, King Si-

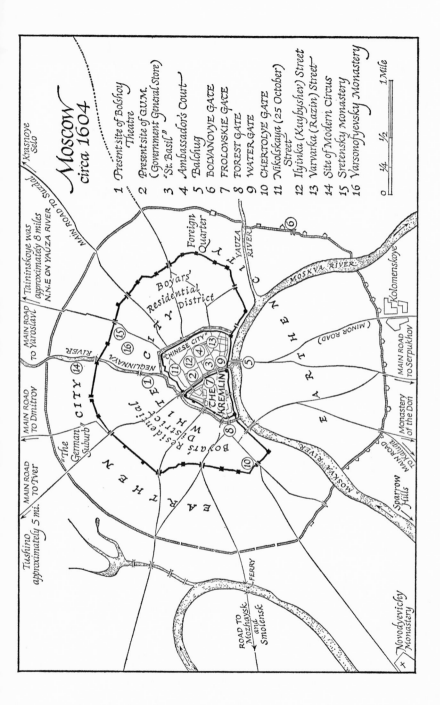

Moscow
circa 1604

1 Present site of Bolshoy
   Theatre
2 Present site of G.U.M.
   (Government General Store)
3 "St. Basil"
4 Ambassador's Court
5 Balchug
6 Bolvanovye Gate
7 Froloyskie Gate
8 Forest Gate
9 Water Gate
10 Chertolye Gate
11 Nikolskaya (25 October)
   Street
12 Ilyinka (Kuybyshev) Street
13 Varvarka (Razin) Street
14 Site of Modern Circus
15 Sretensky Monastery
16 Varsonofyevsky Monastery

0   ¼   ½   1 Mile

Krasnoye
Selo

MAIN ROAD TO SUZDAL

Taininskoye was
approximately 8 miles
N.N.E ON YAUZA RIVER

MAIN ROAD
TO YAROSLAVL

Tushino
approximately 5 mi. TO TVER

MAIN ROAD
TO DMITROV

MAIN ROAD
TO TVER

"The
German
Suburb"

RIVER

NEGLINNAYA

Foreign
Quarter

YAUZA
RIVER

Boyars'
Residential
District

WHITE   CITY

"CHINESE CITY"

Boyars' Residential District

KREMLIN

CHE

EARTHEN

MOSKVA RIVER

Kolomenskoye

(MINOR ROAD)

MAIN ROAD TO SERPUKHOV

Monastery
of the Don

MAIN ROAD
TO KALUGA

MOSKVA RIVER

Sparrow
Hills

ROAD TO
Mozhaysk
and
Smolensk

FERRY

Novodevichy
Monastery

gismund sent two examples of fancy human cast-iron where flex-ible blades of Toledo steel were called for. Furthermore, as royal messengers to a nation where protocol, prerogative and blue-blood were still the mainstays of diplomatic effectiveness, the King chose to send one of the lesser Castellans, far down on the scale of senato-rial rank, as head of his special embassy, with the same Gosiewski as second in command who was even then returning from Moscow after failing to accomplish his first mission. This put an extraordi-nary burden on the senior envoy, Nicholas Oleśnicki, Castellan of Małogość, a man in his pompous late forties.

Whether or not they were intended actually to accompany Pan George and Marina, Oleśnicki and Gosiewski did not cross the Russian border until nearly a week after the great calvacade. Once they were inside Muscovy, however, they sent some of their serv-ants back to Warsaw (or Kraków) and entrusted themselves to the pristavy supplied by Dimitry for the Empress Marina.

Difficulties began almost immediately, especially in the matter of food and drink, and provender for their horses. They had to buy a good deal for themselves, at what seem to have been rather high prices, and on occasion tavern-keepers refused to accept their Polish money. When they sent a letter of complaint to Vlasyev, they got a polite and wordy answer but little relief. Nevertheless, they moved on with reasonable speed, considering the many bridges they had to cross near the headwaters of the Dnyeper — one hun-dred and forty in forty-five miles.

The two ambassadors followed a road that took them to the south of the Moskva River, and on the morning of Marina's entry into the capital they were in the outskirts, near the Sparrow Hills, today named for Lenin. There they received orders from Dimitry to precede Marina, which gave them an opportunity to observe the huge, ornate tents set up for her, as well as her state-coach. It is worthy of note that they confirmed in their official reports that nothing like the coach had ever been seen in Poland, a realm famed for the luxury of its private conveyances.

Crossing the Moskva River by a "specially prepared" bridge, they came to the lower end of Red Square, before the so-called Cathedral of Saint Basil. At that point, they were received by Dimitry's representatives, Prince Grigory Konstantinovich Volkonsky, of Dimitry's Council, and a Foreign Office Secretary, as he might be called today.

Prince Grigory recited that "The Most Illustrious and Unconquered Autocrat and Great Lord Dimitry Ivanovich, by the Grace of God Caesar and Great Prince of all Russia and many Tatar Empires and other Muscovite Kingdoms subject to him" had sent them to greet, in the name of His Imperial Highness, "the Ambassadors of the Most Illustrious Great Lord, Sigismund III, King of Poland, Grand Duke of Lithuania, Russia, Prussia, Samogitia, Mazovia, and other Kingdoms," and so on.

Then the ambassadors were conducted up the street now named for the communist activist Valerian Kuybyshev to the Ambassadors' Court, a three-story establishment where visiting diplomats were accommodated, along with their retinues up to a thousand or so in number. It was a rambling wooden structure built after the fire of 1591, which some said had been set by Boris Godunov to make people forget the murder of the Tsarevich Dimitry. Great outside staircases led up to the main floor, and there were turrets at the corners of the building, as well as a huge tower which gave a magnificent view over the whole city.[2]

During the week before the arrival of King Sigismund's ambassadors, however, Pan George Mniszech had posted ahead of his daughter and had reached Moscow on April 24, as has been mentioned. Dimitry, boyishly, rode out incognito to observe whether his father-in-law was properly welcomed, and despite Muscovite protocol received him in solemn audience the next day. With Pan George came Stanislas Mniszech and Prince Konstantin Vishnevetsky.

The audience was surrounded with the usual stiff formality of the Kremlin, with the usual boyars in long gem-laden kaftans, the usual four figures in white satin, and the usual wealth of gold chains and jewels. Prince Mikhaylo Skopin-Shuysky stood at Dimitry's right, as port-glaive. In the background was a solitary boyar whose charge was to carry the Imperial handkerchief. He alone was unusual.

Pan George knelt to kiss the Tsar's hand, then retreated a few steps to intone the harangue which was considered *de rigueur.* "It is hard for me to make up my mind," he admitted, "whether I should marvel rather than rejoice . . . O Fortune, how inconsistent you are with men, and how you do play with them! . . . Now must I greet Your Imperial Majesty on this throne, and kiss Your Majesty's hand — a hand which I used to cherish before out of friendship, as a host to his guest, but which I now bow before . . ." and so on. The greatness of God, and the cold of the winter near Novgorod Seversky alike served as inspiration for Pan George's eloquence.

Dimitry was touched to the quick. According to one of the Poles who were present, before the speech was over Dimitry "was weeping like a beaver." [3]

Fortunately, protocol did not permit Dimitry to answer personally. Afanasy Vlasyev did the honors, as always, after which Pan George was provided with a chair facing the throne, where he sat while young Stanislas and Prince Konstantin made proper obeisance. Dimitry then rose, presumably having made use of the Imperial handkerchief, and invited Pan George to join him at dinner, while Basmanov took charge of the other two guests mentioned, as well as a number of unmentioned Polish gentlemen attendant upon Pan George.

Again, everything was glowing with gold and silver and sparkling with jewels — table service, cups, door-hinges, and all. Dimitry sat alone, at a silver-gilt table covered with a cloth of gold brocade. Mniszech, his son, and his son-in-law sat at a second table, lower than the Tsar's and at a short distance away. The remaining guests were at a third table, slightly more remote.

Since the repast was as rich as the decorations, and the variety of food was as great as the variety of cups and serving plates, the dinner lasted several hours. As was customary in Moscow, the courses were consumed without benefit of any liquid refreshment whatsoever. But towards the end, an ocean of liquor began to flow into the endless reserves of drinking vessels on hand. Only the first cups of wine were served from the Tsar's table, with the major-domo designated to attend the guests delivering these personally, each with a brief speech: "Dimitry Ivanovich, Emperor, Tsar and Great Prince of all Russia, extends this grace to you." Beyond this, the serving of wine, mead, beer and brandy was relatively unceremonious, in the eyes of the Poles.

A score of Muscovite subjects just arrived from Siberia were presented to Dimitry before the banquet was concluded. Their presence was particularly worthy of notice because of the fact that they had started out when Boris Godunov was Tsar, had later heard that their ruler was Fyodor Borisovich, and had finally arrived to greet Tsar Dimitry Ivanovich. The Polish gentleman whose account of the affair has been followed here suggested that these newcomers were pagans from Japan, but it is more likely that they were Mongolians.

Finally, the Tsar indicated that dinner was over. Each guest then passed before his table, in strict order of rank, and received from Dimitry's own hand, two Hungarian plums. By this gift the Tsar indicated that he was well pleased.[4]

A few days later, Dimitry invited Pan George to ride out with him to inspect the tents which had been prepared for Marina outside the city walls. The scene was exceedingly festive, what with halberdiers running on ahead (despite a hot day), and Dimitry cantering in sumptuous attire at the head of the party. Pan George rode immediately behind, on the right hand of Prince Vasily Ivanovich Shuysky, completely restored to favor, and with a retinue of boyars and members of the Imperial Guard.

A jovial lunch followed the tour. Then a circle of armed men marked off an arena, and a number of bears, rounded up for the occasion, were let loose. When all was in order, Dimitry himself rode into the ring, charging the largest bear of all and killing it with a superb thrust of his pike. Beyond the fact that such behavior was fervidly considered wrong for a Tsar of Russia, it was highly dangerous. Firearms was still far from effective or accurately reliable, and a slip on the part of either horse or rider would almost certainly have been fatal.

Although the bear was dead, another kind of slip occurred. Such un-Tsarlike behavior under the very nose of Prince Vasily Shuysky was a grave mistake. That cunning, shifty old man had resumed his relentless plotting against the young, open-minded and often naïve ruler. Bear-fights were added to the lengthening list of things to serve as bases for disparaging rumors.

Just then, however, an odd incident frightened the Shuysky cabal into extraordinary caution and a period of silence. A female "blessed idiot" named Elena began an independent series of rumors, all pointing to an early death for the Tsar, but without specifying whether it was to come at the paws of a bear or the hands of a man. Elena had a great reputation as a saint and prophetess, and Boris Godunov visited her during the winter when Dimitry was fighting at Novgorod Seversky. Boris asked her about the future. In answer she provided a bit of mummery that seemed to say that he would be buried soon. When he could get nothing further out of her, Boris left, deeply disturbed. Strangely, he was indeed buried within a very few months.

Dimitry, when he heard about her, laughed at her predictions, and to the great relief of the conspirators refused to ask when, how, or by whose hand he would die. But even that refusal to believe in superstitions was eventually turned against him. To the people of Moscow, Elena was a saint, with the divine gift of prophecy. That she was an idiot made no difference.

About the same time Shuysky heard of another development, curious in the extreme, which he and his fellow plotters quickly turned to their advantage. The Cossacks of the Terek River, far away on the slopes of the Caucasus and the shores of the Caspian Sea, learned of the great privileges won by their brothers, the Cossacks of the Don, and got together with their neighbors, the Cossacks of the Volga, to hatch a plot of their own.

Tsar Fyodor the Angelic had had a daughter, Feodosia, who died in 1593, an infant in arms. At the time there had been rumors (against Boris Godunov, of course) that Feodosia had been a boy, but that Boris had substituted a baby girl for him, and done away with the boy for fear he would grow up and become Tsar. The Cossacks of the Terek decided to produce that non-existent boy and turn Boris's fears into a fact.

After casting about a little, the Cossacks located two possible candidates: a lad named Dimitry in Astrakhan, and one named Ilya in Murom, less than two hundred miles from Moscow itself. Dimitry begged off on the grounds that he had never been to Moscow, and that he knew nothing about things there or how to behave like a Tsar. Ilya's past, on the other hand, had been adventurous, including voyaging with merchants on the Volga and other rivers, and becoming a Cossack after the death of his mother and father. He turned up in Astrakhan in 1604, and from there went to Tersky Gorodok, in the heart of the Cossack country. Upon being asked, he was happy to become the Cossack candidate for the son of Fyodor the Angelic. The fact that he must have been at least twenty, while the "son" of Fyodor could not have been over fourteen, had no bearing.

By this time the Dimitry who was called the Pretender was on the verge of moving towards Moscow, but the Cossacks of the Terek had not yet heard of him. After a brush with the voyvode of Tersky Gorodok over Ilya, they slipped out to sea, some four thousand of them, and sailed to Astrakhan. Denied admission to the city, they then sailed up the Volga, entertaining themselves royally by robbing all the merchants they could lay hands on. Between Astrakhan and Kazan, they are said to have augmented their resources by some three hundred thousand rubles — an enormous sum of money in those days.[5]

By this time, Dimitry had reached Moscow. Learning of the presence of the Cossack band, with the "son" of Fyodor as their leader, within five hundred miles or so of the capital, he made a highly astute move. Instead of attempting to fight and capture these hardy sons of the steppe and the wilderness, he wrote a letter to Ilya, who was by then known as "Pyotr," saying that if he were really the son of his brother, he must come to the city as quickly as he could, for a great reception and high honors were waiting for him there. Ilya-Pyotr accepted the invitation and was well on his way when Pan George and the Empress Marina arrived.

Prince Vasily Shuysky helped himself to this incident with great alacrity. With the aid of his expert rewriters of history, Prince

Vasily gave out that Dimitry invented and was supporting Ilya-Pyotr himself, for by accepting a fake son of the angelic Tsar as his real nephew, he was bolstering his own fake claim on the throne by a second imposture. For everyone knew that Ilya-Pyotr was the bastard son of Ivan Korovin, a citizen of Murom on the Oka.

Dimitry all the while persisted in ignoring or refusing to believe in Shuysky's disloyalty. When the "old man," for he was prematurely old, returned from exile, Dimitry not only permitted but even encouraged him to marry. Boris Godunov had steadfastly refused to allow this, presumably for fear that an heir to that branch of the Shuysky family would spell the end of his own dynastic hopes.

At the same time, Prince Fyodor Mstislavsky also received permission to marry. He too had been denied this privilege by Boris Godunov, for similar reasons. But neither of the scions of the House of Rurik at any time showed any gratefulness for their reinstatement to wealth and position by the young Tsar. Mstislavsky accepted favors and prominence passively as his due; Shuysky, likewise as his due but with active duplicity.

Pan George Mniszech seems not to have noticed Prince Vasily's untrustworthiness any more than did Dimitry. To be sure, his son-in-law the Tsar kept him so occupied that he could hardly have had time to think about such things; and then, if he had suspected anything, it would be difficult to discover it in surviving documents. He had no occasion, of course, to write to Dimitry while he was in Moscow, and later, when Shuysky had made himself Tsar, he certainly could not have testified that he did not trust him. Nevertheless, nowhere is there even a hint of such an attitude on his part.

It is true that Mniszech had not yet arrived when one of the secretaries, Timofey Osipov according to one contemporary, took Holy Communion and strode madly to the palace. There he pushed himself into Dimitry's presence and addressed him, before everyone, in these words: "You are really the unfrocked monk Grishka Otrepyev, and you are not an undefeated Caesar, nor the Tsar's son Dimitry, but a sinful slave and a heretic." [6]

Osipov is supposed to have been tortured and sent into exile (but significantly, not killed) without revealing who inspired him to commit this insensate act. Although some writers have suggested that it may have been Shuysky, the details of the story have every appearance of being a later invention. Just the same, something did happen, and a secretary was sent into exile. The sole significance of the report lies in the fact that such assaults on Dimitry's genuineness were not uncommon and could easily have reached Pan George's ears if he had chosen to listen.

A better documented instance of the same sort took place just before Mniszech reached Moscow, when Prince Vasily criticized the Tsar for eating roast veal at a public dinner, especially since it was still Lent. Dimitry brushed the comment aside, but a member of his Council named Mikhail Ignatyevich Tatishchev spoke up for Shuysky, without even elementary courtesy or caution. Dimitry was angered by his attitude, and ordered him to leave the table. Later there was talk of exile, but Pyotr Basmanov persuaded Dimitry to restore the antagonistic boyar to his graces. Although in the days of Ivan the Dread, or even Boris, Tatishchev would possibly already have been executed, Dimitry willingly forgave him. The glories of benevolence as sung by Seneca may have reached Dimitry through the Jesuit fathers, but Basmanov should have known that he was sowing kindness in a very barren field indeed.

During the week following Pan George's arrival Prince Vasily in fact labored more assiduously than ever on his schemes for ridding Russia of the young man for whom his distaste seems to have been mounting rapidly. He had learned that the people loved Dimitry, that they wanted him for Tsar, and that no amount of rumor-mongering about his violations of ancient customs or about his imposture in the matter of his descent would move them. He had even learned that Dimitry would probably continue to trust him, and that his warped life was safe. So, as the month of May approached, he turned to new tactics.

Instead of relying entirely on his own family, Shuysky sought the support of Prince Vasily Vasilyevich Golitsyn, the courier who had brought word to Dimitry in Putivl that Basmanov had surrendered, and Prince Ivan Semyonovich Kurakin, a third-or-so cousin. Both of these princes were descended from the Lithuanian Gedimin, and the Kurakins particularly were not noted for taking second place, even when it belonged to them.

In order to unite themselves against a common foe, the trio swore to a single aim: to kill the "unfrocked monk, Dimitry-Grishka." As to which of them was to reign when they were successful, they concurred that "no-one should seek vengeance for bygone injuries, but rule the Russian empire in accordance with the council of all." Each conspirator undoubtedly had preconceived notions as to the meaning of this cryptic agreement.

So many echoes of so much plotting reverberated softly in the streets and houses of Moscow that the Saxon immigrant, Konrad Bussow, began to be deeply interested. Bussow, a former mercenary soldier in the service of Boris Godunov who had established himself in some sort of business and acquired a little property, had known Basmanov before the appearance of Dimitry. Now that Dimitry was Tsar, and Basmanov in the most trusted position of all the Muscovites in Dimitry's service, Bussow found occasion to see him rather frequently. By the spring of 1606 they seem to have become friends, and Bussow took advantage of an invitation to visit Basmanov in company with "a distinguished German merchant," to inquire of him the truth about Dimitry's identity. Was he the true heir?

Basmanov answered with remarkable openness:

> You Germans have a father and a brother in him. He is fond of you, and has raised you to higher and better positions than any Emperor has done before. You are also true to him, that I know. Pray that God will protect him, and I will do that with you. Even though I admit that he possibly is not the son of Tsar Ivan [*ob er wohl zwar nicht des Iwans Sohn ist*], still he is now our Lord; we have accepted him, even sworn an oath to him, and we will never get a better lord in Russia.[7]

Shuysky's rumors did not create that feeling in Basmanov, and it is very likely that many more in Moscow suspected or believed that

Dimitry was not Ivan's son. Yet all surviving reports lead to the inescapable conclusion that Dimitry was enormously popular with the people, defects and bad habits notwithstanding. They would be loyal to him, much in the same way as Basmanov, though without the same intensity. Shuysky could not shake the people. The ears he found to listen were the ears of the princes of the blood and the more self-seeking boyars. By the time Marina arrived these ears were buzzing with unpleasant anticipation.

Friday, May 2, thus finally arrived. Marina entered Moscow in triumph such as no living Muscovite had seen before. For hers was a *foreign* triumph. Stately boyars were there, to be sure, and Russian troops. And Russian cavalry rode with their great war-drums sounding. But the war-drums were drowned out by the Polish cavalry, in full armor, beating Polish drums and blaring and squealing with Polish trumpets and shawms. Not even the clumsy bawling and rattling of cornets and side-drums played on by Russian musicians at the three city gates could drown out the strident Polish fanfares. It was a strange ceremony for Moscow.

Many of the onlookers asked old-time German residents if it was customary in *their* country for knights to ride to weddings in full armor, or for baggage wagons to carry five or six light cannon or heavy guns each. Shuysky had long been claiming that their Tsar was not the son of Ivan, and indeed not a Russian. Here was evidence of it. Not only was the Tsar friendly with the Germans and other foreigners, but especially did he favor the Poles, the hated Poles. Worse, he armed them. Against whom? His own people?

Shuysky's partisans were ready with the answer. Dimitry had surrounded himself with Polish troops and German mercenaries in order to wipe out ancient Moscow and her inhabitants. The Russians must bow down to Poland. They must become Poles. The absurdity and maliciousness of this imputation was strikingly evinced the very next day during the audience granted to Sigismund's ambassadors. But that side of the coin of course was never shown to the public by Prince Vasily Shuysky and his henchmen.

As has been mentioned, the Polish ambassadors, Nicholas Oleśnicki and Alexander Korwin Gosiewski, arrived in Moscow a matter of minutes before Marina's procession began. That day was given over to her. The next morning, however, a state reception was prepared for the leading members of Marina's entourage, and Oleśnicki and Gosiewski were included.

The group arrived at the Great Palace at ten. While the ambassadors waited briefly, Marina's suite was ceremoniously admitted before the Tsar, surrounded by his customary "Byzantine" court. But for the longer shadows on the floor and the heavier, darker design of the throne-room, they could have been gaudy barbarians from the West before the purple and porphyry mystique of the Great Palace in Constantinople.

Martin Stadnicki, as Master of the Empress's Court, addressed the Tsar on behalf of the guests from Kraków. Without hesitation he proclaimed Dimitry's Imperial title. He spoke briefly. And with comparable brevity Afanasy Vlasyev thanked him in the name of his master.

By then, a specially designated boyar had gone to the entrance of the palace to receive Sigismund's envoys. Apparently this separate treatment was designed by Dimitry to reflect the annoyance he felt at the attitude of the King toward his titles and himself. After reciting the Tsar's titles in full, the boyar announced on behalf of the envoys: "The Ambassadors Nicholas Oleśnicki and Alexander Gosiewski of the Most Serene and Great Lord Sigismund III, by the Grace of God King of Poland and Grand-duke of Lithuania, etcetera, do obeisance to Your Lordship's Grace." Sigismund had been deliberately stripped of the title "King of the Swedes, Goths and Wends" which was his by inheritance.[8]

Oleśnicki was imperturbable. Upon being brought before the throne, he bowed properly and addressed Dimitry according to the instructions he had received. Giving full vent to Sigismund's style, including Sweden and so on, he greeted the Tsar merely as "Great Prince of Muscovy," and went leisurely on to state that he and his companion had been sent to congratulate Dimitry on his accession to the throne, and to bring the King's brotherly greetings. Thereupon he handed to Afanasy Vlasyev a personal letter from the King to Dimitry.

Vlasyev, without a doubt delighted at the opportunity thus given him to be officious, took the letter, studied the address on it carefully, whispered something in the Tsar's ear, received an answer, cleared his pompous throat and stated:

Nicholas and Alexander, envoys to the Most Serene and Undefeated Autocrat from the Most Serene King of Poland and Grandduke of Lithuania, we have just presented this letter to our Sovereign Lord [and he enumerated all the titles in detail]. The title of Imperial Giace is missing, and it is therefore from the Most Serene King to some great prince of all Russia or other. His Highness is Lord of his vast empire; and I return the letter to you to deliver back to your master.

The astounded envoy took the letter, and turned to Dimitry scornfully:

I will take the letter respectfully, but what then? It is an unprecedented affront to the King, to all the distinguished Poles now standing before you, and to all our land, where we just recently saw you loaded with favors and goodwill. You contemptuously reject His Highness's letter from the very throne on which you sit by the grace not only of God, but of my master and of the Polish people.

This far from discreet riposte scandalized all the Russians present as much as it did the Tsar. But Polish outspokenness in the presence of royalty, or even directly to royalty, had been shocking parts of Europe for some little time. Less than ten years before, Queen Elizabeth I of England had pinned back the ears of a similar Polish envoy, saying: "That is not the speech of an ambassador!" Dimitry handled the situation according to his best lights.

Although he had no intention of driving the envoy away, Dimitry took advantage of the opportunity to display his diplomatic and oratorical gifts. Removing his crown and handing it to an attendant, he began by quietly saying that it was unheard of for a crowned monarch to argue with foreign envoys. "But," he continued, "your King obstinately tries my patience." Then, with mounting earnestness, he explained:

It is known and proven that I am not just a prince, nor just a lord
and a tsar, but a great emperor over my immeasurable domains.
That title was given me by God, and it is not an empty title, like
the titles of some kings. Neither the Assyrians nor the Medes under the Roman Caesars had any real right to such a title. Can I be
contented with the title of prince and lord, when I count among
my servants not only princes and lords, but even tsars? I have no
equal in these northern regions. I have need only of God. And do
not all European monarchs call me Emperor? Why does Sigismund
not want to? — Pan Oleśnicki! I ask, would you accept a letter addressed to you which omitted your title of nobility? Sigismund had
in me a friend and a brother, such as the Republic never had before. But now I see there is only malevolence.

This effort at peacemaking only heightened Oleśnicki's temper-
ature and rudeness. He accused Dimitry of ingratitude and of forgetting the King's kindnesses. Then he roundly declared that it
was irrational of Dimitry to demand a new title when he had no
right to it. Turning to the boyars, he called them to witness that
the Russian rulers had never thought of calling themselves Caesars,
which was not true, and called down upon the Tsar's head the
wrath of God for the bloodshed which would be the inevitable
consequences of such limitless pride.

Seeing that Oleśnicki was getting completely out of hand, Dimitry changed tactics and attempted to pass the matter off, saying that
Oleśnicki could kiss his hand, not as ambassador, but as an honored
acquaintance. But the Pole was so enraged that he spat out: "Either I am an ambassador, or I cannot kiss your hand."

There can be no doubt that Dimitry was thoroughly disgusted
by then. Nevertheless, he decided to yield. As Vlasyev later wrote,
"the Tsar did this because he was on the eve of his marriage, and
was disposed to be conciliatory and to want peace around him."

With some semblance of propriety restored, Dimitry intimated
that Vlasyev should accept Sigismund's letter, which was accomplished. Then the ambassadors were shown their seats, and Dimitry officially inquired for the health of the King. In so doing, he
remained seated.

Oleśnicki observed with his customary intransigence that Dimitry must rise on asking the question, out of respect to the King. Dimitry answered that it was his custom to inquire first, and to rise afterwards. This he then did, and Oleśnicki assured him that his master was in good health — at least when he last saw him.[9]

With the audience thus terminated, Dimitry issued commands for an honorable escort to accompany the ambassadors to their quarters. Soon after, he also sent the secretary Ivan Gramotin to them to say that they could live as they pleased in Moscow, without any sort of surveillance or constraint. Customs were changed in Russia, he said, and peaceful love of freedom had taken the place of suspicion and tyranny. Indeed, hospitable Moscow rejoiced that so many Poles were now her guests, after years of mutual distrust and enmity. And as a last and definite hint that his mind was not in any way altered with regard to the matter of titles, he authorized Gramotin to say that he would restore Sigismund's Swedish title, which had been discontinued by Boris Godunov, in exchange for his own imperial style. However, he concluded, these matters could wait until after the celebration of his wedding.

During the whole audience, Mniszech had exerted every effort to restrain both sides of the argument. Once or twice he succeeded in calming Oleśnicki a little. There were also a few details which have been omitted but which testify to Dimitry's efforts to keep protocolary dignity alive. But on the whole there can be no doubt that the morning was an embarrassing one to Poles and Russians alike. Pan George and his friends and relatives cannot have been pleased with Oleśnicki's insolence and boorishness, while the Russians were concerned over the Tsar's lenience. The oddest fact of all, perhaps, was the *disappointment* of the ambassadors at their treatment.

Dimitry had in fact issued an invitation to them to dine with him, which they had refused with somewhat ill grace, and he had given them rich presents. What in part underlay their undiplomatic conduct was their suspicion that Dimitry was not being completely open with them. They seem to have regarded his stubborn insistence on the imperial title as a cloak for insincerity toward Sigismund. And in this they were both right and wrong.

Dimitry, for reasons already stated, had to clear himself from suspicion of even dreaming of turning Russia over to the Poles. Furthermore, there could be no doubt that imperial notions had been part of the atmosphere of the Kremlin since the arrival of the Greek Princess, with her double-headed eagle which remained in use until 1917, and her intransigence in dealing with other nations — which seems still to remain. Yet it was immature on Dimitry's part to expect to force Sigismund to acknowledge such developments by arguing with his ambassadors.

For their part, the ambassadors were not trained diplomats, and exercised their Polish freedom of speech in the wrong place at the wrong time. They knew the formulas of diplomacy, undoubtedly, but not its basic concepts. Afanasy Vlasyev, for all his curious clumsiness, was by far the better trained diplomat. At the same time, in an attempt to explain some of their evident distrust, it may be argued that they suspected that Dimitry, because of his known interest in Unitarianism, and his friendliness toward such extreme Protestants as the Buczyńskis, was secretly aiding the revolt against Sigismund which was rapidly becoming overt. Gosiewski was a known creature of Sigismund. Oleśnicki probably was also very much "trusted."

Furthermore, Sigismund had vaulting aspirations, for his son as well as for himself. These may have formed part of the core of the trouble, for all of the reasons can hardly be traced after three and a half centuries. But in brief it can be said that many years of tension between Russia and Poland had culminated in the confrontation of an ambitious and unpopular King and an ambitious and uncertain young Tsar. Before long, the war gauchely threatened by Oleśnicki was bound to come.

As if in support of Oleśnicki's menace, Marina herself began to fuss quite unimperially. Certainly not eighteen, Marina had become a spoiled darling, ruined by the part she almost unquestionably played of her own free will in saving her father from financial beggary and political disgrace. In 1604 she had been promised the crown and fabulous resources of a Golconda called Russia. In 1606 she was in that Golconda, about to receive the crown. But Golconda proved to be a golden prison. Her hum-

mingbird mentality had looked for the reception accorded the
Queen of Sheba, and she had found herself a Cleopatra in chains of
pearl in a Rome named Moscow.

Showered with the gold and jewels of fairy-tales, the Empress of
all Russia was subject to the strict rules of an Orthodox convent.
As a child she had had servants. During the ride to Moscow great
ladies had attended her. But in the capital of her empire, not one
Polish lady-in-waiting supplied her wants. A single day of such
treatment was enough. Marina let the Emperor of all Russia know
what she wanted.

Dimitry began by sending a Polish maître-d'hotel and Polish
chefs to her, with full authority to produce whatever Marina
wanted by way of food. From Marina he got few thanks, but from
his subjects came endless complaints. The Muscovite cooks announced their umbrage to the world in general. It was not that
they could not roast, boil, fry or grill as well as the useless Poles,
but that the little Tsaritsa, and even the Tsar himself, wanted
cooks who were heretics. They wanted to eat food forbidden by
the Church, and to break the laws of fasting.

That this must have been true was only confirmed by Marina's
loud grumbles that she was infested with Greek Orthodox priests
whose interminable chanting she had to tolerate. Dimitry tried to
alleviate the trouble by sending her a Polish orchestra. With their
strumming, these individualistic and Italianate (if not Italian)
musicians hoped to while away the time for the imprisoned pout-
ing angel. To what avail? Only that all Moscow could whisper
and protest that Marina was profaning a holy place with balls and
masquerades.

Yet the whole matter of Marina's stay in the convent was nothing but an overt demonstration of a piety on the part of the Tsar
that was not genuine, because of an urge that *was* genuine to celebrate his marriage in the most Orthodox form practicable. He and
Marina were by both civil and divine law already man and wife.
But that marriage had been performed under alien — heretic, if
you will — skies, and by heretic priests, including Cardinal Maciejowski. For Marina to be crowned Tsaritsa of all Russia, she had to

be married according to Orthodox ritual, and (since Dimitry considered it indispensable) crowned after the Orthodox fashion. For Marina, whose objective this coronation had long been, it would have seemed a trifling matter to wait out the few days custom decreed. She would not.

Slowly, Prince Vasily Ivanovich Shuysky collected his bits of information, listened to his spies, and wove his dangerous web. While the people reveled in the thought that their radiant, wild and glorious Prince was about to marry the woman he loved, Pole though she was, the stern, deceitful princes and prelates of the old order piously plotted. Their plotting took time, for their real opponent was not the man they wanted to murder. It was the Russian people. They adored Dimitry.

CHAPTER 15

CORONATION AND ZENITH

Marina had arrived on Friday. Sunday came on May 4, according to the Muscovite calendar, but for Marina it was a joyless Sunday. According to the Catholic calendar, it was Pentecost, or Whitsunday, yet in the Convent of the Ascension, Catholic mass was impossible. She could not even be visited by a Catholic priest — even on the day when the Apostles were filled with the Holy Ghost.

Dimitry tried to console her. He gave her a magnificent casket worth fifty thousand rubles. And he solicited cooperation from her father by adding another hundred thousand zlotys to what he had already given him, making a total of at least eight hundred thousand — truly a king's ransom. But neither of them succeeded in persuading Marina to remain in "prison." She was determined to leave the convent.

Dimitry had many other things on his mind, but he finally compromised by bringing her to the palace a day and a half before the festivities were scheduled to begin. Meanwhile, he had a serious difference of opinion with the Russian clergy, in addition to some (still slight) concern over the continuous reports of mutiny in the making.

Shuysky, despairing of getting the help of the common people, now tried to win over the eighteen-thousand-man army collected by Dimitry for his proposed campaign against Ghazi Giray, Khan of the Crimean Tatars. To this end he employed a number of what would now be called noncommissioned officers who came

from Novgorod the Great and who had long been friendly to the
Shuysky family. These he invited to his home one night, along
with some boyars and merchants.

At this clandestine meeting, Prince Vasily explained that Dimitry was a pretender who had been chosen to play the rôle of the
Tsarevich only to rid the realm of Boris Godunov. "They," whoever they were, had thought that he was an intelligent and brave
young man who would be a pillar of the Orthodox Church and a
defender of ancient customs. Instead, the man they had made Tsar
loved foreigners above all, despised the Holy Faith, profaned the
temples of God, expelled the clergy from their homes so that foreigners could live in them, and finally was going to marry a Pole.
Grave dangers threatened Moscow through this man's love for the
Poles.[1]

One of those present apparently drank too much and was soon
picked up by some German halberdiers for calling the Tsar a heretic and the Tsaritsa a pagan. They brought the culprit to the palace, where Dimitry heard at least a part of what had happened at
Shuysky's home. But Shuysky had boyars who belonged to his
cabal always in attendance on Dimitry, and they spoke up immediately. The man was drunk, they said, and the Germans were blab-
mouths. The Tsar should not pay any attention to such tales. He
had nothing to fear, even if there was a mutiny, for he had more
than the necessary strength to crush it. Anyway, nobody would
dare start a mutiny.

These boyars knew Dimitry only too well. He was not born a
coward or inclined to suspicion. For the moment he agreed with
the boyars who said there was nothing to fear.

But for three days in a row, officers of his foreign guards brought
written reports to him that something evil was afoot. On the first
day, Dimitry put the papers in his pocket and said, "That is all
nonsense." Then he got annoyed when the reports were repeated,
and finally got angry, in his own strange way. Whom did he punish? The loyal men who brought bad tidings.

Dimitry's proneness to irritation, particularly at this time, was in
a sense not surprising. The religious leaders in Moscow regarded
Marina with a cold, suspicious eye. Dimitry had already spent a

great deal of time in a vain effort to make his point of view understood. The Poles were Christians, he insisted, as well as the Muscovites, and nothing could stand in the way of his marrying another Christian. Yet the Orthodox clergy refused to comprehend.

The ceremonies which took place in Kraków were to them as non-events — they had never happened. Dimitry would not be married to Marina until their union was celebrated in Moscow and according to the Orthodox rite. Dimitry was willing to accept that point of view. The marriage would take place. In fact, he wanted it that way. But this was only the introduction to the truly thorny problem.

Dimitry was, everyone believed, of the Orthodox Faith. Marina was admittedly a Catholic. This being the case, could the Tsar marry a Pole who was a Catholic? If he could not, what must be done to make Marina acceptable, eligible in the eyes of the Church? It was on this issue that real and vociferous disagreement appeared.

There was no argument among the clergy that she must become Orthodox. She could not remain Catholic. But just how was her Orthodoxy to be made manifest? What must she do?

According to the extremists, Hermogen of Kazan and Iosif of Kolomna, Marina still had to be baptized again. She had not been baptized at all, they explained, and therefore was a heathen. If she was to be married in an Orthodox church and crowned with the holy crown of Muscovy, she must undergo the triple immersion of baptism according to the Eastern rite. It was no matter of theirs that the Catholics accepted Orthodox baptism as valid — of course it was. But the Orthodox Church would not recognize Catholic baptism.

Many bishops disagreed on this matter, however, for the Orthodox doctrine had never been officially proclaimed, and would not be for another dozen years or more. Dimitry naturally backed the dissenting bishops, and the argument was at last settled in favor of accepting Marina's baptism. Passions had run so high before the vote was taken that Hermogen was hustled back to his see and prohibited from visiting the capital in the future.

The less exigent members of the clergy announced then that they would rest content if Marina indicated her acceptance of the Orthodox Faith by being anointed with the holy chrism. In the Eastern Orthodox Church this was symbolic of Confirmation, the second Mystery, after Baptism. Dimitry promptly supported this solution to the problem, for quite obvious, and not entirely guileless, reasons. Marina was to be crowned. Unction with the chrism was part of the coronation. One and the same unction could be taken as confirmation and coronation.

This opened the way to double interpretation of the ceremony, the Poles regarding the unction as part of the coronation ceremony, while to the Russians it could only be considered as acceptance of Orthodox doctrine. Although there is no proof that Dimitry so analyzed his thoughts on the matter, his evident lack of religious scruples probably justifies the assumption. A torn fragment of the order established for the ceremony bears witness to Dimitry's care that no religious convictions or conventions should be offended.

Marina's brief stay in the purgatory of an Orthodox convent was concluded during the night of May 6 to May 7. The moon, if weather permitted it to be seen, had already set behind Sparrow Hills, leaving the open spaces and lanes of the Kremlin submerged in stygian gloom. A hundred pairs of three-branched candlesticks threw a funeral luster over the state-coach which stood ready for the Empress. Bodyguards and boyars'-sons stood around in a silent semicircle. The convent door opened, and a wisp of a girl slipped out, mounted the steps into the coach and was swallowed in its murky interior. Whips cracked. Slowly the cumbersome vehicle moved over the wooden-paved street to the new palace, a quarter of a mile away.[2]

It was two o'clock when Marina reached her apartments. There, to greet her, stood Princess Mstislavsky and Princess Shuysky, whose further identification is now impossible for lack of surviving documentary details. Both were thickly painted with white, and their eyebrows plucked and re-penciled halfway up their foreheads, according to local custom, so that they looked like white masks — one Pole called it "obscene." This custom was said to be for the purpose of concealing their faces from men's stares, but on that night there were no men present, beyond two who carried lights into the palace. The two great princesses received Marina without a word, only nodding their heads. Then they led her to her room.

Later on that same May 7, the matter of Marina's wedding-and-coronation robe was finally settled. She had brought with her a long, tight costume in the style of the French court, which then reigned supreme in Kraków, with a ruff two feet in diameter, over which her hair was to be tightly curled and decorated with pearls and diamonds. But no sooner had the Russians gotten wind of this than a cry of "Shame!" arose. It was indecent, Orthodoxly obscene, for a woman to display her hair and her figure for all to see. Furthermore, no Tsaritsa had ever been crowned in anything other then the national costume: a *kokóshnik* completely hiding the hair and a long robe drawn tight around the neck but with straight lines below, beneath which boots emerged, with huge heels fitted with iron supports.

Marina protested (screamed, would possibly be more accurate) that she would not appear in such a scandalous disguise. Dimitry expostulated, first to her, then to the boyars. Finally he had recourse to his Council. Taking her side, he argued that she had been accustomed to Polish styles since childhood, and that she would be ill at ease in an unfamiliar garb. It has been suggested that he even added that clothes were the special province of women, and that national politics could not be accepted as a sound argument.

A glance at the boyars of the Council would have told him that his pleas and explanations were so much wasted breath. And in fact before long he realized once more that their minds were as unbending as their bodies. He gave in. "Very well," he said, "I will not abrogate my country's customs. I will comply with the wishes of my Councillors, so that they will have no cause to complain that I want to introduce too many changes and novelties." Then he turned to Marina. "It is only for one day," he said. "Please wear Russian dress."

Marina by that time had nothing further to offer. She too obeyed the will of the boyars. Yet it must be added that no sooner was the great day over than Dimitry showed his true stuff. At his command, new Polish dresses were quickly made ready, and he brought them to her in person. She was to wear *those* from then on, "in his honor," he apprised her — with humor, it is to be imagined.

The next morning, Thursday, May 8, came the culmination of Marina's march to glory. At midnight the Kremlin bells began to ring, announcing the coming festivities. By dawn, Dimitry's messengers were already hurrying through the city, loudly exhorting the citizens to drop their work, or not to begin it. All the day was to be dedicated to rejoicing. Their appeal was far from ignored.

In spite of this, the Poles in general were concerned, if not precisely alarmed. Rumors of trouble had reached their ears, and Mniszech, Vishnevetsky, and other magnates had collected groups of armed men in the houses where they were living, or in the surrounding gardens. Some of them tried to communicate this uneasiness to Dimitry, and perhaps in some measure succeeded. For broad daylight saw eight hundred streltsy take up posts along the streets where any of the guests might pass, and throughout the Kremlin. Perhaps because of this precaution Moscow was calm, and even gay.

Soon workmen began once more to stretch crimson cloth over the paths where the Tsar's sacred feet might tread. Noblemen and princes, Muscovites and Poles, streamed through the ancient gates, the Poles conspicuously armed with glittering sabres, and accompanied as always by grooms bearing muskets. In Cathedral Square, between the Facetted Palace and the campanile of Ivan the Great, they gathered, impatient for the Tsar and Tsaritsa to appear.[3]

Meanwhile, in the banqueting hall of the Great Palace, a much smaller group stood, among them Dimitry himself, so weighted by his coronation robes studded from head to foot with diamonds and other precious stones that only a sturdy young man could have walked in them. After a slight pause, Marina entered, accompanied by the Princess Mstislavsky *in loco matris*, and the Lord Palatine of Sandomierz, Pan George Mniszech.

Marina's robe, much lighter in weight but only slightly less dazzling than the Tsar's, was of red velvet, garish with diamonds, rubies, sapphires and pearls, with wide Russian sleeves, and her feet were shod in morocco boots. She wore a diamond crown. Her poise, her diminutiveness, and perhaps her vanity, were the more manifest in such a great hall among so few people. Only the closest relatives of the bride and groom and especially distinguished princes and boyars were admitted: the Mniszechs, a few unnamed boyars, Prince Vasily Ivanovich Shuysky and his brother Dimitry, Grigory Fyodorovich Nagoy (Marfa's brother), and a handful of wedding attendants.

When all had taken their places, the Archpriest of the Cathedral of the Annunciation, who was also Imperial Father Confessor, recited the prayers according to the ritual of betrothal, and the ushers sliced the cheese wedding-cake and distributed napkins. After this relatively brief ceremony, the wedding-party moved on to the Facetted Palace, where all the boyars and court officials were already waiting, along with Sigismund's ambassadors and other distinguished Poles.

There the Russians saw an unheard-of novelty. In the great square salon, whose thirty-foot vaulted ceiling was supported by a giant central pillar, a second throne had been set up alongside the one used by Dimitry's predecessors. Near it stood Prince Vasily Shuysky, who had apparently hurried on in advance of the bride and groom.

As Marina's doll-like figure approached, he proclaimed: *"Nayasnéyshaya velikaya Gosudárynya, Tsesaréva María Yúryevna!* [Most Serene Great Lady, Caesar's-wife Maria daughter-of-George.] By the will of God and of the Unconquered Autocrat, Caesar and Great Prince of all Russia, you have been chosen to be his spouse. Assume, then, your Caesarian majesty, and with the Sovereign rule over us!"

As soon as Marina had seated herself and her unwieldy robe had been adjusted, Boyar Mikhaylo Nagoy brought before her the

Crown of Monomakh and the *bármy,* worn by the Tsar on state occasions. These Marina was commanded to kiss, in token of submission to the power of her lord, the Tsar. Thereupon she was conducted by the Archpriest to the adjacent Cathedral of the Assumption. The cortège accompanying her has been described as "flowing slowly like a river of gold" to its destination.[4]

The door of the Cathedral was normally firmly closed to Catholic "heretics." But on this occasion it was flung wide, and Poles and Russians mingled in seeming brotherly love as they crowded up to watch the parade. It was a display of wealth and pomp worthy of an Oriental pen to describe, for there was much of the incredibility of a story from the Arabian Nights. Marina, for whom the display was made, was the daughter of a bankrupt Polish senator of far from royal Moravian origin. And the Tsar who offered all this had not long since been hunted by the police as an unfrocked monk and impostor.

Rows of bodyguards and streltsy lined the path of the procession, as civil servants and court-attendants marched ahead, followed by Polish guests, ushers, pages, and other human accessories to the wedding. Then came Prince Vasily Vasilyevich Golitsyn, Shuysky's knave, bearing the sceptre, and the Boyar Pyotr Fyodorovich Basmanov with the orb. Dimitry stalked slowly behind these, accompanied by Pan George Mniszech. In their wake, Marina glided with scarcely perceptible steps at the right hand of, and slightly before, the Princess Mstislavsky. Then, at a respectful distance came the boyars, members of the Council, courtiers, and secretaries of the various governing bodies of the empire. A huge crowd of people stood silent in the small square.

It was a ceremony unique in the annals of Russia. Never before had a living Tsar granted such status to his wife that she be allowed to succeed him, if he died childless. Dimitry even assigned the revenues from some districts directly to Marina during his lifetime. The common folk who stood and stared at the spectacle had good reason for excessive curiosity.

On entering the cathedral, Marina kissed the proper ikons, and followed the Tsar to an elaborate dais in the center. On this stood a gilded, bejeweled throne for the Tsar — undoubtedly the one Shah Abbas had given Boris Godunov — and a silver one for Marina. By these was a third seat of state for the Patriarch Ignaty.

While Marina took her seat, Dimitry spoke briefly, presumably about Marina although there is no record of his subject, and was answered by the Patriarch, who then offered a prayer before endowing her with various symbolic emblems: the life-giving cross, the bármy, a diamond fillet with pendants called the "diadem," and, after ladies-in-waiting had removed her kokóshnik, her crown.[5] At that the choir burst into a chant imploring long life for the Lady, the Orthodox *Tsesaréva Maria* (even her baptismal name had to be altered!), while the Patriarch placed the "Chain of Monomakh" around her shoulders and annointed her. Thus Marina became Tsaritsa even before she was in the eyes of the Russians legally married to Dimitry, although she was significantly not given either the sceptre or the imperial orb.

After the clergy and the boyars had kissed Marina's hand in token of fealty, all except the leading members of the court filed out of the cathedral. A solemn hush descended over the few who were present as the Archpriest of the Cathedral of the Annunciation united the Tsar and Tsaritsa in holy matrimony. Thereupon came the most difficult moment for Marina. She and Dimitry were invited to approach the altar and take Holy Communion.

Months before, both Dimitry and Pan George had written to the Pope requesting a dispensation for Marina, so that she might take communion according to the Orthodox rite without endangering her relations with the Catholic Church. Pope Paul seems to have wanted to permit her to satisfy her future subjects in this way. But it was a matter beyond his proper authority and, as has been mentioned, he referred it to the Holy Office for decision.

That body, after studying the communications from both Kraków and Moscow at leisure, met on March 2, 1606 (new style). The Pope himself presided. There was no discussion, so the matter was promptly put to the vote. The result, as laconically transcribed in the Archives, was that "in a meeting in the presence of the Holy Father the petitions as shown on the reverse were presented, and the reverend councillors gave their votes, and with one exception these were negative." Both Dimitry and Marina were aware of this ecclesiastical veto.

Archbishop Arseny of Elasson, a Greek who had come to Moscow at the time Iov was created Patriarch and had been given one of the cathedrals there, took part in the ceremony of May 8. He has left an account of what he saw, heard and thought, and he is considered trustworthy. In part, he wrote:

> After the wedding ceremony, both of them [Dimitry and Marina] showed no wish to receive Holy Communion. This greatly saddened those present, not only the Patriarch and the Bishops, but all those who saw and heard it. Such was the first, indeed the heavy affliction [for all]; the source of scandal, and the origin of many, many evils for the Muscovite people and for all Russia . . .[6]

For a people as fanatically religious as the Muscovites of 1606, refusal to take Holy Communion was brandishing insolence at God. Marina had theretofore been regarded as a pagan; now she might be considered godless, and even antichristian. And Dimitry with her.

From then on, what did it matter that both of them scrupulously complied with all the outward, and empty, gestures of being one with their people? Wine was poured for them, for instance, and when they had wet their lips three times the bottle was broken on the floor, and stamped into a thousand pieces. An ancient custom, but what of it? And when they walked out of the cathedral, hand in hand, wearing their scintillating crowns, with Marina leaning lightly on Prince Vasily Ivanovich Shuysky, gold and silver coins were thrown into the crowd. The crowd scrambled for them, but what of it?

Suddenly, trumpets blasted and kettledrums rattled, the signal for cannon-salutes and an insane clangor of bells. A radiant Dimitry greeted his people. But from them came only low, inarticulate cries. A nameless chill hung over the square, that early mid-May afternoon.

Dimitry apparently paid no heed. Taking a handful of coins, he gaily threw them at a group of Polish guests. These, tired and bored after standing for hours at a ceremony which they did not understand and which they considered barbaric, did not pick them up. Worse, those who accidentally caught a few on their hats shook them off disdainfully.

This insult to their Tsar hardly pleased the common people of Moscow, for they still loved him, and some of the Poles suffered various contusions from the "unintentional" shoving of people who wanted to see their sovereigns. To make matters still sorrier, the Poles voiced their opinions of ruler and ruled alike, loudly and in plain language. Long sentences in Russian and Polish are seldom mutually comprehensible. Isolated words usually are. The frail, fleeting Slavic brotherhood of the morning had already dissolved in the irritated air.

In the palace that night, Pan George Mniszech and a handful of boyars dined with the bride and groom. The meal did not last long, due to the late hour, and all soon rose from the table. The boyars accompanied the couple as far as their bedroom door, and Mniszech and Prince Shuysky went with them to their bed, as was customary. After their departure all was quiet in the palace.

Moscow seemed calm. Only the Poles celebrated and were noisy in expectation of the coming wedding-banquets, further royal gifts, and the distribution of honors. But in the homes of Prince Vasily Shuysky and his cabal there were no festivities, no high spirits, and no idle dreams. From courteous and subservient attendance on Marina, Prince Vasily quickly turned away to weave the net of his conspiracy tighter.[7]

According to the Orthodox calendar, May 8 was the Feast of Saint John the Divine. The next day was both a Friday and one of the several Feasts of Saint Nicholas the Thaumaturge — not a Great Feast, still not a day to be taken lightly. Yet that morning after the marriage of Dimitry and Marina an unwelcome band of chanticleers in the enthusiastically combined persons of bass-drum beaters and blaring trumpeters sallied noisily from the Kremlin out through the streets and byways of the capital to announce the glad tidings of the wedding festivities of the Unconquered Caesar, Dimitry Ivanovich, Tsar and Great Prince of all Russia.

The Orthodox Church, and the Catholic as well, required a certain degree of abstinence that day, and perhaps among the Orthodox a little more than routine attention to things spiritual. The peace of the morning for Orthodox and Catholic alike was thus broken by the rat-a-tat-tat and tarantara that greeted the sun when it rose and relinquished its cacophonous summons only at midday. Soon, revels worthy of the Rome of the Caesars would shake the respectable ramparts of Ivan's dread Kremlin.

The wedding festivities began with a gala dinner for both Muscovites and Poles. King Sigismund's ambassadors logically were among the latter, and were invited with gay politeness by the Tsar himself. They accepted with corresponding courtesy, but attached a condition — which was far from unusual with them. At least one of the two, they informed Dimitry, expected to be seated at the table with him, just as Afanasy Vlasyev had sat at the King's table after Marina's wedding by proxy in Kraków.

Since this condition could not be met, Dimitry sent Vlasyev to explain why. "What you demand is unheard of," Vlasyev explained to Oleśnicki. "No-one is ever seated at the table with the Tsar. Your King entertained me on an equal footing with the ambassadors from the Emperor and from Rome, and there was nothing remarkable about that. Our sovereign is not *less* than the Emperor or the Bishop of Rome. Not at all. The great Caesar Dimitry is greater than they. Your 'Pope' is the same as his 'Popes' [priests]!" Obviously, Vlasyev enjoyed this brief opportunity to show his little liking for the Poles.

Oleśnicki put up with the rude language, but at the same time decided for himself and Gosiewski not to attend the banquet. His refusal had no influence on the other Poles, with the exception of Pan George Mniszech, who clearly had to keep on good terms with people as close to the King as the two ambassadors. At the last minute he tried to explain to Dimitry that Oleśnicki was right, but without success. And when Dimitry repeated that he could not have an ambassador seated at his table, even as the guests were already assembling, Pan George accompanied the bride and groom only to the door of the banqueting hall. There he suddenly complained of an attack of gout, and went home. Neither he nor the ambassadors seem to have been missed.

Dimitry and Marina sat on a dais, with bodyguards armed with battle-axes behind them. Priests asperged the couple with holy water. Then boyars began to serve them from huge platters and bowls of gold and silver. Stanislas Mniszech's orchestra struck up a tune.

While the Poles marveled at the inexhaustible supply of precious metals and priceless gems, the Russians showed some disgust at the costumes worn by the Tsar and Tsaritsa. Gone were the stiff robes of ancient usage. In their place, Dimitry wore a sprightly hussar's tunic of the kind worn in Poland, and Marina was also attired in good Polish style. Both of them undoubtedly looked their best in such clothing, but Moscow universally regarded it as un-Muscovite, and objectionable. Still more offensive was the fact that only a handful of Poles (all of them relatives of Marina), and no Russians, were invited to attend the Tsar in his private apartments after the feast.

Nevertheless, it was not only the Russians who eventually took umbrage. Once Dimitry was free of the stifling court abracadabra, his tongue was loosed, and his questionable gift of bravado was indulged beyond reasonable bounds, undoubtedly aided by the free-flowing bowl. He regretted not having lived a good many centuries earlier, when he could have known Alexander the Great, his paragon of paragons, so that he could have matched wits and tactics with him, and shown his profound devotion at the same time. By comparison, the Emperor Rudolf was a nobody (which was hardly an exaggeration, despite his illustrious ancestry), and King Sigismund fared little better. In fact, he did not even spare the Pope and the Abbé of Sambor entirely.

All of this was turned into a theoretically hilarious bit of entertainment by the Italian buffoon, who was there for just such purposes. Still, the Poles could find no real cause for offense. Ready as they were to fight for fatherland and faith, Dimitry stopped short

of supplying the spark to set them off. He remained, despite the
cheap boasting and badinage, Tsar of all Russia. None dared con-
tradict him in that capacity.

When the drollery began to pall, Dimitry suggested a dance.
Stanislas Mniszech and Prince Konstantin Vishnevetsky accepted
the idea with alacrity, and the musicians obliged with lively Polish
airs. But this was not dramatic enough for Dimitry. Restlessly
looking for further excitement, he remembered the Polish soldiers
who were on duty outside. Opening the great doors of the hall, he
called them in, to have a glass of wine. Then, summoning a chamberlain, he sent for some coins and gave each of them a present,
promising great wonders for the future.

The soldiers, greedy to show off (and get more coins), implored
his permission to organize an impromptu tourney. Hesitantly, re-
luctantly, Dimitry agreed, but when one rider was hurt and a horse
killed in short order, he called the entertainment off. It was time
to retire in any event. Tomorrow would be another festive day.

On Saturday, Marina was honored by a large number of personages who came bearing wedding gifts. At the head of the procession was the Patriarch, followed by representatives of the clergy.
Then came the leading Muscovite merchants, and after them the
foreigners. Another banquet closed the day's diversions, and
closed it on another unpleasant note. Although Dimitry and Marina were not personally present, the foreign agents were better
placed with relation to the empty throne than the native magnates.
Once again tongues wagged over the Tsar's predilection for everything which was not Russian.

Several untoward incidents occurred during these two days, including Dimitry's loss of a diamond ring which Isaac Massa valued
at thirty thousand rix-dollars.* Then a Pole was wounded by one
of the streltsy. Many people blamed the profanation of the holy
day for these mishaps.

At the same time, it seems that Prince Vasily Shuysky was profit-
ing by all such matters to improve the chances of stirring up a
successful revolt. Anything which contributed to public disap-

* Worth between $250,000 and $500,000 today.

proval of Dimitry was indeed pleasant news to him and his cabal. But the best news of all was word that three thousand of Shuysky's malcontents had successfully entered Moscow without their hidden arms being found.

By then Ambassador Oleśnicki had been convinced by Mniszech that he and Gosiewski should accept an invitation from Dimitry, if issued, to attend a banquet on Sunday. This done, the peacemaking voyvode hastened to the palace and persuaded Dimitry not only to provide the invitation, but to accord Oleśnicki the most favored position possible in the seating arrangement. Finally, another trip to the ambassadors' quarters extracted a promise from both of them not to demand anything more, and not to stir up an argument over the value to Russia of a close association with Poland.

But Dimitry himself was on the verge of making trouble before the banquet started. Referring to the places he had assigned to the envoys, he said to Oleśnicki that he had not invited King Sigismund to the wedding, and therefore Oleśnicki was not attending the festivities as proxy for the King, but as a simple ambassador. Therefore he saw no reason to honor him exceptionally. And he added gratuitously, "If Emperor Rudolf came to Moscow, I would not seat him at my table." At that point, Mniszech managed to intervene, keeping Dimitry from saying anything further. The dinner, the most elaborate yet presented, began in comparative peace and friendship.

On this occasion, the ladies of the nobility attended for the first time. Dimitry and Marina also wore their crowns for the first time since the wedding, as well as Polish costumes once more. But the most remarkable event was Pan George's insistence on serving Marina himself, hat in hand, like a palace flunky rather than a father. Poles and Muscovites alike were astounded at such a gesture from an old man.

When the meal was over, many, many toasts were drunk. Since there were always sensitive matters from the point of view of protocol and prerogatives, the ambassadors never relaxed their guard. Still, Dimitry playfully maneuvred an embarrassment for Gosiew-

ski. Declaring that he was ready to forget all the nagging differences between them, he drank to the health of that junior envoy.
Gosiewski, overwhelmed at the honor, rose to acknowledge it.
Quickly Dimitry told him that he must come to his table to do
that. Gosiewski, perhaps prompted by Oleśnicki, saw in this some
threat to the dignity of the King of Poland, and refused to budge.
One of the Buczyńskis was near at hand, however. Fearing another
tempest from the Tsar, he quickly whispered in Gosiewski's ear:
"For the love of God, go! — Unless you want to create a scandal
. . ." Gosiewski meekly complied.

Finally, when all the toasts had been drunk, and the plums
passed out, a group of high officials approached the throne to receive certain letters which they were to carry to Shah Abbas I, in
his new capital of Isfahan. Before leaving, they kissed the hands of
both Dimitry and Marina.

Sunday did not end, however, without a new cause for complaint
against the Tsar. In the morning, permission had been granted to
the Lutheran pastor, Martin Baer, to conduct services in the palace
for the German captains, doctors, and other German (or Lutheran) gentlemen resident in Moscow, for whom a trip to the
German colony in the suburbs would be a long ride. At the same
time it was noted that Dimitry had not been seen in any Orthodox
church himself. By nightfall, new rumors were on foot: The Tsar
was no longer a true believer in the Holy Orthodox Faith. And
this was "confirmed" by stories that, although the great imperial
bathroom had been ready day and night, neither he nor Marina
had yet followed the ancient Russian customs in bathing.

The next morning, two halberdiers picked up a loose-tongued
"rogue" spreading such talk and brought him to Dimitry for questioning. Apparently Dimitry was taken aback by what the man had
to say, for he promptly commanded his entire guard to take up per-
manent residence in the palace, at least until the whole matter
could be thoroughly investigated.

But the boyars on duty in the palace were of Shuysky's faction.
Once more they covered up the rascal's stories by saying that he
was a drunken fool who would not make any more sense even if he

were sober. Besides, they added, the Tsar was paying too much attention to German tattlers. He was far too powerful to let himself be misled by such nonsense.[8]

That of course was enough for Dimitry. It was not the first time that he had heard tales, and it was not the first time that he refused in the end to be tantalized by them. Especially during the festivities of his wedding-week.

CHAPTER 16

THICK AND UNWHOLESOME
THOUGHTS AND DEEDS [1]

Aꜰᴛᴇʀ ᴛʜᴇ ꜰêᴛᴇ of Sunday afternoon and evening there was a slight respite. Doubtless the guests were glad. Certainly the Shuysky cabal was overjoyed. Shuysky's plot, born of ambition and hatred, was now full-fledged. It had an organization, a plan, and two additional leaders: Prince Vasily's brothers Dimitry and Ivan. The diminution in required attendance at court allowed more time to settle the preliminaries for action, in detail. Meanwhile, the common people and the boyars loyal to Dimitry *knew* nothing, although an air of foreboding rested heavily over the city.

Monday and Tuesday there was music in the Kremlin. Some said that a bear-hunt or something of the sort was planned, along with another mock assault on a made-to-order fortress, but these did not materialize. Something seemed to have gone out of the guests, and the entertainment was flat and purely formal.

In the city — in the Chinese City, and the White City, and the Earthen City — otherwise sensible people began to see things in the sky, omens of disaster. One day, Tuesday or Wednesday, in mid-afternoon, huge clouds suddenly rolled up out of the west (where Poland lay) and took the shape of mountains and caverns. Then a lion was clearly visible, which was soon replaced by a camel, and then by a giant who was seen to enter a cavern in the clouds. Finally, the great mass reformed, and there was a whole city in the sky, with towers from which dark smoke poured. The young Dutch merchant, Isaac Massa, saw this, and so did his landlord and many friends, and they were frightened. But others only laughed.

On Thursday, May 15, fresh rumors reached Dimitry, which troubled him just enough for additional guards to be placed everywhere. They did not interfere with the resumption of festivities. Dimitry invited Oleśnicki and Gosiewski to a ball, informing them that it was purely social. There would be neither Tsar nor Ambassador, he said. Etiquette would be suspended for the day.

Oleśnicki took him at his word, arrived without his usual pomp, mingled with the crowd, and permitted others to enter the salon before himself. When he finally did go in, he greeted a number of the guests, and invited a lady to dance with him. As was proper among ladies and gentlemen then, he kept his jeweled cap on his head, which would be highly improper in the presence of a king. Dimitry spotted him at once. Beckoning to Martin Stadnicki, he informed him that anyone wearing a cap in his presence would have not only the cap removed, but the head with it, and sent him to convey this information to Oleśnicki. Oleśnicki looked at Dimitry, only to find a gaze that admitted no discussion. "There is no Ambassador," he muttered, removing the cap, "but the Tsar is still here."

Later, the Ambassador met a number of boyars in the palace apartments for the purpose of discussing certain matters for which King Sigismund had sent him. The chief point on this occasion was the proposed campaign against the Turks. After proper eulogies on the intelligence and farsightedness of the Tsar, Oleśnicki questioned the boyars closely about the plans for such a campaign — when it was to start, how many troops would be involved, and so on. The boyars listened with incredulity. Who were they to disclose state secrets to foreign envoys? There was an acrimonious dispute, which ended in an appeal to the Tsar. Word was sent back that he would discuss the matter personally in a few days.

Oleśnicki was not the only Pole who was disappointed in the Tsar. Stanislas Niemojewski, a courtier who had a long interview with Dimitry on May 16, as will be seen shortly, accused him of being over-ambitious, haughty and impatient even with his most trusted associates. But this severe judgment was modified by the concession that he was amiable, quick to take offense but quick to forgive, moderate of habits and intolerant of drunkenness, in favor of progress but without real religious faith. In short, very human, and with great capabilities.

Conflicting reports of the same sort were made also by the Carmelite monks who passed through Russia on their way to Persia in March, and by Father Sawicki, who stressed Dimitry's "sins of the flesh," voluptuousness and pride. But here it appears to be the Catholic Church speaking — Dimitry was no longer the pliable convert, the faithful son of the Holy Father. Beyond that, it is as difficult to place a finger on the real cause of the Polish disillusionment as on that of the implacable enmity of the "old family" Muscovite princes. In both cases, there seems to be surprise, shock and distaste in discovering a monarch who had his own ideas about what should be done with Russia — Holy Russia, basking in the mystic obscurity of an unregenerate medievalism.

Nevertheless, one phase of the Russian ferment, not directly connected with religion or with Dimitry's ideas about progress, was immediately derived from the cavalcade of Poles which swept through to Moscow with Marina. There were, as has been said, some two thousand of them, many well armed and mounted. They seemed like a conquering army, and they treated the Muscovites as trash, dregs, and muck. But if the Polish nobles indulged in open and often indecent abuse in the city streets, their men — their grooms, or valets — behaved like animals. They desecrated churches, started rows anywhere at any time, and outraged decent girls.

As for Father Sawicki, his sorrow over Dimitry's seeming abandonment of piety and loyalty to the Pope was mitigated even on the day of Oleśnicki's tribulations. That same Thursday, May 15, Dimitry sent word to Sawicki that he would like to receive him in audience. He had written the Polish Provincial, Father Decio Striveri, three months before, urgently asking him to come to Moscow, but Striveri had not appeared. It is possible that Dimitry had gotten word that he could not come. In any event, Father Sawicki talked privately with Dimitry, with no other person present. What happened at the time can be known only through Sawicki's report.

According to this, he kissed Dimitry's hand and offered the usual protocolary greetings. Dimitry burst out with sincere evidence of friendship and gratitude for things past. He assured Sawicki that he had not forgotten any promises, and that his feelings had not changed. Sawicki then presented to Dimitry a letter from Claudio Acquaviva, General of the Society of Jesus, along with some small devotional objects and little tablets of gold and silver with indulgences which he had received from Pope Paul. They bore the Pope's image.

Dimitry thanked Sawicki effusively and, rising from his chair, began to pace up and down the room. Since Sawicki just stood there, Dimitry took him by the arm, leading him back and forth as he talked. Religion came up, and Sawicki took advantage of that subject to tell Dimitry that he had been sent to be of help to the Tsar, to receive his orders, and to carry out what he commanded, so far as he could. Dimitry then came back at him with his plan to build a college in Moscow, immediately, and to send for teachers from abroad.

Sawicki barely had time to comment on this when the Tsar switched to the subject, ever present in his mind, of the huge army which was only awaiting his command to march — against whom, he did not say. From that his volatile mind bounced over to the subject of King Sigismund and his unwillingness to recognize Dimitry's titles. Sawicki felt that there was some connection between the huge army and Sigismund, and a brief silence at that moment strengthened this thought. He ventured to say: "Let us hope that Providence will never permit enmity and discord between two such puissant princes." To this he added the question, should he return to Poland or remain in Moscow.

Dimitry so promptly and emphatically said that he should remain that Sawicki was encouraged to say that he hoped that in the future he could present himself at the palace whenever he had occasion to consult the Tsar. Dimitry did not hesitate, but strode over to the door and dictated orders to that effect to the secretary then on duty. And with that he excused himself. He had spent more than an hour with Sawicki, it was late, and he still had to pay his daily visit to his mother.

Sawicki concluded his report with an expression of vague uneasiness, caused by things that happened on the way to and from the palace, and by the attitude of the Muscovites. He did not go into details, but he concluded with the laconic statement that both he and Father Czyrzowski wondered how it would all end.

Meanwhile, some three hundred princes, boyars and magnates gathered under Prince Vasily Shuysky's leadership to put an end to the defilement of the Muscovite Orthodox throne, the blood-stained throne that under Ivan the Dread had rested on corporal, and under Boris Godunov on political, assassination.[2] Dimitry's crime was far greater. He associated with foreigners, he despised superstition, he scorned Byzantine ceremony, and he planned progress and the elevation of the Muscovite state among the nations of Europe. For that he must be murdered. Then the land would be safe and holy once more under the discipline of a Tsar to be freely elected by them — by Shuysky's three hundred. It has a very modern ring.

Not only these immediate backers of Shuysky, however, sought Dimitry's destruction. There were also hordes of commoner followers of the Shuysky clan, ignorant men who had received favors, money or privileges so far as it was within Shuysky's power to give. There may even have been priests, offended by Dimitry's "heretical" views, and certainly there were many discontented elements right among the Tsar's own guard, among the streltsy, for example. All that was needed was a leader who would give the signal. Then, they were certain, the proletariat of Moscow itself would join in the revolution.

These nameless souls were fervid supporters of Dimitry, but they were restive. They hated the Poles, who had brought the hatred on themselves. But more than that, a great popular movement against the old regime was germinating under the superficial calm of the masses. It was momentarily halted by the popularity of Dimitry, and in any case it still lacked precise aim or definition. Any popular war-cry would free it for action. The Poles, for instance. The masses would fly to attack the Poles. Once they were roused, the cabal did not concern itself about the outcome.

So much activity centering around the Shuyskys, however well covered, could not but be remarked by Dimitry's supporters. The day before Father Sawicki's audience a cry of alarm ran through the Polish billets and residences scattered throughout the city. Dimitry was apprised. Yet such was his calm, and so eager were the Poles to continue the festivities, that no precautions were taken.

Then on May 16 the rumors surged up greater than before. People began burying their money and jewels in anticipation of a major revolt. Again Dimitry was warned and begged to take preventive measures. "In the name of Heaven," was his comment, "don't talk about that any more. I know the people of my empire. Nobody is against me, and I am master of life and death here." This remark was made to Pan George himself, who had hoped to open his son-in-law's eyes to the danger.

A German that same day informed Dimitry that a massacre was planned for the very next morning. Dimitry only sent a secretary to the guards to threaten punishment for the faint-hearted. The secretary made so bold as to visit the two ambassadors, Oleśnicki and Gosiewski, as soon as he had completed his mission to the soldiers. He remained there until late at night.

In the meantime, as we have seen, Dimitry spent a large part of the evening with Stanislas Niemojewski. By profession Niemojewski was a merchant. Known to Princess Anne, King Sigismund's sister, he had been entrusted by her to take to Moscow an extremely valuable collection of jewels — diamond chains, rubies, emeralds, topazes, pearl collars, and so on — which she had hopes of selling to the Tsar. Niemojewski had chosen that evening to show them.[3]

Dimitry, who had naturally had access to the treasure chests of Ivan the Dread and his predecessors, discussed the glittering baubles with some amateurish appreciation, and ended by asking Niemojewski to leave the jewel-box with him for a few days. He might be interested in buying some or all. But just at the moment there was a masquerade to think of.

As Konrad Bussow later wrote, slightly misquoting Publilius Syrus, *"Citius venit periculum cum spernitur"* — danger arrives faster when you despise it. And to this he added, "And Saint Paul

says, in I Thessalonians 5, 'When they shall say, Peace and safety;
then sudden destruction cometh upon them.' " That same night,
when an out-of-season wintry blast chilled the fields and the hearts
of men, Prince Vasily Ivanovich Shuysky, descendant of Rurik the
Viking in the twenty-first generation, called his faction together.

The time had come, he harangued them, when the people of
Moscow were ready to revolt. It was time to strike. The holy city
was in the hands of foreigners who insulted its inhabitants. And at
great length he repeated all the charges against Tsar Dimitry,
who was "not even a Russian, for does he not wear Polish dress?"
A Polish account, not entirely to be trusted, gives all the details.

The cabal had already agreed that Dimitry must be murdered,
but Dimitry was still the idol of the unwashed and often drunken
mob, and his assassination, unless carefully planned, might result
in extreme danger for the assassins themselves. Fanatic crowds
were prone to wanton destruction, not to mention the most primitive sort of butchery. To involve the people, and yet distract them
from the chief work at hand, a scheme was devised as sly as it was
underhanded. Availing themselves of the universal dislike of the
Poles, the conspirators would raise a hue and cry, shout through
the streets that the Poles were murdering the Tsar, rush to the
Kremlin "to protect him from the Poles," and in the confusion do
their dirty work.

With that decided, they retired to their respective homes. It was
all worthy of the cowardly mentality of Prince Vasily Shuysky.

A blood-red gibbous moon was sinking beyond the bastion
named for the Forest Gate at the west corner of the Kremlin as the
gray light of the dawn appeared over the Yauza River and the
endless woodland beyond the eastern horizon. It was somewhat
after three o'clock, and in those northern latitudes the sun would
soon rise. In the Kremlin, Tsar and Tsaritsa slept soundly. Even
the tumultuous Poles, in their widespread lodgings, slumbered undisturbed. Gaiety, debauchery, and even fear had found rest.

Suddenly the tocsin was sounded from the bell-tower of the
Church of Saint Elias in the Chinese City. It was the preconcerted
signal. All the church-bells of Moscow rang out in wild alarm —

three thousand churches, each with five or six or a dozen bells. A hundred thousand Muscovites, according to one account, "myrmidons . . . thick as hailstones," according to another, ran madly into the streets, men and boys, and even little children, all armed with something — bows and arrows, cudgels, muskets, hatchets, sabres, pikes. "Their madness lent them weapons," wrote Bussow, adapting a line from Virgil. Prompted by Shuysky's agitators in their midst and brandishing whatever they carried, the horde ran toward the Kremlin, crying, "Who is killing the Tsar?" Shuysky's leaders, already on the scene, egged them on: "The Poles are murdering the Tsar."

Dimitry awoke with a start. Calling Basmanov, who always slept nearby, he sent him to learn the cause of the deafening clangor. Other members of Shuysky's group were among the men in the antechamber and quickly reassured Basmanov. They did not really know, but were sure that it was merely some house on fire.

By that time the yelling of the approaching mob reached Dimitry's ears, although he could not make out what they were shouting. He sent Basmanov out again to learn exactly what was on fire, if it was a fire. Then he leaped out of bed and began to dress.

Basmanov now found the outer rooms of the palace and the entrances filled with unknown Russians, armed with spears and big sticks. Alarmed, he called out, "What are you doing here? What do you want? What does all this uproar mean?"

"Let him —— his mother," they roared. "Bring that fake Tsar out, and you'll get your answer." [4]

In a flash Basmanov knew that his fears were fulfilled. The alarm-bells were the signal for treachery. Calling to the sturdy German lancers who were on guard — for some reason only thirty, when there should have been a hundred — to have their weapons ready, he ran back to the Tsar's bedchamber.

"*Bedá, gosudár!* We're in for it, my lord," he cried to Dimitry. "The people want to kill you, and you're the only one to blame. Why did you not believe the Germans, who were telling the truth?"

But he was not able to finish his reproofs. An insolent boyar who had managed to get past the German lancers broke into the bedchamber and defied Dimitry, insolently. "You abortion of an emperor," he shouted, "haven't you got enough sleep yet? Why don't you come out and tell the people about yourself?"

Basmanov's sabre lopped the intruder's head from his shoulders before he finished scoffing. Dimitry then dashed out to the antechamber where the bodyguard was, to get his great "curtle-axe" (a huge cutlass).[5] When he could not find it, he took Wilhelm Schwarzkopf's "partisan" (a murderous long-handled spear) out of his hand and marched into the next room, where the halberdiers were standing, motionless, on guard. It was filled with commonpeople, backers of Shuysky, who jeered and taunted him.

"Ya vam nye Boris!" Dimitry bellowed, brandishing the partisan at the crowd. "Don't think I'm Boris!" [6]

A volley of shots at himself and the bodyguard was the answer to this. Dimitry had to retreat to the antechamber, while Basmanov, seeing the group of boyars standing there, called out that they ought to watch what they were doing, and keep out of so scandalous a mutiny. They should do what was right by the Tsar.

Mikhail Ignatyevich Tatishchev, one of Dimitry's Council, stepped up impertinently: "—— your mother!" he growled, "and your Emperor!" [7] And with that he whipped out his long knife, such as all boyars carried under their kaftans, and ran it through Basmanov's heart. Emboldened by this, the other boyars gave Tatishchev a hand, picked up Basmanov's body and threw it from the outside porch onto the ground, seventy-five feet below. Such was Basmanov's reward for his first unbreakable loyalty to any man.

Basmanov had been feared by the rank and file of people, not only for his indomitable bravery, but for his steadfastness. Only a Tatishchev — Sapieha had once called him "an impertinent liar" — would have dared face Basmanov. With him gone, the hired mob broke loose precisely as Shuysky had expected. They ran like a pack of blood-thirsty wolves at the guards, barking for that "thief" Dimitry to come out.

Dimitry heard and came. But he and his small guard could do nothing against "a red-hot baker's oven," as Bussow picturesquely described the overheated rabble. With little more than bare hands, the mob tore planks from the wooden walls, fought their way up to the guards, and overwhelmed them. Taking their weapons, they then turned on Dimitry.

Resistance was hopeless. Dimitry and fifteen Germans barely managed to get through the door into the next room, which they barricaded. The Germans, with the few weapons they had saved, confronted an angry horde. Dimitry threw his partisan into his bedchamber, just beyond, and stood for a moment or two, pulling at his unruly red hair as if in self-reproof or powerless anger. Then without a word stalked after the great spear.

The mob shot through the door time and time again, so that the Germans had to stand aside or be killed. Finally, heaving an enormous beam against it, they broke in. Then at last the guards longed for a good battle-axe or musket instead of the fancy but completely impractical armor and weapons of an honor-guard. Had all three hundred of these heroic troops been together and armed as they should have been, the howling, undisciplined rabble would have been overcome in short order, and they knew it. But regrets would not win the battle.

The Germans retreated again, this time into the Tsar's bedchamber, which they again barricaded. But Dimitry was not there. He had slipped past the Tsaritsa's room through a secret door into an outside chamber, some say a bathroom. Knowing that he must find help, he sprang to the ground.* Although it was a jump that would have killed an ordinary man, it only wounded Dimitry. But even these wounds, a sprained or perhaps broken leg and cracked ribs, prevented him from a dash to the barracks where help was available.

Meanwhile, the mob broke into the bedchamber and took the Germans prisoners. Almost incomprehensibly (or did they have orders?), they did not harm them, but only asked where the Tsar was. Since no-one knew, they ransacked the rooms and stole a fortune in gold and precious stones.

By that time, a group of rebel princes and boyars burst into the

---

* According to Bussow, it was a hundred feet beneath.

rooms of the Tsaritsa's ladies-in-waiting, who were wide awake and in a panic by then. Marina, a tiny girl in spite of the majestic rôle she had chosen to play, heard them coming and hid under the ample skirts of Pani Kazanowska, imperious, imperturbable, and corpulent.

The princes and boyars, behaving more like boors and churls than noblemen, bawled out, "Where are the Tsar and Tsaritsa?" The Polish ladies answered, "You know better than we do where you left the Tsar. We have been told not to expect him."

The Russians then cried, in gutter-language, "You scum of womanhood . . . where are you keeping that Pole? . . . your Empress?"

Pani Kazanowska, unbending and icily, asked, "What do you want of her?"

The answer came, as Bussow wrote, in "pure Moscow-ese," which he translated into pure Latin, not to sully the pages of his memoirs. It cannot be put into "pure" English.[8]

Then one prince took one Polish lady to his home, by force, and another another, without regard to their distinguished fathers or brothers. Within the year, Bussow adds tactfully, many who were virgins had become mothers.[9]

But Pani Kazanowska remained untouched, along with the Tsaritsa under her skirts, despite all threats and repeated demands, "Where is the Empress?" But at last that indomitable woman answered, "We accompanied her this morning, very early, to the domicile of her father, the Voyvode of Sandomierz. She is undoubtedly still there."

By then the streltsy on guard at the Chertolye Gate, to the west of the palace, heard groans. On investigating, they saw Dimitry lying on a slope not far away. Helping him up, they started to take him back to the palace, when some of Shuysky's crew spotted this and shouted to the boyars to come and see what they had found.

The princes and other undignified dignitaries leaned out of the windows. Spotting their prey on the ground below, they darted from Pani Kazanowska and the Tsaritsa under her skirts and ran down the stairs to the courtyard. Had the streltsy taken their Tsar to their barracks they would have done him a far greater favor than this misguided effort to help. But a tragedy of errors had been in progress for a fortnight.

When the streltsy saw that the boyars had come to murder, not to save, the Tsar, they opened fire. One or two boyars were killed. But the mob arrived on the scene and completely overpowered the streltsy. Egged on and even joined by the blue-blooded princes and punctilious nobles of the realm, the rabble seized the wounded Tsar and treated him, says Bussow, like the prisoners in Plautus's play — they "pulled and pushed at the same time, and that is a great iniquity." So, fighting and mauling the defenseless man, they carried him up again to his apartments. There, what had been gay and beautiful was now wrecked and shapeless.

The bodyguards were still standing in the antechamber, under guards of their own, when the Tsar was dragged in. He looked at them, tears welling up in his eyes. One of them took his out-stretched hand, but not a word was spoken while the rabble hus-tled him into his private apartments. One German knight, Wil-helm Fürstenberg, slipped in after them, possibly to try to help, possibly merely to see what was going on, but a boyar ended his curiosity with a blow from a partisan.

At that, one of the Russians said, "See what faithful dogs these Germans are! Let's get rid of all of them." But others said not to harm them, and the princes and boyars for their own reasons re-fused to grant permission to murder the Germans.

With that the vicious martyrdom of Dimitry began. Bussow likened it to the tormenting of Christ at Golgotha. One pulled him forward, another pushed him back. Several stripped him of his robes and put a dirty shirt over him, shouting, "Behold the Tsar of all Russia!"

One laughed, "I have a Tsar like that at home in my stables." Another spat out filth. Still another hit him in the face, crying, "Son of a whore, who are you? Who is your father? Where is your home?"

To this Dimitry finally made tired, suffering answer: "You all know who I am — your crowned Tsar — and the son of Ivan Vasilyevich. Ask my mother in the monastery! Or take me to the Place of the Skull, and give me leave to speak."

This was the last thing Shuysky's gang wanted. The populace of Moscow loved their Tsar, and they had been kept out of the Kremlin by force. Only Shuysky's men had been admitted, for a popular revolt would have overthrown Shuysky, not Dimitry. At that point, two treacherous petty-courtiers, Grigory Valuyev and Ivan Voyeykov, pushed their way to the front, guns in hand. Said Grigory, "Why argue with a heretic? I'll give this Polish piper an Orthodox blessing!" And the two of them shot him point-blank.[10]

Prince Vasily Ivanovich Shuysky, who owed his life to Dimitry's mercy, rode up to the palace then, and told the murderers they must make short work of Dimitry. Perhaps he feared action from the mob milling outside the Kremlin.

With such encouragement, everyone in the building tried to get at their victim, but there was no more room. So the ones who were left out cried to the ones who were in the rooms, "What good word did the Polish hooligan have for us?"[11] And the answer came, "He said he was not the real Dimitry, but that he was the son of Ivan Vasilyevich." Thereupon from all sides came shouts, "Crucify him, kill him!"

The princes and boyars took their sabres and long knives from their scabbards. One struck Dimitry on the head from the front, while another cut a big piece of flesh from his back, which hung for a while by a bit of skin. A third cut him on the arm, a fourth on the leg, and a fifth drove his sword through his body. And at last they dragged the bleeding corpse out the same door through which Basmanov had been dragged not long before, and threw Dimitry "down from aloft, with a cord fastened about his privities," according to one account. "You loved him when he was alive," they cried down. "Don't be divided because you're dead."

By then the people of Moscow, who had loved their Tsar, came to the realization that they had been duped into participating in his murder. It was too late to save him now. But there could be revenge.

The death of Dimitry was the birth of unheard-of mob bestial-

ity. Pan George Mniszech's domicile, the old palace of Boris Godunov, had already been surrounded by several hundred Muscovites in Shuysky's employ, provided with small cannon, to prevent
him and his soldiers from making an attempt to run to Dimitry's
defense. Seeing this, the people ignored that building, and ran instead to the billets where the Tsar's musicians lived. All hundred
or so of them, men and boys, were cut to pieces in cold blood.

Finding the Kremlin too crowded with Shuysky's mob, the populace then streamed out again through Frolovskie Gate and across
Red Square in all directions, seeking Poles to kill, to slake their
blood-thirst. The confusion was as indescribable as the uproar.
Marina's brother, Stanislas, and his retinue were able to defend
themselves in their solidly built palace, and many a Muscovite lost
his life attempting to take the place by storm. But others who had
little or no means of protecting themselves could only try to hide.
Some crept under the roof-beams, some into noisome cellars, and
some burrowed under the fodder for their horses outside in the
courtyards, or even in the dung-heaps, both human and animal.

Hundreds, dressed only in night-shirts just as they sprang out of
bed, were clubbed to death, or run through with spears and pikes,
or decapitated, wholly or partly, by swishing sabres. These were
all men, adolescents and boys. The women, young and old, were
carried off, privately.

Prince Konstantin Vishnevetsky and the two Polish ambassadors, showing a bold front in the fortress-like ambassadorial palace,
and backed by some seven hundred armed men, shouted to the first
mob that assaulted the place that they would shoot blazing arrows
from the great tower over the whole city, and set fire to every house
within range if the mob did not go away. Indeed, they demanded
that responsible leaders appear and swear not to molest them.

A similar stand was taken by Dimitry's old Polish cavalry, who
had ridden with him all the way from Sambor. At the same time,
leaders were found in the mobs who swore by Saint Nicholas and
the Crucifix not to molest these bold groups, but they were not
trusted. Heralds for the Poles loudly proclaimed that fact, and a
counterattack was prepared. Someone then sent for Prince Vasily

Shuysky, who rode up through the crowd with a bodyguard, to guarantee safety. His word the Poles accepted, largely in ignorance of his treachery.

Some Poles found time to flee from the city, to take refuge in the new "German suburb" to the east. But their choice was unfortunate, for these Germans were traitors who had deserved execution for their misdeeds in the Livonian wars, had been baptized Orthodox, and were more vicious than the native Muscovites. As Bussow put it, the unhappy Poles escaped the bears to run into a pack of lions. The "lions" took their horses and their clothes, murdered them, and threw their bodies into the convenient Yauza River.

All the while alarm bells jangled in a frightful din, punctuated by the sharp cracks of gunfire and the screams of the wounded and dying. The Muscovites ran madly through the streets howling all the while, "Seki, seki! Kill, kill!" There was no mercy, no quarter. Whom they caught they murdered, for they were giving vent to their hatred of the Poles.

The tale of one Polish merchant is typical. Caught in his home, he offered to buy his life with gold. But when he was led out toward the Kremlin, someone said "for judgment," he had to step over the bodies of his faithful servants, chopped to pieces on his doorstep. In a state of mind which can be imagined, he was brought through the streets, bound, only to run afoul of another Russian, who shouted, "Kill him!" He fell on the ground to implore his life, but no prayer would avail. While he was crying for mercy, he somehow got free of his bonds, and jumped up shouting: "You call yourselves Christians. Where is your Christian pity? Save me for Christ's sake, for my wife's sake, and my children's sake . . ." and so on. But the Russian struck at him with his sword, making a cut eight or nine inches long. The Pole tried to run away, but was caught by his original captors, who then showered him with slashes that ended his suffering, but not his indignities. His murderers took to quarreling among themselves over his blood-soaked shirt and breeches.

The orgy lasted until noon, and in those hours somewhere between seventeen hundred and two thousand Poles were summarily murdered. Along with the Poles, German jewelers and merchants from Augsburg who had brought precious stones and fine cloths to Dimitry's wedding were murdered and robbed. All of these victims of mob terror and violence were stripped stark naked and thrown into the streets and squares, soon to be found by countless stray dogs. While the dogs feasted, Russian quack doctors circulated, cutting the fatty tissue from the corpses for medical use. Not one body was carried away, or even moved, for three days after. Even that veteran of the horrors of war, Konrad Bussow, wrote, years later, "This 17th of May will be remembered so long as the world exists."

But what of Marina?

The same princes and boyars who had shown such boundless contempt for Dimitry hesitated before the imperious demeanor of Pani Kazanowska. They knew that Marina was the daughter of a Polish senator, and that the senator and other members of the family were there in Moscow. They also knew that the King of Poland and the Republic itself would not take lightly any serious offense against these Polish nobles. Violent action and fecal language gave way to respect.

The conspirators asked that the lady be told that they knew who *she* was, but who and what that impostor and rogue was who had posed as Dimitry, heir to the throne, she, Marina, would know better than anyone. So much for Dimitry. He was dead. But if Marina wanted to give herself up, and be free to join her father, she had only to return to them all the presents she had received from the false Tsar. They would not harm her, but they clearly suspected — or by then knew — that she was not with Pan George, but somewhere in the palace.

Marina apparently then emerged from under Pani Kazanowska's skirts. Without hesitation, she gave the princes and boyars everything she had, even the dress that was on her back, and asked to be sent safely to her father. After a long discussion, and several messages between the palace and Pan George's beleaguered residence, thousands of rubles were restored to the Treasury, and Marina was escorted to safety, and virtual imprisonment.

Dimitry's body meanwhile lay in the courtyard where it had fallen, near Basmanov's. His skull was split, and twenty-one wounds were counted on his stark-naked body. The crowd roped Basmanov and Dimitry together. Across Cathedral Square they hauled them, past the bell-tower of Ivan the Great, shivering with reverberating bells, and over the wooden-paved street toward the Frolovskie Gate. On the way, they stopped in front of the monastery where the Tsaritsa-nun Marfa lived. They called for her.

When she came to the gate, the mob cried, "Is this your son?"

"You should have asked me about that when he was alive," she replied. "Now he is obviously not mine any longer." And she raised her eyes toward heaven.[12]

The mob, catching only the words "not mine," rolled on through the gate into Red Square, where they set up a platform on the Place of the Skull. Then the two bodies were arranged on it, so that Dimitry's feet were on Basmanov's breast, and in such fashion that all could see that the dead man was Dimitry, and not some other carcass of the hundreds then strewn about the city.

Soon after, a Russian nobleman came riding from the Kremlin with a bagpipe and a monk's robe, and an ugly mask which was to have been used in the masquerade planned for that day. He put the robe on Dimitry's belly, the bag of the bagpipe on his chest, and the mask partly over his face. The pipe he shoved between the open lips. This done, he ranted: "You have had others pipe enough for you. Now *you* play the pipes for us a while." [13]

Others then came up, nobles and merchants as well as ordinary people, bringing horse-whips to lash the dead bodies, and crying out: "You wretched monk, how much evil you have brought on our land! The Treasury is empty. And you are the cause of our misfortune." Even the women came and mocked and abused the dead Tsar beyond belief. Few there were who honored the fallen hero now.

For three days, Dimitry and Basmanov lay there, while all Moscow made hideous sport of them. But again popular superstition began to sweep over the city. The night of May 19, flickering lights danced over the bodies, up from the sides of the platform.

But when the watchmen on duty came up to look closer, they vanished. Mad with fright, the guards ran to officials in the Kremlin, and brought them to look. The officials also saw the little fires, and were startled. And so it was that the next morning orders were issued to transport the bodies to the God's-acre outside the Bolvanovye Gate, and bury them. Basmanov's half-brother, Prince Vasily Golitsyn, then intervened and asked permission to bury Pyotr Basmanov decently. It was granted.

Dimitry, after the streets had been cleared of Polish dead, was trundled out alone. But further signs to frighten the superstitious were not long in coming. As the wagon went through the city gate, a gust of wind blew up, and tore off the roof of one of the towers of the wall nearby. Other whirlwinds did damage as far away as the Yauza Gate.

Later, in the graveyard, workmen busy with the burial of Polish bodies, noticed that two doves insisted on perching near the remains of Dimitry whenever he was left unattended, and they began to spread rumors. Then, they threw the body in a ditch with a lot of others, planning to cover it with earth the next day. But in the morning they found it outside the graveyard gate, although that had been shut tight. When that report was made, the body of the Tsar was buried more securely, and earth packed down hard on top.

The effort was in vain. On Tuesday, May 27, Dimitry's corpse was found in a churchyard, far from the public burial-place. By then, the entire capital was frightened. According to Konrad Bussow, some said that Dimitry must have been a strange man, that his dead body would not stay buried. But others whispered that he was the Devil himself, who had come to plague the people.

Finally, many claimed with heated obstinacy that Dimitry had in truth learned black-magic from the wild Laplanders. These alarming magicians had the power to come back to life after they had died or were killed. Dimitry had learned this art from them. But there was one sure remedy for this fearful danger. This remedy was explained to the authorities, and it was quickly put into effect.

On May 28, 1606, a great pyre was heaped outside the walls, and Dimitry was laid upon it. A light was applied, and for hours the flames roared high, until every trace of Dimitry was consumed. Then the ashes were collected, gingerly. A cannon was brought up, and what they had collected was rammed into the barrel. A charge of powder, then, and a match! And with a giant roar all that was left of Dimitry was blown into the sky, in the direction of Poland, whence he had come.

Only then did Moscow believe that Dimitry Ivanovich, called the Pretender, would never again appear.

EPILOGUE

Prince Vasily Shuysky and his faction had had one basic objective: to void the throne of Dimitry, whoever he was. Their secondary goal was to place a Tsar of their liking in his place. This Tsar, it need hardly be said, was Prince Vasily himself.

To attain their basic objective, Shuysky's princes, boyars, magnates and merchants allowed — indeed, encouraged — every kind of violence by the common people until Dimitry was disposed of. Then, when it was convenient they began to step in to halt the senseless slaughter. It was not part of their plan to permit such shedding of Polish blood that the powerful Republic would step in to exact punishment and costly wergeld. They knew that Muscovy was too torn by the "episode" of Dimitry to resist the disciplined troops of Zamoyski's successors, Chodkiewicz and Żółkiewski.

By nightfall of May 17, total calm had descended over the city. Patrols circulated through the streets avoiding the dogs and the dead bodies. Shuysky and his cabal met in conference, more or less in secret. Armed men stood guard in all the palaces and private homes where the surviving Poles resided. Marina had already joined her father.

Two days later, Prince Vasily Shuysky was elected Tsar and Great Prince of all Russia, not by popular assembly, as had been the case with Boris Godunov, but by the clique which had joined him in the murder of Dimitry. He was chosen because, they said, he was nearest to the dynasty of Ivan the Dread. And to prove this, Prince Vasily falsified his genealogical tree, modestly.[1] He claimed descent from Alexander Nevsky, ancestor of Ivan, instead of that prince's brother, Prince Andrey of Suzdal, which was correct. He seems to have thought thereby to make himself more welcome in the eyes of the people. He did not.

On the day of Shuysky's "election," Father Pomaski from Sambor died of wounds received during the razzia. He had been celebrating mass at the time. He and Matthew Domoracki were among the few whose names are recorded and who played a conspicuous part in the tragedy of Dimitry's brief reign. The great bulk of the dead had not lifted a finger for the Tsar.

Dimitry's Russian backers on the other hand generally escaped, largely because the inspired "popular" uprising was against the Poles. Thus, by the time Prince Vasily had become Tsar Vasily, the friends of the overthrown regime had already escaped. Chief of these were Mikhail Molchanov, one of the murderers of the young Tsar Fyodor Godunov, and Prince Grigory Petrovich Shakhovskoy, son of the Voyvode of Chernigov who had joined forces with Dimitry, and a "full-blooded organizer," according to some of his contemporaries.[2]

Molchanov in fact not only fled but also with astounding rapidity turned to fight back against Tsar Vasily Shuysky. He had been ardently for Dimitry. Dimitry had been murdered by Shuysky. And Molchanov saw no reason to follow the precepts of Saint Paul. He would not wait for the Lord to claim His vengeance. So he fled prepared — with a bagful of "mementos" from the Tsar's treasure-chest (which might come in handy) and a declaration that Dimitry had not been assassinated, but was still alive.

In this way, by the time Dimitry's ashes were so violently scattered over the earth the story of his salvation was already being spread by the tongues of rumor. Unwittingly, Shuysky himself helped the rumor and thus was one of the authors of a revolt against his own authority.

By an egregious blunder, Prince Vasily appointed Prince Shakhovskoy as Voyvode of Putivl immediately upon Dimitry's death and sent him off with the news of his accession to the throne. Shakhovskoy not only took the letters of credence supplied by the new

Tsar, but also collected the Great Seal of State and two Polish aides dressed as Russians.

Just beyond Serpukhov, the trio had to be ferried across the Oka River. Once on the other side, Shakhovskoy asked the ferryman if he knew them. The man did not. Then said Shakhovskoy mysteriously: "Tell nobody, but you have just ferried the Tsar of all Russia across. People in Moscow wanted to kill him, but we have escaped, and we'll soon be back with a huge army." And he pressed six Polish gold pieces into the man's hand.

Of course, Shakhovskoy did not return immediately with an army. But his story of Dimitry's escape spread over southern Russia just as Dimitry's story of being saved at Uglich had spread three years before. By the time the Prince reached Putivl, a new rebellion was in flower.

There Dimitry's standard was raised — had not the Putivlyans protected him before? His proximate re-appearance was announced. And once again emotion swept through the common people of Muscovy. For all his quirks, it seemed that Dimitry symbolized the "good Tsar" for whom they longed.

As yet neither Molchanov, who was in Poland by then, nor Shakhovskoy was able to produce the man whose salvation they had announced. Molchanov himself seems to have considered acting the part, but before long (for unclear reasons) turned to an ex-serf of Prince Andrey Telyatevsky, by name Ivan Isayevich Bolotnikov. Bolotnikov had been a fugitive in the Ukraine among the Cossacks, a raider against the Turks, a galley slave, and what not. Upon escaping to Venice, he passed through Poland about the time Dimitry was there, but arrived in Russia too late to take part in any pro-Dimitry celebrations. He was apparently in Putivl when Dimitry was murdered.

Bolotnikov saw in the election of Vasily Shuysky a return to the old oppression of peasants and serfs, which had certainly been promised some relief by Dimitry. He therefore immediately put his not inexperienced hand to work against the new Tsar. When word of the return of Dimitry from the dead was noised about, Bolotnikov quickly found the men who knew something about it.

With surprising speed he gathered a group of followers, and before long he was at the head of the first and possibly the strongest and longest-lived revolution against Tsarist tyranny in the history of Russia before 1917. He called himself, modestly, the Voyvode of the renowned Tsar Dimitry.

Bolotnikov's enormous and undisciplined army of Cossacks, serfs, runaways, and desperadoes defeated the troops of Tsar Vasily Shuysky as early as August, 1606, and by the end of November was fighting under the walls of Moscow. Repulsed on December 2, however, they had to retreat to Kaluga. Then a few months later several thousand Don Cossacks joined Bolotnikov's forces, augmented by refugee Russians, all under the "Tsarevich" Ilya-Pyotr. With their help, he trounced Shuysky's army in May, 1607. Nevertheless, fortune gradually turned against him. During the coming winter, the "Tsarevich" was captured and executed, and in March, 1608, Bolotnikov also fell before the Tsar's troops. He was first blinded, and then drowned in the far north, at Kargopol.

All this while, the Ataman of the Don Cossacks, Ivan Martinovich Zarutsky, had been collecting rebels throughout the south. All of Russia was in ferment. Thus, scarcely had Bolotnikov been cut from the scene than a second "Pretender" appeared in the region west of Moscow, calling himself Dimitry Ivanovich. By the summer of 1608, he had gathered up another great army, undoubtedly incorporating elements from Bolotnikov's, and set up his "capital" at Tushino, a village now just inside the modern Moscow Belt Parkway, to the northwest. From the name of his capital, he was given the name "Tushino Brigand." In that capital he virtually succeeded in thwarting the government in Moscow, weakly and dividedly headed by Tsar Vasily Shuysky.

During these two years, 1606 to 1608, Shuysky had in truth had cares to bow the shoulders of Atlas himself. In addition to the internal tempest shaking his government, he had under guard three groups of dangerous subjects of King Sigismund III. Although Sigismund at first was himself struggling with a revolt that fell just short of civil war, Shuysky suspected that any offense to the Republic would rather unite the Poles under their king than contribute to weakening him. He therefore had to solve the triple problem somehow himself.

First in order of pressing importance was the debris of the Polish army. By the time of Dimitry's murder it was a mixture of old soldiers who had come with him, augmented by the still older troops released from prison by him, and the large body which came with Marina. There may also have been some scattered volunteers who trickled into Moscow all through his reign. Shuysky gathered these into what may be called a concentration camp as soon as he could, and held them until there was a chance to let them return peacefully to Poland during the winter of 1608–1609. Father Czyrzowski was back in Poland by mid-February, and one of his letters suggests that the bulk of the army was by then there too.[3]

Shuysky's second perplexity was what to do with the two ambassadors from Sigismund to Dimitry. Since they were not accredited to Shuysky, they demanded to be given their papers immediately, along with proper facilities for travel out of Muscovy. At their insistence, a group of boyars called them to the palace as early as May 27. There, under the presidency of Prince Fyodor Ivanovich Mstislavsky, Prince Dimitry Shuysky, Prince Golitsyn, and Boyars Nagoy, Romanov, and Tatishchev interrogated both of them. These Muscovite dignitaries who had so recently groveled before Tsar Dimitry now rose to their full height and importance, and turned into accusers and calumniators.

Mstislavsky read a long document which purported to prove that Dimitry was the unfrocked monk Grishka Otrepyev — his uncle Smirnoy had appeared on the scene again and testified to this. The source, then, of the trouble was specifically and unquestionably Poland. That country, the representatives of which stood before him, had consciously and informedly perpetrated this hoax on the realm of Muscovy.

Oleśnicki may have been startled at this, but he did not hesitate even so long as the flicker of an eyelid. (If he was not awed by the Tsar, a mere boyar could surely not trouble him!) The Muscovites, he said, were the first to recognize Dimitry as the true Tsar, adding: "You Boyars, you urged him to come to Moscow, you

crowned him, and you swore fealty to him. Why do you blame the
Poles for following in your steps?"

Since there was much artfully prepared evidence on both sides,
and neither party wanted to tell the real truth, the confrontation
soon became thorny indeed. Tatishchev, characteristically, had recourse to insults, which Mstislavsky attempted to oil over with piety and well-worn pronouncements on the sinfulness of man. Un-
moved by any of this, Oleśnicki ended by demanding their papers
without further mutual recrimination. The boyars unwillingly
consented to present their case to the Tsar, who had not yet been
crowned.

The coronation took place, without great pomp, on Sunday,
June 1. Oleśnicki had already sent a message asking for quick action, but it was Thursday before Tatishchev arrived at their residence (or place of detention). He came equipped with a tiresome
documentation of Polish relations with Dimitry and distressing
news. Prince Volkonsky and a Secretary of the "Foreign Office"
would ride to Poland to arrange the details of forthcoming Russo-
Polish relations. On their return the matter of Oleśnicki and Gosiewski would again be considered. Only at that moment did the
proud ambassadors realize that they were prisoners of the Tsar.
Long months they then had to wait, ill-fed, ill-clothed, and extremely well guarded.

Finally the new Tsar had to turn to the question of the ex-
Tsaritsa Marina and her father. Everything they had was taken
from them: Pan George's money, his horses, his stock of wine; Marina lost even the jewels she had had before she met Dimitry. She
was allowed only a few dresses to cover her nakedness. Yet up to
the time they left, Mniszech made every effort to keep the halo of
Tsaritsa hovering over his daughter's head. With what only can
be called gall, he went so far as to suggest that Shuysky marry Marina, and thus unite the crowns. Shuysky chose a Muscovite princess.

Pan George was interrogated as well as the ambassadors, and his
obstinacy produced somewhat more marked hostility than had
Oleśnicki's. During this "Star Chamber" inquiry, Muscovite self-

excuses and spurious explanations reached remarkable heights of untruth, with the name of Grishka Otrepyev resounding like some phrase from a litany involving scapegoats. All this was finished by about June 15, however, when the Mniszechs were transferred to Vlasyev's home for detention. (Vlasyev himself had been exiled in disgrace.) Two months later, father and daughter, accompanied by their relatives and the remaining Catholic clergy, were transported to Yaroslavl, down the Volga from Uglich.

But by then the tale of the salvation of Dimitry had been tricked out in all its details and was scurrying across the limitless plains to Poland, whence it spread to Rome and all Europe. This confused the reports of Dimitry's murder to such an extent that an account of the twilight of the Dimitry saga in western Europe must fall outside the scope of this Epilogue.

For nearly two years the Mniszechs were kept in Yaroslavl, until Tsar Vasily Shuysky at last reached an accord with Poland. Bolotnikov was dead, and King Sigismund had won out over the rebels in Poland. It looked as if peace might be possible between the two countries as well as inside each, despite the continued presence of the Tushino Brigand — elaborately "holed in" at the gates of Moscow. In view of this, on July 13, 1608, a treaty was signed, valid for three years and eleven months, which provided for the return of all Poles from Muscovy to their native land.

Pan George and Marina were recalled from Yaroslavl, and promised safe-conduct out of the country if Marina would renounce all claims on the title of Tsaritsa. Pan George would return to the quiet of Sambor, and his daughter to the pleasant company of the Bernardine Fathers. They had no alternative but to accept. Oleśnicki and Gosiewski and all the other Poles could not do less. Thus, before long, guarded by five hundred horsemen, the great trek west began.

Not far from Moscow there was an "alert," and Gosiewski joined Father Sawicki and other friends in deciding to return to the city for reinforcements. Later, they started again and safely reached Moscow. Oleśnicki and the Mniszechs, on the other hand, refused to sacrifice speed for circumspection. They rode sturdily on.

The Tushino Brigand was well aware of their movements. Indeed, he had a number of Poles on his staff who supplied the intelligence, military and ordinary, which he apparently lacked. A detachment of horse "surprised" the calvalcade — though it is far from clear that there was any element of surprise anywhere — and abstracted Pan George and Marina from their escort without great difficulty. John Peter Sapieha, a cousin of the Lithuanian Chancellor, was at hand, and he led them to the ersatz Dimitry in his headquarters. They had left the walls of Moscow less than five miles behind.

Precisely what happened is shrouded in mystery and confusion. The outcome is none the less clear. Marina emerged from the foray "re-wedded" to her "Dimitry," to whom she confirmed the title of Tsar and Great Prince of all Russia. More candid tongues labeled her "mistress of an impostor," although she was apparently really married to the Tushino Brigand and bore him a child.

Poland at last intervened, partly, if not largely, because of Sigismund's urge to get the Crown of Monomakh for himself or his young son. Both the Brigand and Marina were not long in falling by the wayside, the former murdered on December 12, 1610, by a converted Tatar prince. Marina then fled to the Cossack Ataman Zarutsky with her infant son, seeking to have him declared Tsarevich of all Russia.[4]

By this time Shuysky had unwisely called on Sweden for help, and that inevitably moved Sigismund. Smolensk was besieged by the Poles late in 1609. In the spring of 1610, however, hope was reborn when Prince Mikhaylo Skopin-Shuysky, Dimitry's former port-glaive, led his cousin's troops to victory. He was rewarded by being poisoned on April 23 at a banquet given by the Tsar's brother, Prince Dimitry Shuysky. Tsar Vasily apparently was alarmed, undoubtedly justly, by a vision of young Prince Mikhaylo being chosen Tsar, at his own expense. The one man who could stop Sigismund was thus removed. Tsar Vasily poured tears over the Skopin-Shuysky tomb in the Cathedral of the Archangel Michael.

Two months and a day later, the Russian forces under Prince

Dimitry Shuysky were routed by the Hetman Żółkiewski. The Poles were marching on Moscow, irresistibly now. Elsewhere in the empire rebellion blazed.

On July 17, one Zakhar Lyapunov marched to the Kremlin at the head of a vast throng, to the palace where Tsar Vasily lived. "How long is the blood of Christendom to continue to flow for you?" he demanded. A scene followed, ending in Red Square with the deposition of the Tsar. Two days after, Vasily Ivanovich Shuysky was forcibly shorn a monk, and the throne of Muscovy was once more empty. The Patriarch Hermogen, the unyielding Metropolitan of Kazan, appointed by Shuysky to replace Dimitry's Ignaty, ruled the empire.

A move followed to put the son of Sigismund on the throne. Sigismund backed this, and perhaps the idea was his own from the start. Conditions were placed on the Polish Prince's candidacy, however, one of which was insurmountable. Young Wladislaus must be baptized into the Orthodox Church. Resistance grew on both sides, the Russians refusing a Catholic prince, the Poles refusing the baptism. Meanwhile the last shred of Russian authority disappeared. The Patriarch Hermogen was arrested, and with him the Metropolitan Filaret, in civil life Fyodor Romanov, son of the brother-in-law of Ivan the Dread and of a princess of the Shuysky family.

The Polish authorities then made the mistake of tyrannizing completely over Moscow, and revolt was inevitable. A butcher of Nizhny-Novgorod (now called Gorky), Kuzma Minin, and Prince Dimitry Mikhaylovich Pozharsky, a descendant of Rurik the Viking, gathered a resistance force about them late in 1611. They were so successful that the Poles surrendered Moscow to them a year later. Then, under a government of questionable right but unquestioned might, a winter was spent in an attempt to decide on a new Tsar.[5]

Prince Pozharsky was perhaps more influential than anyone else, and in the end the powerful Cossack Ataman Zarutsky agreed on Pozharsky's choice of the "natural" Prince, Mikhail Fyodorovich Romanov, son of Filaret, aged sixteen. He was described as "young and stupid," but he was connected with the ancient dynasty of Ivan the Dread on his father's side, and through his mother a direct descendant of the House of Rurik. In this way on February 21, 1613, the *Time of Troubles* came to an end with the election of the first Romanov Tsar. Most strangely, fifteen years before it had been the House of Romanov where Boris Godunov said that Dimitry had been "conjured up" to plague him.

The year 1612 saw the death, in Warsaw, of Vasily Shuysky, in relative freedom but not allowed to return to Moscow. Pan George Mniszech died the year following, after witnessing the abject appearance of the ex-Tsar before the Polish Court. He had then spoken bitterly of Shuysky's deceit and its tragic consequences. Yet none had echoed his lamentations. Not all the blame was to be laid to Shuysky.

Marina, after adventures that beggar description, was brought once more to Moscow in July, 1614, and in chains. Five hundred men guarded her and her son lest some daring band attempt to rescue her. At the Serpukhov Gate the little boy, aged four, was publicly hanged. Marina died not long after, in prison in Kaluga.

The drama ends with the death of Ksenia Godunova, long since known as the nun Olga, in Suzdal, in 1622.[6] Before she died, she did obeisance to Tsar Mikhail Romanov, who as a favor promised to bury her alongside her father, mother and brother. Mikhail did not forget his promise.

APPENDICES
NOTES AND COMMENTS
BIBLIOGRAPHY
INDEX

APPENDIX A

THE PRONUNCIATION
OF RUSSIAN AND POLISH

THE TRANSLITERATION OF RUSSIAN

The system of transliteration used in this book is the same as that worked out for my *Alexander Pushkin: Boris Godunov* (Columbia University Press, New York, 1953), with a few improvements. It is substantially the one employed by the *Current Digest of the Soviet Press*, Washington, D. C., and in a measure "approved" by the American Council of Learned Societies. Its aim is to represent the *sound* of the Russian words with some measure of consistency, with all possible fidelity to the Russian system of spelling, and without the use of diacritical marks.

The Russian Vowels

"hard"	"soft"	diphthongs
a as in f*a*ther	*ya* as in *ya*rd	*ay* as in *a*ye (yes)
e as in *e*ver	*ye* as in *ye*t	*ey* as in th*ey*
y as in m*y*th	*i* as in pol*i*ce (prefixed by a faint *y*)	*y* (for unstressed *iy* and *yy*) — as in tru*ly*, but closer to *ee***
o as in *oa*th, verging on *ou*ght	*yo* as in *yo*re, verging on *yaw*n	*oy* as in b*oy*
u as in bl*ue*	*yu* equals *you*	*uy* as in American slang h*ooey*

Since the Russian "soft" *ye*-sound is enormously more frequent than the "hard" *e*-sound, the simple *e* is used here except where *ye* is needed

---

* *Stressed iy* is so indicated.

for euphony: Belsky, Lenin (properly Byelsky, Lyenin); but Dostoyev-
sky and Sergeyevich (the latter properly Syergyeyevich).

The Russian Consonants:

In my system of transliteration, the consonants have (roughly) their
English value, but the following details should be noted for greater
accuracy:

    g is always hard, as in "gate, get," etc.

    kh is used for the heavy sound of *h*, as in "hawk" (compare Ger-
    man *ch* in Ba*ch*). Khomyakóv sounds almost exactly like home-
    ya-COUGH. There is no *k*-sound whatsoever in the Russian letter
    transliterated by *kh*.

    l when not followed by *ya, ye,* etc., is "deeper" than ordinary *l* in
    English; something like *-ll* in "will." (It is very close to the final *l*
    in Brazil as the name is pronounced in that country.)

    zh represents the sound in measure and azure; it equals French *j*
    in "jour."

Russian Stress

Since the position of the stress-accent in Russian is as important as it is
unpredictable, all names listed in the Index show an acute accent over
the stressed vowel. (Where two accents are indicated, either is permis-
sible.) For purposes of illustration two names are given here, with a
popularized approximate pronunciation:

Dimítry Ivánovich — di-MEE-try i-VAHN-o-vich

Borís Fyódorovich Godunóv — bo-REESE FYAW-do-ro-vich guh-doo-
    NAWFF

HINTS ON THE PRONUNCIATION OF POLISH

When the Latin alphabet was adopted in Poland, centuries ago, diacritical marks and combinations of letters were used to represent the
rich variety of Polish sounds. The result looks more formidable to
English readers than the actual pronunciation justifies.

    Briefly, the Polish vowels have the same sound as the Russian, with
the addition of *ą* (which is the same as the French nasal vowels in
"enfant") and *ę* (which is equal to the nasals in "vin" and "main").

    Polish consonants are somewhat as in English, with a number of
exceptions. Furthermore, there are subtle gradations of sound which

are difficult for English-speakers to hear, let alone to copy. The following table of exceptions must therefore be taken as only very rough:

ch and *h* are like *h* in "hawk," but more guttural.

dz and *dż* are both very close to English *j* in "jaw."

l is like the English *l*, but *ł* has a thick sound more like an English *w*.

s is the same as *ś* in "sow" except before *i*.

s before *i*, and *s* and *sz* are all close to English *sh* in "she."

z is the same as *z* in "zone" except before *i*.

z before *i*, and *ź*, *ż*, and *rz* are all pretty close to the *zh*-sound in measure, and French *j* in "jour."

In proper names, and in almost all Polish words, the stress falls on the next-to-last syllable: Lawicki, la-VEET-sky. For that reason Polish names are not marked for stress in the Index.

All Polish baptismal names are translated into their English equivalents, since patronymics are not common in Polish, and for simplicity's sake: George, for Jerzy; Sigismund, for Zygmunt; Andrew, for Andrzej (AHN-jay).

APPENDIX B

GENEALOGICAL TABLES

TABLE I ~ The BEGINNINGS

The Main Trunk of Muscovite Rulers

[A Viking *named Rurik (Hrærekr)*
established himself in Novgorod the Great
in 862. He founded the first Muscovite
(Russian) *dynasty.*]

GENERATIONS

Rurik (Semi-legendary) ---------------- 1
? ~ 879

Igor m. Olga ---------------- 2
?~945 | ?~969

Svyatoslav ---------------- 3
? — 972

Hugh Capet St Vladimir, "The Great" ---------------- 4
KING OF FRANCE ? ~ 1015

Robert II *Yaroslav "The Wise"* ----------------5
? — 1051 ca. 980 ~ 1054

Henry I, m. Anna *Vsevolod, m. Irene* *Izyaslav* 6
1005 ~ 1060 1029 ?~1093

Philip I *Vladimir, "Monomakh"* *Svyatopolk* ------ 7
1053 ~ 1108 1053 ~ 1125

Louis VI *Yury, "Dolgoruky"* *Yaroslav* ------- 8
1081 ~ 1137 ? ~ 1157

Louis VII *Vsevolod II, "Big Nest"* *Yury* ------ 9
ca. 1121 ~ 1180 1154 ~ 1212

Philip II *Yaroslav II* *Svyatopolk* ------ 10
1165 ~ 1223 1191 ~ 1246 (Probable
(*Ancestor of* *ancestor of*
Kings of France, *the Princes*
Scotland and England) *Ostrogski*)

TABLE II ~ THE ESTABLISHMENT OF MUSCOVITE SUPREMACY

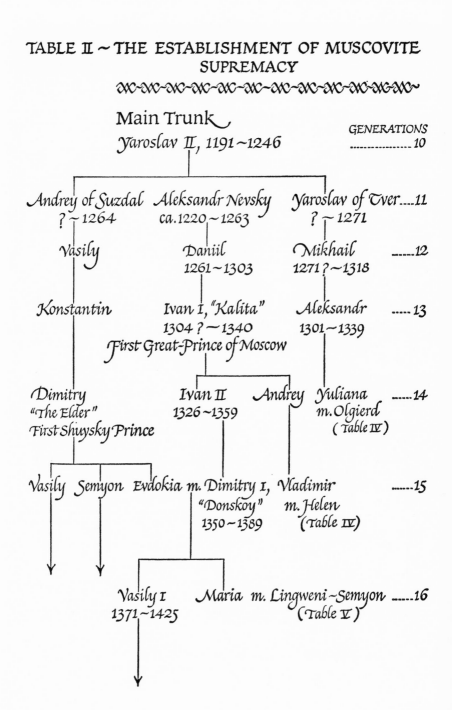

Main Trunk
Yaroslav II, 1191~1246

Andrey of Suzdal   Aleksandr Nevsky   Yaroslav of Tver.....11
? ~ 1264   ca.1220~1263   ? ~ 1271

Vasily   Daniil   Mikhail 12
                     1261~1303   1271?~1318

Konstantin   Ivan I, "Kalita"   Aleksandr   13
                     1304? ~ 1340   1301~1339
             First Great-Prince of Moscow

Dimitry   Ivan II   Andrey Yuliana 14
"The Elder"   1326~1359   m. Olgierd
First Shuysky Prince   (Table IV)

Vasily Semyon Evdokia m. Dimitry I, Vladimir 15
                        "Donskoy"   m. Helen
                        1350~1389   (Table IV)

             Vasily I   Maria m. Lingweni~Semyon 16
             1371~1425   (Table V)

TABLE III ~ The FIRST SEVEN TSARS

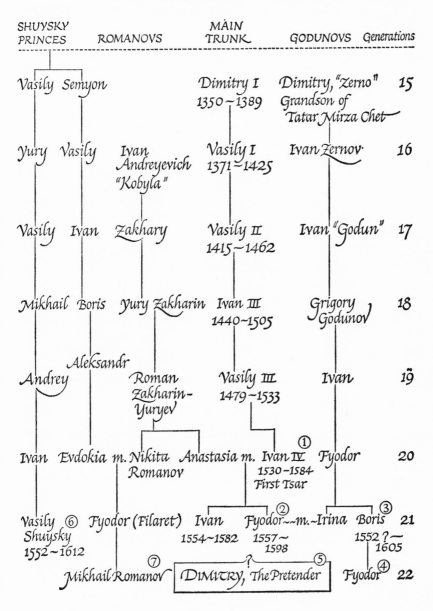

SHUYSKY PRINCES	ROMANOVS	MAIN TRUNK	GODUNOVS	Generations
Vasily Semyon		Dimitry I 1350~1389	Dimitry, "Zerno" Grandson of Tatar Mirza Chet	15
Yury Vasily	Ivan Andreyevich "Kobyla"	Vasily I 1371~1425	Ivan Zernov·	16
Vasily Ivan	Zakhary	Vasily II 1415~1462	Ivan "Godun"	17
Mikhail Boris	Yury Zakharin	Ivan III 1440~1505	Grigory Godunov	18
Andrey	Aleksandr — Roman Zakharin-Yuryev	Vasily III 1479~1533	Ivan	19
Ivan	Evdokia m. Nikita Romanov	Anastasia m. Ivan IV ① 1530~1584 First Tsar	Fyodor	20
Vasily ⑥ Shuysky 1552~1612	Fyodor (Filaret)	Ivan 1554~1582 Fyodor ② ~m.~ Irina 1557~1598	Boris ③ 1552?~1605	21
	Mikhail Romanov ⑦	DIMITRY, The Pretender ⑤ ?	Fyodor ④	22

TABLE IV ~ Connections Between the Ruling Houses of Muscovy, Poland and Lithuania

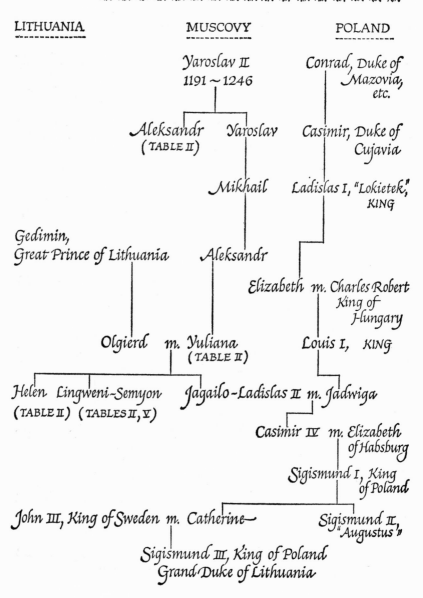

LITHUANIA   MUSCOVY   POLAND

Yaroslav II 1191~1246 — Conrad, Duke of Mazovia, etc.

Aleksandr (TABLE II)   Yaroslav   Casimir, Duke of Cujavia

Mikhail   Ladislas I, "Lokietek", KING

Gedimin, Great Prince of Lithuania   Aleksandr

Elizabeth m. Charles Robert King of Hungary

Olgierd m. Yuliana (TABLE II)   Louis I, KING

Helen (TABLE II)   Lingweni-Semyon (TABLES II, V)   Jagailo-Ladislas II m. Jadwiga

Casimir IV m. Elizabeth of Habsburg

Sigismund I, King of Poland

John III, King of Sweden m. Catherine   Sigismund II, "Augustus"

Sigismund III, King of Poland Grand Duke of Lithuania

TABLE V ~ The House of Mstislavsky

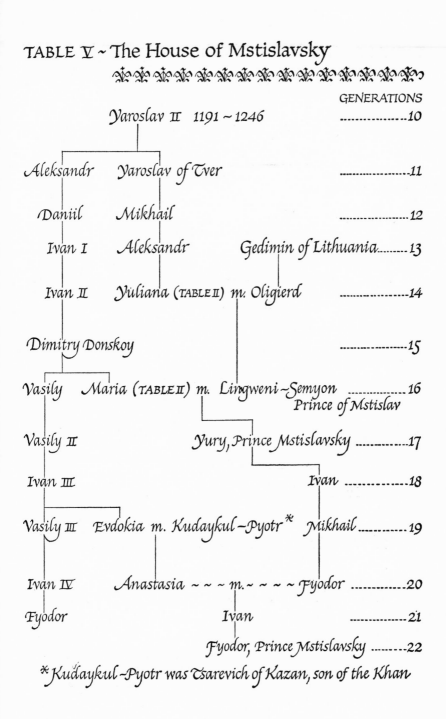

			GENERATIONS
	Yaroslav II 1191 ~ 1246		10
Aleksandr	*Yaroslav of Tver*		11
Daniil	*Mikhail*		12
Ivan I	*Aleksandr*	*Gedimin of Lithuania*	13
Ivan II	*Yuliana* (TABLE II) *m. Oligierd*		14
Dimitry Donskoy			15
Vasily	*Maria* (TABLE II) *m. Lingweni ~Semyon*		16
		Prince of Mstislav	
Vasily II	*Yury, Prince Mstislavsky*		17
Ivan III		*Ivan*	18
Vasily III	*Evdokia m. Kudaykul ~Pyotr**	*Mikhail*	19
Ivan IV	*Anastasia ~ ~ ~ m.~ ~ ~ ~ Fyodor*		20
Fyodor	*Ivan*		21
	Fyodor, Prince Mstislavsky		22

* Kudaykul ~Pyotr was Tsarevich of Kazan, son of the Khan

TABLE VI ~ The House of Vishnevetsky (Wiśniowiecki)

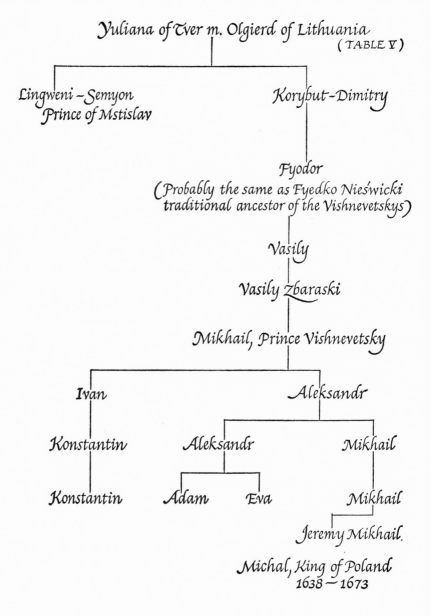

Yuliana of Tver m. Olgierd of Lithuania
(TABLE V)

Lingweni – Semyon
Prince of Mstislav

Korybut – Dimitry

Fyodor
(Probably the same as Fyedko Nieświcki
traditional ancestor of the Vishnevetskys)

Vasily

Vasily Zbaraski

Mikhail, Prince Vishnevetsky

Ivan

Aleksandr

Konstantin

Aleksandr

Mikhail

Konstantin

Adam   Eva

Mikhail

Jeremy Mikhail.

Michal, King of Poland
1638 – 1673

RUSSIAN AND POLISH TITLES

Ataman — Russian (and Polish) *atamán*. Cossack chief, or captain. The origin of the word is uncertain, but it is probably not related to *hetman* (see below).

Boyar — Russian *boyárin*. The boyars were civil officers in origin, the highest in the land, and their rank was to all purposes hereditary, although new ones could be, and were, created. In principle, they formed the council of state for the ruler. The word was borrowed from Danube-Bulgarian, a Turkic language, and its meaning can vaguely be conveyed by "magnate."

Boyars'-son — Russian *syn boyársky*. A sort of petty-nobleman in Russia. (The plural form *déti boyárskie*, "boyars'-children," was also common.) See the *Bolshaya Sovetskaya Entsiklopediya*, 2nd ed., XIV, 137, for a brief explanation. Suffice it to say that it was a title (the lowest, perhaps), rather than a descriptive phrase.

Castellan — Polish *kasztelan*. With a very few exceptions, the castellans ranked next after the palatines (voyvodes), although the Castellan of Kraków, for example, for complicated historical reasons outranked the Palatine. Both the English and Polish words are derived from Latin *castellanus*, "governor of a castle."

Courtier — Russian *dvoryanin*, Polish *dworzanin*. In Russia this title was applied to the junior civil officers, ranking below the boyars. The English term is unfortunate in its connotations, but any other one would be cumbersome. The source of both words is common Slavic *dvor*, "court."

Dyák — a Russian word, translated as "Secretary." These civil servants were a cross between cabinet ministers and chiefs of governmental departments. The word was borrowed from Middle Greek *diákon* and is therefore "related" to English "deacon."

Hetman — Russian *gétman,* Polish *hetman.* Commander-in-Chief of the Cossacks. In Poland, the *Hetman wielki koronny* was the "Marshal" of the Polish army. Borrowed from eastern Middle German *häuptmann,* modern *Hauptmann.*

Okólnichy — a Russian word. A member of the body of boyars attached to the court and closest to the Tsar. A "privy councillor." From Russian *ókolo,* "near, around."

Oprichnik — a Russian word. The title was invented during Ivan the Dread's reign for members of the "separated state" which he set up in 1564. "The *Oprichniki* swore an oath that allowed neither God nor man to come before his [Ivan's] commands" (Bernard Pares, *A History of Russia*). See this or any history of Russia for details.

Pan — a Polish word. A courtesy title applied to noblemen (or gentlemen), along with its feminine counterparts, *Pani,* "lady," and *Panna,* "young lady." It corresponds in meaning and use to Spanish *don.* The word was abbreviated from an old form, *župan,* "district leader." (On *don,* see Diego de Hermosilla: *Diálogo de la vida de los pajes de palacio* [1573], 50–56, as edited by Donald Mackenzie [U. of Penna. dissertation, Valladolid, 1916], which shows that the practice was not so very ancient in Spain.)

Pietyhorcy — a Polish name for what are commonly called light horse, or light cavalry. The name is derived from the Polish for "five mountains," and it is said to have been taken from the Tatars of the Five-Mountain Horde.

Prince — Russian *knyaz,* Polish *książę.* The princes mentioned in this book were descended from Rurik or Gedimin or both. Whereas, however, sons of kings and princes in western Europe were generally called dukes, counts, earls, and so on, especially in the later generations, the descendants of princes were all princes and princesses in Russia and Poland. Hence the great number of persons so styled.

Prístav — a Russian word (old-fashioned plural *pristavy*). A superintendent, surveillant, inspector, warden. In this book, a police officer charged with caring for ambassadors and other visitors. Translated "sergeant" by Fletcher in the sixteenth century. Derived from a verb meaning "to charge with, to appoint as overseer."

Starosta — a Polish title, meaning an administrative officer, usually with military background. The usual translation is "subprefect." In Russian, a *stárosta* was merely a village "elder" (overseer). This reflects the original meaning of the word.

Streltsý — plural of Russian *streléts,* "archer." The corps of streltsý was established about 1550 by Ivan the Dread. It bore some slight resemblance to (and may have been inspired by) the Imperial Roman Praetorian Guard.

Szlachta — a Polish word, broadly meaning "noblemen, nobles, nobility." Possibly more used of the petty-nobility than of the great magnates (*cf.* Russian boyars'-son). Derived from Old (or Middle) High German *slahta,* "family," implying the *known* families.

Voyvode — Russian *voyevoda,* Polish *wojewoda.* Literally, "army leader." In Poland the title was used, interchangeably with *Palatine,* for heads of districts; see *Castellan.* *Voyvode* is often spelled *voivode,* but I have used *voyvode* as a compromise between the various equivalent Slavic forms.

APPENDIX D

WHO WAS
GRIGORY (GRISHKA) OTREPYEV?

WHEN THE RESURRECTED Dimitry, long mentioned in rumor, finally appeared on the scene in the late summer of 1603, Tsar Boris Godunov instituted an inquiry. Before long, the Patriarch Iov (probably helped by Boris's cousin, Semyon Godunov) announced that a former monk of the Chudov Monastery (in the Kremlin) named "Grishka" Otrepyev had run away to Poland, and that Grishka was now undoubtedly passing himself off as the Tsarevich Dimitry, son of Ivan the Dread.

After much equivocation and hesitation, this identification finally became "official," and for two and a half centuries almost no-one doubted that the man who reigned as Tsar Dimitry Ivanovich was in actuality the unfrocked monk, Grishka. The "identity" is still in question, under various aspects, as is briefly mentioned in Appendix E, but a few words as to the historical character Grigory Otrepyev are appropriate.

The Otrepyevs were a branch of the Nelidov family, one of whom, David, received the nickname *Otrepyev*, "Tatters," from Ivan III in 1497. David had three known grandsons, Ignaty, Ivan and Matvey. Ignaty's progeny is of no relevance to the story of Dimitry. Ivan, however, had a grandson named Borislav-Bogdan at the same time that Matvey had one named Bogdan, or Bogdan-Tikhon, or Bogdan-Yakov (in addition to Smirnoy-Nikita and Pyotr-Lukyan). Grigory Otrepyev was called Bogdanovich (son of Bogdan), but nowhere is it clearly stated *which* Bogdan.

Grigory's recorded history is limited. Contemporary chronicles say that his father died when he was young, and that his mother taught him to read and write. He was shorn a monk at the age of fourteen, under Trifon Vyatsky, probably in a monastery by the Dedino estate of the Romanovs. (The estate was near Kostroma, some sixty miles down the Volga from Yaroslavl.) He lived with the Romanovs for a while, and with their relatives, the Cherkassky princes — but just when is not clear. Soon he began the life of a vagabond. Again, the facts are hazy, but it is obvious that his vagabondage was later inflated by the chroniclers into an almost monstrous libertinage because of the association of his name with the Dimitry who was called the Pretender.

Although there is confusion and disagreement among the sources as to the details of Grigory's life (by then generally called Grishka), he seems to have been in Moscow at the time Boris became Tsar, or within the year following. He committed some "error" against Tsar Boris, in company with another petty nobleman named Mikhail Trofimovich Povadin, eluded capture, and before long turned up in the Chudov Monastery, where he was safe. Exactly what he did is not known, but it may have had some connection with Boris's persecution of the Romanovs.

In the end, however, about the time of Sapieha's embassy to Moscow (1600–1601), he sought refuge in Poland, accompanied by Povadin, who had become a monk called Misail, and another fugitive monk by the name of Varlaam Yatsky. One registered fact is that "in the year of the creation of the world 7110, the thirty-first day of August [August 31, 1602]," a book was given to "us, Grigory, and Brothers Varlaam and Misail," by Prince Ostrogski, in Kiev. A later hand added the words "Tsarevich of Moscow" to the name Grigory. (Note: Nowhere does Prince Ostrogski state that he recognized Dimitry as Grishka Otrepyev.)

To all *practical* purposes, Grishka Otrepyev disappears from the scene with this. He was identified with the Dimitry who reigned from 1605 to 1606, and this made it impossible for Grishka to lead an independent life. Nevertheless, Captain Margeret wrote that he was living in banishment imposed by Dimitry because of his perennial drunkenness, in 1606. (If true, it is probably the only instance of a man being banished for drunkenness in Muscovite history.) At the same time, it is not strange that Tsar Vasily Shuysky made no effort to locate Grishka, for that would have proved that the wrong man was murdered on May 17.

So far, so good — or so bad. Nineteenth century historical studies in Russia brought the matter of the Time of Troubles, and more specifically Dimitry called the Pretender, once more to the fore. And these culminated around the turn of the century in the detailed investigations of Pavel ("Paul") Osipovich Pierling, S. J., and Evgeny Nikolayevich Shchepkin, and the ably presented hypothesis of Aleksey Sergeyevich Suvorin. None of these adds any fact whatsoever to the known life of Grishka, but all three bear directly on the subject of Appendix E: *Who Was Dimitry?*

APPENDIX E

WHO WAS DIMITRY?

IN A SOMEWHAT DIFFERENT Russian context, Sir Winston Churchill said, "It is a riddle wrapped in a mystery inside an enigma; but perhaps there is a key." * There is a strange pertinence to Dimitry, called the Pretender, and a key may indeed be supplied — but not a solution.

First of all, as more than one writer has pointed out, it is improper to call Dimitry an "impostor" or a "pretender." He was convinced that he was the son of Ivan, or at least so close a connection that he had a better right to the throne than anyone else. Even though a few historians have doggedly maintained that he was an ignoble clown masquerading as the son of the Dread Tsar, none of the post-Romantic age has been able to visualize a basically false Dimitry. In the laconic phrase of more than one German writer, he was (perhaps) "deceived, but not a deceiver" (. . . *ein Betrogener, kein Betrüger*).

If Dimitry was not a shabby fake, then, these points must be taken into consideration:

1. If the Tsarevich Dimitry did not die on May 15, 1591, Dimitry called the Pretender could well have been he.
2. Or Dimitry may equally well have been the monk Grishka, as recounted in nearly all the contemporary Russian sources — everything heretofore said notwithstanding.
3. Or, he may have been the son of Ivan IV by another wife or concubine, which is hardly tenable.
4. Or, he may have been the son of Ivan's son Ivan, killed in 1582.
5. Farther afield, he may have been a bastard son of King Stephen

* Broadcast on October 1, 1939, quoted in *The Second World War: I. The Gathering Storm* (Boston, 1948), 449.

Báthory of Poland. (This suggestion was obviously inspired by Dimitry's royal air, the urge to justify Polish intervention in Russia, and the conviction of almost everyone that he could not have been a "nobody.")
6. More specifically, he may have been a waif of noble (or even "royal") extraction adopted by the Otrepyev family — with or without clear reasons.
7. He may have been the scion of some princely family, of the heritage of Rurik (or Gedimin), trained from a very early age in the belief that he was the Tsarevich Dimitry,
   a. by a princely family at odds with Godunov, or
   b. by a powerful group of boyars and dyaks whose motives remain obscure (beyond a general dislike of Boris Godunov).

The guesses and ad-hoc theories for explaining one or another aspect of the riddle called Dimitry may be taken up first. They form the points numbered three to seven.

The idea, in number three, that Dimitry was the son of Ivan IV by another wife (or concubine) appears to be nothing more than a guess, to account for Dimitry's insistence on the patronymic *Ivanovich* and yet to allow for the usually accepted record of the Tsarevich's death.

Only a shade more probable is the suggestion, in number four, that he may have been the son of Ivan's son, whose wife was pregnant in 1582. There is a curious bit of evidence in favor of this in a letter written to Dimitry by Antonio Possevino, S. J., from Venice, on July 10, 1605 (n.s.). In that letter, Possevino (who had been Papal peacemaker between Poland and Russia and had known Ivan personally) three times altered the word *father,* referring to Ivan, to *grandfather.* Possevino was one of the best-informed men of his day with regard to Muscovite affairs. Did *he* know who Dimitry was? Or did he only know who he was not, and therefore made an alternative guess?

As to number five, Poles of that day, and this, have now and again advanced the theory that Dimitry must have been the son of their great King Stephen Báthory. Stephen had no legitimate children, but there is no evidence that he had any *affaires-de-coeur* either. Since everything tends to show that Dimitry must have been a Great Russian (*i.e.,* Muscovite) by birth, this conjecture can hardly be sustained.

Numbers six and seven are interlocking, in that both contain the surmise that Dimitry was trained from early youth to believe that he was the Tsarevich. If he was not the Tsarevich, and was adopted by the Otrepyevs, it is difficult to understand why the action was taken, unless it was merely that the childless Bogdan wanted a son. But then why try to turn him into Dimitry?

By virtually the same token, why should the Romanovs, say, start training a boy to pretend to be the son of Ivan when the real Tsarevich was not yet dead, or, after his death, when it was still possible for Tsar Fyodor the Angelic to have a son? (In fact, he did have a daughter.)

Or if it was a plot by a group of boyars or dyaks (or even princes) to rid themselves of Boris, how could they have trained a *sincere* "pretender" when the "trainee" was old enough to know that he was not the Tsarevich? The boyar and/or secretary plot could hardly have been born until it was pretty obvious that Boris would be the successor to Fyodor, and this would not have happened before the death of Fyodor's daughter in 1594. By then, the "pretender" would have had to be twelve years old.

These guesses and surmises have been mentioned primarily to show what a variety of figments of superheated imaginations history has recorded. It remains now to look into the first and second possibilities. They should be taken together, although it has not been common practice to do so.

To begin with, despite the vast amount of evidence to the contrary, it is quite conceivable that the Tsarevich did not die on May 15, 1591. A great deal of later falsehood must be taken as a historical necessity if the Tsarevich survived, but under any circumstances the record is fairly full of prevarications of one sort or another. (As has been pointed out in the text, Prince Vasily Shuysky changed from *yes* to *no* and back again no less than seven times when he was asked if Dimitry was or could be the Tsarevich. Perforce he lied.)

The astute Russian journalist and publisher, Aleksey Sergeyevich Suvorin (see Bibliography) pointed out sixty years ago that after the Tsarevich lay "dead" in the courtyard at Uglich, no-one paid any attention to him for four days, beyond taking the body to the Church of the Savior. Nor is there any mention of *anyone's* observing that it was the Tsarevich whom they buried — not even his mother, who, curiously, was not interviewed by anyone.

Coupled with this disregard for the "dead" Tsarevich is the puzzling ride of Afanasy Nagoy, the Tsaritsa's cousin, to Yaroslavl, to his friend the English agent then there, Jerome Horsey. Judging by Horsey's letter of June 10, 1591, to Lord Burghley (see Bibliography, under Edward

A. Bond), Nagoy reached Yaroslavl not before May 20 or 21, and therefore did not leave Uglich until about May 19 — the distance being less than seventy miles overland. Yet Nagoy was riding *in haste* to ask Horsey to give him "some good thing for the passion of Christ 'his' sake," to help the Tsaritsa. Horsey gave him some "pure salad oil" and a box of Venice treacle,* and Nagoy "hied him post away."

Most strangely, Horsey did not admit Nagoy into his "compound," although he had fifteen men armed to the teeth, Nagoy seems to have been alone, and the two were good friends. This attitude, according to Suvorin, hints that Horsey's letter was far from telling the whole truth, and that Nagoy may have had a body of men with him. From this he moves on to speculate that the medicine was really needed for the Tsarevich, whom Nagoy was secretly taking down the Volga from Uglich to Kostroma, some fifty miles beyond Yaroslavl.

If this was the case, and if Nagoy had trusted Cossacks with him to guard the wounded boy, then the delay in reaching Yaroslavl would be explained. The party would have slipped down the Volga, and by that route Yaroslavl was one hundred and forty miles from Uglich — just about what a boat could cover in four to six days, perhaps at night only, and certainly in secret. (The Cossack bodyguard is postulated to account for the early rumors of the "saved Tsarevich" down by the Don and the Dnyeper.)

This somewhat fantastic tale is in a sense borne out by the fact that Afanasy Nagoy was not interrogated regarding the death of Dimitry when the Commission arrived in Uglich. They arrived on May 19, when Afanasy was already far away. Then, too, there is the business of the other Nagoys, who were still in Uglich, "protecting" the corpse in the church from thieves. This seems an odd idea, unless, as Suvorin suggests, they were protecting it from investigators who might recognize that it was not the body of the Tsarevich.

Finally, there is a third strange fact. By the time Shuysky and his aides reached Uglich, it is reported that the Tsarevich, for unexplained reasons, was no longer recognizable. With little further ado, the body was buried, and remained so until 1606, when Shuysky the unreliable ordered it exhumed to prove that the Dimitry who was called the Pretender was not the Tsarevich. Then, fifteen years after death, the

---

* *Venice treacle* — a medicinal paste, with some sixty-odd ingredients, supposed to prevent or counteract poisoning, but apparently rejected as "impure" by the Orthodox Church in Muscovy.

Tsarevich was found in a state of perfect preservation, including a hand full of nuts which he was not known to have had when he died. Shuysky, who had possibly not seen the boy since he was two, and could not have recognized him when he was eight and a half, now, in 1606, did recognize him, and the Tsarevich was canonized for a saint. So much for the possibility that the real Tsarevich was not killed at all, either by himself or by anyone else.

This leads to the matter of the Otrepyevs and their wayward scion Grigory. As Suvorin correctly says, Grishka Otrepyev is almost inescapable in any contemporary account of the Dimitry who was called the Pretender. His advent in Kiev coincides with the presumed time of Dimitry's arrival there. And there are many other coincidences between the lives of Grishka and Dimitry, so far as the latter is known or admitted. But in the winter of 1605–1606 a Grishka Otrepyev appears alongside of Dimitry in Putivl — unless a French captain and two Polish priests are untrustworthy witnesses. Dimitry naturally could have hired the man to play the part (although difficulties arise even there), but the event has led the Russian historian Evgeny Shchepkin to assume the existence of two Grishkas.

Since there were two Bogdan Otrepyevs, there is no reason to deny the possibility of two sons of Bogdans, both named Grigory — especially since the recorded family-tree of the Nelidov-Otrepyev family does not show any particular preference for one or two baptismal names. (Out of fourteen names recorded, only Ivan and Bogdan are repeated.) But Shchepkin's thesis is vitiated by the simple fact that, beyond the Putivl event, there is no evidence at all for a second Grigory-Grishka, and almost everything militates against it.

Returning then to the existence of one Grishka and one Dimitry, and the remarkable parallels between their known or surmised lives, there arises the strong likelihood that they were one and the same person. Yet even in this tentative proposition there are two reasons to hesitate. One is that it is far from easy to associate the historical *record* of Grishka with the historical *personality* of Dimitry. Then there is the problem of imagining a Grishka trained, prepared or even capable of playing the rôle of the Dimitry who flashed across the Muscovite scene for three years.

Suvorin, to this biographer's mind, is right in pointing out that (1) to prepare Otrepyev for the part of Dimitry long in advance "would not be Russian"; and (2) the Cumaean Sybil could not have foreseen events to the extent that such highly unlikely preparation would have led to anything. In fact, circumstances tend to show that preparation, as such, was not necessary in any case. The ground was ready for "Dimitry."

The entire problem, Suvorin claims, would be solved if Grishka Otrepyev were not the *son* of one of the Bogdan Otrepyevs, but an *adopted* child. The conflicting accounts of Grishka's parents (and "uncle" Smirnoy's uncertainties) provide Suvorin with an opening, and he reaches the conclusion that Grishka was not an Otrepyev at all, but the real Tsarevich Dimitry, entrusted to the Otrepyev family to nurse, protect, and rear. The fact that the grandfather of one of the Bogdans (a cousin, not a brother of Smirnoy) was definitely settled in Uglich long before 1591 lends some sort of support to the idea.

Briefly put, if the Dimitry who was called the Pretender was identical with Grishka Otrepyev, and Grishka in turn was the Tsarevich (saved from death and brought up by the Otrepyev couple as their son), all the confusing story is logical, consistent, and believable.

The Tsarevich was almost certainly an epileptic, as Suvorin says, but boys do outgrow manifest epilepsy, while retaining a certain tendency to fly off the handle, so to speak. This is almost precisely the character of Dimitry. Then, an epileptic would not remember too well what happened to him as a child. Here again is Dimitry, who, in Suvorin's words, "remembered the past as in a dream." Someone, somehow, saved the boy after his attack (perhaps Afanasy Nagoy), realized or dreamed that he was in danger, and gave him to one of the Bogdan Otrepyevs to raise as their son. Then, perhaps with a little prompting, the princes who were opposed to, and persecuted by, Tsar Boris gradually realized that the Tsarevich Dimitry was still alive. Years passed, and they put the boy in the Chudov Monastery to learn to read and write, and to see how the empire was governed. Thus the princes, boyars, dyaks, and all those mentioned in the foregoing list of "points" regarding Dimitry, were not *preparing* him; they were *training* him.

During those years, Dimitry-Grishka sowed wild oats as well as studied. As Grishka, he acquired a reputation which was hardly in keeping with the man destined someday to be Tsar. Therefore, when the time came for him to slip across the border into the safety of Poland (perhaps into the scholarship of Poland as well), he had to shake off the name of Grishka, and all possible identification with him. Wild oats had to give way to good grain.

Suvorin brings out many details in a highly plausible way, such as Dimitry's shaving and going bare-headed (both totally un-Russian at the time) to remove any resemblance to the known Grishka. By then his sickness had abated to a degree that permitted him to take stock of his position, and his chances of regaining the throne. Once he was assured of Polish help, he took his stand, confident of the future.

As history has shown, there was nothing of the dissolute youth or the studious monk about Dimitry, but a fearless even if temperamental prince. He faced his mother, who could hardly have recognized him after fourteen years, without demurring. Eleven months later, he confronted Shuysky's paid mob with "I am no Boris!" and with "Take me to the Place of the Skull! I will tell you who I am."

Those are hardly words of a prepared impostor, or of a Grishka Otrepyev of the petty nobility of Uglich, Suvorin contends. And to conclude he all but clinches his argument with the telling point that even Boris was suspicious that Dimitry was genuine. It was not the Pretender whom Boris feared, but Dimitry. It was not the shade of Dimitry, but Dimitry himself. Realizing the truth at last, says Suvorin, Boris knew that "his only weapon was to use the *name* Grishka Otrepyev." That *name* was to hide the horrible truth.

Suvorin's hypothesis and the circumstantial evidence he brings to back it deserve serious consideration. Two world wars and a great revolution have altered the face of Russia since he wrote. No Soviet, and only one exiled, Russian had since taken up the study of Dimitry's career (Shmurlo, and he somewhat superficially). No-one at all has subjected Suvorin's suggestions to modern historical analysis. It is beyond the scope of this biography to do so. Yet one basic point may be made here, for the general reader as well as the historian for whom the subject may still be unplowed ground.

With or without benefit of all that has been published, unprejudiced and careful investigation of available sources leads not only to the inescapable conclusion that Dimitry himself was convinced that he was genuine, but also to the presumptive truth that in some way he really was.

NOTES AND COMMENTS

A WORD OF caution is unavoidable in regard to the story told in this book. This is because of the unusually strong prejudices of writers, both contemporary and modern, about the events described. These have been nationalistic or religious in origin, with a good deal of political or social theory influencing the later writers.

For example, Russian accounts of Ivan the Dread vary according to the time of writing: under the Tsars, he was painted in rather bloody colors; under Stalin, he became a man of genius. More recently, the stand is less definite. (See Cyril E. Black, ed.: *Rewriting Russian History* ["Vintage Edition," New York, 1962], 230–32.)

Similarly, with regard to the death of the Tsarevich Dimitry, the traditional accusation of Boris Godunov as his virtual murderer has only recently begun to be questioned, despite the fact that it is nearly a century since the basic contemporary document was first properly and fairly studied. The first unbiased study by a scholar appeared only in 1954 (see Prologue and notes).

The account which I have prepared for the life of Dimitry called the Pretender has one basic assumption. It is that Dimitry firmly believed in himself as the rightful heir to the Muscovite throne. While it may of course be argued that I am wrong, I have found no firm evidence that Dimitry ever doubted his inborn right. As a consequence I have subjected to unusually careful scrutiny all accounts which have perpetuated rumors of behavior incompatible with such a heritage. The fact that he is known to have been abstemious weighs heavily in investigations of his reputed licentiousness, and, while I have taken pains to mention the rumors, I have felt obliged to point out their sources and to question their veracity. Beyond this, I have followed primarily those original chroniclers who present the most consistent characteristics in Dimitry. For I believe that people who are sane do not tend suddenly and without evident provocation to indulge in iniquities. If they do, then I have deliberately distorted the personality of the man.

GENERAL SOURCES

To eliminate repetition, it can be said here that my basic general historical sources were: Karamzin's *History of the Russian State,* especially Vol. 11; Solovyov's *History of Russia,* especially Vol. 8; and Klyuchevsky's *Course in Russian History,* especially Lessons 41 and 42. Karamzin and Solovyov particularly have been referred to constantly. Since the pertinent passages are easy to locate, specific references have been reduced to a minimum.

In addition, I have had before me three major works which can be called biographies of Dimitry: Prosper Mérimée's *Les faux Démétrius,* Aleksander Hirschberg's *Dymitr Samozwaniec,* and Reverend Paul Pierling's *La Russie et le Saint-Siège,* Vol. III. I am indebted particularly to Hirschberg and Pierling for citations of manuscript sources not available to me.

In all cases, specific references have been held to a minimum. Principal special sources, for example, are given at the beginning of the notes for many chapters, to avoid excessive footnoting. In addition, the longer chapters are divided into sections by small raised numbers, to facilitate reference to important occasional sources. Where there is no number, the sources for a chapter are grouped together.

Finally, only essential notes and comments have been supplied, since readers acquainted with Russian, Polish, German, French, and so on can easily find the pertinent passages in the source; those unfamiliar with any of these languages will have no need for specific guidance. Regrettably, very little of the source material is available in English.

TITLE

The Tsar's style actually read ". . . of all Rus'," which was the old name for Russia. The country was commonly called the "Muscovite

State [or Empire]," although the name "Russia" is found in some official acts as early as the reign of Boris Godunov.

PROLOGUE

Rurik the Viking (properly Ryurik) is first mentioned in 862 A.D. He
died in 879. For some account of him, see any history of Russia (e.g.,
that of Bernard Pares). For an attempt to identify him, see Charles
Marshall Smith's *Northmen of Adventure* (London, 1932), consult
index.

On Ivan IV: the all too common translation "Terrible" for Ivan's
sobriquet is unfortunate. The Russian adjective *Grozny*, which was
applied to him even during his life, is derived from the noun *grozá*,
"threat, fear, thunder-storm." I adopted Pares's translation "Dread"
some years ago, and feel that it is more satisfactory, although far from
being "perfect." The following studies of Ivan the Dread are well
worth consulting: Hans von Eckardt, *Ivan the Terrible*; K. Waliszewski, *Ivan le Terrible*; Vipper, *Ivan Grozny*; Platonov, *Ivan Grozny* (see
Bibliography for details).

There is a great mass of material, largely in Russian, on the events
following the death of Ivan. In addition to the general work by Platonov, *Ocherki po istorii Smuty*, in Russian, three biographies of Boris
Godunov are useful: Platonov's *Boris Godunov* (available in French),
Kostomarov's monograph on *Boris Godunov* (available in German),
and the new biography of Boris by Constantin de Grunwald, *La vraie
histoire de Boris Godounov*, which benefits by the latest studies of the
period.

The principal contemporary English accounts of Russia are collected in *Russia at the Close of the Sixteenth Century*, edited by Edward A. Bond (Hakluyt Society, 1st ser., XX [1857]). See pp. 21–22
for the passages quoted.

With regard to the death of the Tsarevich Dimitry, a full account
is supplied in Professor George Vernadsky's "The Death of the Tsarevich Dimitry: a Reconsideration of the Case," *Oxford Slavonic Papers*,
V (1954), 1–19. There are also many pertinent suggestions in A. S.
Suvorin's *O Dimitrii Samozvantse*.

For the dynasty of Rurik, and more specifically that of Ivan the
Dread's branch thereof, see Appendix B, Tables I to III.

CHAPTER 1

In addition to the general histories, see Pierling, *La Russie et le Saint-Siège, III,* and Mérimée. For details on the Vishnevetsky clan, see Rudolf Bächtold, *Südwestrussland im Spätmittelalter* (Basel, 1951), 128, 132, and 148.

1. Poland, a kingdom since about 1000 A.D., had entered a dynastic union with Lithuania when the male line of Polish kings was extinguished by the death of Casimir III, "the Great." Casimir's sister's son succeeded to the throne but died in 1382, leaving a nine-year-old daughter, Jadwiga. The Poles accepted Jadwiga as Queen, provided she married a prince of their choice. Agreement was reached, and in 1386 Jadwiga was married to the Grand Duke Jogaila (Jagiełło) of Lithuania, who styled himself King. On the death of Jogaila's son Casimir IV (by his fourth wife) a century later, however, the two countries had separate rulers, until they were reunited dynastically in 1506, by the election of Sigismund I as King of Poland and Grand Duke of Lithuania. Sigismund I was succeeded by his son, Sigismund II Augustus, who succeeded in uniting the two countries politically. On July 4, 1569, he signed a *Writ of Union* which provided, among other things, for separate state functions but one common commonwealth, or "Republic," under an elected monarch to be "proclaimed simultaneously King of Poland and Grand Duke of Lithuania, Russia, Prussia, Masovia, Samogitia, Kiev, Volynia Podlasia and Inflants [eastern Latvia]."

The bulk of the account of Dimitry's appearance at the Brahin estate belonging to Prince Adam is based on Konrad Bussow's *Relation* or *Chronikon,* which was first published in Russian translation by Ustryalov (*Skazaniya*), then in the original German of a second version in the *Rerum Rossicarum Scriptores Exteri,* and has now appeared in Konrad Bussov, *Moskovskaya Khronika, 1584–1613* (Moscow/Leningrad, 1961). For further information, see Ernst Eduard Kunik, "Analectes Historiques," *Bulletin de la Classe des Sciences historiques, philologiques et politiques de l'Académie Impériale des Sciences de Saint-Pétersbourg,* VIII (1851), cols. 305–27 and 353–87, which contains a brief life of Bussow.

I have followed Bussow's account of how Dimitry "revealed" himself for the reason that it appears to be the only contemporary one — although Bussow was anything but present at the time.

On the Cossacks and the Ukraine in general, see W. E. D. Allen's *The Ukraine: A History* (Cambridge, England, 1940), especially Chapters ii and iii.

2. Prince Adam's letter of October 7, 1603, was printed in Wacław Sobieski's *Szkice Historyczne* (Warsaw, 1904), 80–81, transcribed from a manuscript in the Zamoyski Archives. See also the letter of October 20 from Ławrin Piaseczyński, Chamberlain of Brasław, now in the Vitebsk district, Byelorussian S. S. R., to King Sigismund, in V. N. Aleksandrenko's "Materialy po Smutnomu vremeni na Rusi XVII v.," *Starina i Novizna*, XIV (1911), 423–24.

The information from Vishnevetsky's letter which was sent to Rome forms Appendix I of Pierling's *Russie,* as above, while much of the other detail is based on the same work.

For the description of Dimitry, see Karamzin's *History,* Vol. 11, Chapter 2. As to Tsar Ivan's height and other details, the information was obtained by word of mouth in the State Historical Museum, Moscow, September, 1964.

For the details regarding the Mniszech family, see Aleksander Hirchberg's *Maryna Mniszchówna* (Lvov, 1927), 2–5, and footnotes. There is a genealogical tree of the family in Dworzaczek's *Genealogia* (see Bibliography).

CHAPTER 2

The chief sources for this chapter have been well summarized in Pierling's *Russie,* Hirschberg's *Dymitr,* and Mérimée's *Faux Démétrius.*

1. The details are from Hirschberg's *Dymitr* and *Maryna,* so far as the Mniszechs are concerned. The description of Sambor is based on *Dymitr,* 55–57, which in turn follows an official examination, *Rewizyi ekonomii samborskiej z r. 1596.*

The extraordinary pomp of Polish travel is discussed in Władysław Łoziński's *Polnisches Leben in vergangenen Zeiten* (translated from Polish, Munich, n.d. [1920's?]).

The quotation on Polish girls is from Adam Mickiewicz's "Trzech Budrysów" (*Dzieła,* Warsaw, 1948–1950, I, 228). The translation is my own. Unfortunately, the lightness of the original cannot be imitated in English, and some change in the similes is unavoidable if the verse form is to be preserved.

The declaration of Mniszech's servant is in the "Interrogation of Mniszech on the death of Dimitry, May, 1606," in *Sobranie Gosudarstvennykh Gramot i Dogovorov* (3 vols., Moscow, 1813–1822), II, 294.

2. The estimate of Dimitry's "theological luggage" is from Pierling's *Russie,* 58. Pomaski's "reward" is mentioned in a footnote on the same page. It was dated October 31, 1605.

The Hebrew words *thōhū* and *bhōhū* occur in Gen. I, 2, and mean "waste, confusion" and "void." They were used to describe the condition of the earth at the beginning of the Creation. Rabelais appears to have imported the phrase into French, to describe utter confusion, whence it spread over most of Europe by the early seventeenth century.

Any life of Sigismund will supply information on his unusual character, his difficulties with the Polish Republic over which he reigned, and his lack of understanding of the Polish people. The Polish strain in his blood was minimal, since it derived from his great-great-great-great grandmother, the Polish Princess Elizabeth (see Apendix B, Table IV). He was continually at odds with the Great Chancellor, John Zamoyski, and other capable officials. (There is a good account of Sigismund III in *The Cambridge History of Poland* [to 1696], Cambridge U. Press, 1950.)

For a recent, readable account in English of King Sebastian of Portugal and the False Sebastians who cropped up after his death, see E. W. Bovill, *The Battle of Alcazar* (London, 1952), especially pages 155–57.

The details of Sigismund's circular letter are taken from a copy of one to Christopher Zenowicz, Palatine of Brest, in S. L. Ptashitsky's "Despoty Zenovichi v kontse XVI i nachale XVII vekov," *Russkaya Starina,* XXI (1878), 135–36.

On Sigismund's troubles with Sweden, see any good Swedish history; e.g., Andrew A. Stomberg, *A History of Sweden* (London, 1932).

3. Among the papers in the library of Count Delagardia, published by Aleksandr Ivanovich Turgenev in the *Historica Russiae Monumenta* (3 vols., Petropoli [Leningrad], 1841–42 and 1848), III, 404 ff., there is a long document containing "Notes" from the years 1608 to

1615. This gives some detail on the Muscovites who turned up in Kraków in 1604. Two Atamans of the Don Cossacks are there mentioned as having arrived in Kraków shortly after Poroshin: Andrey Korela (or Karela) and Mikhaylo Miezakow (Mezhakov?). In the Archives of Königsberg (now Kaliningrad) there is (or was) a letter from the Don Cossacks to Dimitry, dated November 15 (1604?) to the effect that Korela and Miezakow have been sent, but when they reached Dimitry does not seem to be recorded. I have therefore omitted this reference in the text, since the "Notes" were made at least three or four years later than the letter was written.

Mniszech's banquet is beautifully described in a letter from Claudio Rangoni, printed in Paul Pierling's *Rome et Démétrius* (Paris, 1878), 178–79.

With regard to Dimitry's audience with King Sigismund, there is an account in Mérimée (p. 90) and elsewhere of Dimitry's throwing ing himself at the King's feet in abject fear ("tutto tremante"). This invention has been totally discredited by Pierling in his "Cilli i Massa, Sovremenniki Lzhedimitriya," *Russkaya Starina*, LXXX (1893), 465–86 — if such erudite disproof was ever necessary. The names of those present were recorded by Rangoni, and the quotation is from his dispatch of March 20, 1604, printed by Pierling (1878), 180–82.

Dimitry's speech about Croesus and Cyrus must have been taken from Herodotus, whose *History* was available in Latin in 1604, but hardly in Polish or Russian. Who prompted Dimitry in this instance remains unknown — as does the name of the prompter of a number of Dimitry's moves.

As for Rangoni, I have given a slightly more "diabolical" slant to his moves than Father Pierling would have countenanced. Pierling calmly writes: "il naviguait à pleines voiles dans ces eaux" (*Russie*, 81). I feel that Rangoni's vision of a reunion of the Catholic and Orthodox Churches had become so lifelike that he employed all sorts of means, short of falsehood and force, to accomplish his ends. He may certainly be excused for it.

With regard to the scenes of Dimitry's participation in thoroughly un-Orthodox rites (based on Pierling and Hirschberg), it should be pointed out that here is the first hint that Dimitry, called the Pretender, could not have been a mere actor who had learned his part well. His faith in himself was too great.

CHAPTER 3

1. The Wawel is a low hill on the banks of the Vistula, south of the old walled town of Kraków. It contains the citadel, the royal palace, and the cathedral.

To "turn on the heat," if somewhat slangy, is a fair imitation of Rangoni's own words: "a far caldo offitio" (Pierling, *Rome et Démétrius*, 183).

Nicholas Zebrzydowski, whose wife was a cousin of Zamoyski, was one of the most powerful men in Poland. Any history of Poland will provide some information on his character, and there is a fairly full account of his life in the Polish Encyclopedia of Orgelbrand.

With regard to Dimitry's first confession and his brief hesitation before Sawicki, there are two possible explanations, *both* of which may be correct. First, Dimitry had absorbed a good deal of agnosticism at Hoshcha, and his later life showed that religion rested lightly on his shoulders. Second, his agreement to join the Catholic Church was evidently based on necessity. Then, while he never faltered in his conviction that he was the rightful heir to the Russian throne, it may be doubted whether he was completely certain that he was specifically the son of Ivan the Dread. (He could have been the son of Ivan's son, Ivan, and still have been Dimitry Ivanovich, rightful heir to the empire.)

With regard to Easter, in 1604 the feast was celebrated on the same day throughout Christendom for the ninth time since the calendar reform of 1582.

Dimitry's letter of April 24, 1604, to Pope Clement is reproduced in Paul Pierling's *Lettre de Dmitri dit le Faux à Clément VIII* (Paris, 1898). The translation is mine.

2. There seems to be no record of Dimitry's route from Kraków to Sambor, other than that the caravan stopped at Sanok. On the basis of similar contemporary expeditions of which there is a record, however, it may be guessed that Pan George and Dimitry (and company) moved at the slow rate of two to four Polish miles a day. Although the length of a Polish mile seems not to have been "standardized," there is some evidence that in the Kraków region, early in the seventeenth century, it amounted to about seven and a half kilometers, or a little under five modern statute miles.

The phrase "pride, pomp and circumstance" is from Shakespeare's *Othello,* III, iii, 354.

The record of the stop at Sanok is in Hirschberg's *Dymitr,* 55. The information regarding Pan George's visit to Kraków and the letters to Zamoyski and the Ostrogskis comes from the same work, pp. 58–61. Hirschberg's sources include the Żółkiewski letters, some of which have not been available to me. Nevertheless, not even his tireless scrutiny of the Polish archives has produced much evidence on Marina's activities, attitude, and so on.

The quotation from Pushkin is from my *Alexander Pushkin, Boris Godunov* (Columbia U. Press, 1953), 98–99.

On the contracts signed with Pan George, see the *Sobranie Gosudarstvennykh Gramot i Dogovorov, II,* 159–62 and 165–66. The texts are not quite the same in the Polish and Russian versions as printed, although the translation presented no problem. It is perhaps worth noting that to me Dimitry's signature in Russian (*Tsare[vich] Uglitsky*) appears more practiced and firmer than his awkward Polish "printing" of *Dmitr Carewicz, Ręką swą* ("by his own hand"). Both signatures have been reproduced, along with a handsome Russian seal.

As for Marina's exotic titles, that was the custom of the day in Poland. Medenitsa (Ukrainian S.S.R.) is a small town about twenty-five miles east-by-south of Sambor.

The million zlotys amounted to an enormous sum in those days, although it is not possible to determine its purchasing power in terms of modern currencies. It nevertheless appears certain that a zloty contained two and a quarter pennyweight of pure gold, which, figured at the present United States value of $35 per ounce, would bring the total to $3,942,000.

Ostyor is sometimes transliterated *Oster,* although it is accented on the last syllable and rhymes with "for." The text of Ratomski's message to Dimitry is quoted by Hirschberg, *Dymitr,* 54, from the Borghese MSS in the Vatican Archives.

The story of the attempted assassination of Dimitry is in Johann Peter von Ludewig's *Reliquiae manuscriptorum,* VI, 355–56. Ludewig says that the anonymous author was a "R. legatus," but which royal legate is not stated. For an extended summary of the incident, and further information on Varlaam, see Evgeny Nikolayevich Shchepkin's "Wer war Pseudodemetrius I?" in the *Archiv für slavische Philologie,* XX (1898), 291–92 (see Bibliography for details).

CHAPTER 4

Of the several biographies of Boris Godunov, the most recent and in many senses the best is Constantin de Grunwald's *La vraie histoire de Boris Godunov* (Paris, 1961). It should be remembered that Aleksandr Pushkin's play and Modest Musorgsky's opera (based thereon) were inspired by Karamzin's account. This combination, disregarding the opera, set the pattern for telling the story, and while both Platonov and Kostomarov moved toward correcting the melodramatic errors, it remained for M. de Grunwald to set the record at least a little straighter. My own sketch of Boris's life, in my translation of Pushkin, was written before Professor Vernadsky's monograph on the death of the Tsarevich and before M. de Grunwald's book, but it already anticipated the conclusions I can now express in this book.

1. The Polish Ambassador, who arrived in Moscow on October 16, 1600, was Leo Sapieha (1557–1633). Details are available in M. de Grunwald's life of Boris Godunov, pp. 142–44, although he has confused Leo with his younger brother Andrew. Solovyov provides even more material (see Vol. VIII, Chapter 1).

The episode of Prince Gustav is related in all histories. There is a rare play on the subject, in Swedish, by Lorenzo Hammarsköld, *Prins Gustaf* (Strängnäs [near Stockholm], 1812), in which the name of Gustav's paramour is given as Aldonza, "a Spanish lady." I do not know where the author learned this, or if it is pure fiction. (Parenthetically, Lorenzo's brother was great-grandfather of Dag H., noted Secretary of the United Nations.)

My source for the first rumors about Dimitry is Isaac Massa (see Bibliography), p. 67. There were earlier whisperings (1600), but "Boris paid no attention to them at all, at that time" (Massa, p. 60).

The story of Boris and the Romanovs is well told, and in considerable detail, by M. de Grunwald, pp. 157–65. For that and Belsky as well, see also Solovyov, Vol. VIII, Chapter 2.

On Boris and the "empty name," see my translation of Pushkin's *Boris Godunov*, 72–73.

On the Russian youths who were sent to England, see S. Konovalov, "Anglo-Russian Relations, 1620–4," *Oxford Slavonic Papers*, IV (1953), 80–82.

2. Ivan's policy in the Ukraine is outlined in both Karamzin and Solovyov. See also S. F. Platonov's *Smutnoye Vremya* (Prague, 1924) and *Ocherki po Istorii Smuty* (St. Petersburg [Leningrad], 1899). There is more detail in the monograph by E. N. Kusheva, "K istorii kholopstva v kontse XVI — nachale XVII vekov," *Istoricheskie Zapiski,* XV (1945), 70–96.

The quotation from Pushkin is again from my translation of *Boris Godunov,* 70–71.

The story of Marfa's visit to the Tsar is in Massa, pp. 114–15. Hirschberg (*Dymitr,* 63) supplies the date, April 7/17, 1604, by quoting a letter from Michael Ratomski. Karamzin (XI, Chapter 2) claims that Marfa knew it was not her son, but was happy about the Pretender because he frightened Boris.

The fullest study of the "discovery" of the culprit, Yury (Grishka) Otrepyev is in Shchepkin's "Wer war Pseudodemetrius I?" *Archiv für slavische Philologie,* XXII (1900), 321–432 (see Bibliography for details).

Prince Boris Kanbulatovich Cherkassky married Fyodor (Filaret) Romanov's sister, Marfa (Martha); his niece Maria had been Ivan the Dread's second wife and is said to have egged him on, in his unbridled career.

Smirnoy Otrepyev was the brother of Bogdan, "father of Grishka." According to Shchepkin, however, there were two Otrepyevs named Bogdan, second cousins, and one of them had no children of his own. On Smirnoy's uncertainty about his "nephew," see Pierling's *Russie,* 93–95.

CHAPTER 5

In this chapter, in addition to the usual sources, I have made great use of Stanislas Borsza's *Expedition of Tsar Dimitry to Moscow,* a manuscript account printed in Polish and in Russian translation in *Russkaya Istoricheskaya Biblioteka,* I (1872), columns 365–426, and John Zabczyc's *Mars moskiewski krwawy* (Kraków, 1605), both of whom were members of the expedition, supplemented by Pan George Mniszech's "Diary" as printed in the *Sobranie Gosudarstvennykh Gramot i Dogovorov,* II, Item 80.

1. For an ample description of Smirnoy Otrepyev and his discussions in Poland, see Solovyov, Vol. VIII, Chapter 2.

On Dimitry and his relations with the Jesuit fathers, as well as their experiences on the way to Moscow, see John Wielewicki, *Dziennik spraw domu zakonnego OO. Jezuitów u św. Barbary w Krakowie od r. 1600 do r. 1608 (włącznie)*, Kraków, 1886. (This is volume X of the series *Scriptores Rerum Polonicarum*.) Mention of Dimitry begins on page 49 of this work, but it may be said that the story is of prime importance only from page 69 on. I have relied on Wielewicki extensively, as have others who have written on the subject.

On Glinyany, see *Istoriya Ukrainskoy S.S.R. v dvukh tomakh,* I (Kiev, 1956), 136.

The story of Khrushchov is told in full by both Karamzin and Solovyov. He is apparently the same as the boyars'-son of that name mentioned in Solovyov, Vol. VII, Chapter 3, toward the end. It is possible that Nikita Sergeyevich Khrushchov of contemporary history came from the same family. The interrogation of Khrushchov is in the *Sobranie Gosudarstvennykh Gramot i Dogovorov,* II, 173–78.

On the title *Hetman,* see Appendix C.

Mniszech's letter of September 18, 1604, is in Pierling's *Rome et Démétrius,* 201–2. The translation is mine.

On Kiev, the *Istoriya Kieva* (Kiev, 1963), I, 126–37, is curiously brief in its historical notes for the period in question, although there are a few interesting illustrations.

The details of Dimitry's entrance into Kiev, along with the picturesque and laconic description of his army, are taken from Hirschberg, *Dymitr,* 71–72.

2. In addition to Karamzin, for Dimitry's declarations on crossing the Dnyeper and so on, see *Akty sobrannye Arkheograficheskoyu ekspeditsieyu* (1836), II, 76–77 and 89–99. The translations are mine.

On Chernigov, see Mikhail Nikolayevich Tikhomirov's *Drevnerusskie Goroda* (2nd ed., Moscow, 1956), 338–45, and Rudolf Bächtold's *Südwestrussland im Spätmittelalter* (Basel, 1951), with a number of references (see index).

The balance of the account of the happenings at Chernigov is derived primarily from Borsza's account, already mentioned.

CHAPTER 6

1. On Novgorod Seversky, see Tikhomirov, 347–48, and Bächtold (refer to index).

The story of Prince Igor Svyatoslavich is told in the famous Russian epic, *Slovo o Polku Igoreve*, the history of which is so remarkable that its "genuineness" has been doubted. The Russian text of this "Tale of the Campaign of Igor" has been published, with modern Russian translations and copious notes, under the general editorship of Varvara Pavlovna Adrianova-Perets (Moscow/Leningrad, 1950). There are also translations in various western European languages, and a considerable body of critical literature has sprung up, far from entirely in Russian. Aleksandr Porfiryevich Borodin drew largely on the *Slovo* for the libretto of his opera *Prince Igor* ("Knyaz' Igor"), a task in which he was to some extent aided by the great Russian nineteenth-century critic, Vladimir Vasilyevich Stasov.

The Basmanov family was noted for its army-commanders as early as the middle of the sixteenth century. It was a branch of the Pleshcheyev family of Chernigov, founded by Aleksandr Fyodorovich Bakont "Pleshchey" (perhaps "the Extravagant") early in the fourteenth century. Danilo Pleshcheyev, son of the boyar Andrey Mikhaylovich, adopted the sobriquet "Basman" (a Turkish word in origin), thus giving rise to the Basmanov family. During the infancy of Ivan IV, Danilo's son Alexey took the side of the Shuyskys, but later supported the Tsar. He and his son were favorites of Ivan's, but by 1568–1569 he was caught in a plot. The son, Fyodor, was so handsome that his close association with Ivan gave rise to whispers of indecent behavior, but neither beauty nor amity saved him from the implacable Tsar. He was executed while still a young man in 1571, leaving two infant children, Ivan and Pyotr. His widow, said to have been a sister of Prince Andrey Vasilyevich Sitsky, soon married Prince Vasily Yuryevich Golitsyn, and the two Basmanov orphans were brought up in that princely house. Between 1571, then, and 1584, three Golitsyn princes were born, all half-brothers of Ivan and Pyotr Basmanov, The Naum Pleshcheyev of Chapter 8 was about a fifth cousin of Ivan and Pyotr.

The four lines of bad poetry are from Zabczyc's *Mars moskiewski krwawy*, bottom of leaf D2ʳ. They are a fair example of the Ronsardian alexandrines in which this invaluable account is written.

The district of Komarichi (*Komaritskaya volost'*) was virtually the

cradle of the Bolotnikov revolt of 1606–1607. It is on the divide between the Desna-Dnyeper and Oka-Volga basins, across which Dimitry's route to the capital lay. See Ivan Ivanovich Smirnov's *Vosstanie
Bolotnikova, 1606–1607* (Leningrad, 1951), end map, for the location
of the district.

On Putivl, see Tikhomirov, 346, and Bächtold (see index).

Mérimée (*Les faux Démétrius,* 106) mentions several reports to the
effect that Prince Vasily Mikhaylovich Mosalsky-Rubets, Voyvode of
Putivl, voluntarily brought some eighty thousand ducats to Dimitry
at this time. Since the accounts are far from clear (although in part
confirmed by Karamzin), I have omitted the story from the text. It is
quite possible, but neither essential to the action nor entirely credible.

2. Although Borsza is again my chief source, the report on the battle
by Captain Jacques Margeret (then with the opposing forces) is valuable. The passage translated is on pages 113–14. Between Margeret's
account and Karamzin's comment, Pushkin found the basis for a remarkable scene in his play *Boris Godunov* (see my translation, pp.
110–13).

Again, in the case of the battle of Dobrynichi (which merited attention in the *Great Sovyet Encyclopedia,* 2nd ed., XIV, 614, while that of
Novgorod Seversky did not), I have followed Borsza and Margeret,
principally. The passage translated from Margeret is on pages 115–16.

The scene from Pushkin's *Boris Godunov* is quoted from my translation, pp. 130–31.

CHAPTER 7

1. It is fundamental to note, in the history of Dimitry, that while that
dynamic young man rushed into Muscovy to find a temporary setback
in January, 1605, the previously energetic and capable Tsar Boris Godunov fiddle-faddled with diplomatic protests, conveyed by such third-
rate envoys as the presumed uncle of Dimitry, Smirnoy Otrepyev, and
the obscure Posnik Ogaryov (often transcribed Ogarev despite the
sound of the word). Indeed, in the very days when Dimitry was lick-
ing his wounds and wondering whether to retreat into Poland, Ogaryov was presenting a dubious case for his Tsar in Warsaw, which at
times brought more confusion than clarification, and which is virtually the springboard for Evgeny Shchepkin's lengthy inquiry into *Wer*

war Pseudodemetrius I? Had Boris lived, it is possible that he might have won out in the end. At the same time, it is glaringly obvious that he set about winning in a strangely ineffective way. Unfortunately, no biographer of Boris has dug very deeply into the mass of material on the subject which Shchepkin shows to be available outside of Russia.

A second point to be remembered is that Dimitry's recovery from defeat and his final march on Moscow were both due largely to the Cossacks. The Russian historians, both contemporary and subsequent, have generally been so eager to place the "blame" for Dimitry on the Poles that they have failed to notice that few Poles indeed were in Dimitry's camp after Dobrynichi.

With regard to Dimitry's more detailed manifesto as to who he was and how he was saved, Shchepkin gives a lengthy extract from a manuscript in the Hofbibliothek in Vienna which may contain much of the same material (Shchepkin, I, 294 fn.).

The original text of the communication carried by Ogaryov is transcribed in part by Solovyov, Vol. VIII, Chapter 2, from which I have translated the extract given.

The extract from Sapieha's remarks is taken from Rangoni's dispatch of February 26, 1605, quoted in Pierling's *Russie*, 108 fn.

2. On the appearance of Grishka Otrepyev, see Pierling, *ibid.*, 420–21, which contains further references. It is unfortunately often difficult to estimate the credibility, total or partial, of many of the sources; witness, for example, Solovyov's long analysis of the Varlaam account in fn. 65 to Vol. VIII, Chapter 2.

As to the description "sorcerer," and the subject of magic and sorcery in general, Muscovy was certainly no freer of superstition than any other country of the time. It should not be forgotten that even Sir Isaac Newton, in the *late seventeenth* century, wrote over a million solemn words on magic, earning himself the title of "The Last of the Magicians" (see Lynn Thorndike, "Mediaeval Magic and Science in the Seventeenth Century," *Speculum*, XXVIII (1953), 692–704).

With regard to Fyodor Godunov's famous map, there is some discussion of this in Heinrich Michow's *Das erste Jahrhundert russischer Kartographie* (Hamburg, 1906), 41–49.

As for Korela, there is an entertaining account of his activities in Mérimée, 123–25.

The town of Kromy, though mentioned as far back as 1147, was thoroughly inconspicuous until 1595, when the fort was built there to guard against attacks from the Crimean Tatars.

There is a new life of Ghazi Giray in the new edition of *The Encyclopedia of Islam* (Leiden and London, 1954–   ), II, 1046–47.

The *Dikoye Pole* (literally "wild country") was the no-man's-land between the Muscovite empire and the Crimean Khanate. It lay mostly in the upper reaches of the Don, but extended as far west as the eastern tributaries of the Dnyeper and the Desna.

Merick's account of the death of Boris Godunov was printed in *Sir Thomas Smithes voyage and Entertainment in Rushia* (London, 1605), pp. H 2^r – ^{v}. Some of the more picturesque tales of what happened may surely be discarded, but the account of his death in Karamzin is worth reading. (The pertinent footnotes to Vol. III, 5th ed. [1843], are the source of some of the information in my text, and are worth consulting in any event.) See also de Grunwald's life of Boris, already mentioned.

CHAPTER 8

There is a fine description of Tsar Boris and his son receiving an embassy in 1603, in Otto Blümcke's *Berichte u. Akten der hansischen Gesandtschaft nach Moskau im Jahre 1603* (Halle a. d. Saale, 1894), 100–1. Fyodor's personal traits are glowingly described by Kubasov, as quoted in fn. 308 to the 5th ed. of Karamzin, Vol. III. His eyes were large and black, his complexion very white (with no implication of pallor or sickliness), and he was of medium height and well-developed.

Prince Katyrev-Rostovsky (who lived until 1640) enjoyed the favor of Tsar Boris, seems to have played a somewhat equivocal rôle after April 13, 1605, was exiled by Tsar Vasily Shuysky, and enjoyed the imperial favor once more under Tsar Mikhail Romanov. He is chiefly noted for his contemporary chronicle, published in two versions in *Russkaya Istoricheskaya Biblioteka,* Vol. XIII.

Prince Vasily Shuysky had an astounding ability to change his mind with regard to Dimitry. But it is most regrettable that this ability was not the product of indecision or uncertainty. It was purely selfish, when it was not cowardly. Nikolay Ivanovich Kostomarov, in his *Russkaya istoriya v zhizneopisaniyakh yeya glavneyshikh deyateley,* lists in his biographical sketch of Prince Vasily no less than seven instances of his swearing and forswearing, from the time of his first report on the Tsarevich's death in 1591, to the day of mob-rule, May 17, 1606.

There is no easy way to get around the double-dating in a story which involves two such countries as Poland (or France) and Russia (or England). It would be just as absurd to convert Russian dates to the new style as to hold Poland to a calendar which it had abandoned.

My source for the events at Kromy has been (chiefly) Borsza's account, which seems generally reliable as well as picturesque.

Lawicki's letter, from which I have translated the passage, is dated June 15, 1605. It is transcribed in Pierling's *Russie*, p. 166 fn.

I have followed Solovyov, Vol. VIII, end of Chapter 2, in my analysis of Basmanov's denying his oath to young Tsar Fyodor. Considering Basmanov's background, he was astoundingly loyal — but later.

The idea of the people longing for a "good Tsar" was developed by Stalin in an interview with Emil Ludwig, which was published in 1938. I have taken the reference from Smirnov's *Vosstanie Bolotnikova*, p. 28. It is an apt and simple way of expressing the evident attachment to the idea of a Tsar which was still very strong in Russia in 1605.

Dimitry's words to the Jesuit fathers are taken from Barezzi's *Relazione*, 44.

The description of the fighting at Kromy is taken from Massa, p. 123.

The Shakespearean phrase referring to the divine origin of kings is in II Henry VI, V, i, 105.

The extracts of Dimitry's message are translated from the *Akty sobrannye*, II, 89–91.

Pleshcheyev was distantly related to Basmanov, as mentioned above. Gavrila Grigoryevich Pushkin was undoubtedly a collateral ancestor of the great poet, Aleksandr Sergeyevich. See also my translation of *Boris Godunov*, 179.

The lines from José Hernández's poem, *Martín Fierro*, are translated from lines 91–92 in the edition of the Biblioteca Argentina, Buenos Aires, 1937.

I have based my account of the death of young Tsar Fyodor largely on Massa, 136–37, Margeret, 124–25, and Bussow, 34–35. At the same time, I have woven in such bits from Karamzin's account as can fill in the picture. Several of Karamzin's sources have not been available to me, and I have relied on his footnotes for these. The details of the actual murder of Fyodor are again from Karamzin, fn. 347, ed. as above.

I have borrowed from Pushkin the idea that the crowd stood silent when the two princes emerged. It is possibly imaginary, but surely is entirely in keeping.

CHAPTER 9

Bussow, Margeret and Massa have by now become the principal sources, although there is still something in Borsza. Karamzin's powerful pen cannot be disregarded, however, especially since he had access to sources which I have not been able to consult personally, and which appear to be generally hard to locate. One great advantage Karamzin offers over other relatively modern (*i.e.*, non-contemporary) sources is that his literary-dramatic sense often counterbalances his historic prejudices, so that an understanding word escapes now and then despite his basic scorn for the "impostor" Dimitry. Three generations had to slip by before Evgeny Frantsevich Shmurlo could declare that Dimitry cannot be called "false" or "an impostor" for the simple reason that *he* was convinced that he was genuine. (See Shmurlo's *Kurs russkoy istorii* [Prague, 1933], Vol. II, 182–191.)

1. I believe that Karamzin's presentation of Dimitry's problem over Fyodor is very fair and have based the opening paragraphs of this chapter on it. (See Karamzin, Volume XI, last paragraphs of Chapter 3.) On the other hand, Hirschberg's interpretation of the attitude of the assassins is not only more modern in approach but undoubtedly quite to the point (*Dymitr,* 122). It should be noted that Margeret (124ff.) and Bussow (35) are not entirely in accord as to what happened.

The Varsonofyevsky monastery stood about three hundred yards from the Neglinnaya River and five hundred north of the Chinese City walls — about ten minutes walk from the modern Bolshoy Theatre. The popular name for the monastery is taken from Bussow, 35, along with other details.

The story of Merick is based primarily on *Sir Thomas Smithes voyage,* and the Borsza account (see Bibliography). Merick's report of January 11/21, 1606, is in P. R. O., State Papers, Foreign, Russia (S.P.91. 1, 211), London. For general background, and a few details, see T. S. Willan, *The Early History of the Russia Company: 1553–1603* (Manchester U. Press, 1956); consult index under both names. From the Russian point of view, there are passages devoted to Dimitry and the Englishmen in Inna Lubimenko, *Les relations commerciales et politiques* (see Bibliography), 130–32.

2. The Biblical passage is from Matthew, X, 16. The source is Father Lawicki's letter of September 21, transcribed in Aleksandrenko, 397–402 (see Bibliography).

There is something so "operatic" about the whole scene between Dimitry and the Germans that I have not been able to resist the temptation to mention *Tannhäuser,* although there is no real parallel at all. The factual details are taken from Bussow, 36. Where the Germans are involved, I believe that Bussow's word may be taken as reliable.

Pushkin's *Boris Godunov* has an inspired scene where the people are begging Boris to be Tsar, which conjures up a picture of the sort of thing that happened when Dimitry arrived in Moscow (see my translation, 12–15).

The appearance of the Kremlin from across the Moskva in Dimitry's time may be fairly accurately guessed from the drawing made by the Dutch artist, Pieter Pickaerdt (various spellings), in 1707. Although many of the wooden buildings had been replaced during the century, the general effect must have been about the same. See *Istoriya Moskvy,* I, 217 (see Bibliography).

On the so-called Cathedral of St. Basil, see Giles Fletcher's *Of the Russe Common Wealth,* in *Russia at the close of the sixteenth century* (Hakluyt Society, 1st ser., XX [1856]), 118–19. Théophile Gauthier has described the indescribable building as "an immense crouching dragon."

Several historians have questioned the importance of the stories about Dimitry's laxity in religious matters. I am inclined to agree that it has been exaggerated, but have reported this version as illustrative of what may very well have happened. (A good example of "typical" Orthodox venom is to be found on p. 57, Tom V, of the *Polnoye Sobranie Russkikh Letopisey.*)

On the symbolic hand-washing, see K. Waliszewski's *Ivan le Terrible* (Paris, 1930), 88.

3. Shakespeare's phrase, "I'll pour this pestilence into his ear," is from *Othello,* Iago's monologue, II, iii, 362.

Solovyov has a good description of the "stolid burghers" and their difficulties with secrets, early in Vol. III, Chapter 8. Even so, there is considerable disagreement, even among contemporary sources, as to just when all this took place. I have avoided being specific, but feel that I have placed the whole event in approximately its correct chronological setting.

Dimitry included his "mother," the Tsaritsa-nun Marfa, in the formal oath he drew up on June 11/21 (*Sobranie Gosudarstvennykh Gramot,* 202–3).

A portrait of Prince Skopin-Shuysky, unfortunately somewhat retouched, is one of the earliest surviving portraits by Russian artists. It is reproduced in its present state in E. S. Ovchinnikova's *Portret v Russkom Iskusstve XVII veka,* Moscow, 1955.

The list of members of Dimitry's Council is in the *Sobranie Gosudarstvennykh Gramot,* 207–10.

The description of Marfa's arrival is based largely on Massa, 140. Both Solovyov's and Karamzin's accounts are colored by their respective *partis pris.* Mérimée's version (pp. 176–79) is perhaps the fullest and least influenced by preconceived notions. It is an exceedingly difficult episode to analyze.

CHAPTER 10

While the events of Dimitry's life up to his entry into Moscow are well (though often conflictingly) attested, from this point on no contemporary chronicle is without copious comment, and no history exists (to the best of my knowledge) which does not offer extended accounts of what went on. For that reason, reference to each and all of my sources would be tedious and repetitive. I have therefore restricted the Notes and Comments for this and the succeeding chapters to such matters as seem to merit particular attention. The numbers in the text consequently refer to specific events, quotations, interpretations, side-lights, and so on, and various subjects are not grouped together as heretofore. It is a question of cutting the coat according to the cloth.

1. The whole passage, including the two quotations, is taken from Borsza's account, *Russkaya Istoricheskaya Biblioteka,* I, cols. 400–2.

2. In the opinion of Evgeny Shmurlo, Dimitry's real enemy was society, the society of the time. This amounts to the same thing, since it was Dimitry's behavior in that society which caused his downfall.

3. The description of Ivan IV's inspections of his artillery is based on Jenkinson's "Description of Russia," first printed in Richard Hakluyt's *The Principall Navigations Voiages and Discoveries of the English Nation* (London, 1589; republished in photo-lithographic facsimile by the Hakluyt Society, 1965 [see Bibliography]), 340.

4. There is a good photograph of the "chariot" sent by Queen Elizabeth in Charles Oman, *The English Silver in the Kremlin, 1557–1663* (London, 1961), facing p. 29, along with descriptive text on pp. 29–30. I am indebted to Professor David B. Quinn, University of Liverpool, for calling my attention to this work.

5. The description of Boris's palace is taken from *Istoriya Moskvy*, I, 216. Due to conflicting reports, it is difficult to say precisely what Dimitry did with the old building, but it is logical to assume that he "pulled down" (Pierling) only the superstructure.

6. Samuel Maskiewicz was the Pole who called Dimitry's palace beautiful. He wrote a description of the building.

7. The *yuródivye* have been mentioned in the previous chapter (see also Notes and Comments, Chapter 9, n. 2). My quotations are from Fletcher, pp. 117–19. According to Augustus J. C. Hare's *Studies in Russia,* fn. to p. 211, Peter the Great commanded the clergy to turn these "impostors" over to the civil authorities so that the latter "may drive out the evil spirits from them with the knout."

8. It is interesting to note that the Venetian Ambassador to Rudolf II, Francesco Soranzo, wrote from Prague on August 29, 1605 (new style), that another sister still remained unwed, living in Graz, "and if the new Muscovite [ruler] were not as determined as people say he is to marry the daughter of the Polish Palatine of Sandomierz . . . they [the Habsburgs] would arrange to give him this other daughter to make doubly sure his professed inclination towards the Emperor and his demonstrated affection for the Catholic Church" (Aleksandrenko, 356–57).

9. An anti-Turkish league had been in the air long before, in the days when Possevino was in Moscow, 1581–1582, but nothing came of it (Günther Stökl, "Posseviniana," *Jahrbücher für Geschichte Osteuropas,,* XI [1963], 223–24). Dimitry may have learned something about this from the Jesuits. Antonio Possevino was a Jesuit himself, and still active in Dimitry's day.

CHAPTER 11

1. The chapter-title is borrowed, with modifications, from George Pettie's *A Petite Pallace of Pettie his Pleasure,* 257: ". . . marriage is a daungerous thinge, and daintely to be dealt with all . . ."

2. Pope Paul's letter of July 12 is transcribed in Turgenev's *Historica Russiae Monumenta,* 57–58.

3. Rangoni's "report" is transcribed as Appendix 1 to Pierling's *Russie.*

4. This evidently means only the wedding by proxy, in Kraków (Hirschberg, *Dymitr,* 166 and fn. 1). Dimitry did not invite the King to Moscow.

5. It must always be remembered that the Tsar sat in such majesty as was not known in western Europe. Due to the Byzantine customs introduced by Sophia Palaeologue, he was more like the Emperor of China than even the Holy Roman Emperor — who was accorded very little real respect. By marrying Dimitry, Marina acquired the same mystique in the eyes of the Muscovites. Sigismund was a mere elected King of a Republic. Vlasyev saw nothing strange in sitting down to dinner with *him;* Marina, because she was Empress as soon as the wedding was over, was quite another matter.

6. Jean Le Laboureur's comment was made a good two generations later, but the description holds true in any case.

7. A few extracts from Alidosi's dispatches have been printed in Aleksandrenko, 382–84.

8. Historical records rarely if ever supply motives. It is therefore impossible to know whether Buczyński approached Dimitry because of his preoccupation with rumors, or whether Dimitry determined to send him to Kraków on the delicate religious mission. It is probable that both notions were in existence at the time Vlasyev left, but nothing was done until two months later.

9. I have suggested that Dimitry could hardly have been so base as was rumored. If, then, it was only a rumor, who started it? That is what I have attempted to suggest. (A transcription of Mniszech's letter is in *Sobranie Gosudarstvennykh Gramot,* II, 241–45.)

10. The behavior of certain elements of both Polish and Russian society with regard to these matters is a veritable model of deceit, hypocrisy and treachery. It is beyond anything suggested even in Machiavelli's chapter on "In what manner Princes ought to keep their words" (*Il Principe,* Chapter 18).

CHAPTER 12

1. The Biblical reference is Acts, XVII, 22.

2. The entry of the schismatic Prince Vishnevetsky (Adam) is given as August 9 (new style) in a letter of Father Lawicki dated August 16 (Aleksandrenko, 392–93) — or July 30 and August 6 respectively, Muscovite calendar.

3. "Fall down flat" — the reference is of course to the walls of Jericho (Joshua, VI, 5). It should be noted in addition that some decried Dimitry for a tyrant, as well as a heretic. Levesque makes a point here so forcefully that it is worth quoting his comment in detail: "How was it, if Dimitry had so ferocious a character, that he only put in prison those who called him an Apostate? How was it that he inflicted the death penalty on one single man, apparently more guilty than the others? Scurrilous epithets mean nothing in history: we can know the character of men only by their acts." (*Histoire de Russie,* III, fn. to pp. 207–8.)

4. The Russian translation of Gosiewski's speech "in secret" is transcribed in *Sobranie Gosudarstvennykh Gramot*, 213–16, while extracts from Dimitry's reply are given on pp. 216–17, in Polish as well as Russian. There is a footnote that the Polish text is in John Buczyński's handwriting. It may therefore well be that Buczyński's departure for Kraków was purposely delayed until after Gosiewski had left Moscow (on October 27, old style).

5. The modern historian is Hans von Eckhardt, and the quotation appears in the English translation of his *Ivan the Terrible* (New York, 1949), 62.

6. Queen Elizabeth I's letter to Tsar Fyodor the Angelic regarding his titles is in Hakluyt's *Voyages*, III, 422–27.

7. An Italian translation of the letter to Charles of Sweden even got into print, in Barezzo Barezzi's *Avisi et lettere ultimamente gionte*, Venice, 1606.

8. Mikulin is the ambassador who took leave like a dancing bear. The record of his voyage appears in *Puteshestviya Russkikh Poslov XVI–XVII vv.* (AN SSSR, Moscow-Leningrad, 1954), 156–205, with copious notes, 402–417. No explanation is given, however, of why Boris chose this non-professional diplomat to go to London. Finally, the editors of this volume limit themselves to stating that the head of the streltsy was *very likely* the same as the ambassador. I should probably have followed suit.

9. My chief source for the entire scene is Massa 154–57.

10. The identity of the Scottish commander seems to have been settled by A. Francis Steuart's *Scottish Influences in Russian History* (Glasgow, 1913), 22–27, and further confirmation is suggested in Purchas's *Pilgrimes*, XIV, 183–84, and 198–99.

11. Dimitry's letter to Paul V is in *Sobranie Gosudarstvennykh Gramot*, while the letters of credence have been printed in the *Scriptores Rerum Polonicarum*, X, 105–06.

12. The use of Hungarian gold ducats is interesting. The Kingdom of Hungary had all but ceased to exist by 1605.

13. Dimitry's answer has been preserved in a Latin version (Pierling, *Rome et Démétrius*, 168–69), and there is an Italian account of matters he entrusted to Rangoni (*ibid.*, 169–70).

14. The "no-one" who translated the letter was probably John Buczyński. There is a transcription of the text in Pierling, *Rome et Démétrius*, 171–72.

15. According to Bussow, 41, the mock-battle took place "about Shrove-Tuesday," which came on March 4 (old style) that year. Both Bussow and Per Persson (Petrus Petreius) mention hard substances in the snow-balls, and Persson adds the detail of sand and ice (*Rerum Rossicarum Scriptores Exteri,* see Bibliography), I, 181.

CHAPTER 13

1. The sources of my information on the early printing presses are: for Nieśwież, *Istoriya Belorusskoy S. S. R.* (AN SSSR, Minsk, 1961), I, 145; for Moscow, P. Beryozov, *Pervopechatnik Ivan Fyodorov* (Moscow, 1952), 112, 139–40 and 142.

2. The bridge is said to have been maintained, one half by Radziwiłł, one half by a representative of the Tsar. According to Stanislas Niemojewski's *Pamiętnik*, 2, the name of the river was the Iwata (in Polish), and the bridge over it was perhaps seven to eight miles beyond Bayevo. This means that it was the same river that divides the Byelorussian S.S.R. from the Russian Socialist Federated S.R. today. In the twentieth-century Imperial War Department 1:50,000 maps, the name Ivata is applied only to the upper reaches of the river.

3. While it is dangerous to attempt to explain early seventeenth-century values in terms of today, a comparison can be made between different countries in the same epoch. The comparison I have used is taken from Captain John Smith's *A Description of New England* (London, 1616), 22. Even here, I am assuming that by "florin" is meant the

gold coin which went under various names according to country of issue, and was worth between 6s. 8d. and 9s. in terms of English currency of the period. On that basis, 5,000 florins would be between £1,666 6s. 8d. and £2,250, in comparison with Smith's estimate of £2,000 for the two ships.

4. There is a great deal on Smolensk in Tikhomirov's *Drevnerusskie Goroda*. See especially pp. 352–61. Bächtold has less, but is worth consulting (see index).

5. Mozhaysk was of little importance then (and still is), and I have been unable to find any confirmation of the existence of a miraculous statue of Saint Nicholas.

6. Although there is some slight discrepancy in detail between the various accounts of Marina's entry into Moscow, the dazzling glory of the parade is in no way diminished by such matters. All the contemporary writers dip their quills in purple and gold to describe what they saw — or heard about.

7. It is unfortunate for English readers that the only full-length biography of that strange girl-woman named Marina is not only in Polish, but even then difficult to find. For those interested, however, Aleksander Hirschberg's *Maryna Mniszchówna* (Lvov, 1927) is well worth reading.

CHAPTER 14

1. The matter was not so much for the ambassadors to travel with Marina, as for them to be in Moscow at the time of her wedding and coronation. For various reasons, they did not actually meet Marina until they reached the capital.

2. There is a reproduction of a sketch of the Ambassadors' Court (*Posolsky dvor*) in *Istoriya Moskvy*, I, 568. This was drawn by Augustin Meierberg, Austrian ambassador to Moscow, in 1661–1662, but there is no record (apparently) of any basic alteration in the appearance of the building, although it was enlarged sometime before 1678.

3. The phrase is in the so-called "Journal of Marina," in Ustryalov's *Skazaniya sovremennikov o Dimitry Samozvantse* (see Bibliography). I do not know the origin of the comparison.

4. Hungarian plums are still rated very high in Russia, and are grown there. They are dark blue in color. It should be noted that the western European "dessert" was not in vogue in Russia at the time, nor indeed popular in England.

5. While it is impossible to estimate the value of 300,000 rubles in terms of modern currencies, it is worth noting that the total revenue of Tsar Boris for one year was reported as 1,430,000 rubles (Fletcher, in *Russia at the Close of the Sixteenth Century*, 53).

6. The Osipov incident is reported in Palitsyn's *Skazanie*, 113. Since Palitsyn can hardly have been in Moscow at the time (*ibid.*, 23), it cannot be determined how factual the report is.

7. According to Bussow (p. 62), Basmanov directed the words quoted to Bussow himself. The incident begins Bussow's Chapter 8, and follows his account of the events from Marina's arrival in Moscow to the death of Dimitry. My text from here on is based largely on Bussow.

8. The account of the doings of Oleśnicki and Gosiewski follows the "Diary" they prepared in Moscow in 1606, which is printed in Turgenev's *Historica Russiae Monumenta*, II, 92–126 (so far as Dimitry is concerned).

9. There is a parallel account of the audience in Niemojewski's *Pamiętnik*, 32–41, which I have followed.

CHAPTER 15

1. Solovyov has summarized the attitude well in Vol. VIII, Chapter 3, toward the end.

2. I have followed Karamzin's inspired description of this scene, Vol. XI, Chapter 4. Otherwise, Bussow has been my chief source of information.

3. My description of what *happened* has been based on what was *supposed to happen,* according to the surviving remnants of a "wedding-ceremony" document, transcribed in the *Sobranie Gosudarstvennykh Gramot,* 289–93. It is generally taken as reliable in detail. I have, however, added a good deal from Massa's narrative (presumably based on reports he got on his return to Moscow), 168–71.

4. The description is from Pierling's *Russie,* 303.

5. The typically Russian elements in the coronation robes were the *bármy* (a word of uncertain origin), a sort of tippet or shoulder-piece, adorned with pearls and sacred medallions, and the diadem, which was not a crown but a narrow, jeweled band. The kokóshnik was considered suitable headdress for royalty even as late as the coronation of Nicholas II.

6. Translated from Pierling's French translation from A. Dimitrievsky's *Arkhiepiskop Elassonsky Arseny i memuary ego iz russkoy Istorii* (*Russie,* 304), which has not been available to me.

7. The vicious antagonism of the petty, self-seeking Shuysky clique was the outgrowth of fear, transmuted into hatred. Dimitry sought to modernize Muscovy, too fast and with the wrong instruments — the reckless, self-confident Poles. And in the end, it was the Poles who gave Prince Vasily something concrete to hate. Indeed, without this "last straw," Shuysky might well have had to suffer the distasteful lordship of Dimitry to the end of his own uncreative, negative life.

8. The tale of the "rogue" is from Bussow. It is evident that all through this period the Germans were keeping close watch on the people, for the Tsar's sake, and were informing Bussow what they heard. The Germans were right, as Dimitry admitted when it was too late.

CHAPTER 16

1. The chapter-title was inspired by Shakespeare's *Hamlet*, IV, v, 81–82: "the people muddied, Thick and unwholesome in their thoughts and whispers . . ."

2. These details are in an autograph letter from Francesco Simonetta, who succeded Rangoni as Nuncio in Kraków, to Cardinal Borghese, dated December 13, 1608. The letter is printed as Appendix III to Pierling's *Russie*, 449–50. Simonetta says he got his information from the two ambassadors to Dimitry, and from Mniszech's nephew Paul, all three of whom had apparently returned from Moscow by then.

3. See Niemojewski's *Pamiętnik*, 69.

4. For the rest of this scene I have followed Bussow in the main. He undoubtedly obtained his information from Germans who were present. Unfortunately, Bussow's account has been available to me only in two bowdlerized versions, one a transcription of the original German *(Rerum Rossicarum Scriptores Exteri)*, the other in a Russian translation (Ustryalov, *Skazaniya sovremennikov*). The original German here is: "er solt seine Mutter geheyen." In the notes to the Russian translation, the German is given as: "er sollte seine Mutter vexiren." In view of a common gutter-Russian phrase, however, I strongly suspect that the word I have left blank should stand for an unprintable indecency. (On July 27, 1965, *The New York Times* reported that a recent article in *Izvestiya* attacked current "verbal hooliganism" in Russia, and asked the opinion of readers. One of these wrote that the Russian language "is especially rich in obscenities, but nobody in authority tries to keep them [the Russians] in bounds.")

5. I have used the obsolete curtle-axe (or curtal-ax) in place of the more common cutlass as betokening a heavy slashing sword as distinct from a more delicate weapon. Bussow refers to a *Pallasch*, Russian *palásh*, a word derived from Turkish *pala*, "scimitar," through Hungarian.

6. Another version of what Dimitry said is: *"Ya tebé ne Boris búdu"* (Bussow, 47). The meaning is the same. (Bussow translates it as: "Ihr solt nicht den Boris an mir finden.")

7. Bussow resorts to Latin to translate the language of the distinguished courtier and councillor: ". . . infer stuprum tuae matri, una cum Imperatore tuo."

8. With reference to this passage, bowdlerized in Ustryalov, in fact simply cut, the editor-translator says in his footnotes that he is convinced that Bussow calumniated the princes and boyars. Nevertheless, he supplies the original text, "in all probability invented":

> "*Volumus nos omnes, unus post alium stuprum inferre, unus in p. . . , alter in v. . . ; audivimus Polonicas meretrices vestras plurimum concubitus bene sustinere posse; nec ipsis unus vir sufficere." Et postea nudabant sua equina pudenda (proh Sodomia!) coram toto Gynaeceo, dicentes: "videte, meretrices, videte nos multo fortiores sumus Polonis vestris. Probate nos!"* (Ustryalov, I, 383–84.)

9. Bussow expressed this also in Latin: *"ut intra actum anni tempus ex virginibus matres fierent"* (Bussow, 48).

10. Grigory Valuyev came of a Lithuanian family which had migrated to Russia and become Orthodox, in the early fourteenth century. He rose to some sort of fame through murdering Dimitry, joined Skopin-Shuysky, soon turned traitor to Vasily Shuysky, but in the end was honored by Tsar Mikhail Romanov. Ivan Vasilyevich Voyeykov "Menshy" (junior) achieved fame by the same act. After murdering Dimitry, he joined Shakhovskoy (see Epilogue), and supported the impostor Petrushka. He and a cousin of the same family-name were killed, apparently in Putivl.

11. I have used "hooligan" to translate the German *Schmarotzer* since that word has been adopted by the Russians themselves to label such individuals.

12. I have chosen the account of Marfa's attitude and words which seems to me the most in keeping with her unwillingness to commit herself during the entire time. This is the account also preferred by Solovyov, and is taken from the *Lyetopis o myatezhakh*, 100–103.

13. As mentioned by Mérimée (279), among others, it is remarkable that no-one made much use of the name Grigory Otrepyev, the vagabond Grishka, at this time. Dimitry was a "Polish piper," but not the man with whom Godunov had identified him, and with whom Shuysky was to exert every effort to identify him.

EPILOGUE

Few comments, I believe, are needed on the matters treated here. The general history is available in any full history of Russia. A very few additional sources may be mentioned for the record: Ivan Ivanovich Smirnov's *Vosstanie Bolotnikova* (Leningrad, 1951), for Bolotnikov's revolt; *Rękopism Hetmana Żółkiewskiego* (Moscow, 1835), for the "Polish Intervention"; Kostomarov's monograph on Tsar Vasily Shuysky, in his *Russkaya istoriya v zhizneopisaniyakh yeya glavneyshikh deyateley* (2 vols., St.-Petersburg [Leningrad], 1873–1874); and, among others, Jacob De La Gardie's *Thet Swenska i Ryssland Tijo åhrs Krijgz-Historie* (Stockholm, 1671). They are not specifically referred to below.

1. See G. M.: "Zametka o rode knyazey Shuyskikh," *Russkaya Starina,* LXXXVII (1896), 118–25, which contains the necessary evidence.

2. "Full-blooded organizer" is at least close to the original "vsey krovi zavodchik" (Smirnov, *Vosstanie Bolotnikova,* 101).

3. See Notes and Comments, Chapter 16, 2. Oleśnicki, Gosiewski, and Paul Mniszech, at least, seem to have been back in Kraków by mid-December, 1608. Father Czyrzowski's presence there on February 13 is attested in Pierling, *Russie,* 338.

4. The whole of this sordid, tragic story is told in Hirschberg's *Maryna Mniszchówna.* For those who read French but not Polish, Mérimée's *Les faux Démétrius* (pp. 307, et seq.) provides an account which is still sound, after more than a century.

5. The story of Minin and Pozharsky is told in considerable detail in *Istoriya Moskvy,* I, 325–45. There is also Sergey Vladimirovich Bakh-

rushin's *Minin i Pozharsky* (Tashkent, 1942), but this has not been available to me.

6. The following *bylina* (folk-poem, heroic poem) was recorded in 1619 by Richard James, then chaplain of the English merchants in Moscow, and has been preserved in the Bodleian Library at Oxford. It forms a fitting conclusion to the tragedy of Dimitry, Boris, and Ksenia:

> The little bird is mourning,
> The tiny quail is crying,
> "Woe is me that I must weep, so young!
> They want to set the green oak on fire,
> To pull to pieces my little nest;
> They want to slaughter my little ones,
> And lay hands on me, the tiny quail."

> In Moscow the Tsarévna laments:
> "Woe is me that I must weep, so young,
> Because a traitor comes to Moscow.
> Who but the unfrocked Grísha Otrépyev!
> For he wants to take me prisoner,
> And in prison he will shave my hair,
> And command me to become a nun.
> But I do not want to be a nun,
> And lead a lonely monastic life;
> The dark cell must be thrown wide open
> That I may catch sight of fine young men.
> And you, halls and courts so dear to us,
> Who will wander now along your ways,
> Now that our royal life has ended,
> Now that Borís Godunóv is dead?
> And you, *teremá* so dear to us,
> Who will find peace and rest within you,
> Now that our royal life is ended,
> Now that Borís Godunóv is dead?"

[Note: The *teremá* were the lofty apartments where the Tsar's family lived in semi-oriental surroundings.]

BIBLIOGRAPHY

Because there is a surprising amount of source material for the period covered by the life of Dimitry, called the Pretender, most of it in Russian, I have limited myself here to those volumes which have contributed *something,* be it a drop or a bucketful, to the present biography.

Basic bibliographies exist, and one or two specialized studies of fairly recent publication have ample indication of sources. Nevertheless, so many currents of history flow together in the period under consideration that a full bibliography would be unmanageable. I must therefore apologize, particularly to any scholar who may be led to read what I have written, for the shortcomings of this section of my book.

Here and there, I have added a brief note of explanation of value or content, and — rarely — an indication of works I have not been able to consult, for one reason or another (mostly, inavailability). Beyond this, I can only add that I trust that some literary detective will someday utilize the guides and "charts" I have here provided and pursue the investigation further, until it is determined *Who Was Dimitry.*

PRELIMINARY NOTE:

Paul Pierling's *La Russie et le Saint-Siège,* listed below, contains a valuable basic bibliography. It is at the same time more comprehensive and less specifically pertinent than my own.

CONTEMPORARY MANUSCRIPTS

While I have consulted a number of manuscripts in the British Museum and the Public Record Office in London, in the Archivio Segreto Vaticano, Vatican City, and elsewhere, I have found but two unprinted sources pertinent to Dimitry. The first of these, bound in two volumes, is discussed in Pierling's "Un manuscript . . ." The second, not mentioned or even noticed by anyone before, I discovered by chance in Darmstadt, in October, 1965.

Archivio Segreto Vaticano. Polonia 173. Del Secretario Malacrida à li Nuntij in Polonia.
—— *Polonia 174.* Registro delle lettere scritte a Mons. Vescovo di Reggio [Rangoni], Nun.o al Rè di Polonia, che comincia li 4 di Giug. 1605.
(One continuous document, bound in two volumes, of considerable pertinent interest. Partly in deplorable condition, it apparently has never been printed, although there is some discussion of it in Pierling "Un manuscript du Vatican . . ." listed below.)
Hessische Landes- und Hochschulbibliothek, Darmstadt. Handschrift 1971, Band 5, fol. 235^r–242^r. This consists in a German version of the history of Dimitry and how he escaped, and contains nothing new. Preceding it, fol. 233, however, is the portrait of Dimitry which has been used as a frontispiece. There is neither signature nor indication of source, but there can be no question that it was brought by Sigismund Myszkowski to Darmstadt in October, 1605.

PRIMARY PRINTED SOURCES

Akty, sobrannye v bibliotekakh i arkhivakh Rossiyskoy imperii Arkheograficheskoyu ekspeditsieyu Akademii nauk, Vol. II. St. Petersburg (Leningrad), 1836.
Eigentliche Beschreibung der königlichen Hochzeit in Polen: . . . Kraków, 1606.
Historica Russiae Monumenta. See, Turgenev.
Moskovskaya Tragediya, ili razkaz o zhizni i smerti Dimitriya, ed. by S. D. Sheremetev, with a translation from the Latin original. *Tragoedia Moscovitica . . .* published by G. Grevenbruch, Cologne, 1608. St. Petersburg (Leningrad), 1901.

Polnoye Sobranie Russkikh Letopisey. 8 vols., St. Petersburg (Leningrad), 1846–1859.

Poselstwo od Zygmunta III. Króla Polskiego do Dymitra Iwanowicza, Cara Moskiewskiego — Samozwanca — z okazyi jego zaślubin z Maryną Mniszchowną. Wrocław, 1837.

Povest vremmenykh. "La Chronique de Nestor," traduit en français d'après l'édition impériale de Pétersbourg. 2 vols., Paris, 1834–1835.

Puteshestviya Russkikh Poslov XVI–XVII vv. Ed.: D. S. Likhachev. Moscow/Leningrad, 1954.

Rerum Russicarum Scriptores Exteri. 2 vols., Petropoli (Leningrad), 1851, 1868.

Russia at the Close of the Sixteenth Century. Ed.: Edward A. Bond. Hakluyt Society, 1st ser., XX (1857).

Russkaya Istoricheskaya Biblioteka. Vol. I. St. Petersburg (Leningrad), 1872.

——— Vol. XIII. St. Petersburg (Leningrad), 1891.

Scriptores Rerum Polonicarum, Tomus Decimus. "Historici diarii domus professae Societatis Jesu Cracoviensis, annos novem 1600–1608." Kraków, 1886.

Sir Thomas Smithes voyage and Entertainment in Rushia . . . London, 1605. *See also,* Boldakov.

Sobranie Gosudarstvennykh Gramot . . . *See,* Rumyantsev.

Tragoedia Moscovitica . . . *See, Moskovskaya Tragediya* . . .

Aleksandrenko, Vasily Nikiforovich. "Materialy po Smutnomu vremeni na Rusi XVII v.," *Starina i Novizna,* XIII (1909), 185–455.

Barezzi, Barezzo. *Avisi, et lettere ultimamente gionte di cose memorabili succedutte* . . . *in Moscovia* . . . Venice, 1606.

——— *Relazione della segnalata e come miracolosa conquista del paterno Imperio conseguita dal Serenis. Giovane Demetrio Granduca di Moscovia in quest' anno 1605* . . . Venice, 1605.

The same, translated into French as *Discours merveilleux et veritable de la Conqueste faite par le jeune Demetrius* . . . Arras, 1605. Reprinted by Prince Augustin Galitzin, Paris, 1858.

The same, translated into Spanish as *Relacion de la señalada y como milagrosa conquista* . . . Lisbon, 1606. (Very likely the source used by Lope de Vega for his drama. *See below,* Literary Works.)

Note: This work has been seriously attributed to Antonio Possevino, S.J. (1533–1611), by Pierling, in "Barezzi ili Possevin?" *See below,* Secondary Sources.

Boldakov, I. M., ed. and tr.: *Sbornik materialov po russkoy istorii na-chala XVII veka* . . . St. Petersburg (Leningrad), 1896. (With a supplement by Evgeny N. Shchepkin.)

—— *Sera Tomasa Smita Puteshestvie i Prebyvanie v Rossii.* St. Petersburg (Leningrad), 1893.

Bond, Edward A. *See, Russia at the Close of the Sixteenth Century.*

Brereton, Henry. *Newes of the present Miseries of Russia.*

Bussow, Konrad. "Chronicon Moscoviticum." Original German in *Rerum Rossicarum Scriptores Exteri;* Russian translation in Ustryalov's *Skazaniya sovremennikov* . . . Both versions are included in the new edition, *Konrad Bussov,* Moscow/Leningrad, 1961.

Gardie, Jacob de la. *Thet Swenska i Ryssland Tijo åhrs Krijgz-Historie* . . . Stockholm, 1671.

Hakluyt, Richard. *The Principal Navigations Voyages Traffiques & Discoveries of the English Nation* (London, 1598–1600). 12 vols., Glasgow, 1903–1905.

—— *The Principall Navigations Voiages and Discoveries of the English Nation* (London, 1589). Facsimile, with introduction by D. B. Quinn and R. A. Skelton, and a new index by Alison Quinn, Hakluyt Society, extra ser., 39, 1965.

Herckmann, Elia. "Narratio." *See, Rerum Rossicarum Scriptores Exteri.*

Hirschberg, Aleksander, ed.: *Pamiętnik Stanisława Niemojewskiego (1606–1608).* Lvov, 1899.

James, Richard: ["Six Russian Folk-Poems"]. *See,* Simoni: "Velikorusskiya pesni."

—— ["Dictionary"]. *See,* Larin, Boris Aleksandrovich.

Jansonius, Petrus. *Itinerarium, Oder Aussführlicher Bericht/* . . . *von der Ruessen oder Muscowiter Religion/Ceremonien/Gesetzen/Policey/* . . . Hamburg, 1619.

Larin, Boris Aleksandrovich. *Russko-Angliysky slovar-dnevnik* RICHARDA DZHEMSA [*James*], *1618–1619.* Leningrad, 1959. (Of later date, but contains important minor points.)

Klyuchevsky, Vasily Osipovich. *Skazaniya inostrantsev o Moskovskom Gosudarstve.* Petrograd (Leningrad), 1918.

Ludewig, Johann Peter von. *Reliquiae manuscriptorum omnis aevi Diplomatum ac monumentorum ineditorum ad huc.* 12 vols., Frankfort/Leipzig, 1720–1741.

Margeret, Captain Jacques. *Estat de l'empire de Russie et grande duché de Moscovie.* Paris, 1821. (Reprint without alteration, of edition of Paris, 1669.)

Massa, Isaac Abrahamszoon. *Histoire des guerres de la Moscovie (1601–1610).* 2 vols., Brussels, 1866. (*See also, Rerum Rossicarum Scriptores Exteri.*)

―――― *Légende de la vie et de la mort de Démétrius.* Amsterdam, 1606. (No copy is known, but it has been postulated by Prince Galitzin. See below, Russell, *Reporte.*)

Meusel, Johann Georg. *Der Geschichtsforscher.* 7 parts, Halle, 1775–1779.

Mukhanov, Pavel Aleksandrovich. *Autentyczne świądectwa o wzajemnych stosunkach pomiędzy Rossya a Polska szczególniéj zaś za czasów samozwańców w Rossyi.* Wrocław, 1840.

Niemojewski, Stanisław. *Pamiętnik. See,* Hirschberg.

Nowakowski, Franciszek K. *Źródła do dziejów Polski, zebrane i wydane przez* . . . 2 vols., Berlin, 1841.

Obolensky, Prince Mikhail Andreyevich. *Sbornik Knyazya Obolenskaya.* 12 parts, Moscow, 1838–1859. (See especially Nos. 8 & 10.)

Palitsyn, Avraamy. *Skazanie Avraamiya Palitsyna.* Moscow/Leningrad, 1955.

Persson, Per. "Petri Petrei Chronica Moscovitica." *See, Rerum Rossicarum Scriptores Exteri.*

Ptashitsky (Ptaszycki), Stanislav. "Despoty Zenovichi v kontse XVI i nachale XVII vekov," *Russkaya Starina,* XXI (1878), 125–38, and XXII (1878), 503–11.

Purchas, Samuel. *Hakluytus Posthumus, or Purchas His Pilgrimes.* 20 vols., Glasgow, 1905–1907.

Rostopchin, Graf Andrey Fyodorovich. *Chetyre skazaniya o Lzhe-Dimitrie* . . . St. Petersburg (Leningrad), 1863.

―――― *Tri zapiski vremyon Lzhe-Dimitriya* . . . St. Petersburg (Leningrad), 1862.

Rostowski, Stanislaus. *Lituanicarum Societatis Jesu Historiarum Libri Decem.* Paris/Brussels, 1877.

Russell, William, translator. *The Reporte of a bloudie and terrible Massacre in the Citty of Mosco, with the fearfull and tragicall end of Demetrius the last Duke, before him raigning at this present.* London, 1607. (Note: It is generally agreed that this is a translation of "La Légende de la vie et de la mort de Démétrius," reported in Friedrich von Adelung's *Kritischliterarische Uebersicht der Reisen-*

den in Russland . . . (St. Petersburg [Leningrad], 1846) as having been published in Amsterdam in 1606. No copy of this survives. Prince Augustin Galitzin suggests that Massa was the original author, in his *Récit du sanglant et terrible massacre arrivé dans la ville de Moscou, ainsi que de la fin effrayante et tragique du dernier duc, Démétrius, 1606.* Paris, 1859.

Simoni, Pavel Konstantinovich. "Velikorusskiya pesni, zapisannya v 1619–20 gg. dlya Richarda Dzhemsa [James] na kraynem severe Moskovskago tsarstva," *Sbornik Otdeleniya Russkago Yazyka i Slovesnosti,* Imperatorskoy Akademii Nauk, LXXXII (1907), No. 7.

Talbot, Carolus H. *Res polonicae Iacobo I Angliae regnante conscriptae ex archivis publicis londoniarum.* "Elementa ad Fontium Editiones," VI, Institutum Historicum Polonicum Romae. Rome, 1962.

Thou, Jacques-Auguste de. *Histoire universelle de J.-A. de Thou, depuis 1543 jusqu'en 1607.* Vol. I, London [Paris?], 1734.

Turgenev, Aleksandr Ivanovich, ed.: *Historica Russiae Monumenta.* 3 vols., Petropoli (Leningrad), 1841–42 and 1848.

Ustryalov, Nikolay Gerasimovich: *Skazaniya sovremennikov o Dimitrii Samozvantse.* 2 vols., 3rd. ed., St. Petersburg (Leningrad), 1859.

Wielewicki, Jan. *Dziennik spraw domu zakonnego OO. Jezuitów* . . . (This constitutes Vol. X of the series *Scriptores Rerum Polonicarum,* which see.)

Zabczyc, Jan. *Mars moskiewski krwawy.* Kraków, 1605.

Zółkiewski, Stanisław. *Rękopism Hetmana* . . . Moscow, 1835.

ENCYCLOPEDIAS, GUIDE BOOKS, SPECIALIZED DICTIONARIES

Bolshaya Sovyetskaya Entsiklopediya. 2nd ed., 51 vols., Moscow, 1949–1958. (With later index and continuing supplements.)

Cracovie et ses environs. Kraków, 1846.

Moskovsky Kreml. Moscow, 1964.

Po Kremlyu. Kratky putevoditel. Moscow, 1960.

Słownik Geograficzny Królestwa Polskiego . . . 15 vols., Warsaw, 1880–1904.

Andreyevsky, Ivan Efimovich, and others, eds.: *Entsiklopedichesky slovar.* 41 vols., 1890–1904, with 2-vol. supplement, 1906. St. Petersburg (Leningrad), Brockhaus and Efron.

Benson, Morton. *Dictionary of Russian Personal Names, With a Guide to Stress and Morphology.* U. of Pennsylvania Press, 1964.

Bovet, Marie-Anne de. *Cracovie.* "Les Villes d'Art célèbres," Paris, 1910.

Dworzaczek, Włodzimierz. *Genealogia.* Nauki Pomocnicze Historii, Institut Historii Polskiej Akademii Nauk. 2 vols., Warsaw, 1959.

Grossmann, P., and Knöbel, J. *Führer durch Moskau.* Moscow, 1882.

Léger, Louis. *Moscou.* "Les Villes d'Art célèbres," Paris, 1910.

Orgelbrand, S. *Encyclopedja Powszechna* . . . 18 vols., Warsaw, 1898–1904.

Radó, A. *Guide-book to the Soviet Union.* Berlin, 1929.

Tupikov, Nikolay Mikhaylovich. *Slovar drevne-russkikh lichnykh imyon.* St. Petersburg (Leningrad), 1903.

SECONDARY AUTHORITIES

Byl li Lzhedimitry I Grishka Otrepyev? Vozrazhenie G. Kostomarovu na sochinenie ego: "Kto byl pervy Lzhedimitry." St. Petersburg (Leningrad), 1865.

Cambridge History of Poland, The . . . *(to 1696).* Ed. by Reddaway, Penson, Halecki and Dyboski. Cambridge U. Press, 1950.

Die falschen Demetrier und der Aufstand der Strelitzen . . . Torgau, 1826.

Istoriya Byelorusskoy S.S.R. 2 vols., Minsk, 1961.

Istoriya Kieva, v dvukh tomakh. Vol. I, Kiev, 1963.

Istoriya Moskvy, v shesti tomakh. Vol. I, Moscow, 1952.

Istoriya Polshi, v tryokh tomakh. Vol. I, Moscow, 1956.

Istoriya, S.S.S.R. Tom I. S drevneyshikh vremyon do 1861 g. 2nd ed., Moscow, 1964.

Istoriya Ukrainskoy S.S.R. v dvukh tomakh. Vol. I, Kiev, 1956.

Adelung, Friedrich von. *Kritisch-literarische Übersicht der Reisenden in Russland bis 1700, deren Berichte bekannt sind.* 2 vols., St. Petersburg (Leningrad), 1846.

Alef, Gustave. "The Adoption of the Muscovite Two-headed Eagle: A Discordant View," *Speculum,* XLI (1966), 1–21. (Received after this book had gone to my publisher. Professor Alef suggests that Ivan III's adoption of the Byzantine eagle for his coat-of-arms was inspired by the Habsburg *Doppeladler.* The article presents a soundly based hypothesis.)

Allen, William Edward David. *A History of the Georgian People.* London, 1932.

―――― *The Ukraine: A History.* Cambridge U. Press, 1940.

Artsybashev, Nikolay Sergeyevich. *Povestvovanie o Rossii.* 3 vols., Moscow, 1838–1843.

Bächtold, Rudolf. *Südwestrussland im Spätmittelalter.* Basel, 1951.

Bagrow, Leo: *History of Cartography,* revised and enlarged by R. A. Skelton. London, 1964. (Brief mention of Massa and young Fyodor Godunov.)

Bakhrushin, Sergey Vladimirovich. *Nauchnye Trudy, I: Ocherki po istorii remesla, torgovli i gorodov Russkogo tsentralizovannogo gosudarstva XVI — nachala XVII v.* Moscow, 1952.

Baudouin de Courtenay, Ivan Aleksandrovich. *Strona językowa oryginału listu "Dymitra Samozwanca" do papieża Klemensa VIII-go z dnia 24 kwietnia roku 1604.* Kraków, 1899. In *Rozprawy Akademii Umiejętności, Wydzial filologiczny.* Ser. 2, tom 14.

Belov, Evgeny Alekseyevich. "Ob istoricheskom znachenii russkago boyarstva do kontsa XVII v.," *Zhurnal Ministerstva Narodnago Prosveshcheniya,* CCXLIII (1886), Jan., 68–127, Feb., 233–305; CCXLIV (1886), March, 29–75.

Beryozov [Berezov], Pavel Ivanovich. *Pervopechatnik Ivan Fyodorov.* Moscow, 1952.

Black, Cyril E., ed.: *Rewriting Russian History.* New York, 1962.

Blümcke, Otto. *Berichte und Akten der hansischen Gesandtschaft nach Moskau im Jahre 1603.* Halle/S., 1894.

Caro, Jacob. "Zur Demetrius-Frage," *Historische Zeitschrift,* Neue Folge LII (1902), 264–76.

Chaykovsky, Andry. *Moskovsky Tsar Dmitro Samozvanets.* Kolomiya, Ukr. S.S.R., 1928.

Cherepnin, L. V. " 'Smuta' i istoriografiya XVII veka," *Istoricheskie Zapiski,* XIV (1945), 81–128.

Cherniavsky, Michael. "Khan or Basileus: An Aspect of Russian Medieval Political Theory," *Journal of the History of Ideas,* XX (1959), 459–76.

―――― *Tsar and People.* Yale U. Press, 1961.

Chopin, Jean M. *Révolutions des peuples du Nord.* 2 vols., Brussels, 1843. (Antiquated, but of some interest for analysis of Poland, Sweden and Russia in the days of Godunov and Dimitry.)

Ciampi, Sebastiano. *Bibliografia Critica delle antiche Reciproche Corrispondenze . . . dell' Italia colla Russia, colla Polonia, ed altre parti settentrionali.* 3 vols. in 2, Florence, 1834–1842.

Dlugopolsky, Svyashchennik Ananiya: "Vishnevets i knyazya ego," *Vestnik Zapadnoy Rossii,* VI (1868), vols., II–III.

Dobrotvorsky, A.: "Kto byl pervy Lzhedimitry?" *Vestnik Zapadnoy Rossii,* IV (1866), parts vi–vii. (Superficial, but the copy available to me was incomplete.)

Doroshenko, D. "Die Namen 'Ruś,' 'Russland' und 'Ukraine' in ihrer historischen und gegenwärtigen Bedeutung," *Abhandlungen des ukrainischen wissenschaftlichen Institutes in Berlin,* III (1931), 3–23.

Eckardt, Hans von. *Ivan the Terrible.* New York, 1949. (Translated from German.)

Gennadi, Grigory Nikolayevich. "Portrety Lzhedimitriya Pervago i Mariny Mniszek, II," *Russkaya Starina,* XV (1876), 873–74.

Godet, Robert. *En marge de Boris Godunov.* Paris/London, 1926. (Valuable collection of notes having to do primarily with Musorgsky's opera.)

Golubtsov, I. A. "'Izmena' Nagikh," *Institut Istorii RANION, Uchonye Zapiski,* IV (1929), 55–70.

Grabowski, Tadeusz. *Literatura aryańska w Polsce 1560–1660.* Kraków, 1908.

Graham, Stephen. *Boris Godunof.* London, 1933.

Grunwald, Constantin de. *Histoire de Moscou et des moscovites.* Paris, 1963. (Relatively brief text to accompany lavish illustrations.)

——— *La vraie histoire de Boris Godounov.* Paris, 1961.

Hamel, Iosif Khristianovich. *England and Russia . . .* Translated by John Studdy Leigh. London, 1854.

Hare, Augustus J. C. *Studies in Russia.* London, 1885. (Of interest only for comparison with 1605 and 1965.)

Hirschberg, Aleksander. *Dymitr Samozwaniec.* Lvov, 1898.

——— *Maryna Mniszchówna.* Lvov, 1927.

Howe, Sonia E. *The False Dimitry. A Russian Romance and Tragedy, described by British eye-witnesses.* New York [1916?]. (Popularized extracts from primary printed sources.)

Hrushevsky, Michael. *A History of Ukraine.* Ed. by O. J. Fredericksen, preface by George Vernadsky. Yale U. Press, 1941. (Translation of Hrushevsky's short *Illustrated History of Ukraine,* of 1911, prepared while he was working on his ten-volume history. The latter can be consulted, but contains very little not to be found elsewhere.)

Jasnowski, Jozef. "England and Poland in the XVIth & XVIIth centuries (Political Relations)," *Polish Science and Learning, No. 7,* Oxford U. Press, 1948.

Jurgėla, Constantine R. *History of the Lithuanian Nation.* New York, 1948.

Karamzin, Nikolay Mikhaylovich. *Istoriya Gosudarstva Rossiyskago.* 12 books, unfinished. 5th ed., 3 vols., St. Petersburg (Leningrad), 1843. (With notes and index, I. Eynerling, ed.) Also available in French and German, under the title *History of the Russian Empire (State).*

Karzinkin, A. *O medalyakh tsarya Dimitriya Ioannovicha, Lzhedimitriya I* . . . Moscow, 1889.

Kazansky, Pyotr Simonovich. "Izsledovanie o lichnosti pervago Lzhedimitriya," *Russky Vestnik,* CXXX (1877), 463–501; CXXXI (1877), 5–33 and 472–507.

Klyuchevsky, Vasily Osipovich. *Kurs Russkoy Istorii.* New ed., vols. 1–5 of *Sochineniya* (Works), in 8 vols., Moscow, 1956–1959. Also available in French and English, under the title *History of Russia* (or its equivalent).

Konovalov, Serge. "Anglo-Russian Relations, 1620–4," *Oxford Slavonic Papers,* IV (1953), 80–82.

Kopiyssky, Z. Yu. "Iz istorii torgovykh svyazey gorodov Belorussii s gorodami Polshi (konets XVI — pervaya polovina XVII v.)," *Istoricheskie Zapiski,* LXXII (1962), 140–83.

Kostomarov, Nikolay Ivanovich. *Kto byl pervy Lzhedimitry? Istoricheskoye izsledovanie.* St. Petersburg (Leningrad), 1864.

——— "Lzhedimitry pervy: Po povodu sovremennago portreta, 1606 g.," *Russkaya Starina,* XV (1876), 1–8.

——— *Russkaya istoriya v zhizneopisaniyakh yeya glavneyshikh deyateley.* 2 vols., St. Petersburg (Leningrad), 1873–1874. (German translation, *Russische Geschichte in Biographien;* Vol. I, Giessen, 1891.)

——— *Smutnoye vremya Moskovskago Gosudarstva v nachale XVII stoletiya.* 2 vols., St. Petersburg (Leningrad), 1866–1868.

Kot, Stanislas. *Socinianism in Poland.* Boston, 1957.

Kunik, Ernst Eduard. "Analectes Historiques," *Bulletin de la Classe des Sciences historiques, philologiques et politiques de l'Académie Impériale des Sciences de Saint-Pétersbourg,* VIII (1851).

Kusheva, E. N. "K istorii kholopstva v kontse XVI — nachale XVII vekov," *Istoricheskie Zapiski,* XV (1945), 70–96.

Leem, Knud. "An account of the Laplanders of Finmark, their language, manners, and religion," in Pinkerton, John, *A general collection of voyages* (17 vols., London, 1808–1814), I, 376–490.

Leitsch, Walter. *Moskau und die Politik des Kaiserhofes im XVII Jahrhundert. I Teil, 1604–54.* Graz/Köln, 1960.

Levesque, Pierre-Charles. *Histoire de Russie.* 5 vols., Paris, 1782. (A remarkable work for its day.)

Librovich, Sigizmund [F.]. *Nepolomitsky Tsarevich.* St. Petersburg (Leningrad), 1903. (An elaborate attempt to prove that Dimitry was the son of King Stephen Báthory of Poland.)

Lorentz, Friedrich. *Der falsche Demetrius.* Berlin, 1862.

Łozinski, Władisław. *Zycie polskie w dawnych wiekach, wiek XVI–XVII.* 2nd ed., Lvov, 1908. (German translation, *Polnisches Leben in vergangenen Zeiten,* Munich, n.d.)

Lubimenko, Inna. *Les relations commerciales et politiques de l'Angleterre avec la Russie avant Pierre le Grand.* Paris, 1933.

M., G. "Zametka o rode knyazey Shuyskikh," *Russkaya Starina,* LXXXVII (1896), 118–25.

Manley, Sir Roger. *The Russian Impostor: or, The history of Muscovie, under the Usurpation of Boris and the Imposture of Demetrius, late Emperors of Muscovy.* London, 1674. (A silly work, as jumbled as his spelling.)

Mérimée, Prosper. *Demetrius the Impostor.* Translated by Andrew R. Scoble. London, 1853.

——— *Épisode de l'histoire de Russie — Les faux Démétrius.* Paris, 1853.

——— "*Skazaniya sovremennikov o Dimitrii Samozvantse. —* Mémoires contemporains relatifs au faux Démétrius, traduits et publiés par M. Oustrialof. Pétersbourg, 1837. 5 vol. in 8°," *Journal des Savants,* Paris, 1852, 88–100 and 159–74.

Michow, Heinrich. *Das erste Jahrhundert russischer Kartographie.* Hamburg, 1906.

Milioukov, Paul, Seignobos, Ch., and Eisenmann, L. *Histoire de la Russie.* 3 vols., Paris, 1932–1933.

Müller, Gerhard Friedrich. *Sammlung russischer Geschichte.* 9 vols., St. Petersburg (Leningrad), 1732–1764. *See* vol. V, 180–380.

Nazarevski, V. V. *Histoire de Moscou depuis les origines jusqu'à nos jours.* Paris, 1932.

Nerman, Ture. *Svensk och Ryss.* Stockholm, 1946. (A popular study, from the Swedish viewpoint.)

Novoselsky, A. A. *Borba Moskovskogo gosudarstva s Tatarami v pervoy polovine XVII veka.* Moscow/Leningrad, 1948.

Oman, Charles. *The English Silver in the Kremlin, 1557–1663.* London, 1961.

Ovchinnikova, E. S. *Portret v Russkom Iskusstve XVII veka.* Moscow, 1955.

Pantenius, Theodor Hermann. *Der falsche Demetrius.* Bielefeld/Leipzig, 1904. (*Monographien zur Weltgeschichte,* XXI.)

Pares, Bernard. *A History of Russia.* 3rd ed. revised, New York, 1937.

Pavlov, Nikolay Mikhaylovich ("Bitsyn"). "Pravda o Lzhedimitry," *Russky Arkhiv,* XXIV, ii (1886), 525–66. (Followed by an exchange of opinions with Kostomarov, up to p. 604.)

Pierling, Pavel Osipovich ("Paul"), S.J. "Barezzi ili Possevin?" *Russkaya Starina,* CIV (1900), 193–200.

—— "Cilli i Massa, Sovremenniki Lzhedimitriya," *Russkaya Starina,* LXXX (1893), 465–86.

—— "Dimitri dit le Faux: à propos du nouveau livre de M. Waliszewski," *Revue des Questions Historiques,* LXXXI (1907), 213–22.

—— *Dimitri dit le Faux et les Jésuites.* Paris, 1913.

—— *Dimitri dit le Faux et Possevino.* Paris, 1914.

—— *Dimitry Samozvanets.* Moscow, 1912. (Translation of *La Russie et le Saint-Siège, III. See below.*)

—— *Iz smutnago vremeni: statyi i zametki.* St. Petersburg (Leningrad), 1902. (Contains some of the articles listed independently.)

—— "Iz Smutnago Vremeni: Dnevnik Andreya Lavitskago," *Russkaya Starina,* CIV (1900), 689–706.

—— *Lettre de Dmitri dit le Faux à Clément VIII.* Paris, 1898. (Discussed in S. Ptaszycki's *Pismo pervago samozvantsa k Pape Klimentu VIII* . . . [St. Petersburg, 1899] and Baudouin de Courtenay's "Strona językowa oryginału polskiego listu 'Dymitra Samozwańca' do papieża Klemensa VIII-go . . ." *Rozprawy Akademii Umiejętności, Wydział filologiczny,* ser. 2, Tom XIV [1899].)

—— "Un manuscrit du Vatican sur le Tsar Dimitri de Moscou," *Revue des questions historiques,* XII (1894), 540–48.

—— "Nazvanny Dimitry i Adam Vishnevetsky," *Russkaya Starina,* CXVII (1904), 123–38.

—— *Rome et Démétrius* . . . Paris, 1878.

—— *La Russie et le Saint-Siège; Études diplomatiques.* Vol. III,

Paris, 1901. (Contains an exhaustive bibliography up to the year of publication.)

Platonov, Sergey Fyodorovich: *Boris Godounov, Tsar de Russie (1598–1605)*. Paris, 1929. (Translated from Russian.)

────── *Drevnerusskie skazaniya i povesti o Smutnom vremeni XVII veka kak istorichesky istochnik.* St. Petersburg (Leningrad), 1888 (1913).

────── *Ivan Grozny.* Berlin, 1924.

────── *Ocherki po istorii Smuty v Moskovskom Gosudarstve, XVI–XVII vv.* St. Petersburg (Leningrad), 1899.

────── *Smutnoye Vremya.* Prague, 1924.

Pogodin, Mikhail Petrovich: *Istoriko-kriticheskie otryvki.* 2 books, Moscow, 1846, 1867.

Przezdziecki, Count Renaud: *Diplomatic Ventures and Adventures.* London, 1953.

Rovinsky, Dmitry Aleksandrovich. *Materialy dlya Russkoy ikonografii.* 12 parts, St. Petersburg (Leningrad), 1884–1891.

────── *Podrobny slovar Russkikh gravirovannykh portretov . . .* 4 vols., St. Petersburg (Leningrad), 1886–1889.

────── *Podrobny slovar Russkikh gravyorov XVI–XIX vv.* 2 vols., St. Petersburg (Leningrad), 1895.

Rumyantsev, Nikolay Petrovich, ed.: *Sobranie Gosudarstvennykh Gramot i Dogovorov.* 3 vols., Moscow, 1813–1822.

Samarin, Yury Fyodorovich. *Iezuity i ikh otnoshenie k Rossii.* Moscow, 1866.

Schaum, M. "Tragoedia Demetro-Moscovitica. Istoriya dostopamyatnykh proisshestvy sluchivshikhsya so Lzhe-Dimitriem . . ." *Inostrannye Sochineniya i Akty Otnosyashchiesya do Rossii,* No. 1, 1847.

Shambinago, Sergey Konstantinovich. "Novy dokument o Samozvantse," *Russkaya Starina,* CX (1902), 313–16.

Shchepkin, Evgeny (Yevgeny) Nikolayevich. *Kratkiya Izvestiya o Lzhedimitrii I.* Odessa, 1900.

────── "Wer war Pseudodemetrius I.?" *Archiv für slavische Philologie,* XX (1898), 224–325; XXI (1899), 99–169 and 558–606; and XXII (1900), 321–432. (By far the most searching study of the identity of Dimitry, although his conclusions may be questioned.)

Shennan, J. H. "Church and State in Russia," *History Today,* XIII (1963), 520–29.

Shmurlo, Evgeny Frantsevich. *Istoriya Rossii.* Munich, 1922.

—— *Kurs Russkoy Istorii.* 3 vols., Prague, 1933.

Skribanowitz, Hermann. *Pseudo-Demetrius I.* Berlin, 1913. (I have been unable to consult this personally, but it appears to contain little if anything new.)

Smirnov, Ivan Ivanovich. *Vosstanie Bolotnikova, 1606–1607.* Leningrad, 1951.

Smith, Charles Marshall. *Northmen of Adventure.* London/New York/Toronto, 1932. (Interesting for study of Rurik the Viking.)

Sobieski, Wacław. *Szkice Historiczne.* Warsaw, 1904.

—— "Zabiegi Dymitra Samozwańca o koronę, polską," *Rozprawy Akademii Umiejętności, Wydział historyczno-filozoficzny,* Ser. 2, Tom 27, 1909.

Solovyov (Soloviev, etc.), Sergey Mikhaylovich. *Istoriya Rossii s drevneyshikh vremyon.* Modern ed. in 15 vols., Moscow, 1959– . Also available in French.

Steuart, A. Francis. *Papers relating to the Scots in Poland.* Edinburgh, 1915.

—— *Scottish Influences in Russian History.* Glasgow, 1913.

Stökl, Günther. "Posseviniana," *Jahrbücher für Geschichte Osteuropas,* XI (1963), 223–36.

Suvorin, Aleksey Sergeyevich. *O Dimitrii Samozvantse. Kriticheskie ocherki . . .* St. Petersburg (Leningrad), 1906. (A journalist's study of the evidence presented by Pierling, Shchepkin, and other historians.)

Sytin, P. V. *Iz istorii Moskovskikh ulits.* Moscow, 1952.

Szelągowski, Adam. *Z dziejów współzawodnictwa Anglii i Niemiec, Rosyi i Polski.* Lvov, 1910.

Tazbir, Janusz. *Świt i zmierzch Polskiej reformacji.* Warsaw, 1956.

Tikhomirov, Mikhail Nikolayevich. *Drevnerusskie Goroda.* 2nd ed., Moscow, 1956.

Turkawski, Marcel. "Carewicz Dymitr w Polsce," *Prezgląd Lwowski,* XXIII (1882), 15–21, 90–94, 164–67, 207–13, 335–38, 493–96; and XXIV (1882), 182–85, 253–57, and 296–99.

Ustryalov, Nikolay Gerasimovich. *Russkaya istoriya.* 2 vols., Sanktpeterburg (Leningrad), 1855.

Vernadsky, George. "The Death of the Tsarevich Dimitry: a Reconsideration of the Case," *Oxford Slavonic Papers,* V (1954), 1–19.

—— *A History of Russia.* New rev. ed., Yale U. Press, 1944.

—— "Die Tragödie von Uglič und ihre Folgen," *Jahrbücher für Geschichte Osteuropas,* III (1955), 41–49.

Vilenskaya, E. S. "K istorii russko-angliyskikh otnosheny v XVI v.," *Istoricheskie Zapiski*, XXIX (1949), 123–34.

Vipper, Robert Yuryevich. *Ivan Grozny*. Moscow, 1947. (English translation.)

Waliszewski, Kazimierz. *Ivan le Terrible*. Paris, 1930. (Re-issue of 1904 ed.)

—— *Les Origines de la Russie moderne. La Crise révolutionnaire (1584–1614)*. Paris, 1906.

Willan, T. S. *The Early History of the Russia Company*. Manchester U. Press, 1956.

—— *The Muscovy Merchants of 1555*. Manchester U. Press, 1953.

Winter, Eduard. *Russland und das Papsttum, Teil I*. Berlin, 1960. ("Die Diplomatie der Päpste in der Zeit der russischen Wirren." Band 6.)

Zalozieckyj, V. R. "Stilhistorische Untersuchung der Monomachkappe," *Abhandlungen des ukrainischen wissenschaftlichen Institutes in Berlin*, I (1927), 140–67.

LITERARY WORKS

Ankersmit, J. H. *Pseudo-Demetrius. Drama in drie tafereelen*. Deventer, 1871.

Barbour, Philip L. *Pushkin's Boris Godunov*. See, Pushkin.

Bisaccioni, Conte Mayolino. *Demetrio di Russia* (Novella). 1643.

—— *Il Demetrio Moscovita, Historia Tragica* . . . 1649. (The latter work is in the British Museum, the former mentioned in various encyclopedias. I have not consulted either.)

Bodenstedt, Friedrich von. *Demetrius*. Berlin, 1856.

Börjesson, Johan. *Erik XIVs Son. Sorgespel i fem akter*. Stockholm, 1847.

Gottschall, Rudolf von. "Die Demetrius Dramen," *Studien zur neuen deutschen Litteratur*, Berlin, 1892, 95–133. (Emphasis on Schiller's *Demetrius* [*see below*] and various attempts to complete it.)

Grimm, Hermann. *Demetrius*. Leipzig, 1854.

Hammarsköld, Lorenzo. *Prins Gustaf*. Strängnäs (Sweden), 1812.

Hebbel, Friedrich. *Demetrius. Trauerspiel*. Hamburg, 1864.

Khomyakov, Aleksey Stepanovich. *Dimitry Samozvanets*. In collected works, Vol. IV, Moscow, 1909.

Mérimée, Prosper. *Les débuts d'un aventurier.* Paris, 1892. (In *Les deux héritages.*)

Mordovtsev, Daniil Lukich. *Lzhedimitry, istorichesky roman iz Smutnago vremeni.* [Fiction.] In complete works, 25 vols., Petrograd (Leningrad), 1914.

Ostrovsky, Aleksandr Nikolayevich. *Dimitry Samozvanets i Vasily Shuysky.* In Vol. IV, new ed. of complete works, 16 vols., Moscow, 1949–1953.

Pix, Mary. *The Czar of Muscovy, A tragedy* . . . London, 1701.

Pushkin, Aleksandr Sergeyevich. *Boris Godunov.* Russian text with translation and notes by Philip L. Barbour. Columbia U. Press, 1953.

R—ev, G. *Lzhedimitry I. Tragediya v desyati bylinakh.* Novgorod, 1864.

Scherr, Johannes. *Der falsche Dmitry.* Vol. III of *Menschliche Tragikomödie,* 12 vols., Leipzig, 1884.

Schiller, Johann Christoph Friedrich von. *Demetrius.* (Unfinished.) In collected works, ed. Körner, Stuttgart and Tübingen, 1812–1815, and many editions since.

Sumarokov, Aleksandr Petrovich. *Dimitry Samozvanets.* Vol. III of *Rossiysky Theatr,* 43 vols., St. Petersburg (Leningrad), 1786–1794.

Tolstoy, Aleksey Konstantinovich. *Dramaticheskaya Trilogiya. III. Tsar Boris Godunov.* St. Petersburg (Leningrad), 1895.

Vega Carpio, Félix Lope de. *El Gran Duque de Moscovia y Emperador Perseguido.* First ed., *Comedias,* Part VII, Madrid and Barcelona, 1617. (Best ed., *Obras de Lope de Vega,* Real Academia Española, Vol. VI, Madrid, 1896, in which there is a study of the play by Marcelino Menéndez y Pelayo [pp. cxxxiii–cxxxix].)

[Note: The foregoing does not pretend to be complete. An exhaustive search would undoubtedly turn up a number of additional literary works based on the life of Dimitry.]

INDEX

Divided for ease of reference into two sections, Geographical and Historical, the Index covers only the text, Appendices D and E, and a few primary references in the Notes and Comments.

To save space, in lengthy references to a given name, where a single page interrupts the sequence, the passage is listed as if it were continuous. For example, under *Boris Godunov* the indication 94–131 ignores the lack of mention of his name on pages 99, 114, 119, and 127.

Well-known places are not further identified. Less noted place-names are followed by their respective districts, etc., in parentheses, and occasionally by the names of the countries. The lack of complete consistency in this, and a few other matters, may be excused on the grounds of economy.

All Polish names are stressed on the next-to-last syllable. Such "accents" as appear are therefore matters of Polish orthography. Russian names, on the other hand, because there is no simple rule, all bear an indicated stress-accent, except for a very few instances of uncertainty or lack of knowledge for the years 1600–1610. After all, the purpose of the Index is to guide, not to supplant, curiosity.

The following obvious abbreviations are used:

ASSR — Autonomous Socialist Soviet Republic
BSSR — Byelo-Russian ("White Russian") SSR
ČSR — Czechoslovak Socialist Republic
EstSSR — Estonian SSR
RSFSR — Russian Socialist Federated SR
UkrSSR — Ukrainian SSR

GEOGRAPHICAL SECTION

HISTORICAL SECTION

386

INDEX

Lake Peipus

Livonia

BALTIC SEA

Courland

Riga

DVINA

Pomerania

Gdańsk

E. Prussia

Varmia

Minsk

MO

VISTULA

Poznań

Słonim

Mir
Nieświez

52°

Warsaw

BUG

P O L I S H -

PRIPET MARSHE

PRIPET

Silesia

L I T H U A N I A N

Lublin

R E P U B L I C

Hoshcha

Kraków

Jarosław

Ostrog

Lvov

Glinyany
Zalozhtsy

Sanok

Sambor

Skałat

Strzyzov

CARPATHIAN

MTS.

Vienna

E

20°

Dimitry's *Route to Moscow*

→ → →

••••••• Polish Boundary

Statute Miles
0   100   200
50   150

(Under Turkish Hegemony)

20°